SONDHEIM & CO.

SONDHEIM & CO.

CRAIG ZADAN . . . .

2ND EDITION

HARPER & ROW,
PUBLISHERS, New York,
Cambridge, Philadelphia,
San Francisco, Washington,
London, Mexico City, São Paulo,
Singapore, Sydney

Author's note:

Chapters 1–19, 21, and 29 were originally written in 1974. Each of these chapters has been revised and updated, and several chapters (17, 18, 21, 29, and the appendixes) have been expanded. Chapters 20 and 22–28 were written in 1986.

SONDHEIM & CO. (Second Edition). Copyright © 1974, 1986 by Craig Zadan. All rights reserved. Printed in the United States of America. No part of this book may be used or reproduced in any manner whatsoever without written permission except in the case of brief quotations embodied in critical articles and reviews. For information address Harper & Row, Publishers, Inc., 10 East 53rd Street, New York, N.Y. 10022. Published simultaneously in Canada by Fitzhenry & Whiteside Limited, Toronto.

Designer: Kathleen Westray and Ed Sturmer, Design and Printing Productions, New York City

Library of Congress Cataloging-in-Publication Data

Zadan, Craig.
    Sondheim & Co.

    Discography: p.
    Includes index.
    1. Sondheim, Stephen.   2. Composers—United States—Biography.
3. Musical revue, comedy, etc.   I. Title.   II. Title: Sondheim and company.
ML410.S6872Z2   1986   782.8'1'0924   [B]   86-45165
ISBN 0-06-015649-X   86 87 88 89 90 MPC 10 9 8 7 6 5 4 3 2 1
ISBN 0-06-091400-9 (pbk.) 86 87 88 89 90 MPC 10 9 8 7 6 5 4 3 2 1

CONTENTS · · ·

INTRODUCTION
vii · · ·

1. EVERYBODY HAS TO
GO THROUGH STAGES
LIKE THAT
3 · · ·

2. ''I'VE NEVER EVEN
KNOWN A PUERTO
RICAN!''
11 · · ·

3. MUSICAL PRODUCTION
33 · · ·

4. NO FITS, NO FIGHTS,
NO FEUDS, NO EGOS?
37 · · ·

5. MUSICAL LIBRETTO
61 · · ·

6. SEND IN THE CLOWNS
65 · · ·

7. MUSIC PUBLISHING
78 · · ·

8. THE WAY THE
COOKIES CRUMBLED
81 · · ·

9. MUSICAL DIRECTION
96 · · ·

10. ''THE LESS SAID,
THE BETTER''
99 · · ·

11. CASTING
108 · · ·

12. WAITING AROUND
FOR THE GIRLS
UPSTAIRS
113 · · ·

13. MUSICAL STAGING
132 · · ·

2/21/90 &

14. AN EMBARRASSMENT OF RICHES
135 . . .

15. ORCHESTRATION
154 . . .

16. THE GAME IS NEVER OVER
161 . . .

17. ORIGINAL CAST RECORDINGS
173 . . .

18. IS HANS CHRISTIAN ANDERSEN EVER RISQUÉ?
181 . . .

19. FOR WHOSE BENEFIT?
201 . . .

20. EAST SIDE STORY
209 . . .

21. SONGWRITING
229 . . .

22. MURDER, HE WROTE
243 . . .

23. POSTER ART
263 . . .

24. ''IT'S *STILL* BACKWARDS''
269 . . .

25. POP RECORDINGS
287 . . .

26. ART ISN'T EASY
295 . . .

27. ONE LAST LOOK AT WHERE IT ALL BEGAN
319 . . .

28. PERPETUAL ANTICIPATION
337 . . .

29. WITH SO LITTLE TO BE SURE OF
359 . . .

APPENDIX A: SONDHEIM PRODUCTIONS
369 . . .

APPENDIX B: SONDHEIM CAST ALBUMS
395 . . .

ACKNOWLEDGMENTS, FIRST EDITION
398 . . .

ACKNOWLEDGMENTS, SECOND EDITION
400 . . .

INDEX
402 . . .

INTRODUCTION · · ·

In the twelve years that have passed since the publication of the first edition of *Sondheim & Co.*, Stephen Sondheim, in many respects, has changed quite a bit. His work has gone in new directions that even his diehard fans never anticipated.

Until recently, Sondheim has been a cult figure, hardly a household name; but his influence has paved the way to a new hope for the American musical theater.

Having written the lyrics for *West Side Story*, *Gypsy*, and *Do I Hear a Waltz?* and the music and lyrics for *A Funny Thing Happened on the Way to the Forum*, *Anyone Can Whistle*, *Company*, *Follies*, *A Little Night Music*, *Pacific Overtures*, *Sweeney Todd*, *Merrily We Roll Along*, and *Sunday in the Park with George*, he is the only composer–lyricist in Broadway history to win the Antoinette Perry (Tony) Award for three consecutive years. Today, he holds five Tonys, as well as the Pulitzer Prize for Drama (won for *Sunday in the Park*). His musicals are the most anticipated of any Broadway season.

His songs, as always, continue to be adventurous and complex, demanding almost as much effort from the listener as they do from the man who writes them. Sondheim strives to be not merely a songwriter but a dramatist as well, interweaving his songs deeply into the fabric and character of his shows. There have been complaints over the years that his shifting rhythms and asymmetrical melodies make his songs "unhummable" and "unmelodic," that the subjects of his songs are "elitist" or "dark," foreign to present-day audiences weaned on songs with simple hooks.

But the argument that his songs don't stand on their own, out of the context of his shows, has been gradually broken down—initially by a surprisingly popular Broadway revue of his songs, *Side by Side by Sondheim* (1975). The "pop"ularization of his work continued that year with the success of Judy Collins's Grammy Award–winning recording of "Send in the Clowns." And finally Barbra Streisand's *The Broadway Album* (1985), a multimillion-selling phenomenon, brought Sondheim to a new and broader audience, reaching people who discovered his soaring melodies and crackling lyrics, in many cases for the first time.

The man himself has also changed. Sondheim's appearance used to be intimidating: often he was attired carelessly in a dark turtleneck, his hair long and scraggly, falling over his forehead. If Cole Porter represented utter elegance, Sondheim was determined dishevelment.

Today he is trim and handsome. With his neater haircut and silvery beard, he bears more of a resemblance to Giancarlo Giannini than to the harried-looking artist of more than a decade ago. Friends say that he is happier than ever before, and that he has mellowed through the years. They admit that he can still be moody and intolerant of small talk, but then he can also sit for hours in his game-filled townhouse on Manhattan's East Side, meticulously dissecting any topic tossed at him. By his own admission he is lazy by nature, loves nothing more than to procrastinate, and, like many gifted artists, is tormented by insecurities and apprehensions in everyday living, as well as in his work.

But his work continues. Today, more than ever before, he maintains and reaffirms his position as the reigning talent and motive force of the American musical theater. Sondheim, along with his distinguished collaborators, has continued to break old traditions by stretching the conventional and rigid musical into a new-fashioned art, a thinking person's form of entertainment.

SONDHEIM & CO.

EVERYBODY HAS TO ... |
GO THROUGH STAGES
LIKE THAT

STEPHEN SONDHEIM, born March 22, 1930, son of a successful New York dress manufacturer, found his early years comfortably upper-middle-class. A precocious child, he skipped kindergarten, read the *New York Times* in the first grade, and even had the sense to be self-conscious about being the smartest kid in the class. "I would purposely drop my *g*'s because I spoke English too well."

When Sondheim was ten, his quiet childhood underwent upheaval when his parents were divorced. His mother moved to a farm in Doylestown, Pennsylvania and sent her bewildered son off to military school, where he reveled in the confining order and rules. "I also loved it because the school had a huge organ with lots of buttons." (His musical training was sporadic. He had a year of piano when he was seven, a year of organ at eleven, a year of piano at fourteen, and another year at nineteen.)

Being in the right place at the right time had a lot to do with Sondheim's initial interest in the musical theater. "Among my mother's acquaintances in Pennsylvania was the Oscar Hammerstein family," Sondheim says. "They had a son, Jimmy, who was my age, and we became close friends very quickly. Since the Hammersteins lived only three miles from us, they gradually became surrogate parents for me."

Around that time, Hammerstein was working on a new musical for Broadway called *Oklahoma!* and before long, with Hammerstein's "nudging," adolescent Sondheim became intrigued with the musical theater.

At the age of fifteen, he and two classmates wrote a musical about campus life called *By George* for the Quaker-run George School, which he attended in Bucks County, Pennsylvania. "I really thought it was terrific,"

Opposite: Stephen Sondheim's first professional publicity portrait, 1957. (FRIEDMAN-ABELES)

Sondheim remembers. "And when I finished it, I not only wanted Oscar to see it but I wanted him to be the first to read it, because I just knew he and Dick Rodgers would want to produce it immediately and I'd be the first fifteen-year-old ever to have a musical done on Broadway.

"So I gave it to him one evening and told him to read it objectively, as though he didn't know me—as something that crossed his desk on a totally professional level. And I went home that night with delusions of grandeur in my head. I could see my name in lights. Next day when I got up he called and I went over to his house, and he said, 'Now you want my opinion as though I really didn't know you? Well, it's the worst thing I've ever read.' And he probably saw that my lower lip began to tremble, and he said, 'Now, I didn't say that it was untalented, I said it was terrible. And if you want to know *why* it's terrible I'll tell you.' " Hammerstein proceeded from the very first stage direction to go through every song, every scene, every line of dialogue. "At the risk of hyperbole," Sondheim recalls, "I'd say that in that afternoon I learned more about songwriting and the musical theater than most people learn in a lifetime. I was getting the distillation of thirty years of experience. And he did indeed treat me as if I were a professional. He taught me how to structure a song like a one-act play, how essential simplicity is, how much every word counts and the importance of content, of saying what you, not what other songwriters, feel, how to build songs, how to introduce character, how to make songs relate to character, how to tell a story, how not to tell a story, the interrelationships between lyric and music—all, of course, from his own point of view. But he was at least as good a critic as he was a writer. Most people think of Oscar as a kind of affable, idealistic lunkhead. Instead, he was a very sophisticated, sharp-tongued, articulate man who did indeed have an idealistic philosophy which prompted him to be attracted to the kind of material he was attracted to.

"I once asked him years later why he didn't write a sophisticated musical. And he said, 'By sophisticated, do you mean one that takes place in a New York penthouse?' And I said, 'All right, yes, if that's the way you want to put it.' And he said, 'Mostly because it doesn't interest me.' Which was a very simple answer—and absolutely true. When he got close to that kind of sophistication, as he did in the second act of *Allegro*, that's when he wrote least well—he just wasn't interested in it."

Hammerstein immediately undertook to teach Sondheim the art of writing for the musical theater and outlined a course of study to follow over the next six years. "He told me to write four musicals," Sondheim

From left: James Hammerstein, Dorothy Hammerstein, Nedda Logan, Oscar Hammerstein, and Stephen Sondheim in 1946 snapshot. (COURTESY OF STEPHEN SONDHEIM)

says. "For the first one, he told me to take a play I admired and turn it into a musical. I chose *Beggar on Horseback* by George S. Kaufman and Marc Connelly, and we actually got permission to do it for three performances at college. Next, he told me to take a play I didn't think was very good and could be improved and make a musical out of it. My choice was *High Tor* by Maxwell Anderson—but I couldn't get permission to put it on in college because Anderson wanted to do a musical of it with Kurt Weill, though they never did it, but it taught me something about playwriting, about structure, about how to take out fat and how to make points. [*High Tor* eventually became a musical for television, written by Anderson and Arthur Schwartz, starring Bing Crosby and Julie Andrews.] For the third effort, Oscar told me to take something nondramatic, like a novel or a short story. I spent about a year writing a musical version of *Mary Poppins*. That's where I encountered the real difficulties of playwriting, which is one of the reasons I'm not a playwright. It was very difficult to structure a play out of a group of short stories, and I wasn't able to accomplish it. For the fourth and last in this series, he told me to write an original, which I completed when I finished college. It was called

Climb High, and its first act was ninety-nine pages long and the second act was over sixty. Oscar had recently given me a copy of *South Pacific* to read and the entire show was ninety pages long, so when I sent him my script I got it back with a circle around ninety-nine and just a 'Wow!' written on it."

Inevitably, Sondheim became a music major at Williams College, although he says he had thought of becoming an English or mathematics major. "But once I took an elective in music during my freshman year," Sondheim says, "the teacher, Robert Barrow, was so sensational that if he had taught geology I would probably have become a geologist. Before Barrow I waited for all the tunes to come into my head. I was a romantic. He taught me first to learn the technique and then to put the notes down on paper . . . that's what music is." Upon graduation, Sondheim won the Hutchinson Prize, a two-year fellowship which he used to study with avant-garde composer Milton Babbitt in New York.

Babbitt: "I was teaching at Princeton, and I tutored very few students individually. In fact, Steve was the last person I've taught privately.

"He had good basic training in music at Williams, a great deal of musical intelligence, and through a certain amount of listening to records and piano playing, he had quite a broad background. He made it clear immediately that he wasn't interested in becoming what one would call a serious composer, but he wanted to know a great deal more about so-called serious music because he thought it would be suggestive and useful."

Babbitt met with Sondheim for one composition lesson a week during which they analyzed a great deal of music. "We did a number of species counterpoint for a structural point of view," Babbitt says, "and hardly ever looked at contemporary music. We also never went into twelve-tone theory at all. His only interests in recent music to speak of were Ravel and Copland, although they were neither near nor dear to my heart. We mostly got deep into Mozart sonatas and Beethoven symphonies from esoteric, detailed points of view.

"Steve came as a sort of Ivy League young man who had decided to go into music after having thought about other alternatives. He learned very quickly. He had a very nimble mind and he was very musical. He worked slowly, even on what might seem to be simple material. He claimed that he was lazy, which he could afford to be, but I think that it takes him a long time to satisfy himself. He was also constantly being diverted with parties. He spent a great deal of time designing games and solving puzzles

—and I might add that most of these games had rather recondite Show Biz references. His social world was also very interesting. It was very Park Avenue, which was a slight dichotomy between a non-Jewish milieu and the fact that he was obviously Jewish. He was terribly bright and one could only wonder how serious he could afford to be. He had money, he was accustomed to the best things in life, he was accustomed to frivolity, he was *not* accustomed to working terribly hard in the serious composer's sense. I could hardly see Steve fighting the world the way serious young composers are obliged to, particularly if they are principled—and Steve was always very principled. And when I say *serious*, I'm using the word in quotes, to define a certain area of activity. No one could have been more serious about his music than Steve and he wanted to improve himself in every conceivable way. He wanted his music to be as sophisticated and as knowing within the obvious restraints of a Broadway musical. After all, very few Broadway composers were all that educated. Richard Rodgers, who was considered the smartest of that gang, had no real connection with the world of serious music, and he was so self-centered I don't think he thought there was much for him to learn. Dick was always a problem, always a thorn in Steve's side. I think Steve admired him and wanted to please him but Dick made that very difficult.

"I remember one thing in particular. Steve had a group which consisted of people who later became prominent in show business. At that time they were nobodies. One of his friends was the now-eminent producer-director Hal Prince, who later presented most of his shows."

Prince: "I remember meeting Steve on the opening night of *South Pacific* in 1948. [Sondheim was with Oscar Hammerstein, and Prince was with Richard Rodgers.] When I finally got out of the army in 1952 I went to work at one point—I believe I was the assistant stage manager of *Wonderful Town*—I remember a conversation that Steve and I had in Walgreen's drugstore . . . sitting there at the counter having sandwiches and milk shakes and talking about the theater and what we hoped our place in it could be . . . what we thought was wrong with it and all the things we wanted to do to fix it."

Another of Sondheim's early friends was Burt Shevelove, who later coauthored the book of *A Funny Thing Happened on the Way to the Forum*. "Burt and he had the kind of relationship," Babbitt points out, "that when things were tough, they would call each other up to see who had finished the London *Times* crossword puzzle first. It was a relationship that was very important to Steve—and Steve was extremely loyal."

Shevelove: "Steve and I met when he was still at Williams. You could tell from the very beginning that he was not just a songwriter. Other than writing birthday songs for friends, Steve could never write a song without some dramatic situation to base it on. We talked even then about plays that could be adapted, ideas that could be made into musicals, but he always thought in terms of theater music. He never said, 'I have a melody here' or 'Wouldn't this be a cute idea for a song?' He still can't think in those terms. He's the only nonopera writer of true theater music around today."

Babbitt: "When *Newsweek* interviewed me about Steve, what they couldn't understand was why he had this great insatiable desire to make it big. I don't have the answers to such things. That would be psychological dilettantism, but it was perfectly obvious that he had grown up in a society of celebrities and he wanted to be a fellow celebrity. There was a great deal of social pressure and he was aware of a certain kind of favorable position one could have under those conditions. He was simply going to make it."

One evening Sondheim joined Oscar and Dorothy Hammerstein for a dinner party at the home of Dorothy Stickney and Howard Lindsay in Bucks County. Spending the weekend was their friend, George Oppenheimer, who was celebrating the news that a pilot he had done for a new television series, *Topper*, had just been accepted for production. But with the acceptance came the warning that as writer of the series he would be expected to turn out scripts in rapid succession.

"They told me that I should look for a young writer to help me," Oppenheimer said. "And at dinner that night as I was presenting my problem, Oscar turned to me and said, 'Your search is over. Here's the perfect guy to work with you.' "

After reading some of the material Sondheim had written at Williams, Oppenheimer nodded his approval and they were soon on a plane to Hollywood.

Oppenheimer: "I just found Steve to be the most incredibly amusing guy. He couldn't have been more than twenty-three years old. And he was one of the most loyal kids I've ever met. I went through hell on the show. . . . We had to get out twenty-nine segments in six months. He did about ten, I did about ten with him, and I did the rest."

Babbitt: "I may be wrong, but I believe that Steve was very unhappy about doing the TV show. He had his problems with his mother, who was out in California at the time, all kinds of domestic and family problems. And his writing seemed to be both for his independence and to begin his career."

When Sondheim returned from Los Angeles, having quit *Topper* when he had saved enough money to rent an apartment in New York, he was invited to usher at the wedding of a friend. One of the other ushers at the affair happened to be Lemuel Ayers, one of America's finest set designers and producer of *Kiss Me, Kate.* Ayers had a property called *Front Porch in Flatbush*, written by two Hollywood screenwriters, Julius J. and Philip G. Epstein, twin brothers who had won an Academy Award for *Casablanca*. Philip had died and this, their last play together, was about their third brother and a group of kids in Flatbush in 1928 all investing in the stock market. Ayers wanted to make a musical out of it. Having been turned down by Frank Loesser, who at the time was busy on another show, Ayers set up an audition for Sondheim, and after hearing some of the material from his four apprentice musicals, hired him on spec to write three songs. The songs turned out so well that Sondheim was hired for this new musical for Broadway, then retitled *Saturday Night*—his first professional job in the musical theater. Eight backers' auditions were held (with a cast that included Jack Cassidy, Alice Ghostley, and Arte Johnson), over half the money was raised, and Ayers suddenly died. As did the project.

Babbitt: "Very frankly, I thought many of the songs were very good but I thought the book was a disaster and I had great fears that if the show was to ever go on it could very well have bombed. It was filled with all sorts of homespun corn which I find offensive and the score bears no relation to anything Steve has written since."

Several years later, there was a major attempt to resurrect the show. On June 1, 1959 (after the opening of *Gypsy*), the *New York Times* theater page carried the news: "It is now official that *Saturday Night* will reach the stage under the joint auspices of Jule Styne and Joseph Kipness. Definite, too, is the engagement of Bob Fosse, director and choreographer of *Redhead*. An early December entry, probably at the 46th Street Theatre."

Sondheim: "When we started auditioning people, I got a terrible feeling in the pit of my stomach that I didn't want to regress. . . . It was a small charming show but I couldn't go ahead with it."

With the abrupt halt of *Saturday Night*, twenty-five-year-old Stephen Sondheim had not reached Broadway as soon as he had hoped, but he did have the best audition portfolio of any unknown songwriter in town.

"I'VE NEVER EVEN KNOWN A PUERTO RICAN!"

G EORGE OPPENHEIMER was on the telephone to Martin Gabel raving about "this bright young songwriter" Gabel had to hear immediately. Gabel agreed, and later that day Stephen Sondheim played his score from *Saturday Night* for a small audience that included playwright Arthur Laurents. The audition was for Gabel and Henry M. Margolis's upcoming production of a musical version of the James M. Cain novel *Serenade* (a project originally announced as a joint venture for Leonard Bernstein, Jerome Robbins, and Laurents, of whom Laurents was the only one to remain). Although almost everyone liked Sondheim's work, the show never required the choosing of a songwriter, since Warner Bros. shortly thereafter announced that they were bringing out *Serenade* as a movie with Mario Lanza.

But the audition proved to be not a total loss when, six months later, Sondheim turned up early one evening for an opening night party at the apartment of Ruth Ford and Zachary Scott. "I was invited by Burt Shevelove," Sondheim says, "and I didn't know anyone there since Burt hadn't arrived yet. Then in the corner I spotted Arthur Laurents. I went over to make small talk and I asked him what he was doing and he said that he was just about to begin a musical of *Romeo and Juliet* with Leonard Bernstein and Jerry Robbins. I asked, just idly, 'Who's doing the lyrics?' and Arthur literally smote his forehead, which I think is the only time I've ever seen anybody literally smite his forehead, and he said, 'I never thought of you and I liked your lyrics very much. I didn't like your music, but I did like your lyrics a lot.' Arthur is nothing if not frank. So he

Opposite (from left): *West Side Story* producers Robert Griffith and Harold Prince, director-choreographer Jerome Robbins, lyricist Stephen Sondheim, and composer Leonard Bernstein at rehearsal, 1957. (MARTHA SWOPE)

invited me to meet and play for Bernstein, which I agreed to because I thought it might be very glamorous to meet Lenny."

"Glamorous?" Arthur Laurents says amusedly. "I remember I thought I was giving him a big break but he wasn't terribly impressed. . . . But they obviously had a very successful meeting."

Bernstein's original intention was to write his own lyrics for *West Side Story*, having already written lyrics for his opera *Trouble in Tahiti*, some of *Candide*, and even some of *On the Town* (specifically, the lyrics to the very popular "I Can Cook, Too"). But there came a point when Bernstein realized that he was not going to be able to do the whole lyric job himself, because the show seemed to have become larger than anticipated, especially from the point of view of all the ballet music to be written and orchestrated, and *Candide* still had to be finished. In addition, he didn't like a lot of things he was doing lyrically, nor was he able to hit the tone of the piece. It was at that point that he felt he should have someone to collaborate on the lyrics.

Sondheim: "When I met him, he said that he had wanted Comden and Green to come in, but they were in Hollywood and couldn't get out of a film contract. I told him that I didn't want to write *just* lyrics, but I played him the score of *Saturday Night*."

Bernstein: "I went wild, I thought that he was a real, honest-to-God talent. The music wasn't terribly distinguished—it sounded like anybody's music—but the lyrics didn't sound like anybody's lyrics by any means."

Sondheim went to Oscar Hammerstein complaining that he didn't want to accept the job if it came through, but Hammerstein convinced him that it was a marvelous opportunity to work with first-rate professionals on a project that sounded original and exciting.

A week later, Bernstein called to offer Sondheim the job officially. "When he reached me," Sondheim recalls, "it turned out that he wanted to co-write the lyrics, which made me even more depressed. But I said yes anyway."

"It was a difficult decision for Steve to make," says Milton Babbitt. "Steve had always regarded himself as primarily a composer and for a long time he felt humiliated a little bit—certainly put upon—and certainly a bit embarrassed that he was to be regarded as a man of words, a lyric writer."

Flora Roberts, Sondheim's agent, with him from the days of *Saturday*

Above: The "Jet Song," *West Side Story* Broadway cast, 1957. (MARTHA SWOPE)

Left: *West Side Story* Jets, movie version, 1961. (UNITED ARTISTS)

Night and still in charge of his business affairs today, remembers that Sondheim thought of every conceivable excuse *not* to accept the job. "Steve would complain, 'I can't do this show. . . . I've never been that poor and I've never even *known* a Puerto Rican!' I told him not to think in those terms. They are star-crossed lovers. They are underprivileged and the haves and have-nots have more to do with their psyches than their economics."

It took two years to get the new musical ready for production, during which time Bernstein took a six-month hiatus to do *Candide* (as it turned out, some of the music in *West Side Story* was from *Candide*, and some of the music in *Candide* was from *West Side Story*), Jerome Robbins went off to direct *Bells Are Ringing*, Arthur Laurents had his *A Clearing in the Woods* produced, and Sondheim went to work on a television program called *The Last Word*. In actuality, however, the show dated back to an idea struck upon in 1949, with three title changes along the way: *East Side Story* to *Gang Way* to *West Side Story*.

"The original idea was Jerry's," Bernstein says, "and it did involve the East Side. The idea was to use the Romeo play, which fascinated Jerry, in contemporary terms to tell of the meeting which had its milieu on the East Side at the Easter–Passover time. We discovered pretty soon that our story was a pretty mixed bag and the Catholic–Jewish, Irish–Jewish situation was no longer the case. The war had changed all that with the influx of Latin Americans. The East Side wasn't what it used to be, therefore the idea was old-fashioned—it would have been *Abie's Irish Rose* all over again and not very topical."

Bernstein, Robbins, and Laurents had their first meeting in 1949 to discuss the writing of their *Romeo and Juliet* musical. "I didn't know Arthur very well," Bernstein says, "but I had been terribly moved by his play *Home of the Brave*, and during that initial conference he had a sudden outburst of hostility which was unusual because we had just met. He announced vehemently, 'I want to make one thing clear before we go any further and that is that I'm not writing any fucking libretto for any goddamned Bernstein opera!' I suppose what he had in his mind was that operas are incontrovertibly known as works of their composers rather than of their librettists. And I understood what he was talking about, since *Aïda*, *Falstaff*, and *Otello* are known as Verdi operas, which is too bad because those libretti have a great deal to do with the success and even beauty of them. Since he knew I was a serious composer and that the show might have operatic overtones—or might even turn out to be an opera—

he wasn't going to get lost on the way. I pacified him and tried to make it clear that I considered him as important as any of us, more so in fact, because we were utterly dependent on what he would do. He is something of a genius at this. I don't know many playwrights who could have accomplished this particular job in so brilliant a way and in so self-effacing a way. He knew exactly how to limit his scenes so that they would set up a musical situation and would not indulge himself in the luxuries of the expository scenes and delineation of character which would lead to a song. In fact, he often encouraged us to take a scene he had written and musicalize it or take a germ of a scene and build a musical segment on it."

After their first meeting, Bernstein and Laurents began working, respectively, on the score and the book. "I remember receiving about a dozen pages and saying to myself that this is never going to work," Bernstein says. "I had a strong feeling of staleness of the East Side situation and I didn't like the too-angry, too-bitchy, too-vulgar tone of it. We talked and slowly the project fizzled out."

Then it was 1954. Bernstein, in Hollywood scoring *On the Waterfront*, ran into Laurents one afternoon at the Beverly Hills Hotel pool. "We were sitting there reminiscing and ruefully saying what a shame that that wonderful idea never worked out," Bernstein says, "and while we were talking, we noticed the *L.A. Times* had a headline of gang fights breaking out. And this was in Los Angeles with Mexicans fighting so-called Americans. Arthur and I looked at one another and all I can say is that there are moments which are right for certain things and that moment seemed to have come."

Returning to New York, they talked to Robbins, who became "wildly excited because here was suddenly the living, breathing reincarnation of the *Romeo* story, and it was topical." At the time, Bernstein had already gotten involved with Lillian Hellman on *Candide* but was doing very little conducting. "Somehow it seemed I could do both by juggling," Bernstein says. "I had written *Wonderful Town* in 1952 to support my little family. I juggled *Candide* and *West Side* in '54 and '55 and in '56 *Candide* finally got on and flopped miserably. I was very worried about it and wasn't surprised that it failed. I was amazed that it ran two months. All through '56 I was working on *West Side* after three years of agony, trying to make an impossible situation possible with *Candide*.

"When Steve came into the picture and we began working together, he became part of the team and the contribution he made was just enormous. It far exceeded even *my* expectations. What made him so valuable was that

he was also a composer and I could explain musical problems to him and he'd understand immediately, which made the collaboration a joy. It was like writing with an alter ego. We also found we shared a love for words and word games and puzzles, to say nothing of anagrams. In fact, I think we spent more time doing puzzles than we did writing lyrics for *West Side Story*."

Just as things were falling into place in the writing of the show, the production end gradually began to drift into dissension.

Laurents: "Cheryl Crawford and Roger Stevens were going to produce the show, after it was turned down by everybody else. Cheryl was known as a lady of great morality, but not the way she behaved on this show. For one thing she would say to me, 'You can't listen to Jerry, he doesn't know anything about writing.' And she would go to Jerry and say, 'You've got to do something about Arthur!' Then after the show was written, Roger came to me and said, 'Listen, I think Cheryl's gone cold on the show but I'll stick.' And Cheryl called a meeting—we were six weeks away from rehearsal and since everyone had other commitments, if we didn't go on time the show would never be done. Cheryl announced that she thought the book was terrible and that it would be insane to proceed. And I asked her how Roger felt, and she said, 'Oh, exactly the same way.' And I said, 'Cheryl, you're an immoral woman,' and we all got up and walked out and went to the Algonquin to have a drink. I remember it was a very hot day and we couldn't get in because I didn't have a tie. We were so desperate that we were talking of having it done for two weeks at City Center."

Bernstein: "We thought at that point that it would not get on. Everybody told us to stop. They all said it was suicidal. I don't know how many people begged me not to waste my time on something that could not possibly succeed. After all, how could we do a musical where there are two bodies lying on the stage at the end of the first act and everybody eventually dies . . . a show that's so filled with hatefulness and ugliness?"

At that time, Sondheim's friend Harold Prince was in Boston with his production of *New Girl in Town*. Prince called one day to tell Sondheim the terrible problems they were having trying to fix the show. "I poured out my catastrophes," Prince says, "and when I was done I said, 'How are you?' And he said, 'Well, we don't have a show.' Which just *killed* me. I asked, 'When were you going into rehearsal?' and he said, 'In about six weeks.' I said, 'Ouch,' and 'Good-bye.' I called him back about fifteen minutes later, having talked to Bobby Griffith, my partner. I knew the show backwards and forwards, though Bobby had not heard it, for Steve had played all the music for me unbeknownst to Lenny, since he didn't want anybody to hear it. So when I called Steve back I told him that Bobby and I could come to New York on Sunday to hear the score while George Abbott rehearsed *New Girl*, but if they wanted us and if we wanted to do it, we would go right back to Boston because we had a show in trouble and we would not talk about their show, would do nothing about getting a theater, would do nothing about raising money, and they would have to just leave us alone."

As promised, Griffith and Prince arrived in New York that Sunday, and after hearing the material, agreed they wanted to present *West Side Story*.

The day after *New Girl in Town* opened on Broadway, the team went to work, within the week raised the $300,000 capital for the show, and went into rehearsal within a few weeks of the original set time.

There was a slight delay since Robbins insisted that Oliver Smith redesign his sets; and auditions got rather sticky since it was such a young show.

Laurents: "In casting *West Side*, we had to make compromises, and I think most of them were made by Lenny and Steve. People didn't expect much acting in musicals then. We had to find people who could move, who could dance. . . . Also to be young enough and to be able to sing that score. At Carol Lawrence's last audition, Lenny leaned over and asked me her age. I replied, 'How old is the part?' I mean you just couldn't hold to that. When we opened in Washington I looked at one of the actor's biographies and I said to the press agent, 'For God's sake, take out that he was in *Oklahoma!*' That was fifteen years earlier and he was thirty-five playing seventeen or eighteen."

Larry Kert received a call from a friend, Chita Rivera, saying that she was going into a new Broadway musical and that he should come and audition. Kert tried out for the chorus and was told that he wasn't Puerto Rican or American enough. He tried out for the part of Bernardo, the Puerto Rican gang leader, and was rejected. Then he auditioned for Riff, the American gang leader. "Though I had rehearsed at night with Jerry Robbins, unbeknownst to some people," Kert relates, "I couldn't make the dancing. By this time, I'd been auditioning for about four weeks. I was also doing an industrial show for Burt Shevelove, and Steve Sondheim heard me do a calypso number in it and asked me to audition for Tony. I said, 'But every day you read that Leonard Bernstein is looking for a six-foot, blond, Polish tenor. I'm a five-foot-eleven, dark, Jewish baritone!' But Steve said, 'Come in and sing.' And I got the part—I was raw material, having never had an acting or singing lesson, which was what they wanted because the show was the star and they didn't want anybody to overshadow their precious *West Side Story*.

"Rehearsals were a very painful experience," Kert said in several magazine interviews. "Jerry Robbins is an incredible man and I'd work for him in a minute, but he is a painful man—a perfectionist who sees himself in every role, and if you come onstage and don't give him exactly what he's pictured the night before, his tolerance level is too low, so in his own kind of way, he destroys you. People thought we were puppets on strings and in some ways we were. But we resented it."

Prince: "Jerry Robbins started *West Side* with a bunch of amateurs who had never played roles anywhere—just a bunch of kids who danced in shows. He would always call them in groups, 'You're the Jets,' and 'You're the Sharks.' He would put up articles about interracial street fighting all over the bulletin boards where he was rehearsing. He would encourage them not to eat lunch together, but to stay in groups. Somewhere in the middle of the rehearsal period, Lee Becker, who was playing Anybodys, came to me and said, 'No one will eat with me!' And that's the key to getting a cast in the right frame of mind. By whatever means, you turn them on so that they feel pretentious about the experience. You've got to do it.

"Jerry's style of putting together a show is different from mine. In those days I just watched. I wasn't a director yet. I found later that if I'm not liked I can't work. I *hate* turmoil. Jerry Robbins is a man who likes the excitement that comes of contest. I hate it . . . whatever it is that generates your own creativity is what you have to find. I love the whole family thing. I end up every show I do with the feeling that we're all

Larry Kert as Tony singing "Something's Coming" from *West Side Story*, 1957. (MARTHA SWOPE)

going to be in touch . . . we're a family . . . but, of course, everyone goes his own way. That's the way life is."

In a published excerpt from a diary kept by Bernstein during the rehearsals came a great rush of excitement: "I can't believe it; forty kids are actually doing it up there on the stage! Forty kids singing five-part counterpoint who never sang before—and sounding like heaven. I guess we were right not to cast 'singers'; anything that sounded more professional would inevitably sound more experienced and the 'kid' quality would be gone. A perfect example of a disadvantage turned into a virtue."

When Arthur Laurents walked into rehearsal one day with an idea for a new number, he met with unanimous rejection. "Nobody wanted 'Officer Krupke,' " Laurents maintains. "They all said that it was a cheap musical comedy number. But I tried to be a little intellectual and talked Shakespeare's clowns and I felt it was really necessary, and then there wasn't that much dissension. We originally did the number with the idea that it would be performed early in the show but because of the scenic scheme it couldn't. And in the end, I think that it was perfect just where it was. What proved it to me was when the movie was done and it was shifted to earlier in the plot . . . without the tension it *became* just a musical comedy number and it laid an egg.

"The strength of the show to me is the *Romeo and Juliet* story. The other thing is the contemporary application, which, unfortunately, is still timely. There are gangs here and there are gangs in England and there's violence all over the world, prejudice everywhere. We haven't changed all that much. But Shakespeare had much more time and space than I did, although I don't feel his version of *Romeo* is any better than mine. A callow lovesick boy is a callow lovesick boy. Unfortunately, I think he is the worst character both in the original and in *West Side.* The main trouble in writing it was trying to establish what they would have cut anyway—the socioeconomic backgrounds. You get a very quick abortive scene with the two boys and another little scene to introduce the girl. When I originally wrote the book I didn't have those introductory scenes but Jerry wanted them and he was right."

One of the techniques Laurents employed in writing the libretto was the use of made-up expressions of slang which were all his own invention. "I told him immediately that if I used real slang, it would date too quickly. But even the Puerto Rican talk, saying *kiddando* instead of *kid*, was all made up. It sounded very jivey. They never used *cool* then—that word came into the language much later. I twisted syllables and did all sorts of things because the show needed a language. It was lyric theater and if you used actual language it would have been flat."

As librettist, Laurents also gave his composer and lyricist titles of songs and even lists of what they should be about. "One of the funny things," Laurents says, "is that I meant for the girl to sing again at the very end when she picks up the gun. The dialogue I wrote was meant as a rough outline for a dummy lyric for what she should sing. And that's what she says to this day—they just never wrote the song, they decided that there shouldn't be one. One thing that Jerry wanted was for the girl to take sleeping pills like Juliet did, but to me it just didn't work in contemporary terms—it just didn't make sense."

Bernstein: " 'Something's Coming' was born right out of a big long speech that Arthur wrote for Tony. It said how every morning he would wake up and reach out for something, around the corner or down the beach. It was very late and we were in rehearsal when Steve and I realized that we needed a strong song for Tony earlier since he had none until 'Maria,' which was a love song. We had to have more delineation of him as a character. We were looking through this particular speech, and 'Something's Coming' just seemed to leap off the page. In the course of the day we had written that song.

"Steve and I worked together in every conceivable way—together, apart, sometimes with the tune first ('Cool' and 'Officer Krupke'), sometimes with the words first ('A Boy Like That'). It just would never occur to me to write a lyric like, 'A boy like that who'd kill your brother.' That looked like a line of prose to me, but when Steve saw it in Arthur's book, he pulled it immediately.

"I had a song called 'Maria,' for which I had the title and some kind of lyric that I'd written which was there when Steve came in. I think it took longer to write that song than any other. It's difficult to make a strong love song and avoid corn. Steve hates 'I Feel Pretty' and 'One Hand, One Heart' and he never loses an opportunity to say so, which always gripes me because I love them."

Sondheim: "On one level, I suppose lyric writing is an elegant form of puzzle. There's a great deal of joy for me in the sweat involved in the working out of lyrics, but it can lead to bloodlessness and I've often been capable of writing bloodless lyrics. There are a number of them in *West Side.*

"You have to also know when and where to use rhyme. One function of rhyme is that it implies education. And one of the most embarrassing

moments of my life was after a run-through of *West Side*, when some of my friends were out front. I asked Sheldon Harnick after the show what he thought, knowing full well that he was going to fall to his knees and lick the sidewalk. But he said, 'There's that lyric, "I Feel Pretty." ' And I thought that the lyric to that was just terrific. . . . I had spent the previous two years of my life rhyming 'day' and 'way' and 'me' and 'be' and with 'I Feel Pretty' I wanted to show that I could do inner rhymes, too. So I had this uneducated Puerto Rican girl singing, 'It's alarming how charming I feel.' You *know* she would not have been unwelcome in Noël Coward's living room. Sheldon was very gentle but I immediately went back and wrote a simplified version of the lyric which nobody connected with the show would accept. So there it is to this day embarrassing me every time it's sung, because it's full of mistakes like that. When rhyme goes against character, out it should go, and rhyme always implies education and mind working, and the more rhymes, the sharper the mind.

"I remember that the tune of 'One Hand, One Heart,' which Bernstein originally wrote for *Candide*, had only a dotted half note to each bar. I realized I couldn't set any two-syllable words to the song, it had to be all one-syllable words. I was stifled, and down in Washington, after my endless pleas, Lenny put in two little quarter notes so that I could put 'make of our' as in 'Make of our hearts one heart.' Not a great deal, but at least a little better. [A number of tunes were switched between the two shows: e.g., "Officer Krupke" from *West Side Story* was originally a song called "Where Does It Get You in the End?," another melody cut from *Candide,* whereas "O Happy We" in *Candide* was originally written for the bridal shop scene in *West Side Story,* etc.]

"Words must sit on music in order to become clear to the audience," Sondheim explains. "You don't get a chance to hear the lyric twice and if it doesn't sit and bounce when the music bounces, and rise when the music rises—it isn't just a question of mis-accents, which are bad enough, but if it is too crowded and doesn't flow, the audience becomes confused. 'America' has twenty-seven words to the square inch. I had this wonderful quatrain that went, 'I like to be in America/O.K. by me in America/Everything free in America/For a small fee in America.' The 'For a small fee' was my little zinger—except that the 'for' is accented and 'small fee' is impossible to say that fast, so it went '*For* a smafee in America.' Nobody knew what it meant!"

Bernstein: "Steve has very bitter prejudices. He is violently opinionated and when he gets hold of an idea that is pro or con something, it possesses him. He is unable to free himself from it because he is a compulsive person and an obsessive person, as you can tell from the game playing and the collecting. But it has its good sides. This compulsiveness and obsessiveness are exactly what produce that first-rate work. He doesn't leave a thing alone, he's a perfectionist, and he suffers all the pains a perfectionist suffers."

In 1957, *West Side Story* opened in Washington to tumultuous raves. And because so much painstaking work was done on the production before and during rehearsals, Sondheim claims that the show was changed the least of any musical he had heard of (up until *Sweeney Todd*). Another help was the precedent Robbins made with this show, initiating an eight-week rather than the standard four-week rehearsal period that had been used prior to that time.

Sondheim: "Our total changes out of town consisted of rewriting the release for the 'Jet Song,' adding a few notes to 'One Hand,' Jerry *potchkied* with the second-act ballet, and there were a few cuts in the book. . . . But we *were* occupied in Washington for a while because Jerry had a strong feeling that there was a sag in the middle of the first act, so we wrote a number for the three young kids—Anybodys, Arab, and Baby John. It was called 'Kids Ain't' and was a terrific trio that we all loved, but Arthur gave a most eloquent speech about how he loved it also but that we shouldn't use it, because it would be a crowd-pleaser and throw the weight over to typical musical comedy which we agreed we didn't want to do. So it never went in. Then we wrote a new opening because everyone felt the opening wasn't violent enough. The new opening, 'This Turf Is Ours,' was *really* violent and everyone thought it was *too* violent, so we went back to the 'Jet Song.' "

Stephen Sondheim (left) and Mickey Calin at *West Side Story* recording session, 1957. (COLUMBIA RECORDS)

Laurents: "I think it was a marvelous collaboration and in this particular case egos never really got in the way. Look, Lenny, God knows, has an ego, but he's a wonderful collaborator. You couldn't ask for anyone better. So was Steve and I think Steve would say that about me. Jerry's in the ballet because I don't think musicals really satisfy him. Because of his behavior on the show, nobody spoke to him on the opening night in New York."

Bernstein: "I remember the day we opened, we were all excited and leaping with joy—everybody except Steve, who was disconsolate and moping around. I asked him what the matter was and he mumbled something, and I suddenly realized without his telling me that he felt he wasn't getting enough credit for what he had done. He wasn't mentioned in the reviews and I knew that the billing needed to be changed, since he was a beginner in the field and deserved the recognition. I felt that he had done so much of the lyric writing, certainly more than I had done, and some whole songs were all his. Collaboration is this great mysterious thing that gets to the point that you don't really know who wrote what."

"Bernstein called me early the next morning," Flora Roberts says, "and he said, 'I want you to know, I got a great education from that young man. I've decided to take my name off as a co-lyricist. I'm calling the music publisher and my agent and we'll reprint the music because it's just not fair.' And I just thanked him. . . . I think, quite frankly, what Lenny did is fairly unheard of in the theater. Too many people get credit for things they don't do, much less remove their names."

Following a triumphant run in Washington, the *West Side* troupe moved to Philadelphia, where the reception was nowhere as good. "Philly is an antitheatrical town," Sondheim says. "Later, when *Gypsy* opened in Philly, I met Mike Nichols, who told me that it was the only city in the world that he and Elaine May would never play again . . . that they'd played hamlets in the Deep South rather than Philly. *I* did three shows there and that's enough."

On September 26, 1957, *West Side Story* opened at the Winter Garden and the critical raves rumbled in.

"The American theater took a venturesome forward step," proclaimed John Chapman in the *Daily News*, "a bold new kind of musical—a juke-box Manhattan opera—the skills of show business are put to new tests—as a result a different kind of musical has emerged—a perfect production."

"Young Mr. Sondheim has gone all the way with the mood in his lyrics," heralded John McClain in the *Journal American*. "His ballads are the lament of the sincere and he can come up with the most hilarious travesty of our times—'Gee, Officer Krupke'—a plaint which should settle the problem of juvenile delinquency forever."

"The radioactive fallout from *West Side Story* must still be descending on Broadway this morning," raved Walter Kerr in the *Herald Tribune*. But his reservations were clear. "The show in general is not well sung. It is rushingly acted, and it is, apart from the spine-tingling velocity of the dances, almost never emotionally affecting."

Henry Hewes in *Saturday Review* had his own reservations: "Mr. Bernstein is an able and intelligent craftsman. But when his music is sad it seems nervous. What this young composer needs is to relax and give himself more deeply and quietly to his work. Mr. Sondheim's lyrics only occasionally rise above adequacy."

And "Hobe" in *Variety* soberly theorized: "The show seems a doubtful prospect for record album popularity and would need considerable revision as film material. It's hard to visualize it for stock, but at a guess, it might be a sensation in London."

"Everyone thinks that *West Side Story* was an enormous hit," Sondheim says, "but it wasn't. The reviews generally were good. In the first review I ever got in the theater from Brooks Atkinson, my name was totally left out. Walter Kerr didn't like my work or Arthur's—but I tell you it's much better being panned than ignored. At least you know your presence is felt."

During opening week, Arthur Laurents accepted an offer to write a piece about their adventurous new musical in the *Journal American*: "We all knew what we did not want—neither formal poetry nor flat reportage; neither opera nor split-level musical comedy; neither zippered-in ballets nor characterless dance routines. We didn't want newsreel acting, blue-jean costumes, or garbage can scenery any more than we wanted soap-box pounding for our theme of young love destroyed by a violent world. What we did was to aim at a lyrically and theatrically sharpened illusion of reality."

"The show, specifically, was not one that people wanted to see," Sondheim contends. "It was a big hit with theater people but not with audiences. Four years later the movie came out and it became a smash. In those four years, take note that there were exactly two singles from the score because everyone said that it's such a shame you can't hum the music. Well, of course, when the movie company put hundreds of thousands of dollars into pushing the film, and when disc jockeys began

From left: Barbara Luna as Anita, Victoria Mallory as Maria, Alan Castner as Bernardo, and Kurt Peterson as Tony in the Lincoln Center revival of *West Side Story*, 1968. (FRIEDMAN–ABELES)

playing the songs—in other words, as soon as everyone got a chance to *hear* the songs a few times—they suddenly discovered that they were hummable and all of a sudden we had all those standards from the show. The very idea of it not being hummable is laughable. But critics and audiences have said that about *my* scores, when in point of fact, *anything* is hummable. Obviously if it can be sung, it can be hummed. When people say it's not melodic, not hummable, it makes my blood boil. It's really a question of how many times you hear it. People have lazy ears. I would say that if people hear a score for the first time and they find it hummable, then it's usually because they were humming it before they came into the theater. . . . It means that it was familiar to them and they knew where the next note was coming from. That's almost invariably true. If you go back over the reviews of the old Rodgers and Hart shows, they said that the songs were at best pleasant. Rodgers and Hart fared no better than Lenny did with *West Side* or I did with *Company*, *Follies*, or *Forum*. In *Night Music*, I finally was told that I wrote a hummable score. Everyone would go out during intermission humming 'A Weekend in the Country.' Can you wonder why? The musical phrase is merely repeated over and over again with nine choruses in ten minutes. Anyone who uses the word hummable is suspect. Hummable really means familiar.''

Sondheim maintains that *West Side*, like *Forum*, relies on theatrical spectacle; that the streamers coming down during the dance at the gym are as important as the rumble. "*West Side* is about the theater," Sondheim emphasizes. "It's not about people. It's a way to tell a story. What was best was its theatricality and its approach to telling a story in musical terms. I had always claimed that it would date very quickly. Not because of the subject matter, but because of the lack of characters. When it was done in revival at Lincoln Center, the critics were disappointed and blamed it on the production. Well, the production was at fault but what the critics didn't realize—and they never realize anything—is that the show isn't very good. By which I mean, in terms of individual ingredients it has a lot of very severe flaws: overwriting, purpleness in the writing and in the songs, and because the characters are necessarily one-dimensional. They're not people. What lasts in the theater is character, and there are no characters in *West Side*, nor can there be. It's the shortest book on record, with the possible exception of *Follies*, in terms of how much gets accomplished with how little dialogue. It's more about techniques, not about people, and Arthur recognized that problem right away and instead of writing people he wrote one-dimensional characters for a melodrama, which is what it is. More happens in terms of the plot of the show than in almost any other musical I could name and with less dialogue, which is how smart Arthur is and how he recognizes that that's the form it must take. Arthur didn't want the show to say something about the human heart; he was interested in having some fun inventing forms for the theater —ways that he could make song, dance, and dialogue blend. The techniques we used then have been used many times since—and sometimes wrongly. In revival the show seemed so terribly old-fashioned, not because we didn't have street gangs any more, but because the forms that were so dazzling in 1957 were not so dazzling ten years later."

Laurents: "A lot of people think of the show as a first. I think of it as an end of an era. I think the merit of the show was the total integration of everybody's talents and it consequently had more fluidity than any show ever."

Bernstein: "I'm one of those who think, in retrospect, that the show did break ground. As a matter of fact, I stopped writing for the theater and accepted the directorship of the New York Philharmonic the same month *West Side* opened. I thought, 'Oh, well, now I've really done my bit for the Broadway theater and I can become a conductor and seriously think about Beethoven and Wagner,' and I was perfectly confident that there would be dozens of kids who would take the next step and pick up on the hints of *West Side*, that I was convinced would lead to some form of American opera. I once drew a parallel between the American musical comedy which was a real living thing, a kind of very special form that had an analogy with the *Singspiel* of Mozart's time, which was also a kind of mixed-up form of half-vaudeville, half-operetta which became something quite marvelous when Mozart came along and wrote a *Singspiel* called *The Magic Flute.* I remember saying after *West Side* that what we needed was for a Mozart to come along and take this thing and make it into whatever it's going to be. I didn't mean myself, by any means, because I don't think of myself on the same plane as Mozart, but I thought I was doing my bit getting to the point with *Candide*, and especially with *West Side*—a show where so much was conveyed in music, including the enormous reliance upon dance to tell plot—not just songs stuck into a book."

As audiences dwindled, after only a little more than a year's run, *West Side Story* went on discount ticket policy and its producers booked the show for a national tour. "It was one of the few business mistakes of Hal's career," Sondheim says. "Hal didn't realize what a large audience there would be once ticket prices were reduced, so he made the mistake of booking a tour too early and the last couple of months you couldn't get into the theater. To make up for that, he brought it back to New York after the tour for a run of about six months—also on reduced prices—and it did quite well."

Prince: "It never sold out for very long . . . not more than a couple of weeks or so. It's an important show, but most shows that are important are not smash hits. That same year *The Music Man* was a smash and it won all the awards. The big money that *West Side* made came later from the movie and the record. Our investors are the beneficiaries of that movie sale, which was very small but with a substantial piece of the gross. When we sold it nobody wanted it. No one cared and then it turned out to be this monumental success. The ledger on *West Side* is very handsome—but not because of its life on Broadway."

Once *West Side* was sold to the movies, speculation began as to who would star in the film. The *New York Times* in May 1959 reported that "Marlon Brando is very anxious to do *West Side Story*; however, he wants to play the young lead and he is worried at 34 whether this will be plausible on the screen."

Without Brando, but *with* Natalie Wood, Richard Beymer, Russ Tamblyn, and Rita Moreno, *West Side Story* was filmed and then released in October 1961 by United Artists. The movie musical was an enormous success, garnering eleven Academy Awards, including the Oscar for Best Picture of the Year.

"The picture failed for me," says Arthur Laurents. "I think film is an extremely literal medium. You either have to be very realistic or surrealistic. One of the very few movie musicals that succeeded for me was *The Wizard of Oz* because it's fantasy, so when they sing it's not odd. I think with the movie of *West Side*, they never even approached the visual. How do you do balletic movement in real streets? The one number that I thought worked well was 'Cool,' and I wondered what would have happened if they used real streets but stripped them down of every piece of set dressing. Jerry Robbins worked on the film as co-director with Robert Wise, as well as choreographer, but he was fired rather early because he was spending too much time, and in the movies, time is money. They gave him an ultimatum that something had to be done by a certain time and he didn't do it so they kicked him off. He was also spending some time directing the actors at one point, and I shouldn't think that would have helped much." Robbins received not only a Best Director Oscar (which he shared with Wise) but was awarded an honorary Academy Award as well.

Although Stephen Sondheim's first Broadway musical brought him little personal acclaim, *West Side Story* did bring him *some* notoriety. In the Sunday *New York Times*, September 29, 1957, three days after the show premiered, an article appeared titled "The Facts Don't Rhyme: *An Analysis of Irony in Lyrics Linking Puerto Rico's Breezes to Tropic Diseases*," by Howard A. Rusk, M.D.

In the piece, Dr. Rusk stated: "Even before *West Side Story* opened, many Puerto Ricans in New York and in the Commonwealth of Puerto Rico objected strenuously to certain parts of the new hit. The objections, however, were not so much to the depiction of the lives of Puerto Rican juvenile delinquents in New York City and their warfare with a rival gang. Rather, they centered primarily on one line of a song that referred to Puerto Rico as 'island of tropic breezes . . . island of tropic diseases.'

"The Puerto Ricans who have cried 'foul' have a point. The lyrics of this and the other songs created by Mr. Stephen Sondheim are clever and effective, but the references to 'island of tropic diseases' is a blow below the belt. This is not based on fact.

"Today, Puerto Rico has no significant disease problems related to its tropical climate. A review of the tropical diseases in Puerto Rico last month showed no cases of cholera, dengue, filariasis, typhus or yellow fever this year and only one new case of Hansen's disease (leprosy). There are only six cases of Hansen's disease on the island. They are known to the public health authorities and constitute no more of a public health problem than the 14 cases who live and work in New York City.

"Mr. Sondheim's lyrics will probably remain unchanged and Puerto Rico's morbidity and mortality rates will continue to decline. In the meantime, *West Side Story* is a dramatic and effective production and Puerto Rico is a healthy island. Would that we in New York City could find as effective measures to control our social blight of juvenile delinquency as Puerto Rico, island of tropical breezes, has found in controlling its 'tropical diseases.'"

Only in A-me-ri-ca.

Opening night at Sardi's: *West Side Story* (from left) lyricist Stephen Sondheim, composer Leonard Bernstein, and producer Harold Prince, 1957. (FRIEDMAN–ABELES)

From left: Associate producer Ruth
Mitchell, producer–co-director Harold
Prince, design assistant Lisa Aronson,
set designer Boris Aronson, stage
manager Fritz Holt at *Follies* production
meeting, 1971. (MARTHA SWOPE)

MUSICAL PRODUCTION · · · 3

ALTHOUGH the blame for most of Broadway's disastrous musicals usually falls on poor direction, choreography, libretti, music, lyrics, and performances, invariably it is the producer who is at fault. If the producer does his job, which goes far beyond the raising of production capital, he will see to it that the correct people are hired and every aspect of the show is well conceived and absolutely ready to go into production. If not, he will postpone or even cancel his project. Not that certain producers actually plan to do less than their best, but in many cases their best just isn't good enough.

"The problem with the theater," said David Merrick several years ago, "is that there are too few producers. You'll notice that I didn't say *good* producers, just *producers*. It takes someone with a dream who tucks a script under his arm, goes out to raise the money, and puts it all together in a professional way. The sad fact is that I'm producing very little these days and that has caused a dent. Realistically, three people alone have presented 75 percent of the successful shows on Broadway in the recent past. Neil Simon (who really produces his own shows), Hal Prince, and myself. The remaining 25 percent is comprised of an odd one here and there."

"What shocks me the most," says Harold Prince in dismay, "is the idiot anarchy that happens to most shows on the road. The naïveté with which shows go into rehearsal is staggering, and the notion that millions of dollars are riding on something where the producers don't know from day to day what they're really doing . . . and with shows that go into rehearsal *knowing* there's something wrong but saying, 'Oh, we'll fix it later.' Actually, the best thing is to be absolutely sure that everything is *perfect*, because you're going to be dead wrong, but you should go in *knowing* the show is in the best possible condition and *then* find out where you're wrong and deal with it. You should never go into rehearsal unless you believe that the show you're doing is going to be the greatest in history and then find out where you made your mistakes."

In the Prince office, which was typical of a large theater organization, production capitalization rarely rested in the hands of the producer himself. The problem of raising funds for each of Prince's upcoming musical productions instead fell to his staff, formerly headed by his secretary and assistant of over sixteen years, Annette Meyers.

"What I really did," she says, "was handle most of the money. I didn't as much in the beginning, but when Hal became a director and began serving in a dual capacity, the job was delegated to me. I don't think raising money was something he enjoyed, and I believe it probably even embarrassed him a bit. But I found it a very exciting function . . . finding new people and the excitement when investors have a hit.

"Most of our investors went all the way back to *Pajama Game*. Some of them were dead or dying. We had gone from having to raise $300,000 for both *West Side* and *Forum*, $550,000 for *Company*, way up to $800,000 for *Follies*, $750,000 for *Night Music*. [Other Sondheim productions were budgeted at $650,000 for *Pacific Overtures*, $1.3 million for *Sweeney Todd*, $1.5 million for *Merrily We Roll Along*, and $2.4 million for *Sunday in the Park with George*.] And it got harder and harder to raise that kind of money. Because of *Follies* we lost a lot of people . . . most of all, because we didn't return the investment, but also for the first time, people who had been with us before just couldn't come up with the money. Some were old and retired, others were leaving the city and buying homes so all their cash was tied up. Two or three actually told me that they had lost faith in the theater.

"There is never a way to tell what is going to be a big money maker. I don't understand why *Follies* was not a success, except most of the theater-buying public was at the age of the people in the show and it was very upsetting. Also *Company* and *Follies* suffered because Clive Barnes's *New York Times* review was not strong and we didn't have that initial surge. Before they opened, I would never have bet on *Night Music* or *Fiddler* as big box-office attractions, but in the case of *Night Music* apparently the timing was right.

"For *Night Music*, we approached preproduction from a different point of view. We did not take a customary full-page Sunday *Times* ad. Instead, we did a mailing from which we got an enormous response. The *Times* ad never brings in enough mail orders even to pay for the ad.

"Theater parties are still important to a degree but they did not buy *Night Music.* Maybe they felt they'd been burned on *Follies.* But they never buy the right shows . . . for many years they mostly bought shows that never made it to New York. When *Seesaw* opened we picked up a lot of their parties. We had only one a week, although we used to be able to take six, but Hal never liked having that many, so we would try and keep it down to three and four.

"And awards? Well, the Drama Critics' Award doesn't help business, but the Tony does boost everything upward for a while. The Tony Award pushed *Company* over the top and paid the show off. It's good to know just where the awards stand . . . their value is important when you don't think of them as ego boosters, but as box-office helpers."

"Personally," said David Merrick, "behind our backs I've always said nice things about Hal Prince and I hear that he's polite about me. In fact, I went around recommending that everyone book tickets to his shows. Steve is without question the world's greatest lyricist. I produced what I consider to be Steve's best work in the musical theater: *Gypsy.* I find it unfortunate that *Company* and *Follies* did not do better, but audiences will not accept serious musicals. They want *Dolly, Mame, Fiddler.* They enjoy sentimental comedy. As for the musical itself, it's too big a convulsion now. How can you possibly make your money back? At this point in my career, and Broadway's career, I don't know what the hell to produce."

Gypsy producer David Merrick (left)
and composer Jule Styne at original
cast recording session, 1959. (COLUMBIA
RECORDS)

NO FITS, NO FIGHTS, · · · 4
NO FEUDS, NO EGOS?

A S SOON as *West Side Story* settled in for its initial Broadway stretch, Sondheim asked Burt Shevelove whether he would like to collaborate on a show for which Sondheim could write both music and lyrics. Though Shevelove had been mainly writing and directing for television at the time (having had a bad experience with a show he had written which closed out of town), he *was* interested in digging up an idea he had been playing around with when he was working at Yale: turning some of Plautus's plays into a musical. Sondheim read the plays, found them "terribly funny," and immediately called Jerome Robbins, who was looking to direct a farce. Robbins also became excited, and a tentative agreement was reached to do what Shevelove referred to as "A Scenario for Vaudevillians." Shevelove enlisted the aid of Larry Gelbart, with whom he had worked in television, to co-write the book, and early in 1958 a first draft of *A Funny Thing Happened on the Way to the Forum* was near completion.

About that time, Sondheim got a call that *Gypsy*, a musical based on the memoirs of Gypsy Rose Lee, had come up as a mutual project between David Merrick and Ethel Merman. Jerry Robbins had expressed interest in the property if Merrick would agree to team with Leland Hayward as co-producer.

Betty Comden and Adolph Green were the first ones given the book to adapt, "but they returned the advance," Merrick says. "They just couldn't figure out a way of doing it." Comden and Green then went off to Hollywood to write the screenplay for *Auntie Mame*, and Merrick began searching for someone else to musicalize his property. Duly impressed with *West Side Story*, he took the project to Arthur Laurents.

"Leland Hayward actually called me," Laurents recalls, "and he asked me to do the show because Jerry said he would only do it if I wrote it. Well, Jerry and I were not on very good terms as a result of his personal behavior on *West Side*, but I wasn't going to allow personal problems to get in the way of a good project and, still, no one can stage a number better than Jerry. Quite simply, the problem was that I wasn't interested in *Gypsy*. I read the book and I thought that it was kind of jazzy, but I didn't see where I came in. But they persisted and I finally came up with the idea of parents who live their children's lives. I told them that if I could figure out a way that the star could top the strip number in the end, then I would do it. Soon after, I devised 'Rose's Turn,' and the whole rest of the show wrote very fast." (Robbins had conceived "Rose's Turn" as a ballet in which all of the characters would appear. Unable to make the dance work, he finally asked that the number be done as a solo song instead.)

Laurents remembers that Irving Berlin had been approached to do the score but turned it down. "Later," Laurents says, "when he saw the show, he said that he was amazed that we got anything out of that book." Cole Porter, who had all but given up on life, turned down the show, and soon everyone who was writing songs came to audition . . . until the day before Jerome Robbins was to go off to Europe for the summer, when Sondheim handed him the first three songs he had written for *Forum*. Sondheim says: "He was mad about them and contacted Leland and told him that he wanted *me* to do the score for *Gypsy*. Of course I was thrilled —until Ethel Merman announced that she would not take a chance on an unknown composer . . . that she'd be perfectly happy to have me do the lyrics, but she wanted Jule Styne to do the music."

"This is not denying Steve's musical talent," Styne says, "but to write for Ethel Merman was a kind of bag he didn't know much about. The extrovert of Merman. . . . but Steve said no to writing just lyrics."

Laurents persisted in pushing Sondheim to accept the lyric-writing chore, but he absolutely refused. Once again, Sondheim had a meeting with Oscar Hammerstein, who told him that he knew how frustrated and disappointed he must be, but that he had never had any experience writing for a star and it could be very valuable. He also pointed out that the show was to go into rehearsal in six months, so the most it would be was six months out of his life.

Ethel Merman (left) as Madam Rose,
Sandra Church as *Gypsy*, 1959.
(FRIEDMAN–ABELES)

Sondheim: "I was heartsick, but I did it. And part of me is glad because I think it's a first-rate show, and part of me is sorry because it delayed my work as a composer just that much longer. It also interrupted *Forum* for six months."

Styne: "Knowing that Steve wanted to write the whole score, I decided that I would never pull rank on him. Steve is very astute. He worked very closely with Arthur. And when we started working, Steve would come over to my place, and God, we had a ball."

Flora Roberts remembers that as soon as *Gypsy* started, Styne gave Sondheim a folder with thirteen melodies, but "Steve told Jule that he couldn't write words just to notes, that he would have to wait for an outline from Arthur."

"Jule is so extraordinary," Sondheim says. "His melodic fertility is

incredible, but he throws it away. He's profligate. If Lenny makes the most out of the least, then the opposite is true of Jule. He's the least economical composer I know. He'd play you something and you'd say that it's not exactly right, but if he'd perhaps do something after the opening strain . . . and he'd say, 'I'll write something else!' And he'd write a whole new piece. It's certainly not laziness. I guess he's so talented that if he writes enough melodies, he assumes one of them will be good and that's very tough for me to adjust to because of my insistence on economy."

"I remember that Steve would get angry with Jule every once in a while," Milton Babbitt says. "After all, Jule does not exactly have Steve's sophisticated ambitions. For example, I remember that Steve was very excited about the triplets in 'Everything's Coming up Roses,' and Jule didn't even know how to notate them. And, of course, Ethel Merman never sang them correctly."

"I knew all the time that Merman was well taken care of," Styne says. "I had all those good notes for her. The other kids that wrote at that time didn't understand that. They were just writing songs . . . just writing character. When you write for a star you've got to take in what the star has to offer. If you don't, you're not doing what the people want to hear. I respected Steve more than I've ever respected anybody, and it was only his second show. I gave him a tune and he gave back lyrics—when I played him the tune for 'Little Lamb,' he just flipped out. Then I think Jerry must have said that I should play Steve a song that was thrown out of *High Button Shoes* in 1947, called 'In Betwixt and Between,' of which the music had reverted back to me. Strangely enough, I had never used it, I had just put it away. That became 'Everything's Coming up Roses.' It had needed a new and easy release, though, because Merman had to rest on it, which must have made Steve recognize immediately that I was a craftsman because I knew the voice and how you couldn't overtax it. Steve didn't have to tailor, he had to write only character. It was I who was catering to her voice. Steve could write those words for anybody, but he left it for me to settle the tune because it was me the star wanted. I came up with odd sounds for 'Mr. Goldstone.' A waltz for 'If Momma Was Married.' Then I played him the song he eventually wrote three sets of lyrics for, which I thought was for somebody else, but he made it into the dance for Tulsa, 'All I Need Is the Girl.' "

The writing of *Gypsy* progressed smoothly from book to lyrics with the continued excellent working relationship between Laurents and Sond-

Opposite: The real Gypsy Rose Lee (left) with Ethel Merman during a production break, 1959. (FRIEDMAN–ABELES)

heim. "The major thing I got from Arthur," Sondheim says, "was the notion of 'subtext.' What that means, simply, is something to give the actors to act. Lyrics, as well as scenes, without subtext, tend to be shallow or surface. When Arthur gave me the idea for 'Some People,' I was afraid it was going to be just a list song about a woman's anger—about how some people settle for this and some for that, but as for me, I've got to get out of here—and it seemed to be just on the surface. What Arthur had wanted her to play was that she wants a plaque that's hanging on the wall behind her father's head. It's worth $88, which is what she needs, and she uses the entire song as an excuse for borrowing money from him, and when he doesn't fall for the song she goes and takes the plaque. Here again, subtext gives the actress something to play. So although she's singing about other things, she can *play* the money and the plaque.

"Oscar Hammerstein once told me how astonished he was to learn that the sculptor of the Statue of Liberty had carved the top of the head as carefully as the rest of the statue, even though he couldn't possibly have known that one day there would be airplanes. That's what you have to do in a lyric, too—every word counts, whether the audience hears it specifically or not. In 'Everything's Coming up Roses' there was very little to say in the lyrics after the title was over, so I decided that I would give it its feeling by restricting myself to images of traveling, children, and show business, because the scene was a railroad station and was about a mother pushing her child into show business. Now that may be of no interest except to somebody in two hundred years doing a doctorate on the use of traveling images in *Gypsy*, but the point is, it's there, and it informs the whole song.

"In *West Side*, the lyrics had a poetic aspect and therefore there was a tendency to become pretentious. The lyrics for *Gypsy* are in the vernacular and the tendency is to become satirical. That was the big problem. The lyrics must be nostalgic—genuine and real—and this is a very thin line to tread. In *Gypsy*, all the climaxes of emotion and action erupt into music because they can't go further without it. A good character song does something that *can't* be done by a line by the book writer. 'Some People,' again, takes advantage of the fact that music can create intensity. A playwright would have to write a whole scene in order to convey the depth of Rose's desire to get to New York. And dialogue couldn't do what 'Everything's Coming Up Roses' does at the end of the first act.

"Not enough songwriters understand the function of a song in a play. They write songs in which a character explains himself—this is self-

Ethel Merman's last major musical marquee for a role she created on Broadway, 1959. (FRIEDMAN–ABELES)

defeating because the song should reveal the character to the audience; the character doesn't have that self-knowledge. We do, he doesn't. But that's the problem in most shows: characters coming out and singing about their drives, which in a way is a logical development of the Rodgers and Hammerstein form, but there are so many other ways to tell a story.

"Jule was appalled when in 'Small World' I wrote a line that said, 'Funny, I'm a woman with children.' Jule protested, 'Well, that means no *man* can sing the song!' And I told him that if I make the song general, then it's got no texture for the show at all. We've got 'You'll Never Get Away from Me,' and 'Everything's Coming Up Roses,' which are general.

But here's this lady who's trying to con the guy into handling her vaudeville act. It's got to be terribly personalized. Later, I changed the lyrics for the sheet music so that a man could sing it, but today nobody has to worry about that sort of thing.

"There was also a song that Jule had been playing at parties for years that I liked a lot. When we first got together on *Gypsy* and he gave me his trunk tunes, I said that we should write the songs fresh, but the tune that might really work is the song that he'd been playing a lot, a tune he had supposedly written for a movie that never got done called *Pink Tights*. It was called 'Why Did You Have to Wait So Long?' and Sammy Cahn had never finished the lyric. So we used the melody for *Gypsy* and called it 'You'll Never Get Away from Me.' What Jule had *not* told me was that Leo Robin had subsequently written a set of lyrics to it for a TV musical, *Ruggles of Red Gap*, with the title 'I'm in Pursuit of Happiness.' If he had told me that a completed lyric had been written to it, I would never have agreed to work with that tune."

Arthur Laurents was pleased during the writing of *Gypsy* that Robbins didn't see the show until it was done. This, however, did lead to a waste of a great deal of money since, according to Laurents, "Jerry saw it as a great panorama of a show and they hired, before anything, animal acts and burlesque acts and vaudeville acts. Some of them never saw a rehearsal and some of them were in and then thrown out. Actually, *Gypsy* is a show about three people and it had this enormous cast in the beginning. But we never discussed it. I didn't want to. I knew what I wanted to do and the only person I collaborated with was Steve. He collaborated in his own way with Jule. The three of us would meet and play songs and we had only one disagreement. They thought 'You'll Never Get Away from Me' would be a hit and I didn't and I still don't like it. I don't think it works." Laurents also recalls with amazement the day Sondheim played "Everything's Coming Up Roses" for Robbins. "He didn't like the title," Laurents notes. "He was in utter dismay, and he said, 'But that's her name!'

"Generally," Laurents says, "I don't think Jerry was very happy with the show. He would always say, 'It's your show, it's a book show.' Also I think he was rather tired. I forget what he was working on, but he didn't feel that *Gypsy* was the kind of show that enabled him to make the contribution that is uniquely his."

Gypsy's major casting problem was finding a leading man to play opposite Ethel Merman. After several fruitless auditions, Laurents, Robbins, and Sondheim spotted an actor on a segment of *Playhouse 90* who they felt had the perfect qualities for the role of Herbie.

"The problem was, I couldn't *sing*," Jack Klugman says apologetically. Sent by the production team to vocal coach David Craig, the actor could not make much improvement in the short time allotted. Klugman auditioned for three weeks, working diligently on "Small World," which he performed dreadfully, although his readings of the scenes were excellent.

Klugman: "I just wasn't very good. I was totally humiliated. One day they asked me to come down and read a few scenes with Ethel. I did. But then Jerry asked me to sing 'Small World' with her and I warned them, 'If she belts it, I'm going to walk right out!' Well, she sang it so softly that her voice cracked—there was so much love in it, such concern, that I picked up and sang the second chorus and sounded like Pinza. When I finished, I walked out of the theater, knowing that I could never audition again for the role. When I got home, they called and told me I had the part. But I didn't have a good voice and I was very self-conscious until one day somebody told me that Steve was going to parties singing 'You'll Never Get Away from Me' and when he'd get to 'Ah, Rose,' he'd stop and say that he couldn't do it as well as Klugman could . . . that when Klugman does it, it's so real and has so much feeling. And before that, I wanted to quit. I said, 'Steve, I'm making a horse's ass of myself. It's a beautiful score. Get a guy in here that you can write a couple of songs for.' And he said, 'No. What you're doing is right. I don't want a musical voice. I want a person I can believe.' He was really marvelous and he really helped me a great deal.

"Something else that I'll never forget, which is just an example of how emotionally involved we all were with the show: We were three weeks into rehearsal and we were at the Amsterdam Theatre, and Steve and Jule came in very late and announced that they'd just finished 'Rose's Turn.' We stopped the rehearsal and Jule sat down at the piano and played it, and Steve got up and sang it with such feeling and such awareness of what it was about that I just fell apart and bawled like a baby. It was so brilliant. I will never forget that moment. When Steve did 'M-m-momma, M-m-momma,' and couldn't get it out, Ethel and I just burst into tears."

" 'Rose's Turn,' " Laurents explains, "was an explosion for which the character had been heading throughout the play. It's an emotional summation in words and music. And because it's so enormous a moment for the character, the conventional song form was thrown out to provide the required freedom. Unfortunately, the form has since become formula and not done nearly as well. In the theater, artistry is as important as originality."

At the end of the rehearsal period, *Gypsy* had an enormously successful run-through in New York. "I've never seen such a reaction," David Merrick says. "But *I* was harder to please. When we got to Philly, we received mixed reviews and there were numerous problems. The audience just seemed to sit there."

On the other hand, Jule Styne reports a much better response—at least for *Gypsy*'s star. "When we opened out of town, Ethel Merman made her entrance and took a bow. And everybody said, 'Jesus Christ!' You know, like it was in a nightclub. When the guys saw it they ran up the aisles. They never saw anything like it. To her, it was a great return. She had been in a show that wasn't so good and there she was back, with the best role in her career."

One of the better reviews, in the *Philadelphia Evening Bulletin*, exclaimed: "There is only one possible reaction to *Gypsy*, and that is unconditional surrender. Jule Styne has written the most serious score of his life." (There wasn't a mention of Sondheim's lyrics.)

"David Merrick was awfully strange out of town," Klugman says. "I remember that I said, 'Gee, I'd like to invest in this show,' and he said to me, 'You don't want to invest in this. It's going to be a bomb. If you want to invest in a musical, invest in *Destry*.' We were up at the Variety Club and Leland and Jule pulled out their checkbooks and said to him, 'How much would you take to get out of this show?' But wisely, he stayed with it."

Fixing the show in Philadelphia meant mostly cutting. It ran nearly three and one-half hours. "We were about forty-five minutes too long," Laurents says. "One day in rehearsal, Jerry turned to me and said, 'Steve says you have twenty-two minutes of cuts marked in the script.' And I nodded yes. And he said, 'When are you going to make them?' And I said, 'When are you going to cut twenty-two minutes from those kiddie numbers?' There was a long pause and he finally said okay and we dumped forty-five minutes."

Robbins, never quite satisfied with the orchestrations, kept asking the orchestrators to redo them, though Laurents contends, "It was one of those things where people were *looking* for things to fix."

At one point, Robbins, without telling anybody, cut "Little Lamb" from the show. "When Jule asked him to put the number back, Jerry refused," Laurents says. "Jule walked up on the stage with great dignity and said, 'Mr. Robbins'—it was suddenly 'Mr. Robbins'—'I have notified my lawyers in New York that I am withdrawing my entire score unless "Little Lamb" is put back in tonight.' And it was put back and that was the end of it."

"Do you know," Styne says in exasperation, "do you know how I had to fight for that overture? Jerry didn't like it. All I know is that when the trumpet player started playing that strip music, the audience went crazy. We were a hit even before the curtain went up."

Throughout the adjustments that were made, Ethel Merman remained optimistic and excited about her new role. "You're going to see a different Merman than the one you've seen before," she announced to the press. "I hope you'll enjoy this Merman as much as the other. I'm almost positive you will. . . . I've had people coming back and saying, 'Gee, I didn't know you could act that well!' But I've always wanted to be a dramatic actress but I never had a chance. I always knew I could act and I would love to do a straight play, but I wonder if the public would accept me as a dramatic actress. I only know that I've never been presented to better advantage than in *Gypsy*. This is the peak of my career. And now, for the

From left: Stephen Sondheim, Ethel Merman, and Jack Klugman at recording studio, 1959. (COLUMBIA RECORDS)

Ethel Merman records "Rose's Turn," 1959. (COLUMBIA RECORDS)

first time, with my children grown up, I'd like to do it in London. I never have done a show there." (And she never did.)

Throughout the career of this Broadway star who had appeared in thirteen shows (from *Girl Crazy* to *Gypsy*), modesty had never stood in the way. She always knew her place in the theater. "When I do a show," Merman explained on a television talk show, "not to pat myself on the back, but when I do a show, the whole show revolves around *me*. . . . And if I don't show up, they can just forget it!"

"Merman was marvelous in rehearsal," emphasized Laurents. "She was very professional and very willing. You couldn't have asked for any star to act better than she did. But she did balk when I brought in an addition to the last scene where she would say, 'I did it for me.' She didn't want to say it. But that was one of the necessities . . . to have her face herself and admit that . . . and to have the girl admit that it wasn't talent, but her mother who got them there. They have to give to each other. Also I had an intention in the last scene that didn't quite come off: that Gypsy *becomes*

Rose. The girl becomes the tough mother, and for all of Rose's toughness, she's just a little girl who wants to be recognized."

Sondheim's amiable relationship with Merman nearly came to an abrupt end when she refused to learn some material he had written for her. "Ethel worked very hard," Sondheim says, "and she told us that we could put anything into the show up until one week before the opening. Thereafter, she would not change a single word, gesture, move, or anything. Two weeks before the opening I thought that 'Some People' needed a verse because the dialogue that precedes the song is on a high pitch and the song starts low. It needed the verse to bring it down. The cue-in is clumsy and it would have helped the song a lot. After it was written, however, she said that she felt it was too angry and she refused to learn it."

"Most of the time," Flora Roberts explains, "a writer has say on what goes into a show since the Dramatists Guild says that the writer's words can't be changed without the writer's consent. The Saturday night while they were in Philly, I was home giving a dinner party and I got a call from Steve asking to know his rights. And I asked, 'In what connection?' And he told me the story. Well, this is where you can have all the rights in the world in a contract, but the human factor is involved. Early Monday morning I called the Guild and said, 'If there's an unnamed star who doesn't want to sing a verse, what are the writer's rights?' And the man at the Guild said, 'Let's put it this way. There was a star named Ethel Merman and she was in a show called *Call Me Madam*, and she sang a dummy lyric for "Hostess with the Mostes' on the Ball" for many weeks out of town and just as she got into New York, Irving Berlin came into her dressing room and said, "I've finally perfected the lyric!" And she said, "Call me Miss Birds Eye. The show is frozen!" So for three years, she sang the dummy lyric.' Well, needless to say, Ethel never did do the verse for 'Some People.' "

Another addition that never made the production was a solo number written for Jack Klugman. "Jule came to me in Philly and said, 'Steve and I wrote a song for you to do when Ethel leaves the restaurant after stealing the silverware. The waitress comes by and says, "Where's that nice lady?" Then you sing, "Nice She Ain't." ' And they played it for me and I said, 'Gee, that's a great number,' but it was a week before we were going into New York and I said, 'Let me think about it and I'll tell you tomorrow whether I want to attempt it.' Well, I went back to the hotel, went to sleep, and had the most horrible nightmares that there were eighteen hundred people out there and someone hit a bell tone and I went off key . . . The next day I walked over to Jule and said, 'Take the song and shove it up your ass!' And that was the end of it."

Another number written for *Gypsy* that was cut from the show out of town was "Momma's Talkin' Soft," which was sung by the kids in counterpoint to "Small World," as their comment on their mother's seduction of Herbie. "The number was cut," Sondheim says, "mostly because one of the little girls was afraid of the height of the scenery and cried every time she got up there, and there was no other way to stage it."

One of Arthur Laurents's concerns was killing a totally unexpected audience laugh at the end of the first act. "There was always that surprise," Laurents says, "when Rose says to Louise, 'I'm gonna make you a star,' which we all thought was very dramatic, but the audience laughed, which I think is a very strange reaction. The first time we had a run-through and they laughed, I thought poor Ethel was going to die. There were all sorts of theories as to why they laughed. I suppose that the audience knows her by then and they were appalled at what lengths she would go to."

Gypsy opened in New York at the Broadway Theatre May 21, 1959, to the enthusiastic tune of the *Daily News*'s John Chapman: "What this town has needed is Ethel Merman. What Miss Merman has needed is a good show. We got her and she got it last evening."

Dorothy Kilgallen in the *Journal American* declared: "Anyone who doesn't think *Gypsy* is a fine, funny, satisfying evening in the theater needs oxygen, a nurse and a pint of blood."

And Brooks Atkinson in the *New York Times* said: "Since *Gypsy* has a literate theme, it has put everybody on his best behavior. Mr. Styne has written his most colorful score," but hastened to add, "Stephen Sondheim's lyrics are hackneyed." (Sondheim received a letter from Atkinson after the review appeared, apologizing for the misprint: the newspaper incorrectly printed *hackneyed* instead of *unhackneyed*, which was what the reviewer said he had intended.)

Merrick: "The show ran only a year and a half on Broadway, which was disappointing because *I* thought it was one of the truly great musicals of all time. It was an unusual show and it was a hit that made a million dollars profit, but it wasn't one of those smashes. I would say that tourists and the garment center group weren't exactly wild about it. Ultimately, I suppose they liked *Hello, Dolly!* a lot better."

Sondheim: "Generally, I've always wanted to have a smash, but I rather doubt that I ever will. From their reviews, *West Side* and *Gypsy* should have been smashes. But audiences generally respond to what a show is about. *Gypsy* is not a terribly likable story. And what makes smash-hit musicals are stories that audiences want to hear—and it's always the same story. How everything turns out terrific in the end and the audience goes out thinking, that's what life is all about.

"In *My Fair Lady* they are told that you, too, can be the belle of the ball even if you aren't educated—which can mean in your own terms ugly, ungainly, old, whatever. It's the Cinderella story. *The Sound of Music* says you can eat your cake and have it—you can get away from the Nazis, marry the man of your choice, *without* compromising your religious goodness. *Hello, Dolly!* says that a loud, middle-aged lady can get the man she wants. Now that may sound cynical, but those are fairy stories and they are what make smash hits. And, I hasten to add, I like them, too. So I'm not putting them down—but that's what's essential for a smash hit.

"*Gypsy* says something fairly hard to take: that every child eventually has to become responsible for his parents. That you outgrow your parents and then eventually they become your responsibility . . . they become your children. It's something that everybody knows but no one likes to think about a lot. And that's why *Gypsy*, at base, in spite of the terrific reviews, wasn't a smash hit.

"People who like the show often say that they wish the curtain had fallen immediately after 'Rose's Turn.' That the last scene seems like an addendum of sorts. But the last scene is what the play is about—the unpleasant truth of it. *I* think it's quite moving. But it's not very cheerful."

Around the time *Gypsy* was sold to the movies, Warner Bros. producer–director Mervyn LeRoy visited the show quite often. "He really screwed Ethel," says Jack Klugman. "He was constantly with her and *promised* that he wouldn't do the picture without her. Then he went and signed Roz Russell for the role. Mr. LeRoy is not a very nice person."

"There was quite a fracas," remembered onlooker George Oppenheimer. "I happened to be in Jule Styne's office that day and Jule came in and the phone started to ring . . . he answered it and his face turned white. It was Ethel, who had just found out that Rosalind Russell's husband, Freddie Brisson—whom she affectionately referred to as The Lizard of Roz—had somehow gotten his wife signed for Ethel's part in the movie. Ethel was screaming at poor Jule over the phone, and in pure desperation he said, 'Look, look, talk to George Oppenheimer . . . *He'll* tell you the position I'm in . . .' And I could hear Ethel say, 'What the

Natalie Wood (left) as Louise, Rosalind Russell as Rose, in the motion-picture adaptation of *Gypsy*, 1963. (WARNER BROS.)

fuck do I want to talk to George Oppenheimer for? I want *you* to do something!' "

Released in 1963, with Russell, Natalie Wood, and Karl Malden, *Gypsy* was a disaster as a motion picture, and the quality of the property drifted from public memory. Some years later, however, there was an attempt to have the show revived, but "the guy who headed City Center," Sondheim explains, "Morton Baum, hated *Gypsy* and would never let it be done."

For fourteen years, revivals of the show were planned, but none materialized until 1971, when a young stage manager from Harold Prince's office, Fritz Holt, and a music publishing executive, Barry Brown, decided to bring *Gypsy* to the British.

Since London had never seen a production of the show (because of Merman's refusal to stay long enough for it to recoup its investment), they felt the West End stage should be just the place to open this long-anticipated musical.

Feelers were sent out to Merman, who gave the expected negative response. The producers approached Angela Lansbury and got a polite turndown. Then the London edition of *Company* opened and Elaine Stritch drew great notices and much publicity. Brown and Holt offered the role to Stritch, and she was more than eager to accept their proposal.

Everything was then looking fine. Elaine Stritch would star, Arthur Laurents would direct his book, Stephen Sondheim and Jule Styne would be around for musical support, Robert Tucker would re-create Jerome Robbins's choreography and, coincidentally, Tucker's daughter, Zan Charisse (niece of Cyd), would play the title role of Gypsy.

But slowly, deal after deal fell through. The two young producers were not able to raise the required capital on Stritch's name, and the promise of a new production of *Gypsy* became ominously distant.

Then, with Arthur Laurents's urging, Angela Lansbury re-read the script. She suddenly became excited—she discovered a new way that the character could be played so that she wouldn't be merely a second-hand Rose. Lansbury set up a meeting with her brother Edgar and his partner, Joseph Beruh (producers of *Godspell*), an offer was made, and with Brown and Holt as co-producers, a theater was slated and an opening date set.

"The reason I was interested in directing the show was because we had a different star," said Laurents at the time. "Not to denigrate Merman, but I wouldn't have been interested in doing it with Merman in London —you could get a stage manager and do it the way it was done before. But with a new star, you could play the show for different values."

Laurents made several changes in the London production which cleared up certain defects that were in the show during its initial Broadway engagement. "The strip never worked on Broadway," Laurents pointed out, "and the last scene between Gypsy and Rose was never well played. With the strip, I always felt the girl should talk, but Jerry was never willing to try it. In London, I wrote lines for her [and Sondheim added two new choruses for "Together, Wherever We Go"] and through her talk you can *see* her evolve as a woman. Now, also, the line of the piece is different. The entire show builds to 'Rose's Turn.' Originally, the whole thing built to 'Everything's Coming Up Roses' and everybody thought the second act wasn't as good as the first. Now, the second act *tops* the first. It's in the relationships. The show is a genuine love story between Rose and Herbie. You *believe* she loves him, and when he walks out, she's lost something. You *believe* she's a mother and you *believe* she loves those kids.

"I've staged 'Rose's Turn' with Angie right in the audience's laps on a runway that lights up. At the conclusion of the number, she gets this standing ovation. With no disrespect to Merman, it's the first time that number has been done the way it should be. It's hair-raising and it's because Angie's an actress. At the end of the number she bows and you can *feel* the audience standing and screaming—but it's so strange. Why is Angela Lansbury taking a bow at this stage of the game? It's the first bow she takes in the show. And she has a rather demented look in her eye. On

Zan Charisse (left) as Louise, Rex Robbins as Herbie, and Angela Lansbury as Rose in the American revival of *Gypsy*, 1974. (MARTHA SWOPE)

the third bow, all the lights go out except for a spot on her. And then a spot picks up Gypsy as she walks on . . . and the audience stops applauding . . . but Rose keeps bowing. Then you realize that it was all in her head. It's very spooky. You see, now the last scene doesn't seem tacked on. At the end, they start to exit the stage, which is lit only by a work light. Gypsy leaves . . . and Rose, in her daughter's fur coat, turns and looks at the runway and the lights start to come up . . . and as she looks at them, they go out. Rose is through. It's very lonely and sad. She misled her life and she's the only person in the show who never gets the recognition she wants. And that's something you can do with a unique person like Angela Lansbury. I say she is unique because I know of no one else in the musical theater who can sing as well as she does and be the actress she is. Directing the show was the happiest experience I've ever had in the theater."

The London opening of *Gyspy* was, as Rex Reed wrote in the Sunday *Daily News*, "the most exciting thing since V-E Day. . . . It was like a football game. People cheered through a fifteen-minute standing ovation, grown men cried unashamed, the backstage area looked like a flower shop on Mother's Day, and no less a jaded observer than Kenneth Tynan remarked: 'In twenty years of London theater, I've never seen anything

From left: Sally Cooke as Electra, Mary Louise Wilson as Tessie Tura, and Gloria Rossi as Mazeppa in "You Gotta Get a Gimmick" from the revival of *Gypsy*, 1974. (MARTHA SWOPE)

Angela Lansbury (left) as Rose, and Zan Charisse as the queen of burlesque, Miss Gypsy Rose Lee, 1974. (MARTHA SWOPE)

like this!' " (Later in the run, Miss Lansbury scored yet another personal triumph when she was voted *Plays and Players*'s Drama Critics Award as Best Actress of the Year—the first time anyone had ever won the award for an appearance in a musical.)

"It's really unfair to compare the two performances," says Flora Roberts. "They were both brilliant on different levels. The best way I can think of describing them is that it was goose bumps with Merman and tears with Lansbury."

With Lansbury, Zan Charisse, and a new American cast, *Gypsy* began a full American tour in the spring of 1974. It opened on Broadway on September 23, 1974, to nothing less than triumphant notices.

"*Gypsy* is simply a powerhouse," wrote Martin Gottfried in the *New York Post*. "It's as if it had been born fresh, beautifully directed by Laurents."

And Clive Barnes in the *New York Times* exclaimed: "Lightning never strikes twice! Right? Wrong! At the Winter Garden Theatre last night, Angela Lansbury shattered the town. . . . Everything about *Gypsy* is right. . . . The music bounces out of the pit, assertive, confident and cocky, and has a love affair with Stephen Sondheim's elegantly paced, daringly phrased lyrics. . . . Mr. Laurents has made Rose into a fascinating person, possibly one of the few truly complex characters in the American musical. . . . [Lansbury] is enchanting, tragic, bewildering and bewildered. Miss Lansbury not only has a personality as big as the Statue of Liberty, but also a small core of nervousness that can make the outrageous real. . . . *Gypsy* is one of the best of musicals and it improves with keeping . . . a musical to think about, ponder and love."

Angela Lansbury won the Tony Award that season as Best Actress in a Musical and the show had a successful, limited engagement on Broadway.

"*Gypsy* holds up so well," says Sondheim, "because it's about people. I believe it's one of the best shows ever written . . . the last good one in the Rodgers and Hammerstein form."

Opposite: Angela Lansbury in the climactic "Rose's Turn," 1974. (MARTHA SWOPE)

Director-librettist Arthur Laurents
(left), and composer-lyricist Stephen
Sondheim at *Anyone Can Whistle*
recording session, 1964. (COLUMBIA
RECORDS)

MUSICAL LIBRETTO · · · 5

"ONE of the biggest problems I've found over the years," Sondheim has said, "is that good bookwriting is the most underdeveloped part of the musical theater and the part that there is most to be learned about. Most playwrights are condescending about musicals. They try and get away with things they wouldn't allow in a straight play. Arthur Laurents, as a librettist, is one of the most significant and talented of our bookwriters. His work, all in a row, is quite impressive. Arthur changes his style for a musical, but never his standards."

"The first thing a librettist must be prepared to do," Laurents once said in an interview, "is to sacrifice ego. You have to be prepared that you are going to be ignored. You have to know that the music is the most important thing and everything has to be built toward it. Again, there's that elusive thing that a musical is larger than life. Steve once told me that he thought *Gypsy* could be a play and I absolutely did not agree. Never. Not the way I wrote it. It's too big. The characters are overblown, the strokes are too bold and too broad. It's the presence of music that supports it. There are fireworks in a scene with about two lines and they are screaming and yelling at each other. Music allows you that style. The absence of music doesn't. A musical needs construction. . . . Probably more than a play because you must construct things to build to a song. Every line must make its point or you don't have it. A musical calls for the most economical writing there is in the theater. Maybe I do it well because I began in radio where you had a severe time limit plus the fact that you had to write what I call visual dialogue.

"The books of musicals need to be written so economically and in such broad strokes that the characters tend to be thin unless they are filled out by the songs they sing. Musicals are larger than life so there is little room for subtleties and there is little room to probe and examine. Also, since songs tend to lighten the atmosphere, there must be an extreme sensitivity as to what might be *too* serious for lyrical treatment. Personally, however, I feel that if you see to it that all is related to character and emotion, all will be well. These are problems, not impossible obstacles, and they can be solved.

"I'm asked almost every day to do musicals, not really because I'm that good, but because there's nobody else. There's a terrible paucity of librettists. Looking at the musical book over the years, it hasn't changed so much as developed an attitude of thin sophistication. By thin, I mean it isn't truly sophisticated. Cynicism is more difficult to criticize on an artistic level. Pessimism seems to be considered art. The writing has become bloodless. I think the musical is asked to carry more weight than it should. I think it's slightly pretentious. The idea is to involve the musical with people. It should be emotional bloodletting or the closest you can come to it in a musical. The emotion should be *big.* It's also become much too polite. People don't suffer, they have migraines. They don't enjoy, they have a slight smile. Such shows make me say, 'Terribly well done . . . where shall we go to eat?' They don't move me. They don't excite me.

"People tell me all the time that they want me to hear 'this terrific score.' How can you have the score if you don't have a book? It's impossible. That's why they all fail. But it seems to be true of all the arts. Steve has a comment on it in *Night Music.* 'Where is craft? Where is skill?' It's very hard to learn your craft. It's very hard to acquire a skill and know how to use it. We live in a rather mindless time with novelists like Kurt Vonnegut, who really writes for teenagers. They can read a book quickly and they don't have to think about it. It's all very simplistic, a word I hate to use, but I'm going to. It's very trendish and very mindless and very unskilled. That's one of the reasons those musicals Steve has done with Hal have to be admired, if for nothing else, for the sheer craft and the skill. You also don't have the saccharine attitude of many of the Rodgers and Hammerstein musicals. The attitudes are much better.

"The musical, you must remember, is America's most distinctive contribution to the theater, and though it's the most popular form of theater in this country, it is a form that has been lacking in content and in artistry. Its potential is largely unexplored. There is no reason that the musical must be trivial to be entertaining and successful. So much of the theater is expectation and it's far worse to get dull disappointment than gallant failure."

From left: *A Funny Thing Happened on the Way to the Forum* composer-lyricist Stephen Sondheim, co-librettists Larry Gelbart and Burt Shevelove, director George Abbott, 1962. (VAN WILLIAMS)

S O N D H E I M & C O .

SEND IN THE CLOWNS ... 6

BACK to work on *A Funny Thing Happened on the Way to the Forum* after his six-month break to do *Gypsy*, Sondheim found confusion rampant.

Leland Hayward, who was initially interested in producing it, had dropped out and David Merrick picked up the option. By this time, Phil Silvers, for whom the musical was written, had read the first act and said he didn't want to do it because it was "old shtick," not realizing that that was precisely the show's intention. Then Jerome Robbins withdrew from the project, mostly because Robbins and Merrick had gotten along so badly on *Gypsy*. Joshua Logan then agreed to direct but pulled out when the authors would not agree to rewrite the book to his taste.

Merrick drew up a new list of directors for the writing triumvirate to consider—all of whom they turned down. Finally, Sondheim and Flora Roberts met with Merrick.

"Steve was very frightened of him," Flora Roberts relates. "But we explained to Merrick that we wanted to put the show in a drawer and let it sit because we didn't know what to do with it. So we returned his $4,000 option payment and that was that . . . until five months later when Jerry came back and said, 'I can't forget that show. Why don't we ask Hal Prince to do it.' Meanwhile, Hal agreed to produce it, Jerry took a vacation in Paris, hadn't signed his contract, and upon returning said that he'd changed his mind *again*."

David Merrick's telling of the story is somewhat different: "When they came to me asking for their show back, it seemed that they felt the only

Zero Mostel (left) as Pseudolus, Jack Gilford as Hysterium, in the original Broadway production of *A Funny Thing Happened on the Way to the Forum*, 1962. (VAN WILLIAMS)

way they could get Jerry was if Hal Prince and Bobby Griffith produced it. And I released it to them on this promise: that if Jerry didn't do it, they'd bring it back to me. They said they would and it was all a gentleman's agreement. And lo and behold, Jerry wasn't doing it and George Abbott, whom I had wanted all along, was. Somewhere, I have a letter from Steve apologizing and saying that he owed me a big favor. So that's where we stand, although I don't expect the favor ever to be paid off."

"I had always wanted to do *Forum*," admits Prince. "I had the same conviction about it that I had with *West Side*, but my partner Bobby Griffith wasn't crazy about it. Finally, he did agree to do it with me, but then he died. I had no shows running on Broadway for the first time since we started in '54, and here it was '61 and I had just had two failures and no partner. It was a very lonely time, but I decided to produce the show by myself. To give you an example of how unattractive it was to people, we gave it to the Theatre Guild, and not only did we *not* get the subscription, but they didn't even approve it for consideration. They thought it was confusing and unfunny. Somehow at the piano and on paper it was a show that, to put it mildly, was attractive to a minimal number of people."

"It was difficult to explain to people what the intention of the show was," Burt Shevelove said. "People are oriented by the shows they've seen before. They said, 'There's only room for one or two dances in it and you don't care anything about the kids.' And we said, 'You're not *supposed* to care anything about the kids.' Also, one set of costumes didn't strike them as a musical. Our reason for putting it on was an affectionate one. Low comedy and farce in America are rarely done and are rarely successful."

After Harold Prince released to the press that Milton Berle would be coming to Broadway as the star of his new musical comedy (in the role originally written for Silvers), Berle, afraid that many of his best lines might be cut during the numerous revisions of the libretto, insisted that script approval be included in his contract. Prince refused and Berle withdrew.

Zero Mostel, who had made a big name for himself in *Ulysses in Nighttown* and *Rhinoceros*, was next offered the role and, unimpressed, passed on it.

Mostel: "I read it and I didn't like it . . . so I turned it down. Then Hal Prince went to my wife and asked why I wouldn't do it and she came to me and said, 'I heard you turned down *Forum.*' And I said, 'Oh, yes, I forgot to tell you.' And she said, 'If you don't take it, I'm going to stab you in the balls.' So I said, 'All right, but this is the last time I'm gonna do something for money for you! Next time I'm gonna do what *I* wanna do!' "

Shevelove: "We weren't completely satisfied with Zero. . . . I don't think any of us were. Anybody can be as difficult as he likes, commensurate with his talent."

Gelbart: "Zero was a giant. He was a giant talent . . . and a giant pain in the ass. But there are very few leading men—and leading men, in the conventional sense, are immediately snatched up for pictures. The theater keeps getting robbed of that kind of guy, but Zero had no major movie career so he could afford to return to the theater."

At long last, with George Abbott set to direct, with Mostel, Jack Gilford, and David Burns signed to head the cast, and with Harold Prince producing, the show began to piece together. "We spent a long time on the plot," Shevelove noted. "Although it's really a series of interconnected incidents, one incident has to start before the incident before it can be solved. You have to work it out almost on graph paper so you know what's going on."

"*Forum* is not generally recognized as being experimental," Sondheim once said, "but I find it very experimental. *Forum* is a direct antithesis of the Rodgers and Hammerstein school. The songs could be removed from the show and it wouldn't make any difference. . . ."

"Except one," Shevelove disagreed. "Without the songs, the show would become relentless. It would exhaust you and you wouldn't get any breathers, any savoring of certain moments. 'Everybody Ought to Have a Maid' is a chance to stop running in and out of doors and conniving. When Steve first started, he only wanted to write songs integrated into the show that would advance the plot and increase your knowledge of the characters. I tried to tell him that the songs don't have to do that. Plays have breathers, too, and in *Forum* the songs can be respites. Sometimes they can serve as background for the comedy, like the wailing during the funeral sequence. Although it has funny lines in it, it also has, during that song, a funny situation. Will that body remain there when they sing 'Bring on the fire!'? So the song enhances that. If it were done without music, it wouldn't have been as effective. You can enhance a play a lot of ways and one of the most delightful is with music.

"In writing the book, we selected the characters from Plautus's plays and created a plot. The only thing extremely un-Roman was making a big thing out of the slave wanting to be free. Although slaves in Roman comedies wanted to be free, it was a very casual thing. But to give it some vague relevance to our times, we made *Forum* about a slave who would do *anything* to be free. It gives an overall theme to all the connecting incidents because they are all basically dependent on the fact that he has to buy his freedom."

"I think," Sondheim said a few years ago, "that the book is vastly underrated. It's brilliantly constructed. We worked on the show over a period of four years. It took Larry and Burt eleven complete and distinct separate drafts, and everybody thinks that it was whipped up over a weekend because it plays so easily. The plotting is intricate, the dialogue is never anachronistic, and there are only two or three jokes—the rest is comic situation. It's almost like a senior thesis on two thousand years of comedy with an intricate, Swiss watch–like farce plot. The style of the dialogue is very elegant . . . the phrasings and grace of that dialogue are better than most of the writing of the musical or nonmusical theater of

the last twenty years. It's almost a foolproof piece—it can be done by any high school class or a group of vaudevillians and the play holds up."

Sondheim also notes that the writing of the score for the show was his own rebellion against all his years with Oscar Hammerstein, suddenly finding that there were ways to write shows outside the Rodgers and Hammerstein tradition. He found it most difficult since he had been trained to use songs solely for dramatic purposes, unlike other songwriters who received their training in revue or nightclub work in which a song must be its own entity without having to relate to anything around it.

"I felt then," Shevelove admitted, "but less strongly about it now, that the score should have been brasher, more songs of the style of 'Everybody Ought to Have a Maid.' There was too much intellectuality in the show. But, again, it was Steve's first time writing music and lyrics for a Broadway show and your tendency is to show all your skills. *Forum* should have tapped one part of him. He was trying desperately to show that he was not just a tunesmith. The songs should have been brassier—from the school of Irving Berlin, as some of them turned out to be."

Sondheim himself says today that a month before the show went into rehearsal, he played the score for playwright and friend James Goldman, who immediately pointed out the incongruities between book and score. But as one member of the production put it, it was the sophistication of the score that brought the show up to a higher level than that required for a musical farce.

Under George Abbott's direction, *A Funny Thing Happened on the Way to the Forum* went into rehearsal and opened in New Haven to disastrous reviews.

Gelbart: "The show didn't work because by the time we had opened, we had put it through a strainer and taken out a lot of complications in the plot, subplot, sub-subplot, as George Abbott suggested. But upon seeing it we realized we had done it a great deal of damage because a lot of fun was in the organized confusion. So we put it all back—and probably a little more."

Prince: "It was very unpleasant on the road. Steve felt unduly pressured. There was a lot of talk about how the book and score didn't mix. The one thing that I quarreled with was the casting of the ingenue and juvenile. Both of them, Karen Black and Pat Fox, *were* replaced, but *not* by people I would have cast. Somewhere earlier I had brought in a girl and boy, namely Barbara Harris and Joel Grey, and I was laughed out of that audition. The point that I was trying to make was that the two young people should have been terribly comic. I still think I was right and if I was doing the show today, that's the way I'd do it. They would probably still fight me, but I'd win. Let's put it this way, in those days they were happy with me just as a producer. And I think I was a good one. The trouble we went through was appalling when we got to Washington."

Richard Coe in the *Washington Post* greeted the show with less than enthusiasm: "It's not a bad idea to have an intimate musical from an old Roman farce, but a good deal more steam will be needed to reassure you that you haven't wandered into amateur night."

"We played one matinee to fifty people," Prince says. "The main review said to close the show, and I think my biggest contribution to the show was that I was very sure about it. When the whole world's falling apart, you should have *somebody* who's sure. I never doubted for one minute that the show would be a smash in New York. The problems all were with the authors—they weren't getting along very well at that point. Steve needed somebody else to tell him what to do. Namely, Jerry Robbins."

The very same Robbins who intended to direct the show from its conception was called down to Washington as play doctor. And the problem proved to be basic.

"We had a perfectly charming opening," Sondheim says. "It was a vaudeville-style number called 'Love Is in the Air,' and about a month before rehearsals I had wanted to change it because Burt, Larry, and I began to realize that it was the wrong number. So I wrote another song called 'Invocation,' which really told the audience what the show was all about. But George Abbott wouldn't have it because he wanted something he could hum, and he didn't think the new song was hummable, and he said that you *have* to start a show with a hummable song. This hummable song cost us $100,000 out of town—that's how much we lost. The first thing Jerry did when he came in was to tell us to change the opening number, to tell the audience what the evening is about because the show is perfectly terrific but they don't know what it's about until it's too late. . . . They don't know that it's low comedy, they think it's going to be a rather charming, delicate evening and certainly won't be ready to laugh at the comics. Well, the minute Abbott heard that, he suddenly agreed. I played Jerry 'Invocation' and he told me that was what the tone of the song should be but that I should write another number, one that Abbott would like. So one weekend in Washington I wrote 'Comedy Tonight.' Jerry staged it over the next week, along with restaging several other musical numbers in the show and reblocking the end chase scene. 'Comedy

Tonight' played the first preview in New York and it not only brought down the house, but the entire show was clearly a hit . . . and it was all a matter of the opening number . . . and all a matter of George Abbott not being able to hum."

Forum's triumphant Broadway opening on May 8, 1962, did not register immediately at the box office, and the Prince office was worried for the first eight weeks of its run, until it began to sell out. Another boost came when *Forum* won a slew of Tony Awards, including Best Musical. Stephen Sondheim, however, was not even nominated for either his music or his lyrics.

Sondheim: "The reviews were generally excellent, but they did tend to describe it as a 'romp.' You'd think that Walter Kerr, who taught drama, would have understood it. He had a good time but he didn't really understand what was going on. As far as Zero was concerned, he was wonderful on the road, but the minute he got to New York and became a

Zero Mostel, singing "Free," during original cast recording of *Forum*, 1962. (VAN WILLIAMS)

From left: John Hansen as Hero, Phil Silvers as Pseudolus, and Pamela Hall as Philia in the revival of *Forum*, 1972. (FRIEDMAN–ABELES)

star from the reviews, he would begin doing things like announcing the results of the heavyweight fight from the stage . . . wish everyone a happy Hallowe'en . . . imitate the other actors. He did that in *Fiddler*, too, which was even less seemly. At least *Forum* seemed to be this loose farce so that, as obnoxious as the ad-libbing was, the audience could take it, but when you do it on a piece like *Fiddler*, it really wrecks it."

Mostel: "There's a kind of silliness in the theater about what one contributes to a show. The producer obviously contributes the money; the bookwriter, the book; the composer, the music; the lyricist, the lyrics; but the actor contributes nothing at all? The theory that it's strong material . . . I'm not a modest fellow about those things. I contribute a great deal. And they always manage to hang you for having an interpretation. Why must it be dull as shit? I don't think theater should be like that. Isn't that where your imagination should flower? But the producer, the director, the authors, all go on their vacations and they come back well tanned and I'm pale from playing the show, and they say, 'It's altered a great deal since opening night.' But I'm not the actor who can do it in a monotone all the time. Suppose you have a bellyache, can't you use it when you're on the stage? Don't you use what you have? Guys who call it shtick give me a pain in the ass. If you have the premise that a guy wants to be free, no matter what crazy things you do on the stage, as long as you feel that it's keeping with that premise, it should be accepted by the audience."

Eleven years later, Mostel opened for a limited engagement, re-creating his role of Pseudolus for the Guber and Gross music fairs, and his stage antics seemed only to have heightened.

"He told some Watergate jokes," Shevelove said angrily. "In the original, at least, Zero stuck to the lines. He did outrageous things, but at least he interpreted the script and played it. You see, the play was written broadly enough to leave the clowning to the actors so they don't feel tied in. It's written in cartoon, two-dimensional style; then the players bring humanity to it, some sort of warmth, some sort of emotion. But I do like the actors to stick to the lines as they are written. When I saw the show 'in the round' recently with Zero, I was horrified. There's a line, and it may be my favorite line in the show. It's when he's looking for a body and says, 'I know Gusto, the body snatcher. He owes me a favor.' I just think it's comic that a body snatcher would owe you a favor. Zero changed it and said, 'I know Gusto, the body snatcher. He owes me a snatch.' Now that's dirty. That's a little child sitting at the table saying cocky, cocky, doodie, doodie, and that's not funny. Most of the laughs that you get when you're doing low comedy are things like, 'She's back!' It's not a funny line, but in its context it's funny. There was a line where he says, 'You go and hide behind that clump of myrrh,' and the girl says, 'Will you call me when the captain comes?' and he says, 'Don't we always?' Because she's been called about eleven times. That night, she said, 'Will you call me when the captain comes?' and Zero said, 'I'll knock on your clump three times.' *That's* perversity."

The motion picture version of *Forum* was a terrible failure both financially and artistically. Directed by Richard Lester (who directed the Beatles in *A Hard Day's Night*, and *Superman II* and *III*), the film was produced for United Artists Pictures.

"In casting Phil Silvers in the role of Lycus," Gelbart says, "they felt they needed to build up the part for him so that it would be as big as Zero's. So they began to invent new story points and lots of twists. *Forum* is a very finely put together Chinese puzzle, and if you change one piece you have to account for about fifty more pieces behind it. They cut a lot of the musical numbers and they lost any continuity of style.

"The next problem was that they asked Zero who he would like to direct it and he gave the producer a list of five: Charles Chaplin, Orson Welles, Mike Nichols, Richard Lester, or Seth Holt. He got Richard Lester, who makes films in which the camera never stops. *Forum* is essentially a very literary piece of work and there arose a great contrast in approach of styles, which developed into an enormous power struggle between Lester and Mel Frank, who was co-author of the screenplay and producer of the film, to the point where Frank was literally not allowed on the set lest he incur Lester's displeasure. Well, it's pretty hard to be funny with all that unfunny stuff happening behind and around the camera. I think the work shows it. Any film in which Buster Keaton is an embarrassment says a lot for how unfunny it is."

Even Mostel became disenchanted with his choice of Lester as director. "The stupid damned thing of Hollywood is to open up a film!" Mostel bellowed. "The great thing about the piece on the stage was that it was one set, sixteen characters, three houses, and you did it very simply. You go to the movie and there's horses, zebras, peacocks shitting all over the place, your father's moustache, orphans, winos, donkeys with hard-ons. . . ."

"I went to the opening of the film in London." Gelbart winces. "It was like being hit by a truck that backed up and ran over you again. It was one of the most painful evenings of my life."

In 1972, following a highly successful revival of *Forum*, directed by Burt Shevelove at the Ahmanson Theatre in Los Angeles, starring Phil Silvers, Larry Blyden, and Nancy Walker, Blyden decided to acquire the sets and costumes and bring the production to New York.

"Steve wrote a new song for Nancy called 'Farewell' for the West Coast revival," said Blyden, "and we kept it in, although Nancy didn't come to New York with the rest of us."

Also added to the score was "Echo Song," a number that was deleted in New Haven from the original Broadway production. And on the way to New York this time around, "Pretty Little Picture" was dropped when Phil Silvers couldn't perform it.

The show was most welcome in revival (this time with Silvers playing the role that was written for him) and received even better reviews than it had originally.

Clive Barnes in the *New York Times* led the jubilation: "Everyone ought to have a favorite Broadway musical. Personally, my favorite for ten years has been *A Funny Thing Happened on the Way to the Forum.* Last night *A Funny Thing* happened once again, and I fell in love with it as desperately as ever. This is the funniest, bawdiest and most enchanting Broadway musical that Plautus, with a little help from Stephen Sondheim, Burt Shevelove and Larry Gelbart, ever wrote. . . . Mr. Sondheim's music is original and charming, with considerable musical subtlety but a regard for down-to-earth show-biz vigor that is precisely what is needed. And, as always, his lyrics are a joy to listen for. The American theater has not had a lyricist like this since Hart or Porter."

"People said a decade ago that the score of *Forum* was tuneless," remarked Shevelove, "and it came out in the light of today as very melodic. Some of the same critics reversed what they said. Now the music makes more sense. Steve is a child of his times, and in expressing himself, he is not being derivative, as most composers are. You see, the critics and audiences were startled originally that a play following Rodgers and Hammerstein and all their descendants could be written so abstractly as *Forum.* But when they came to see it again, they didn't mind the abstraction because they knew what to expect. Audiences go to the theater preconditioned. They didn't laugh at the lyrics originally, mainly because of the music. Most of the time when you write a comic song you put it to a very simple melody so that the lyrics shine out. Well, Steve's music is a little tricky. Today, we hear the music more easily because our ears have changed and the lyrics seem much funnier when the music is easier to comprehend."

Although the revival of *Forum* won two Tony Awards—Best Actor in a Musical (Phil Silvers) and Best Supporting Actor in a Musical (Larry Blyden)—business did not stay on an even keel. But just as it appeared to be holding its own, Phil Silvers suffered a stroke, and the show immediately closed after only 156 performances and a loss of its entire $280,000 investment.

A year and a half later, however, with Phil Silvers back in good health, a production of *Forum* starring Silvers toured the British provinces with a stopover in London. In England, *Bilko* was being rerun and Silvers was very popular. (In the fall of 1987 a new production with Frankie Howerd, who starred in the original West End production in 1963, is scheduled for revival on the West End stage.)

"We were very pleased to have *Forum* back," Shevelove said. "We wanted to do it again to give the younger generation, who weren't old enough to see it the first time, a chance to go."

Larry Blyden (left) as Hysterium, Phil Silvers as Pseudolus, in *Forum* Broadway revival, 1972. (FRIEDMAN–ABELES)

MUSIC PUBLISHING ... 7

THE ORCHESTRATIONS played by Broadway pit orchestras have little to do with music that goes on sale in music shops, since show arrangements are used solely for the stage production. It is the function of the music publisher to create other variations of the score for the many commercial markets—such as the ever increasing educational field in which band arrangements and choral arrangements are published for use in schools—as well as to print and distribute regular sheet music, simplified piano, vocal selections, and vocal scores.

"The outlets are not what they used to be," said Irving Brown, a former vice-president of Chappell & Co., Inc., music publishers. "In the early years, when show music and pop music were one and the same, publishing scores of shows was an enormously lucrative business. Today that's changed. Show music and pop music are at opposite ends of the spectrum, unfortunately.

"Years ago, if you had a hit show everybody would wait for the album and the hit songs. My God, recordings like *West Side Story* sold over a million copies. Many artists recorded the songs before the show opened, while it was still out of town, because of the excitement generated by prepublicity on the shows. But the excitement of songs today doesn't really exist apart from the show itself until an artist, a pop artist, happens to pick it up and have a hit record.

"Chappell at that time had practically all the shows. Steve entered the theater through Oscar Hammerstein, and while Chappell published Steve's music, a situation arose after *West Side* where his music was actually published by Williamson Music—the Rodgers and Hammerstein company—in partnership with Chappell. We did all the administrative work, promotion, printing, publishing, and selling of the music. With *Forum*, Steve decided he wanted his own company, so he formed Burthen Music. Steve held the copyright, Burthen held the publication and allied rights, and Chappell was the selling agent. Steve picked the title of his company because he was tickled by the fact that years ago Jerome Kern never used the word *chorus* on his music—if you look at sheet music it says verse and chorus—Kern would use the word *burthen*. Steve liked the word and that's what he named his music company. Obviously it was a good thing for a successful songwriter to have his own company, because he's not only the author of the music but he shares in the publishing income as well.

"When he did *Do I Hear a Waltz?* Rodgers's company, Williamson, and Steve's company, Burthen, were co-publishers, and Chappell once again was the selling agent. Since that time his other shows went to Tommy Valando."

Valando, who has been in the publishing business for many years, worked for other publishers until he set up his own operation and prospered. In addition to Stephen Sondheim, among the leading theatrical composers and lyricists represented by Valando have been John Kander and Fred Ebb, and Jerry Bock and Sheldon Harnick. His instinctive recognition of talent has made him one of the most respected publishers in the business.

"Steve is a rarity in today's world of show music," Valando once observed. "Obviously the music publisher makes a great deal of money from hit songs and Steve does not write hit songs. His scores for *Company* and *Follies* were brilliant, though they were not big money makers. With *Night Music* we have a smash with 'Send in the Clowns.' Publishing his scores is an investment that will pay off later when people realize *just* how brilliant a songwriter he is. I think in the next few years we'll be hearing things from him that no one will ever expect. He's only beginning to show us his capabilities and his output. I believe in Steve . . . I always have."

Angela Lansbury and Goddard Lieberson
(far right) at the recording session for
Anyone Can Whistle the morning after
the show closed on Broadway, 1964.
(COLUMBIA RECORDS)

THE WAY THE COOKIES CRUMBLED

ANYONE CAN WHISTLE is one of the theater's favorite cult musicals. This experimental Stephen Sondheim—Arthur Laurents invention, which lasted a mere nine performances on Broadway, was problem-ridden right from its first attempt to reach the stage. What remains today are Sondheim's superb score (the original cast album headed by Lee Remick, Angela Lansbury, and Harry Guardino was recorded the morning after the show folded) and recurrent notions of reviving the show because of the popular belief that it failed because it was way ahead of its time.

The *New York Times* first announced the show in October 1961: "For the winter of 1962, Arthur Laurents is nurturing another musical project, *The Natives Are Restless.* The narrative and staging will be Mr. Laurents' handiwork; music and lyrics that of Stephen Sondheim."

But *The Natives Are Restless* (which was retitled *Side Show* before finally settling in as *Anyone Can Whistle*) never came to fruition until over a year later because most producers were shying away from the project. Finally, Kermit Bloomgarden, who had so successfully presented *The Music Man*, became fascinated by the material and tried to raise $350,000 to produce the show. He was apparently having some difficulties for, as *Variety* reported in December 1963: "Robert Fryer, Lawrence Carr and John Herman will join Kermit Bloomgarden in producing *Anyone Can Whistle*."

As more time passed and still no money was being raised, Sondheim went to Diana Shumlin (then Diana Krasny) and asked if she would be interested in coming in as Bloomgarden's co-producer.

"I read the script," Diana Shumlin said, "and I thought it was fascinating and certainly a lot different from anything that had been done up to that point in the theater. I must say, I do get a little nervous when directors stage their own book, and when I found that Arthur was going to direct as well as write the show, I worried about whether he'd be able to keep his objectivity. But I adore Arthur and felt it was a very worthwhile show to put on."

But the entire financing was still not raised, and Sondheim eventually had to ask for an advance from Chappell in order to bring enough money into the production to get the show into rehearsal. "It was very nightmarish," said Mrs. Shumlin, "and everybody was in a terrifying state, which is not a wonderful way to start off a show."

By the time Mrs. Shumlin had entered the scene, the show had already been cast with three Hollywood stars who had never done a Broadway musical.

"One day," says Angela Lansbury, "I received one of those lovely letters one occasionally gets in the mail. The writing was unfamiliar but it looked good. I opened it and it said, 'Dear Miss Lansbury, My friend Stephen Sondheim and I have written a musical and we wondered if you had ever thought of appearing on the musical stage. Have you ever done any singing? Would you be interested in talking to us about it? Sincerely, Arthur Laurents.' And I wrote back and said that I would be very interested indeed—send the book. So I read it and I really didn't know what to make of it. I thought it was nuts, crackers. But there was something about it that sort of appealed to me."

Anyone Can Whistle dealt with Cora (Angela Lansbury), the mayoress of a corrupt town that is going bankrupt. The desperate town council creates a miracle, water flowing from a rock, and soon the tourist trade booms. Nurse Apple (Lee Remick) comes to the miracle with her "cookies" from the town's mental institution, the Cookie Jar, and the crazy cookies accidentally mix with the sane members of society. Dr. Hapgood (Harry Guardino) happens along and manages quite cleverly to separate the two groups, although no one can actually tell who is who. Nurse Apple falls in love with Hapgood and it is then learned that Hapgood is actually a fraud—just another cookie—as a new miracle is "discovered" in a nearby town and the tourist crowds move on.

"It was way ahead of its time," Sondheim said once, "in that it was experimental. It started a technique for me which I've used a lot since and I intend never to use again, I hope: namely, the use of traditional musical

comedy language to make points. All the numbers Angie sang in the show were pastiche—her opening number, for instance, was a Hugh Martin–Kay Thompson pastiche. The character always sang in musical comedy terms because she was a lady who dealt in attitudes instead of emotions. I used that technique later in *Company* in 'Side by Side by Side' and 'You Could Drive a Person Crazy' and a great deal in *Follies*. *Whistle* was also the first time I ever got to write the music I most like to write,

Angela Lansbury leads "The Miracle Song" from *Anyone Can Whistle*, 1964. (FRIEDMAN–ABELES)

which is highly romantic; for example, the title song and 'With So Little to Be Sure Of.' "

"When Steve, Arthur, and Kermit came out to California to see me," Angela Lansbury says, "it was absolutely horrendous. They all wanted to hear me sing and I'd always had this rather small voice that had always been replaced by other voices whenever I had to sing in musical movies. I had never sung on the stage. But Herbert Greene, who was going to be the musical director of the show, agreed to coach some of us first, and he had this extraordinary system of making anyone a singer by doing a curious thing of pressing his fingers on your throat, releasing the tension in the larynx, and then somehow you sang. For my audition I did 'A Foggy Day' and I got the job."

"Actually," Kermit Bloomgarden related, "I had originally wanted Herb Greene to be musical director but Steve didn't want him. He wanted Lehman Engel and I had to tell Herb, who had done all of my musical shows up until then, that we couldn't use him. I engaged Lehman and then, after Angela and Lee worked with Herb on vocal coaching, they insisted that he conduct the show—something which I really believe he instigated. So I was in a very awkward position and I had to go to Lehman, who I must say was very decent about it, and he bowed out. Then Herb came back to New York when we were doing further auditions and he mentioned to Arthur and Steve that he would only be with us a short time. They came to me very upset and I was upset as well. I felt that Herb was being very opportunistic, and when I spoke to him, I told him, 'This is dreadful. You've put me in a terrible spot. You never mentioned this limited amount of time to work with us and I'm embarrassed and very angry about it.' Well, I got a little more time from him and then he went back to the Coast and Arthur wrote him a letter expressing what he felt. It was a very tough letter and I don't blame Arthur for writing it. But then I got a letter from Herb saying that he's not going to do the show because he was 'insulted by Arthur's letter.' And that would have been all right, but Steve now insisted on Herb as musical director. So for a week—it must have cost me $600 in telephone calls—I kept on him. And finally I said, 'What can I do?' And he said, 'Talk to my wife.' And I spoke to his wife and she said, 'Make him feel important.' And I said, 'How more important can you be when the composer says he must have you?' Well, it turns out, finally, that he wanted more money. So I had to agree to give him much more than we had already agreed upon and I was furious. So we started off with a split, with him working with Steve and not having any relationship with me. I think he did everything to screw up the show in terms of cost during rehearsals."

When rehearsals did begin, Diana Shumlin immediately began to worry about the problems they would have with the controversial material, as well as with the cast she inherited when she came in late as the show's co-producer. "At the time," she said, "some of the things that appeared to be first-rate on paper weren't being executed as well as it seemed they could be. Ultimately, Arthur had to do a lot of cutting of ideas he was trying, and of course he had every right to try because you can't tell what's going to work until it's up there. There were also difficulties because you did not have top singers, which places a burden on you to gear those wonderful songs for those people. I felt that while the acting was fine, and the energy was fine, the vocal qualities weren't. And Lee, who is a lovely-looking girl and a very good person to work with, did not have a marvelous voice, and the poor girl had tonsilitis all during rehearsals, out of town and into New York, and had her tonsils taken out a couple of weeks after we closed. Harry's voice eventually went. Angie, more than anybody, had the voice."

An innovative but confused *Anyone Can Whistle* opened in Philadelphia to hostile notices, a bit of audience booing, a fire, and even a few deaths.

Laurents: "During the first preview, a fire broke out in the ladies' room and the whole theater was smoky. I had to go backstage and make an announcement and quiet the audience. Then one night later, in one of the numbers where the actors ran forward, someone overshot the stage and fell into the pit. An announcement had to be made that the only thing that happened was an instrument was dented—which is what I thought. However, the musician with the dented instrument had a heart attack and went to the hospital and died. Then, just before we came into New York, Henry Lascoe, who played opposite Angie, had a heart attack and died. We were just killing them off."

Mrs. Shumlin: "Kermit was very angry with me. We were standing in the back of the theater for the first preview in Philly and I said to him, 'The curtain is going up and it shouldn't be because it isn't ready. I think we're gonna get killed when we open.' And he was furious, but it didn't take a great deal of knowledge to look and realize that the show just wasn't ready. There was a lot of experimentation going on during the rehearsal period and we shouldn't have dared attempt to open so soon, but by then we were pretty much out of money. There wasn't any great reserve and there wasn't enormous business, so we had nothing to fall back on.

Lee Remick as Nurse Fay Apple, Harry Guardino as J. Bowden Hapgood, in "Come Play Wiz Me" from *Anyone Can Whistle*, 1964. (FRIEDMAN–ABELES)

We should have gone to Boston and worked more. Had I come in from the beginning I don't know what I necessarily might have done or not done but I would have never budgeted the show so low. It's certainly not good producing."

Laurents: "We needed a good producer very badly. We spent too much time auditioning for money rather than working on the show and it wasn't sufficiently prepared before rehearsals. I think we did thirty-two backers' auditions for the show, and some of the people Kermit had us audition for were absurd. Once we performed the entire show in his office for a man who I think is dead who was some bigwig at a film company who had a lot of money. Unfortunately, he brought his girlfriend. I say unfortunately because *he* fell asleep and *she* was awake and we had to keep on doing the whole show for the girlfriend of a man who was asleep and obviously not going to put in a nickel."

With the negative Philadelphia reviews, another unforeseen problem arose when Harry Guardino lost his singing voice. "I had always wanted Keith Michell to play the man," says Laurents, "and he wanted to do it but it fell apart because Kermit wasn't able to resolve a billing problem. But when we cast Harry Guardino, we did believe that he would come through. Actually, the leading role in the piece is the man. But Harry's performance wasn't strong enough. When he got bad reviews he went to pieces and just gave up and started drinking. I remember also that the review that destroyed him also destroyed Steve."

"It was very unpleasant for all of us," Sondheim says, "but the problem with Harry was that he had a terrific natural instrument and he refused to take vocal lessons. He was Actors Studio—trained and he failed to realize that, unlike acting, singing is an artificial art that needs as much muscle training as a prizefighter. The second week in Philly his voice went out entirely, he lost all control, and he had to talk the songs. He wasn't even difficult about not going for help and taking vocal training; he just refused."

Bloomgarden, equally upset by the chaos all around him, admitted that he was able to do very little to get the troubled musical out of the precarious direction it was headed. "Out of town was impossible," Bloomgarden said. "I never saw Steve, and Arthur was much more interested in the technical aspects of the sound and what the stagehands were doing than in what the actors were doing. And much more time was spent, not on notes for the actors, not on notes for himself, the writer, and not on notes to Steve in terms of what more could be done musically and lyrically. . . . The show was really not directed and rewritten. The concept never got back to where it had started. I felt the first act should have been wilder, crazier, and lighter, and it only seemed to get heavier. I think Steve and Arthur liked the gloom and the darkness. But it was my fault for not understanding them and for not being more demanding of them. . . . I should have insisted on certain things or threatened to close the show out of town. I should have forced meetings with them which I didn't do. I blame myself for that—if I had done some of those things I think we would have had a better show."

Sondheim explains that the show was about so many things that one of the reasons it was a failure was that they weren't able to establish in the first five or ten minutes exactly what the show was about, which created confusion in the minds of the audience. "Also," Sondheim says, "the first of the three acts was very smart-ass and rather condescending. There was a nastiness toward the audience that was not intended. Essentially the show is about, on one level, nonconformity and conformity in contemporary society, which is not a particularly interesting subject, but which was told in a rather whimsical way, which we thought was fun. On another level, it's about the difficulties of maintaining idealism and romanticism as well as the dangers of them. Our two principal characters were an idealist who turns out to be a cynic and a cynic who turns out to be a romanticist. The mayoress wasn't a real character—she represented the venal side of society. The show also dealt with the need for miracles in people's lives. The hero and heroine tried to expose the miracle for what it was, out of different motives. Though organized religion may be dead, there is an enormous need in people to think that something beyond them and not explainable in terms of ordinary human activity is going on . . . which is another form of idealism or romanticism, contrasted with that of the two characters.

Angela Lansbury as Mayoress Cora Hoover Hooper in *Anyone Can Whistle*, 1964. (FRIEDMAN–ABELES)

"Then we were also taking a number of satirical digs at various fads and attitudes of contemporary society. Remember, that's 1964. That's another reason, contrary to popular belief, the show would not hold up to revival because so much has happened in the last twenty years that *Whistle* would seem hilariously old-fashioned. We had a very daring satire on attitudes toward and from Blacks. There was a song line, 'You can't judge a book by its cubber,' which, then, was most shocking and quite offensive to a lot of people and today would seem like child's play."

One of the most extraordinary aspects of the show was Herbert Ross's extensive choreography, which included not only a great deal of dancing throughout, but also a twenty-minute ballet for which Sondheim composed the music.

"The interrogation sequence which closed the first act," says Laurents, "is still, I believe, the best musical sequence done in the musical theater. Its trouble was that we were never able to top it. I loved it and I loved the ending of the act. You know on the record where it ends with the 'Who Is Who?' section? During that confused yelling, all the lights were out except for a tiny light on Hapgood, and then he turned to the audience and said, 'You are all mad.' There was a blackout, a blast from the orchestra, and the lights came up and the entire cast was seated on the stage in orchestra seats with the balcony rail behind them, looking at programs, laughing and applauding at the audience. It was later used by Peter Brook at the end of *Marat/Sade*. It was startling and at first the audience was shocked. Steve and I were standing at the back of the theater and were clutching at each other with tears in our eyes. It was one of the few times you saw what you had done just the way you wanted it and it worked and we loved it. Subsequently, however, Steve began to feel that it was insulting to the audience, but I still love it and wouldn't have done it any other way."

Another of the many problems in Philadelphia was a distinct and bitter difference of opinion concerning the way the role of the mayoress should be played.

"I was ready to quit," says Angela Lansbury. "I had certain quarrels with Arthur because I couldn't take his direction and it was difficult for me to understand what he wanted. I had trouble understanding because I didn't want to play the part the way he wanted. I found it repugnant. The audience liked the character of the mayoress because she was so preposterous and funny. What happened was that the character overbalanced the rest of the play. And they wanted to replace me. I think they had Nancy Walker waiting in the wings, which I wasn't supposed to know. But there was an awful lot of backstage gossip and carryings-on. It was a great show for people screaming up and down the aisles. I remember screaming my ass off at Steve once. I've never done it before or since. I remember yelling, 'I don't know what you want. What the hell do you want me to do? Tell me and I'll try to do it but for God's sake let's get on with it!' Steve wasn't easy. He was a fence-sitter. He's very good at placating everybody and seeming to be on everybody's side . . . but it was Arthur who wasn't getting what he wanted. He loved all the surface, kind of overt camp qualities of the character and he wanted her played as the nastiest thing on two feet. And I simply could not find this lady in myself. My feeling was that I didn't want to play that character and if they wanted it that way they could go and get somebody else. I felt that there needed to be some vulnerability in a character like that, that would be far more interesting than playing her as an out-and-out bitch which would be merely a caricature. I guess I'm ridiculous, but I can't bear to play certain roles. I wouldn't play Sister George. I was capable of playing a sullen bitch quite well, but that was something I had done on film and I guess they associated me with that. They thought maybe I was that kind of woman. A lot of people do. But it's not in my nature to be that way at all."

"What it was," says Laurents, "somebody told me that Henry Lascoe, that poor man who died, was sabotaging me in the wings telling Angie to play it nicer. And she was not playing it the way I thought it should be played for herself, for me, for Steve, for the audience. Well, Lascoe died and suddenly, since most of her scenes were with him, she had to take over, and immediately the whole bloody thing fell into place and she was sensational."

A new song titled "The Natives Are Restless" was written to replace Angela Lansbury's big opening number, "Me and My Town," because the entire first ten minutes of the show didn't seem to work. But when the first three pages of dialogue were changed, "Me and My Town" stopped the show and remained in the production. A song called "There's Always a Woman," written as a number in which Lee Remick and Angela Lansbury bitched each other at the climax of the show, lasted one performance before it was dropped, and a song called "There Won't Be Trumpets" was also omitted.

"It was after Lee's entrance speech," Laurents says. "Though 'Trumpets' was Lee's only song in the first act, it had to be cut because of a long

Angela Lansbury (left) and Lee Remick in "The Cookie Ballet" from *Anyone Can Whistle*, 1964. (FRIEDMAN–ABELES)

speech she did that brought the house down. Then she sang the song, which she couldn't sing, and the song undercut her. When I called for the cut, there were great cries. It was a song that Steve was very proud of, and rightly so. But it was dropped.

"Actually, there was no need for a song at the end of the show. It should have ended before it did because the piece got romantic and I think it was a mistake, as beautiful as it was, too keep 'With So Little to Be Sure Of.' I think Hapgood should have gone off into the world. He's Don Quixote, actually, and if we were going to end it with them together, it should not have had a conventional musical comedy finish but should have ended in a kind of satirical or funny way. But we were so devoted to one another and so respectful of one another that neither of us would ever push a point like that. It would be different today. Also, the show was so experimental . . . and it was experimental not by design. Steve and I believe in certain traditional concepts and one of them is that content determines form. Well, in *Whistle*, the content was insane, so when I wrote the book it came out insane and the numbers were crazy. It wasn't that we were trying to be different, that's what the material called for. There was even a song called 'The Lame, the Halt, and the Blind,' which was a rather vicious waltz that we never put in the show. I think it went, 'The lame, the halt, and the blind, and anyone out of their mind.'

"I remember Steve and I were talking about style and that while a lot of it was craft and learning, it is mostly an instinctual thing. You either know it or you don't. There were many cases where we couldn't get what we wanted because of the circumstances. There was so much that was wrong and there wasn't time—ten days to do a really difficult musical. There was a scene which was played half in French and half in English with subtitles, and the machine for the subtitles was so cheap it never worked. So you would have to spend your time screaming for another fifty dollars for a machine that would work, instead of working on the show.

"I think the thing that drove me up the wall was in the middle of the problems, the confusion, the changes, Kermit came to me and said, 'There's someone I really want you to listen to. Please pay attention to what he says and listen to his opinion of the show.' Well, it was his sixteen-year-old son! I restrained myself and just walked away."

When *Anyone Can Whistle* reached New York to begin its series of previews, Laurents went to Bloomgarden demanding that the show not open on schedule and insisting upon more time to work. "They began arguing," Diana Shumlin said, "and it turned into a terrible fist fight in Shubert Alley. I had to break it up . . . it was awful . . . but I had to stop it. . . . Kermit had a bad heart."

The opening-night curtain of *Whistle* rose April 4, 1964, at the Majestic Theatre. The major critics hated the show, although some reviewers heralded it as one of the most refreshing musicals Broadway had ever seen.

In the *World-Telegram and The Sun*, Norman Nadel ecstatically proclaimed: "You have no idea how many breathtaking surprises are in store for you. . . . At a time when even the good musicals look like something out of a recent season, it is exciting to encounter one so spectacularly original. . . . There's a merry abundance of theatrical ingenuity."

"An exasperating musical comedy," said Walter Kerr in the *Herald*

Opposite: Angela Lansbury warms up at recording session of *Anyone Can Whistle*, 1964. (COLUMBIA RECORDS)

Tribune. "It isn't very musical and it isn't very comical. . . . It fails to fix a satirical target."

John Chapman in the *Daily News* viewed the show as "an unusual, far-out musical with a briskly syncopated score, educated lyrics, original and frisky dances and an imaginative story which the cast and I had to cope with rather strenuously. This book and the lack of a melody I could whistle impeded my enjoyment of the last two acts which didn't quite fulfill the high promise of the joyously daffy first act."

"An unfortunate let-down of an evening," determined Richard Watts in the *Post*, "paved with the highest intentions. Ponderously heavyhanded and clumsily vague in its presentation of a somewhat obscure thesis."

And Whitney Bolton in the *Morning Telegraph* discerned: "If *Anyone Can Whistle* is a success, the American musical theater will have advanced itself and prepared the way for further freedom from now old and worn techniques and points of view. If it is not a success, we sink back into the old formula method and must wait for the breakthrough. . . . The new musical is not a perfect musical commentary by several chalks, but it is a bright first step toward a more enlightened and cerebral musical theater, a musical theater in which that kind of show can say something about its times and the mores of those times. . . . It has no whistleable song in it, neither has Copland. But Mr. Sondheim is a good, resourceful, sound musician and his score has musicianship redolent in it."

The *New York Times*, then and now the most influential "money" review, was decidedly hostile. "There is no law against saying something in a musical," wrote Howard Taubman, "but it's unconstitutional to omit imagination and wit. In an attempt to be meaningful it forgets to offer much entertainment. . . . They have taken an idea with possibilities and have pounded it into a pulp."

"The show was apparently too sophisticated for them," says Herbert Ross. "You see, it had no musical comedy symbols, which left the audience with few recognizable things, very few anchors for an audience to hold on to."

Harold Prince, merely a spectator of *Whistle*, was not terribly surprised at the show's reception. "I did not think it would work, quite simply. I think the score is dazzling. I think there are places where simplifying the shape of the numbers would have made them more accessible to an audience because audiences are not that good about lyrics and not that good about complicated material. I think the numbers could have been made more *available* to an audience. The book is another matter. It seemed a little too cerebral and a trifle smart-ass. I *love* what it's about and I think that Arthur is a very good writer, but I thought that it came out pretty much on the stage the way I thought it would have to."

"In final analysis," concludes Angela Lansbury, "Arthur didn't dig quite deep enough. He didn't work hard enough on his book. Things were dealt with in too surface a way. If only he had someone else to listen to or if another director came in. I think what the critics were angry about was that when it started off it appeared that he was going to dose them with a phenobarbital, but it turned out to be an aspirin. Arthur's premise that the 'cookies' in life are the only sane members of society, and the so-called silent majority belonged in the nut house, was a bit of a pill and rather heavy for a musical, and rather heavy for a certain kind of audience. They weren't about to be made asses of."

Stephen Sondheim and Arthur Laurents chipped in money to pay for an ad in the *New York Times* in a feeble attempt to keep the show alive, but after the nine performances it was gone. Goddard Lieberson of Columbia Records recorded the original cast album (though the record company was not contractually liable to do the album unless the show ran twenty-one performances) because he felt obligated to see that a permanent record was made of what he considered one of Broadway's more important scores.

"The show had quality," said Kermit Bloomgarden, "that very few shows had. I could be far more critical than the critics about the things that were wrong with it, but when you consider some of the shows that have run . . . *there's* the insanity!"

Longtime friend and mentor Burt Shevelove observed: "Steve was very, very lucky. He had written *West Side*, *Gypsy*, and *Forum* . . . quite an impressive group of hits. Before *Forum* opened, I remember I ran into Oscar Hammerstein, who said, 'You know, Steve won't really be a member of the working theater until he has a flop.' It's not that Oscar had any ill will toward him, but it's true that Steve subsequently learned more about the theater from *Anyone Can Whistle* than from any of the other shows."

That might well be so. The techniques and styles Sondheim experimented with and the work he developed under the tensions of the production of *Whistle* inevitably led to his future triumphs in creating new forms in his work. Looking back on the piece, Sondheim has fond memories of a project he was very proud of writing. "I don't mind putting my name on a flop," he says, "as long as we've done something that hasn't been tried before."

MUSICAL DIRECTION · · · 9

"THE MUSICAL DIRECTOR of a show does far more than conduct the orchestra," explains Paul Gemignani, who was musical director of *Follies* (for the latter part of its New York run and during its brief visit to Los Angeles), *Sondheim: A Musical Tribute*, *A Little Night Music* (replacing Harold Hastings following his death after the show opened on Broadway), *Candide*, *Pacific Overtures*, *Sweeney Todd*, *Merrily We Roll Along*, *Sunday in the Park with George*, and *Follies in Concert*.

"One of the musical director's functions," he says, "is to make sure the actors retain their characterizations night after night. You must develop a fairly close relationship with the people on the stage because ultimately you are the one who's in charge once the curtain goes up, regardless of whether the stage manager is calling cues or keeping the show running from the back. You must keep the pace going with the actors. It's almost as though you're a performer and it's very important that you feel that you are part of the performance so that you can maintain a keen level of concentration. I may not look at the show every minute, but I listen to it all the time, because the actors will do it differently every night and the only way to keep it cohesive is to feel their rhythms. A song might be in one tempo one night and a little faster or a little slower the next. Each scene has its own rhythm and if the rhythm should be down one night you may be able to help them pick it up a little bit, to get their energy up if they're tired."

The musical director's work on a new show usually begins with casting; he also serves as the middleman between the composer and the orchestrator. "Some orchestrators must be watched," Gemignani says. "Jonathan Tunick, for example, needn't be. He has a good ear and he knows not to over-orchestrate. He also knows that when you have an actor who has had little singing experience, you must put more melody in the arrangement, and with a singer with great training, you may not put melody in the arrangement at all. When it comes to actually conducting the song, it is a culmination of what the composer wants, the performer delivers, the orchestrator arranges, and how I feel—with all things considered—it should come out sounding.

"Another problem, which is a union one, is that you can't fire anyone in your orchestra unless he's drunk, because after two weeks they have a run-of-the-play contract. So you must be very tough. I don't allow anyone to relax. It keeps a certain tension, and they know I expect the same performance on Monday as I do on Saturday night. You realize that you have to uphold a musical standard, which is very difficult to do because one of the most boring jobs in the world can be playing in a pit. But if you are professional about it, you can make it a lot less boring. Some conductors come in and want to be everyone's friend and before long the orchestra falls down. But if he's popular with everyone because of his musical ability, he'll have respect and still have everyone wanting to play in his orchestra. There are a lot more good musicians in this town than bad and good musicians don't want to play in a pit that is boring. It's hard to keep an orchestra sounding fresh for every performance, but it's another challenge to keep you on your toes eight performances a week, and make them *all* sound like Saturday nights."

From left: Goddard Lieberson, Sergio Franchi, Elizabeth Allen, Stephen Sondheim, and Richard Rodgers complete the studio recording of *Do I Hear a Waltz?* 1965. (COLUMBIA RECORDS)

"THE LESS SAID, ··· 10
THE BETTER"

"THE ORIGINAL INTENTION," suggested Burt Shevelove, "was to do something that would make a lot of money. If I were to list all of Steve's work, I would never list *Do I Hear a Waltz?* Although there are some very good lyrics, as far as I'm concerned, it was streetwalking."

Immediately after the dissolution of *Anyone Can Whistle*, Arthur Laurents set out to have his 1952 play, *The Time of the Cuckoo*, the story of a middle-aged single woman finding love for the first time in Venice, musicalized by Richard Rodgers. (The play, which starred Shirley Booth, was later, in 1955, turned into a film called *Summertime* starring Katharine Hepburn.) Actually, Laurents had always wanted to do the play as a musical and during the writing of *West Side Story* had even brought the project to Oscar Hammerstein II, who liked the idea but suggested that Laurents wait a few years since the movie had been done too recently. Then, unfortunately, Hammerstein died.

"Dick Rodgers had previously asked me to write songs with him," Sondheim says, "and although I didn't want to write just lyrics ever again, I told Dick I'd be honored to write with him if a project came up that excited me—and I hoped against hope that nothing would. Somehow, Arthur and Mary Rodgers (Richard's daughter), after a great deal of pressure, convinced me to write lyrics for Dick's music for *Do I Hear a Waltz?*"

"The thing I objected to the most," Flora Roberts says, "was not the Rodgers situation, which was another matter altogether. It had to do with making somebody, through friendship, do something that he artistically did not want to do."

"My first mistake," Laurents readily admits, "and a mistake that was most important to me personally, was talking Steve into working on the show. Rodgers was foul to him. I remember when we got a new song one day out of town, Rodgers looked at the lyric sheet and in front of the whole company said, 'This is shit!' Well, needless to say, the lyric was a great deal better than the tune."

"I never thought the play should be a musical," Sondheim says. "The reason, and I still think I'm right, is that it's about a lady who, metaphorically, can't sing. How can you do it as a musical? One way is to do it as a chamber opera or another way is to have a musical in which everyone sings the whole time with the exception of the main character, which I think would have been very interesting—if she wouldn't be able to sing until the climax of the piece, then breaks open in anger and is able to sing."

Although Laurents now agrees that the project should not have been done, he strongly opposes the idea that the lady could not sing. In a piece written by Laurents in the *World-Telegram and The Sun* prior to the show's opening, he wrote: "An attractive lady has been libeled. For over ten years now, she has been called a virgin and worse, and I would like to clear her record. . . . My theory is that the actresses who played her were too old for the part. . . . The story of an aging woman who could not give herself physically is something small and rather dirty. What *I* wrote is the story of a woman who could not give herself emotionally, a woman *young* enough to have a chance at a future. Leona, the original Leona, the Leona I wrote, does sing."

So the casting of *Do I Hear a Waltz?* began with a search for a younger actress to play Leona, the lady who goes to Venice looking for love. Dorothy Kilgallen reported in her column that Anne Bancroft was up for the role. Arthur Laurents relates that Mary Martin wanted to do the part but Rodgers said she was too old. Finally chosen was actress Elizabeth Allen. Her costar was Sergio Franchi.

Brought in to direct the show, making his Broadway musical debut, was John Dexter, at that time assistant director of London's National Theatre (even though *Variety* first reported that William Ball, of the Stratford Shakespeare Festival, would stage the show).

"The whole thing was a mistake all the way around," Laurents further admits. "I don't think anybody's work was any good. What we got was a lot of songs sort of stuck into my book that might have been better if someone else did the adaptation. John Dexter, who had done great things in London, was a deadly error as director. We also made the mistake of deciding that we didn't want any dances in the show originally. It was all supposed to be this great songfest, which it never was."

Hired to stage the musical numbers (sans dancing) was choreographer Wakefield Poole, who eventually became used as a go-between, leveling the steadily opposing factions.

"Rodgers was a strange man," Poole has said. "I did three shows with him and I think I was brought into *Waltz* to be on his side. Arthur Laurents wanted John Dexter as director and Rodgers wanted Joe Layton. But none of them wanted any choreography, which was ridiculous. They gave me a musical number which was originally a song called 'Two by Two.' It was a number in which the entire company strolls. And I said, 'This is a twelve-minute number. What do you want me to do, twelve minutes of walking patterns?' But Dexter never allowed me into creative meetings. He's an opportunist and I think that because of his insecurities, I wasn't allowed to express any opinions."

Although trouble was apparent very early in rehearsals, the bomb exploded at the run-through of the show in New York prior to its New Haven opening.

Poole: "Even though the split in interpretation began as soon as the show got off paper, the real trouble started when Liz Allen had not been told that there would be a run-through and that three or four casts from other shows would be coming. Suddenly, that Sunday morning, we were informed that at two in the afternoon we would be having a gypsy run-through and that our cast could invite anyone they wanted. Liz was furious and said, 'I'm not ready to perform this in front of an audience. I need some preparation. Look at me, I'm a mess!' Her insecurities came through and the pressures of the role were building in her. She felt John pulling her one way and Arthur pulling her the other. And John had an outburst and yelled, 'Fuck you, you pig!' and it turned into one of those screaming nasty fights in front of the whole cast. That afternoon she performed the show with the fevered pitch of Ethel Merman in *Gypsy*, rather than as the vulnerable lady the character was meant to be. From that point on, I served as the intermediary because Liz didn't speak to Dexter until a week before we opened in New York."

Laurents: "Steve will tell you that I behaved quite badly also. After that first run-through I just stomped out. I saw it was a disaster and I went out and bought a coat.

"You can talk concept until you are blue in the face . . . but it's the doing that counts. That's absolutely a primary rule in the theater. Everybody talks and thinks they agree and it turns out they are either talking about two different things or they approach it in ten different ways. What you had on the stage in the case of *Waltz* is best characterized as bland. It had no style. No concept. It had characters and it should have had emotion. You *can* have a good musical with a bad book, but I certainly don't think you can have a good musical with a bad score. There was a song in *Waltz* called 'Stay' that always sounded to me like a lament from the Russian steppes. The first *note* bored me. There were new songs put in but Dick seemed to be afraid of Steve. I think he was afraid of his own talent not being what it was. I think there also was great resentment that we had to *convince* Steve to do the show—Dick took it as a great insult. He was very hard to move and very insulting to Steve. He kept calling me over and making remarks about 'my friend' and 'how dare he.' He had known Steve since he was a child and I suppose that made it very difficult for him. I wasn't exactly enamored of Jerry when we did *Gypsy*, but when you do a show with somebody, you really must put aside personal feelings. And then, you see, Rodgers was the producer on *Waltz* as well as the composer, so if there were any objections, it didn't matter. It was what *he* wanted. Even after the show opened, when I wanted to go in and make some changes since Dexter was gone and the thing was in a shambles, Rodgers wouldn't allow me in the theater."

Jerome Whyte, the late executive of the Richard Rodgers organization and production supervisor of *Do I Hear a Waltz?,* described the administration of the show quite differently. "The working relationship was pretty good compared with many other shows I've worked on. There was a difference of opinion and of course it was all put to a vote. The majority won. There was, I think, one moment of unpleasantness in New Haven where Steve became upset and Dick was momentarily upset, too." (Although Rodgers had agreed to discuss his experiences on *Do I Hear a Waltz?* for inclusion in this book, following the Stephen Sondheim *Newsweek* cover story of April 23, 1973, he changed his mind. In *Newsweek*, Sondheim referred to Oscar Hammerstein as a man who had limited talent and infinite soul, and described Richard Rodgers as a man of infinite talent and limited soul. Rodgers offered little explanation for his reluc-

Opposite: Elizabeth Allen as Leona, Sergio Franchi as Renato, in *Do I Hear a Waltz?* 1965. (FRIEDMAN–ABELES)

tance to talk about Sondheim but succinctly noted, "The less said, the better.")

"I had a kind of feeling that Dick was terribly unhappy with the group," George Oppenheimer related. "Dick wouldn't talk to me, my being the critic for *Newsday*, even though we were very, very close. I'd known Dick for fifteen years and I wasn't aware, until much later, that he was a very strange man. For instance, he *hates* homosexuality, cliques, groups as such, but blinds himself when he wants to."

In the *World-Telegram and The Sun*, Rodgers and Sondheim were interviewed early in their collaboration about their working relationship—and it was all safely respectful.

"Working with Steve," Rodgers said, "is much closer to working with Oscar than with Larry Hart—Larry was not as dependable. Steve has a curious way of making people sing as if they were talking."

"Working with Dick is very different," Sondheim commented in the same article. "I write the lyrics myself—and he composes by himself. Then we get together to work it over. With Lenny and Jule we did more talking first."

Do I Hear a Waltz? opened in New Haven to generally mixed reviews, but there was unanimous criticism about the lack of choreography. Soon a decision was reached and John Dexter offered a statement to the press: "We made one initial miscalculation—Dick, Arthur, Steve, and myself —that there should be no dancing in the show. We found the dancing was transparently necessary."

A call went out for help and Herbert Ross arrived in New Haven, supplying some inspiration to the generally insipid show. With Wakefield Poole assisting him, Ross first had to break through the personality factions that were openly waging battle.

Ross: "There was a total conflict of opinion as to how the roles should be played. Steve and Arthur wanted a dry and tough interpretation and Rodgers wanted a sentimental one; therefore the show lacked any positive quality. I restaged the musical numbers, but there wasn't much that could be done. The show was in terrifically good taste but was passionless. Elizabeth Allen was good, but she wasn't right. The show needed someone who would break your heart. She just wasn't vulnerable enough."

Poole: "Sergio was very sterile. He worked hard, though, and if we had told him to stand on his head, he would have—or at least he would have tried. There was much less pressure with Liz after Herb came in because he is so good at handling people. There was one point where we had a discussion of replacing Liz when we got to Boston, and I even remember Gwen Verdon's name being brought up, but they decided to stick it out with Liz. Dexter remained difficult. Throughout the show, Dexter did things that made a lot of people very angry. For instance, he called all the boys by their first names. The women's names he didn't bother to know. He would stage the show and say, 'Hey, you over there,' or 'Miss, you go there,' which alienated every woman in the show. Though his track record is fabulous, I think that any director who can't communicate with actors is a failure."

Although a great deal was happening in restaging, the visual aspect of the production was faltering as much as the stolidly written material. "The whole concept of the show," Poole says, "was Venice remembered rather than Venice realistically. It went all the way, even to the costumes which were filmy and chiffony, but they didn't work because on the stage they looked cheap."

There also still existed the terrible unpleasantness among the creative people. "When Rodgers would come into the theater," Poole remembers, "everyone would say, 'Here comes Godzilla'—that was his nickname. And I looked around and the whole thing completely freaked me out. Here was Richard Rodgers, one of the most renowned composers in the theater, Steve Sondheim, the most brilliant lyricist, Arthur Laurents, a great playwright, and John Dexter, the fair-haired boy who directed all those things at the Royal Court—and no one is talking. Those brilliant minds and there wasn't an ounce of communication. It was most exasperating."

"The show," Sondheim explains, "most simply was what Mary Rodgers calls a 'Why?' musical. And the theater is full of them. You take a successful property, add songs to it, and put it on the stage. And to adapt such properties is like the dinosaur eating its own tail. Although they never intended it, Rodgers and Hammerstein are partly responsible for this. But what people don't understand is that *Oklahoma!* is very different from *Green Grow the Lilacs*, on which it is based. *Lilacs* is a dark play, but they saw something past it and *Oklahoma!* has its own tone, spirit, and style—it's got its own vitality. The same way that *Carousel* does not depend on *Liliom* for its strength—it's a wholly different piece of goods.

"The reason *Waltz* flopped was that it had no real energy—no excitement whatsoever. That's because it need not have been done. When you see *Hello, Dolly!*, no matter what you think of it, there's a feeling that the

people who put it on really loved it a lot. You never got that feeling with *Waltz*. It was a workmanlike, professional show. Period. And it deserved to fail."

Do I Hear a Waltz? ran for half a year, regaining part of its $450,000 investment due to the lineup of theater parties pre-booked for Broadway's "new Rodgers musical."

Saturday Review began its critical evaluation of the show with a headline that read "Dearth in Venice," and *Newsweek*'s review was equally discouraging: "To make a musical comedy without dancing is plausible, to make one without comedy is possible, but to make one without music is, it would seem, unthinkable. Yet this is what Richard Rodgers and Arthur Laurents have unaccountably tried to do in *Do I Hear a Waltz?* Rodgers has written songs, all right, but they add up to the flattest score the old master has produced in years." Perhaps fortunate this time around, Sondheim received no mention. But ironically, after being totally overlooked for his work on *West Side Story*, *Gypsy*, and *Forum*, he received his very first Tony nomination for his work in the musical theater for *Do I Hear a Waltz?* (though all the awards that season went to *Fiddler on the Roof*).

In an interview in the *New York Times* before the opening of *Do I Hear a Waltz?*, Richard Rodgers somewhat jokingly described his relationship with Stephen Sondheim: "The first time I saw him was when I was working on *Oklahoma!* in 1942. . . . I watched him grow from an attractive little boy to a monster."

The less said, the better.

CASTING · · · 11

THE PROCESS of casting a Broadway musical is usually as vague to most producers as it is to actors. To accommodate the enormous task of finding the right performer for the right role, producers employ casting directors. One of the most skilled in her profession is Shirley Rich, who worked for Rodgers and Hammerstein and Harold Prince before opening her own independent casting office.

"I have my own philosophy of how to treat actors," she says, "having begun as one myself. A casting director must be knowledgeable about every aspect of the theater. It takes a lot of time and energy and patience. I don't feel you can cast unless you cover talent. . . . I don't think you can do it just from interviewing and auditioning actors. You must see them in performance, notice aspects of their singing, acting, dancing, and try to remember them by storing these facts in the back of your mind for future reference.

"Actors by nature are so busy trying to sell themselves they make a lot of mistakes. They often talk too much at auditions. Instead of singing numbers *not* normally done—and they can be found if they look hard enough—such as songs cut from shows, usually every year there is a song that everybody sings. . . . The year of *Man of La Mancha* three hundred out of five hundred actors sang 'The Impossible Dream.' Obviously, the production team sitting out there all day listening to the same song done over and over is going to be much harsher on you if you are the ninety-ninth actor singing the *same* song. And, in general, you're always safer *never* to sing a song written by the composer you're auditioning for.

"An actor who's new to singing should go any time he can to audition. . . . There's only one way to be trained to audition well and that is to audition as much as possible—not in your apartment and not in a coach's studio, but on the stage. The one thing that you've got to be able to do if you are going to remain in a profession such as this, where there is little employment for most of its actors, is to keep your inner confidence, because you are going to go through such torturous weeks, months, years. That's why you should study all the time while you are unemployed. Unless you are working on scenes or working with a vocal coach or dancing all the time, you're never going to make it. You also have to be prepared to find work outside the business while you're studying and training—nobody can make money in show business fifty-two weeks a year.

"A major problem the casting director must face is that some of the most talented people in the world can't give a good audition, and if you go by that and discard these people you would miss some of the most gifted people in New York. So you have to do their readings in different ways and take more time with them. I think frankly, even with a lousy reading, there is something that you're going to see. And then, on the other end of the spectrum, there are actors who come in and give extraordinary readings, get hired, and then the show goes into rehearsal and they never go further than the reading in performance. But when I see someone I believe in, I will go to the moon to help him get the part."

Joanna Merlin, also from an acting background—and today, at times, still active in that profession—took over casting in the Prince office when Shirley Rich exited, at the tail end of casting *Company*.

"Casting begins on a show," she says, "when Actors Equity posts a casting notice and anyone who's a member can come and be interviewed. What that means is that you spend a few minutes with each person trying to find out if the actor is physically right for a role, what his background is, and if he's qualified enough to be auditioned. The big problem is that you don't have unlimited auditioning time. You get a résumé and sometimes that résumé is all made up and you don't know that. You don't really know if the person is right until you audition him and that is the sad thing about the casting business. You can't audition everyone and you obviously will overlook people who are talented. I think that after a while you begin to develop a sense. You can't tell how well someone sings from what's on his résumé and a lot of Steve's scores require legitimate, trained singers. But in addition, Hal believes that actors are very important to musicals, and that you can't use singers who sing terrifically and can't act at all.

"There are many offices where you don't get an audition unless you have other Broadway credits. Hal doesn't feel that way at all. He takes great pride in discovering new people. That's the reason you can look at a lot of his shows and see lots of new faces.

"During the interviewing period we send a breakdown of the parts to agents, which we try to make as complete as possible, and then they send in submission lists. I also make up my own submission list of people I think would be right for a particular part and I give it to Hal. Then, of course, there are the people who are *not* represented. . . . I would say they have as much chance. Or if an agent calls me and says, 'I just heard this girl and she's perfect for the role,' I would absolutely give that girl an audition provided that I trusted the agent. There are some less reliable than others. Then I get together with the musical director who has gone over the music with Steve and we determine what the vocal ranges are, and we start auditioning. I generally screen people with the musical director. We hear them sing and if they want to use their own accompanist they can, otherwise they use the one we have. I try before-hand to give them some sort of idea what kind of music we want to hear. Generally we ask them to bring a ballad because it tells the musical director more about the voice because the notes have to be sustained. If they sing badly I usually don't have them read. If they sing well, then I ask them to read some scenes that they already picked up at the office a few days before and have been preparing. They do the scene with the stage manager, and *sometimes*, even if they're not vocally right, I have them read so I can get some kind of sense of what their acting abilities are for future reference— or should the vocal requirements change.

"After a few screenings they audition for the director, the choreographer, and the writers. I generally read with them at the first audition. Then there is a group decision and the roles are cast after a series of callbacks where the staff decides who is right for which role.

"There are lots of times where people audition and don't get a role but study and then try again. As a matter of fact, Alexis Smith was auditioned in California for *Follies* and was eliminated because she sang so badly. She called later and asked if she could have another crack at it and Hal said he'd see her again. So she flew out from Los Angeles on her own and of course the second time she was terrific. She had been working on her voice and she felt more confident. It's wonderful when an actor feels he's right and pursues it until he's seen. Hermione Gingold was not at all close to the original conception of that role in *Night Music*, but she read the script and asked for an audition. The minute Hal heard her read, it was clear she was indeed right for the role. She turned it into her own and now it's hard to imagine anyone else playing that part.

"The major concern of stars is that they do not like to work in ensemble shows, and Hal's productions are not really framed around a star. They are really more of a group effort. There have been many stars whom we wanted to audition, but once they read the script and realized that they could not use the show as a vehicle, they would not even consider it. But that's all part of the crazy kind of psychology we have to deal with."

Elaine Stritch corners Harold Prince at
the marathon recording session of
Company, 1970. (COLUMBIA RECORDS)

WAITING AROUND ··· 12
FOR THE GIRLS
UPSTAIRS

IN EARLY 1965, Sondheim had dinner with a casual friend, playwright James Goldman, author of *They Might Be Giants*, a play Sondheim had read and admired. At dinner, Sondheim asked Goldman whether he had any ideas for a musical they might do together. Goldman wasn't sure but promised he would try to think of something.

"About that time," says Goldman, "I read a tiny paragraph in the *New York Times* that had to do with the Ziegfeld Girls Club, which I didn't know even existed. I thought that it was enormously evocative and Steve and I proceeded to work on an idea I came up with. I was very interested in the past and in secrets. It seemed to me that the whole notion of a reunion, particularly involving people who haven't seen each other in a long time, was a situation that was fraught with emotional possibilities . . . the whole subject of unfinished business in our lives."

By the end of 1965, Goldman had a first draft of the libretto and Sondheim had five songs written for their new original musical, *The Girls Upstairs*. Several drafts later they gave their property to David Merrick and Leland Hayward.

Merrick: "Steve had always made it clear to me that Hal Prince always gets first crack at his work because of an old relationship they have, but he assured me that I get second. At the time I first heard the show, I said, 'What happened to Hal?' and he said, 'He won't produce anything he can't direct and I don't think he can direct this. I don't think he's a good director.' Which amuses me now. I believed at the time that Hal was a very good director. I had already offered him *Hello, Dolly!* to stage and he turned it down, and then I offered him *Promises, Promises* which he couldn't do because he was involved with *Zorbá!* So Hal was out of the picture on *The Girls Upstairs* and I held on to it for a long time. But I didn't like the subject matter. It just didn't send me. I did like the score but I couldn't see how it was going to work."

Sondheim: "It was mostly that David didn't like the idea that we wanted to team him with Leland Hayward. He wanted to produce it alone. So to punish us all he said that he would not raise a cent for it. It would come out of his office and he'd do all the work, but Leland would have to raise all the money. Leland couldn't, so they dropped it."

Putting their temporarily aborted musical to rest in 1966, Goldman and Sondheim accepted an offer to do a project for ABC's *Stage 67.* "They had this whole series," says Goldman, "and they were going through all the people who did Broadway shows, giving everybody a crack at doing a TV show. We thought the other work wasn't really good and we wanted to do something marvelous. I've always liked the John Collier stories, and *Evening Primrose* had a macabre quality that appealed to Steve."

"*ABC Stage 67* will captivate you tonight," promised the network's *New York Times* ad. "Anthony Perkins stars in a musical play about a mystical night society. . . . Inside a department store fleeing from the pressures of the outside world, an unhappy poet is at last alone. But not quite. In his newfound sanctuary, he suddenly comes across a group of hermits who've been hiding there for years. Among them, a young girl with whom he falls in love. . . . An eerie yet charming story with music and lyrics by the noted *West Side Story* lyricist, Stephen Sondheim. Included in the cast are Dorothy Stickney, Larry Gates and the lovely newcomer, Charmian Carr" (the oldest daughter in the film version of *The Sound of Music*).

Presented by John Houseman (executive producer) and Willard Levitas (producer), and directed by Paul Bogart, the Sondheim-Goldman horror musical was shot on location in Stern Brothers department store, which was at 42nd Street and Sixth Avenue in Manhattan.

Jack Gould, reviewing the telecast in the *New York Times*, said that *Evening Primrose* "tripped over its own inordinate complexity," and Sondheim's songs showed "a hint of melodic sweetness, but the score as a whole proved richer in promise than in realization. The songs were simply too much alike."

"The book was literate enough," said Ben Gross in the *Daily News*. "The music and lyrics, although passable, were in no way as good as the lyrics Sondheim wrote for *West Side Story* and *Gypsy*. And his own music lacked the bounce of the tunes he composed for *Forum*. . . . Although it had an appealing basic idea, *Evening Primrose* was a flower that withered before it could bloom."

"It was one of the worst series ever filmed," explains Anthony Perkins. "I think our project suffered somewhat from being a part of it. And it came off a little stiff because they insisted on doing it on tape instead of film."

Separated from Goldman after *Evening Primrose*, Sondheim "got roped into" working on a project with Jerome Robbins at his American Theater Lab. "He has a fascination with Brecht," Sondheim said later, "and one of the things he was experimenting with was a one-act play called *The Measures Taken*, and he wanted me to do a score for it. I hate Brecht—all of Brecht, and I particularly hated that play. So he asked me to turn to the next play in the book, *The Exception and the Rule*. He had a comic idea for it, so it seemed vaguely possible. And I admire Jerry so much that I would work on almost anything with him, so I put aside my prejudice against Brecht. But after writing the second song, I realized that it was not a show that I wanted to do in any way, shape, or form—it was didactic to a degree that I can't handle. I told Jerry to get Lenny to do the music because I felt that he would understand this kind of thing and I also thought Lenny should do the lyrics."

Leonard Bernstein did agree to do the music but when he refused to do lyrics, Jerry Lieber was called in. (Lieber, primarily a pop song writer, with his partner, Mike Stoller, has written many hit songs, including Peggy Lee's "Is That All There Is?") Then a month or two later, they reached an impasse and asked Sondheim to come in and do some lyrics.

"I was suddenly in a dilemma," Sondheim says. "It became a very peculiar request to do lyrics for something that I had turned down doing music for in addition, but I yielded to their blandishments. We worked three months on it, but, actually, the main reason I agreed to come back to it was that they'd brought in John Guare to do the book and he had a wild and fanciful idea that was brilliant and exciting, and I thought that I wanted to be connected with the project."

Stuart Ostrow, the producer of their new musical, then titled *A Pray by Blecht*, was forced to set a strict deadline to get the show into rehearsal because Bernstein was soon to tour with the Philharmonic, and Zero Mostel, the newly signed star of the show, had to be in rehearsal by a certain date or was committed to do a film.

"The setting of the show," explains John Guare, "was a play within a play, taking place in a television studio. It was supposed to deal with the idea that in 1968 having 'good intentions' was not enough and that it was presumptuous and hilarious to expect that *showing* man's inhumanity to man would change anything in the world. I guess we still had illusions . . . Camelot illusions. . . . Not Lerner and Loewe *Camelot*, Kennedy Camelot. And it was odd, because when we were in the middle of writing it, Bobby Kennedy was killed."

In late August 1968, the *New York Times* ran a story announcing that their new show was due at the Broadhurst Theatre in February. "The score is not for the conventional pit orchestra," Leonard Bernstein said in the article. "It'll be a chamber orchestra. Maybe not in the pit at all, but positioned around the stage in groups . . . but that depends on how it goes in rehearsals. We will use lots of amplification and some electronic music." The *Times* piece elaborated that "the main plot deals with two rival groups of oil concessionaires racing across the desert—the motivation is generated by the impossible relationship between one of the oilmen [Zero Mostel] and his coolie."

At the end of a three-month period, having returned to the ambitious project, Sondheim and company became discouraged and dropped it altogether. "We had written eight or nine songs," says Sondheim, "and although I still loved Guare's notion, Brecht still bothered me a lot. I was ashamed of the whole project, it was arch and didactic in the worst way, and we really couldn't go on with it."

When Sondheim went back to work with James Goldman, Stuart Ostrow asked to take a look at *The Girls Upstairs*. Liking the piece, Ostrow optioned it, brought in Joseph Hardy as director, and work began to bring the show to rehearsal by the end of 1969.

In the meantime, George Furth, an actor friend of Sondheim's, had written eleven one-act plays that he planned to have produced with Kim Stanley playing each of the eleven leads. Anthony Perkins, who was directing numerous shows at regional theaters, expressed interest in staging the show. And Sondheim was asked to read the work for his opinion.

"After Steve read the plays," reports Harold Prince, "he gave them to me and told me that George had written them and would *I* give a friend's advice. I read them and told Steve that although I felt that Kim Stanley was one of the best actresses in the country, I thought it wasn't viable to have her running around having eleven makeup jobs and eleven wigs and being eleven different people. That would be a trick. But I found the writing to be superior and it seemed suddenly to be this terrific idea for a musical. The reason that it seemed to be a musical was that for the last couple of years we had been talking about doing a kind of autobiographical musical which would be about marriage today . . . the plays weren't *all* about marriage, but some of them were. I thought, what if we could construct a musical about New York marriages and if we could create a central character to examine these marriages."

Sondheim was surprised but excited by Prince's suggestion and brought George Furth to Prince's office to discuss the project. Upon reaching an agreement, they began immediately to work on this newly devised modern musical comedy titled *Company*, in which a central character—thirty-five, unmarried, and unable to make a commitment to anyone—was created to observe his married friends' lives.

"The problem," Sondheim says, "was to find the form for it, which we eventually arrived at. It was new for me because we realized early on that the kind of song that would not work in the show was the Rodgers and Hammerstein kind of song in which the characters reach a certain point and then sing their emotions, because George writes the kind of people who do not sing. To spend time exploring the characters was wrong because they were primarily presented in vignettes, and as soon as you'd try to expand them with song it would be a mistake. All the songs had to be used, I'm sorry to say, in a Brechtian way as comment and counterpoint. And as such, next to *Forum*, it was the hardest score I ever had to write. The style was different from anything else that had been going on. You see, I find Brecht humorless and his points so obvious in the text itself that the songs have no surprise or wit for me. We tried to use the form, however, and improve on it. We had our songs interrupt the story and be sung mostly by people outside the scene commenting on the action taking place. You never want to make a statement, but *Company* did become controversial because it dealt with the increasing difficulty of making one-to-one relationships in an increasingly dehumanized society. And one of the reasons we had it take place in front of chrome and glass and steel was that it took place in an urban society in which individuality and individual feeling become more and more difficult to maintain. It's the lonely crowd syndrome. It's *also* about expecting relationships to be what they're not. Chekhov once said: 'If you're afraid of loneliness, don't marry.' Most succinct. In the deepest sense, that's what *Company* is about. . . . To quote from the book of the show, 'You've got to marry *some*body, not just some*body*.' And 'Don't be afraid it won't be perfect, the only

Right: Dean Jones, the original Robert in *Company*, 1970. (FRIEDMAN–ABELES)

Below: Larry Kert replaced Dean Jones as Robert in *Company* a few weeks after the musical's Broadway opening, 1970. (FRIEDMAN–ABELES)

thing to be afraid of is that it won't *be*.' We wanted to achieve a lot of surprise in *Company*. We wanted a show where the audience would sit for two hours screaming their heads off with laughter and then go home and not be able to sleep."

Writing began, with Furth retaining only one and a half of his original one-act plays (the karate play and part of the pot play, with portions of the other discards going into Furth's subsequent endeavor, *Twigs*).

Since *The Girls Upstairs* was still pending, it seemed as though it was going to be a very exciting season for Sondheim with *The Girls* the first half and *Company* the second. But six weeks before rehearsals were to begin for *The Girls Upstairs*, Sondheim and Goldman reached an artistic impasse with Ostrow and Hardy, and Ostrow dropped the show.

"I had read *The Girls Upstairs* five years before," reveals Harold Prince. "I had been in East Hampton working on the final draft of *Cabaret* when Steve sent it to me. I read it as a friend because at that time it was supposed to be produced by David Merrick and Leland Hayward in partnership. I found the script to be awful and I didn't know how to cushion how bad I thought it was. It was about two men who took out two girls who were in the dressing room upstairs, and it was a personal story and they were four people self-pitying and, as far as I was concerned, pitying themselves sufficiently that I didn't have to involve myself in their problem. I then heard some music and, well, with Steve, that's devastating because he's *just* that good. Jim Goldman is a very good writer. He'd written *Lion in Winter*, but this had none of the strength and vitality, none of the self-consciousness, and the best of his writing has an edge of self-consciousness which I like, a literary quality, but these mundane people were speaking down so I didn't feel there was any style in this work. I didn't like it and another year went by and the show wasn't done. Merrick and Hayward dropped it and Stu Ostrow picked it up. They were talking to John Dexter, who had done *Do I Hear a Waltz?*, and despite the fact that that show hadn't been very good, Steve wanted to work with him again, so they were asking him to direct and I read the newer draft for Ostrow. I still didn't like it but because I had now read it for a second time, I began to think about it, and I wrote three thousand words for them of what I thought was wrong with it and what I thought it should be, just as a friend, and I sent them over the letter and there was no reply. They didn't like what I had to say, I suppose, or they didn't want to hear it. It was too all-encompassing. They went on with it with Ostrow and then they inherited Joe Hardy. Then I got the idea for *Company* and we began work. Steve doesn't work very fast and he wasn't getting anything done on the show. The summer came and I was in Germany making the film *Something for Everyone*, and we were on long distance phone at night and he was anguishing because *The Girls Upstairs* was supposed to go into rehearsal in September, and my show, *Company*, was to go into rehearsal in February. But now, suddenly, Joe Hardy wasn't happy with the script and they wanted to postpone, and would I postpone my show a season? And I said I would not. And I served notice: 'I'm working. I'm ready, my set is designed, my costumes are designed, you haven't written any god-damned music, but my show's ready.' And he said, 'I can't write any music, so your show is *not* ready.' He said, 'I feel like a father with a kid and I've been over this kid for five years and I cannot write *Company* until I've done *The Girls Upstairs*.' So I agreed to read their show again . . . and I remembered somewhat what I had said three years earlier, but not entirely, and I couldn't find the notes and my secretary couldn't find my letter and the guys who got the letter didn't like it enough to keep it, so there wasn't anything you could refresh your memory with, but then I did in fact start to think about the show and I thought: I believe I know something that I didn't know before, which is that Jim Goldman has to be made into a brand-new playwright. He's got to be able to write these people *big* and if they're small, *really* small, he's got to be able to use of himself what was so remarkable in his previous plays. I mean, Ben and Phyllis are the Kennedy fellow and the Kennedy wife. They're a king and a queen. Well, if he could write that king and queen in *Lion in Winter*, he could write these characters for me. This show is not *The Girls Upstairs*, this show is *Follies*."

Prince told Sondheim to go ahead and write his score for *Company* because he would produce their other show after *Company* opened. A much relieved Stephen Sondheim went right to work.

Although the first ads for *Company* appeared under Macy's Theatre Club, in the *New York Times*, with Anthony Perkins billed as the star, Perkins went to Prince and Sondheim to ask that they let him out. "I told them," Perkins says, "that I know I agreed to do their show and I will do it, but what I *really* wish was that I was not acting but directing some other show. And they reacted with such class and with such understanding and let me go . . . and just a few weeks after that, I got the job of directing *Steambath* off-Broadway."

"Hal replaced Tony with Dean Jones before they began rehearsals," says Flora Roberts. "Tony would have given the role a lot of thought . . . he might have made you marvelously nervous. But Dean broke your heart . . . he looked so dopey and innocent. He was an inspired choice."

With Dean Jones, Barbara Barrie, Elaine Stritch, and one of the best all-around casts ever assembled for a musical, *Company* plunged into rehearsal under the direction of Prince and the musical staging of Michael Bennett. This untraditional new show was not the easiest to put together. It employed no chorus or group of dancers and no singing ensemble— each cast member doubled as character and company.

"It was very difficult," says Fritz Holt, production stage manager of the show. "Hal was frustrated because the show was hard to rehearse. Usually, the director has the principals in one room and the choreographer has the chorus in another. But in *Company* there was no chorus and Michael had to start and Hal had to wait. George Furth was also very anxious to get on with the scenes and see what he had and whether or not his plays were going to work.

"The 'Company' number took longer to stage than any number I've ever been involved with. We had everyone sit in chairs, like in a classroom. Each person was assigned his 'Bobbys' and 'Babys' and 'Bubis.' It

Larry Kert is given a surprise birthday party by his married friends in *Company*, 1970. (FRIEDMAN–ABELES)

Larry Kert is torn in a tug of war during "Side by Side by Side" and "What Would We Do Without You?" in *Company*, 1970. (FRIEDMAN–ABELES)

took the first morning of rehearsals—four hours—to do the first page. Everyone was scared."

"What I did in *Company*," explains Michael Bennett, "was to choreograph the characters. I think that a lot more of the show was choreographed than most people who saw it realized. I believe that one of the best things I've ever done was the opening number, the 'Company' number. It was heightened reality. The characters were taken and the physicalities of those characters were broadened. I don't think anyone has demanded of nondancers as much movement as I did in *Company*. Usually an actress will give you twenty minutes about how she doesn't dance and you usually don't make her dance. But after all my experiences with shows such as *Coco*, when I got to *Company*, I was determined that everybody was going to do what I told them to do in terms of movement. I knew it was a chance to do something different because there was so much subtext. Lots of times in musicals the characters are so shallow that you really don't have anything to work with.

"But working with Steve is different from working with anyone else. Aside from the fact that you have to wait a long time to get the material from him—which can make you pretty nervous—when it comes, it's terrific and it's written to be done on a stage. It's specific and it deals with the show. There are still composers in the theater who are thinking about writing hit songs, but Steve writes for character all the time. Steve, of all the composers I've worked with, understands more about the musical theater than anyone. His music is something you have to get to know. You have to live with it awhile. You are not going to get show tunes like Rodgers and Hammerstein turned out . . . he's not going to write 'Oh, What a Beautiful Mornin' ' or anything like it. Fine. I don't want to hear 'Oh, What a Beautiful Mornin' ' ever again as long as I live.

"I remember when Steve first played me 'Side by Side by Side,' and I told him that it was a good start but I had an idea for something which utilized the partners. I said I saw the beginning and the ending but I needed something for the middle . . . something like, 'We love you, Bobby, We love you, Bobby,' something over and over. I told him to give me something that I could do in many different styles and that I could do over and over and over so that it becomes grating. He then wrote 'What Would We Do Without You?' And I'm not saying that all these married couples aren't sincere about caring for Bobby in the show, but you need more than friendships or it becomes the old song and dance routine. The only thing that Steve and I had any disagreement on in *Company* was the tug-of-war in that number. He didn't want it used as an image and I felt that that's where Bobby was and I thought it worked. 'Side by Side by Side' was best when you felt you were watching the New Rochelle P.T.A. performing. They were delightful amateurs; that's what made the number work and it needed that 'Look, Mommy, I'm on stage' attitude from all those grown-up people in order to make the fun and excitement of it happen.

"An interesting thing I learned about *Company*," Bennett adds, "was that the actors would find ways of performing the show a certain way that would save energy. I gave more pep talks on *Company* than I've given on any other show in my life. I also rehearsed *Company* more than any show after it opened to keep the energy levels up. I found that it isn't a good thing to build things in a show, to build numbers that require that much energy for a performance because they don't want to give it eight times a week. They don't mind it if they are the star but in an ensemble show like *Company*, it gets boring for them to do. It's also because actors don't have the perspective to know what it's like to watch them from out front so if they don't understand what's making a number work, they don't know how to give you what you want."

Once Prince started staging the book scenes he was very pleased with the form his new musical was taking. "I loved it," he says, "but I found *Company* to be the most difficult experience as a director. It was painful from beginning to end because it took *me* until I was thirty-five to get married and Bobby was thirty-five in the play."

A tough and ambitious *Company* opened in Boston to love-hate notices. Kevin Kelly exclaimed in the *Boston Globe*: "It is destined to become a classic in the American musical theater." But *Variety* reported: "Who cares what happens to 'Bobby Buby' [*sic*] is only one of the problems affecting Harold Prince's unconventional-form musical . . . the songs are for the most part undistinguished. . . . It's evident that the author, George Furth, hates femmes and makes them all out to be conniving, cunning, cantankerous, and cute. . . . As it stands now it's for ladies' matinees, homos and misogynists."

Sondheim: "A lot of the controversy about *Company* was that up until *Company* most musicals, if not all musicals, had plots. In fact, up until *Company*, I thought that musicals had to have very strong plots. One of the things that fascinated me about the challenge of the show was to see if a musical could be done without one. Many of the people who disliked the show disliked it for that reason. They wanted a strong story line and they didn't get one and were disappointed. The second reason was that people were mistaking our saying that relationships are *difficult* for relationships are *impossible*. What we clearly said over and over again was two is difficult but one is impossible. We said it over and over again and yet a lot of people missed it."

Prince: "What happened in Boston was that we had a song for Robert to sing called 'Happily Ever After.' It was the bitterest, most unhappy song ever written, and we didn't know how devastating it would be until we saw it in front of an audience. It scared them and it scared us because it was too complicated. Steve was writing an affirmative song, but he put *everything* in it and that *everything* overrode the affirmation. . . . If I heard that song I wouldn't get married for anything in the whole world."

Sondheim: "It *was* a little bleaker, but 'Happily Ever After' was a scream of pain. Bobby was fighting against something he *knew*, instead of *suddenly* realizing it. But my collaborators kept using the word 'negative' . . . the song was really 'The Lady doth protest too much.' It seemed clear that it was a fellow trying to convince himself that committing oneself to one person leads to grief, anguish, loss of privacy, loss of individuality. It was also related to a larger subject: that you can avoid committing yourself to somebody in today's society because there are so many distractions like drugs, drink, chrome and glass and cars. . . . You can easily live your life enjoying the distractions. But apparently the audience got the message wrong, so I had to change it. In Boston I wrote 'Being Alive' and although I love the song, I feel that the ending of the show was a cop-out. When Bobby suddenly realizes that he shouldn't be alone at the end of the scene, it's too small a moment and you don't believe it.''

Elaine Stritch sings "The Ladies Who Lunch" in *Company*, 1970. (FRIEDMAN–ABELES)

Prince: "I don't agree. The last ten minutes are *not* a cop-out. They're just not as skillfully done as the rest of the show. We worked hard but we never got it quite right. The marriages in the show are not bad marriages —they're just marriages that are holding together because people either live little lies or look the other way. It's called human. What happens to Robert in the end is what we wanted to have happen to him. We didn't ease into it properly and that's what's wrong with the show . . . there'll always be something."

Out of town, a closeted but growing friction began between *Company*'s librettist and its producer-director. "The only time there was ever any visible conflict in Boston," Fritz Holt reports, "was when George Furth personally gave Beth Howland a note before a performance and it screwed up her exit at the end of her scene. Hal was furious and I don't blame him. You just can't do that. . . . And George realized that, he's an actor. He apologized for it and that was that. But it was never evident that there was anything the matter between George and Hal until way after we opened. And that's essential . . . regardless of what's happening, there's a place to determine where your feuds are and where you appear united."

Cleaning up easier discrepancies in Boston, following the suggestion of Flora Roberts, "Side by Side by Side" was moved from the latter part of the second act to the opening of the act to serve as a progress report on Bobby's status with his married friends. "Another Hundred People" was cut (to the horror of everyone connected with the show) until a workable way to routine the number was devised, and then it was put back in. A chunk of "Have I Got a Girl for You" was dropped. And the ending of the show changed several times.

"I remember taking a scene that I had just typed," Fritz Holt says. "It was Stritch's last few lines that George had written as a lead-in to 'Being Alive.' I brought it over to Steve's hotel room and just handed it to him at the door. He looked *terrible*. That was the first time I realized the agony Steve goes through on a show. It's painful and horrifying."

With polishing as complete as possible under the limitations of an out-of-town tryout, *Company* entered New York, receiving wildly enthusiastic notices.

"*Company* is so brilliant it passes over one like a shock wave," said Douglas Watt in the *Daily News*.

Ted Kalem of *Time* and Jack Kroll of *Newsweek* both called the new musical "a landmark."

"So extraordinary in execution that it defies comparison with any musical that has come before it," announced Stewart Klein on WNEW-TV.

But all-powerful Clive Barnes in the *New York Times* did not share the enthusiasm of the majority of the critics. He found the characters in *Company* to be extremely unlikable—the kind that you go out of your way to avoid at cocktail parties. He felt the direction was lacking in variety of pace. He added: "Creatively, Mr. Sondheim's lyrics are way above the rest of the show; they have a lyric suppleness, sparse elegant wit and range from the virtuosity of a patter song to a kind of sweetly laconic cynicism in a modern love song. His music is academically very interesting. Mr. Sondheim must be one of the most sophisticated composers ever to write a Broadway musical, yet the result is slick, clever and eclectic rather than exciting. It's the kind of musical that makes me say, 'Oh yeah?' rather than 'Gee whiz!' but I readily concede that many people will consider its sheer musical literacy as offsetting all other considerations."

In the Sunday *New York Times*, the following week, Walter Kerr called *Company*: "Original and uncompromising. It is brilliantly designed, beautifully staged, sizzlingly performed, inventively scored, and it gets right down to brass tacks and brass knuckles without a moment's hesitation, staring contemporary society straight in the eye before spitting in it. . . . Stephen Sondheim has never written a more sophisticated, more pertinent, or—this is the surprising thing in the circumstances—more melodious score; and the lyrics are every bit as good. . . ." Then, after numerous paragraphs raving about Prince's direction, Bennett's choreography, Aronson's set, and most of the terrific performances, Kerr wrote: "Now ask me if I liked the show. I didn't like the show. I admired it. . . . Personally, I'm sorry-grateful."

"*Company* was the only time," Michael Bennett said, "in my entire career that I couldn't have cared less what the critics said. It was a show that I loved, it was a show that I was proud of, and there wasn't a review in the world that could damage that."

A few weeks after the show opened and was confirmed a "hit," Dean Jones withdrew from the cast. A press release was sent out announcing that Jones had contracted hepatitis and that his standby, Larry Kert (the same Larry Kert who starred in the Prince-Sondheim *West Side Story* thirteen years earlier), would assume the role of Robert.

Jones: "I liked *Company* . . . don't get me wrong. I just felt unsatisfied in the role and I was going through my own divorce at the time. I felt

From left: Dean Jones, record producer Thomas Z. Shepard, and *Company* composer-lyricist Stephen Sondheim, 1970. (COLUMBIA RECORDS)

that the show was antimarriage, perhaps because at the time *I* was anti-marriage. Every night after the performance I would be on the phone with the attorneys. I'd gotten soft on the Coast, I guess. I'm not built for a year's run. I can never do that again. I was miserable and obviously I *didn't* have hepatitis, but Hal was nice enough to let me out."

Prince: "One of the problems was that the character of Bobby had to be the observer. The show was often criticized for his not being the action. There was just a glimmer of something that I noticed with Dean who was having a terrible emotional time. A week before we opened, I said to him, 'If I were to tell you that you didn't have to play this part much longer, would you give me an opening night? You're capable of it. You're mar-velous in this role.' And he just opened up and said, 'If you can do that, I can do anything.' So I said, 'All right, the minute we open, if we are a success, I will replace you as soon as possible, I promise you. Now give me a show!' And it freed him and his opening night performance was wonderful. I had gotten Larry Kert to be his standby long before we ever left for out-of-town tryouts. I didn't have in mind that he would replace

Dean; what I planned was for Larry to play the national company. Larry was a guy who was selling dogs in California and I felt that he should get the hell out of there and back into the theater where he belonged. So Larry replaced Dean . . . it was more of a musical comedy with Larry. The show with Larry wasn't the show we intended . . . it wasn't pointed up as well . . . it was softer . . . the laughs were more indulgent . . . but the *audience* liked Larry better, and had Dean stayed, there's no telling whether the show would have been as successful."

Bennett: "I was very sorry that Dean left. Larry was very busy performing, and Dean was a man who was troubled and it worked brilliantly with the part. In 'Being Alive' Dean suffered; with Larry it was Larry Kert doing the show-stopper. The difference was that Larry performed with the fourth wall gone and with Dean it was there—you were witnessing as opposed to being a part of something. I did think Larry improved enormously in the part and when he went to London he was absolutely wonderful. He had matured a little and Hal and I worked with him and he got a lot better."

"I think that it was inappropriate to have someone starring in that role," states Anthony Perkins. "The character is there to make the other scenes possible and the show is really a musical with a cast of fourteen—all of whom have equal responsibilities. It's brilliant ensemble playing, but it's not a show that features a performer. For some reason, I was the first person to turn up backstage after the opening night performance, and Dean was standing there and he said, 'Man, I really tried. I tried to make this part mine but I couldn't.' I sympathized with him. He was good in that role, but the person who plays that part is always unappreciated. And having turned down the role, I thought to myself, not knowing what the part turned out to be, that when I went to the opening I should bring along my gun because at the end of the first act I'm going to put it against my temple and fire. But I didn't. I thought that it was a brilliant show . . . and I was happy I wasn't in it.'

Called upon for a follow-up review of the show, the *New York Times* ran second-stringer Mel Gussow's review rather than giving Clive Barnes a second crack at knocking the show. Gussow, though a bit late, since the harm of Barnes's review had already taken its toll, reversed the *Times*'s view of *Company*.

In a banner that read "*Company* Anew," Gussow reported, "This is, by design, not a musical about a man, but about a theme: marriage and nonmarriage in an urban society. Intentionally, the hero is underwritten, which makes him especially difficult to play. Jones was effective, but perhaps too passive. Kert apparently realizes that Robert is not merely an observer, that he moves from bemused detachment to a final quest for commitment. . . . The scenes whose impulse comes from the music, and not from the book, seem distinctly superior. On re-hearing, Stephen Sondheim's elegantly intricate score deepens in sophistication, intelligence and lyrical and musical inventiveness. Similarly, Harold Prince's direction seems even more firm and imaginative, giving the show a seamless stylistic unity. . . . *Company* is an original, unconventional work, which may be why some in the audience seemed restless. Perhaps they expected to be glad-handed by a typical Broadway hit, instead of confronted with irony, taste and wit—rare commodities in the musical theater."

Although *Company* was clearly a hit, it was a special show with a limited audience. It never made a great deal of money, but because it was economically produced, it was able to play to half-empty houses and still make back its investment with a modest profit. The show received the New York Drama Critics' Award as Best Musical and six Tony Awards (including Best Musical). Sondheim won the first awards of his career: a Tony for Best Music and a Tony for Best Lyrics.

Company closed in New York after a twenty-month run, about the same time most of the original cast took the show to London, where it opened to some of the best reviews any musical has received in British theater history.

Harold Hobson in the London Sunday *Times* proclaimed: "There are no native composers in this city of the varied brilliance of Stephen Sondheim, who is responsible for both music and lyrics—lyrics that are sometimes sharp as an icicle, and that at others set the mind achingly dreaming of unforgotten joys and irrational sorrows. . . . It is extraordinary that a musical, the most trivial of theatrical forms, should be able to plunge as *Company* does with perfect congruity into the profound depths of human perplexity and misery."

Company ran in London for six months with Larry Kert and Elaine Stritch and for another two months with British replacements, closing at a loss of 75 percent of its investment.

"It was the most extraordinary experience," says Richard Pilbrow, co-producer of the London production as well as London's foremost lighting designer. "It was one of those shows where the investors wrote in to say that they were sorry the show was closing but that they were glad they were involved in it. They'd lost their money happily. *Company* advanced the musical theater in this country . . . we'd never seen anything like it before."

"I think the hardest thing in the world," theorizes Anthony Perkins, "is to make people come to see something different. Bob Fosse once defined the musical comedy to me as an evening when everybody has a good time—even in the crying scenes. I think there's a school of creating a successful musical that would adhere to that, and it might be good to keep in mind if you are anxious to create a commercially successful musical. Let's face it, there's nothing quite as enchanting for some of us as seeing something that is new and adventurous and full of surprise. *Company* was just that . . . and when you try new things you must be willing to suffer critical abuses and even financial losses. Very few would even attempt it; that's why we must be grateful for Hal and Steve. They're an impeccable team."

Company choreographer Michael Bennett (left) and Stephen Sondheim attend Tony Award ceremonies, 1970. (VAN WILLIAMS)

MUSICAL STAGING · · · 13

"**I** BEGAN to direct," says librettist Arthur Laurents, "only because I realized how bad directors are. It was out of self-defense. Go back to Shakespeare and Molière—they each directed. Now I'm not putting myself or anybody else in that class, but authors used to direct, and then it began to change. I think some authors do have the objectivity to direct their own work and some don't. . . . Most don't want to. Generally, we have had this great rash of choreographers directing musicals. But there's rarely a musical that is directed by a choreographer that has good acting performances because choreographers, by nature, are used to dealing only with bodies. Jerry Robbins, in my opinion, is not a director. He's a brilliant stager but he doesn't know how to direct actors. On *West Side Story* he had an assistant and I helped. I can think of, off the top of my head, only one choreographer who can direct book as well as stage dances and that's Michael Bennett. I thought the dramatic work he did in *Twigs* was quite good."

"I've always worked with dancers as actors," Michael Bennett explains. "I motivate my dancers beyond just giving steps to them, which is probably why I have been able to get so much out of people who usually cannot dance. And choreography is much more than doing 'steps'—which is something that a lot of new choreographers don't understand. It's also something that a lot of critics don't understand. I've always suffered from the fact that critics think that choreographers do nothing more than steps. Before George Balanchine coined the word 'choreographer,' they used to have what they called dance directors on shows. At one time people like

Agnes de Mille would come in and do three dance sequences and the director would stage all the ballads and smaller numbers. Then Jerry Robbins and people like that came along and started staging *all* the musical numbers. When you see billing that reads 'musical numbers and dances staged by' it means that any time the music plays in the show, the choreographer staged it. Some directors still stage ballads. Hal Prince is capable of doing it. In *Company* he did 'Ladies Who Lunch' and 'Sorry-Grateful.'

"Musical staging entails many things. It's not only having an actor walk from an upper platform to a lower one, but in addition to the movements you also set up the motivation. A lot of directors are known for staging a show well but not necessarily directing the book and the actors well. I think directing is a gift . . . a gift to be able to communicate to actors what you want from them. Now that musicals are more serious, which we can thank Jerry and thank Hal for, it takes a lot more. You need to know the craft of the musical. Unless you've grown up in musicals, you can't do them well. The best work I've done in the theater is when you can't tell I staged one thing and the director staged the other. I have always, no matter whom I've worked with, tried to make it look like one person did the show. You should never be able to tell where one person's work ends and the next one's begins. It takes a lot of knowledge to do a musical and I feel very strongly that before you start breaking the rules—as so many amateurs in the theater have done—you had better know what the rules are."

Awaiting notes from directors Harold
Prince and Michael Bennett, the cast of
Follies gathers on Boris Aronson's
"Loveland" setting, following its first
run-through in Boston, 1971. (MARTHA
SWOPE)

AN EMBARRASSMENT
OF RICHES · · · 14

"IT'S THOSE 'Girls' Again," read the banner of Lewis Funke's "News of the Rialto" column in the Sunday *New York Times*. "With the opening of *Company* the other night, producer-director Harold Prince disclosed that he now holds the option on *The Girls Upstairs*."

When postproduction of *Company* was out of the way, Prince went right to work on a year-long course of turning the naturalistic *Girls Upstairs* into the surrealistic, Fellini-esque *Follies*.

"The original impulse for *The Girls Upstairs* was something that was much more melodramatic and more foolish," James Goldman explains. "We began with people who were much older. It got rewritten a lot and I had incorporated something I was always very taken with—a device Chekhov used for the curtain, at the end of the third act of *Uncle Vanya*, where people are driven by anguish to the point where someone fires a gun and misses. . . . I think it's very important to borrow nice things from nice places and I attempted to make use of a similar ploy. There wasn't any real murder in our show. I've always taken murder mysteries rather seriously, although most of them aren't any good. Those that are good go into the fact that murder is a very passionate act unless you're dealing with some kind of nut who's going around settling some kind of antisocial grievance. Our show dealt with desperate feelings, but nothing bad ever happened. It was foolish in a nice way, but it never worked."

"We found out," Sondheim recalls, "as we kept writing, it was full of incident, and every time there *was* incident, it was not as good as when there *wasn't* incident. The show took on a Chekhovian quality—the less that happened, the better, and gradually it turned into this incidentless show. Throughout the numerous writing changes we kept the same four characters. The murder mystery plot was a 'who'll-do-it' rather than a 'whodunnit.' At the end of the first act, the four principals each had reason to kill each other and the second act was who'll do it to whom."

With Michael Bennett and the show's authors, Prince took only the characters, the locale, and four of Sondheim's original songs to fashion their new musical. The murder mystery aspect of the show was also dropped.

"Before Hal became involved," Sondheim says, "we never had the past embodied on the stage. We had the principals falling into the past and talking and behaving as though they were twenty years old—they were middle-aged people sort of playing a charade. But Hal said that he thought we were assiduously avoiding the use of flashbacks. We felt that they were corny but Hal explained that they would be corny only if they were *done* cornily. Through a series of discussions, Jim got an idea of how to utilize the flashback images. So during the summer of 1970, the book changed drastically with the addition of the young people, the shadows, the ghosts.

"We also originally had the people at the party gradually putting on a Follies in the midst of getting drunk and having a good time. Our original Follies had been realistic, but both Hal and Michael felt that a literal use of the Follies was a mistake. So the idea of a metaphoric Follies came about. Hal was into the whole 'memory' quality of the show. His image was of that great photo of Gloria Swanson standing in the rubble of the Roxy Theatre. The Roxy opened in the late Twenties with a picture called *The Loves of Sunya*, a film which starred Swanson, and when it was torn down in 1960 she posed in the ruins with her arms outstretched. And Hal said that *that's* what the show should be about—rubble in the daylight.

"The show was *not* about failing marriages. The reason Jim chose the Follies as a metaphor was that the Follies represented a state of mind of America between the two world wars. Up until 1945, America was the good guy, everything was idealistic and hopeful and America was going to lead the world. Now you see the country is a riot of national guilt, the dream has collapsed, everything has turned to rubble underfoot, and *that's* what the show was about also—the collapse of the dream. It's not about how difficult it is to stay married over a period of thirty years. . . . It's how all your hopes tarnish and how if you live on regret and despair you might as well pack up, for to live in the past is foolish."

Above: Michael Bartlett as Roscoe (center) sings as (from left) Alexis Smith, Fifi D'Orsay, Mary McCarty, and the rest of the "Beautiful Girls" make their entrances in *Follies*, 1971. (MARTHA SWOPE)

Left (from left): Gene Nelson as Buddy, Dorothy Collins as Sally, John McMartin as Ben, Alexis Smith as Phyllis, in "Waiting for the Girls Upstairs" from *Follies*, 1971. (FRIEDMAN–ABELES)

Preproduction on the show ran smoothly. Although Prince budgeted the musical at close to $800,000—the highest price tag for a show emanating from his office up until that time—the money came rolling in so abundantly that $60,000 had to be sent back. But the show was obviously going to be Prince's biggest gamble: a musical of controversial and not very cheerful material that required more than an eight-month run at *capacity* business in order to recover its investment (a relatively short time by today's standards), a cast of fifty, a large orchestra, a modern complicated setting, and a breakeven of $85,000 a week (later lowered to $79,000 when royalty cuts were taken by the creative staff).

Prince: "*Follies* was an enormous show. I asked Michael Bennett not only to choreograph but to co-direct it with me and we were busy every living, breathing moment from the time we went into rehearsal. It was like trying to get eighty-five shows on at the same time. It was also a show that was very expensive, but the money needed to be spent . . . we spent it and you saw it and it couldn't have been done any other way.

"We were basically telling the story of four people in their early fifties: two ex-show girls and the stage-door-Johnnys whom they married thirty years ago. Phyllis married Ben, and Sally, Buddy. But Sally, who was in love with Ben, retains her fantasies of rekindling her long-ago affair with him. They came to this reunion and the reunion served as a catalyst for looking backwards . . . 'One last look at where it all began' . . . and as the evening wore on, the people got crazier and crazier until the last fifteen minutes which turned into a metaphorical Follies . . . the rubble disappeared and *through* the Follies they were able to make an adjustment to each other. I think that we have a terrible tendency in life, when things are going wrong, to look into the past and moon over it. The point of the show was that you should *use* the past to look into the future."

Casting the show, Prince and Bennett searched Las Vegas for tall, beautiful show girls to portray the ghosts. As for the principals: "The casting could be looked upon as cruel," wrote Martin Gottfried in *Women's Wear Daily*. "Alexis Smith, Gene Nelson, Dorothy Collins, Yvonne De Carlo, Fifi D'Orsay and Mary McCarty have not been hired just for the sake of camp. They are there to embody the point of *Follies* in their very presence. The audience knows these people from its own past, remembers their faces from a performing youth. Now they are aging and we see them aged, and *Follies* is about aging and age. In a sense these actors are being used as people rather than performers. . . . And since John McMartin is the catalyst in the story, he is the one major cast member who is not a shadow from the past."

Michael Bennett's biggest problem in working with his cast was that each of the principals had rhythm problems. "It was especially difficult," Bennett says, "to do a number like 'Waiting for the Girls Upstairs.' It was really a case of the performers not being able to do a piece of material. They were very unsure and performed it tentatively—and that number cannot be done tentatively.

"We had a lot of time when nobody did anything because we didn't have the material. It wasn't really Steve's fault. He started to write stuff for the Follies that we decided was wrong so he started again. I had to order clothes for numbers and I didn't even know what the numbers were going to be. I hate doing things like that. It made the orchestrations rushed and it put a great deal of pressure on everybody."

From the beginning, the agreement between the two directors was that Prince would direct the scenes and Bennett would direct the concept and the way the show went, as well as staging the numerous musical numbers.

Bennett: "While I was waiting for the music for the Follies section to arrive, I had the show girls walk in slow motion eight hours a day. We had the show staged so that the girls changed with each scene, almost like a new drop coming in."

Prince: "I think one of the most ingenious and marvelous of Michael's concepts was to put the ghosts, the show girls, in black and white costumes with light skin, to contrast the older members of the cast, the present, in full color."

Bennett: "The show girls were on six-inch platforms and the head-dresses they wore were huge and the girls were six feet two to begin with. I wanted it all to look bigger than life. I wanted those girls to be bigger than the Ziegfeld girls could ever have been. It was like looking into a mirror and seeing the past—not the *reality* of the past, but the glorification of it."

Bennett's most acclaimed number in *Follies*, which was also the metaphor of the show, was "Who's That Woman?" performed by Mary Mc-Carty and frequently referred to as the "mirror number." "I started working on staging the number using a concept of Steve's," Bennett says. "It was about a woman who had died and left an empty spot in the chorus line. But you really would have needed about sixteen girls doing precision work to see that somebody was missing. It got to be very depressing and it wasn't clear, so I called Steve one day and I told him that I couldn't make the number work the way he wanted it but that I had a good idea for something that I was sure he would like. Incidentally, the taps that were heard in the theater were not actually coming from the women on the stage. In fact, no one onstage wore tap shoes because not enough people tapped well enough to make the sound, so the taps were done live every night by the chorus boys tapping in the basement, which also helped to create an 'effect' since I wanted it to sound ghostlike. In addition, the end of the number was prerecorded and it was a combination of tape along with live singing on stage that made the number peak as it did.

"Something else that was prerecorded was the 'Loveland' number, and once again, they also sang live onstage. The chaos which ended the Follies section and brought us to the last scene was something that was done in five hours in a hotel room right before we previewed in Boston. Everyone was getting nervous. We needed something to get us out of that portion of the show and I finally said, 'Everyone, just leave me alone and I'll get it done somehow.' I don't know if the audience actually realized just how much was going on: the whole disintegration of an orchestration . . . every song was played with one instrument or another and every performer was on the stage doing different songs or replaying scenes that occurred earlier.

"One argument that I had with Steve was about Vincent and Vanessa —the couple who did the 'Bolero d'Amour' number. Steve didn't like them and I thought they were necessary because it broke up all the purple numbers such as 'Don't Look at Me,' 'The Road You Didn't Take,' 'In Buddy's Eyes,' and 'Too Many Mornings.' There they were in their purple

The *Follies* girls, flanked by their ghosts in the background, perform "Who's That Woman?" in 1971. (MARTHA SWOPE)

clothes singing four of those numbers in a row. I just thought the 'Bolero' number was terribly necessary."

One of the show's greatest achievements in staging was the use of specific lighting and movement techniques which created a cinematic appearance from the stage.

Prince: "I purposely requested that the rehearsal scripts of *Follies* and *Company* read like screenplays. I had a sense that you could do close-ups and dissolves and wipes on the stage which had really been left to cinema prior to both those shows."

Bennett: "One of the most boring holdovers from the traditional musical is the use of rideouts or blackouts. In *Company* and *Follies* we discovered ways of using dissolves . . . of never stopping the action. In *Follies* there was a place for your eye to go every minute."

Goldman: "I think a lot of the images created and carried out in the staging of the show, the way scenes bled in and out, were very movielike. One of the best numbers I've ever seen was 'Who's That Woman?' The physical impression you got from that was anguishing. To see the decay of the flesh—all those bright, young beautiful girls and their lovely bodies with all the sense of youth and the promise of what's to come contrasted against what *actually* became of it. That's devastating . . . very disturbing and very movielike. The theater rarely utilizes visuals to make important

From left: Kurt Peterson as Young Ben, Virginia Sandifur as Young Phyllis, Harvey Evans as Young Buddy, and Marti Rolph as Young Sally perform "You're Gonna Love Tomorrow" and "Love Will See Us Through" in *Follies*, 1971. (MARTHA SWOPE)

Yvonne De Carlo as Carlotta Campion in *Follies* number "Can That Boy Foxtrot!" cut in Boston and replaced by "I'm Still Here," 1971. (VAN WILLIAMS)

statements, but films do. It's putting the picture in front of you and there was a lot of that in *Follies*."

A breathless (and breathtaking) *Follies*, barely pulled together in time to open in Boston, received negative to mixed reviews. *Variety* reported that the show had "too many characters, too many leading players, too many scenes, and the most bewildering plot-line in years." Kevin Kelly in the *Boston Globe* said that "*Follies* is in trouble." "When it sings and dances," wrote Elliot Norton in the *Record American*, "Harold Prince's new *Follies* is generally exuberant and exhilarating, ingenious and extraordinary entertainment. When it talks, however, when its four principals thrash out the follies of their love lives, it is bitter and shallow."

It was only Samuel Hirsch in the *Herald Traveler* who came to the show's rescue: "There's a magic feeling that comes over you when a new musical opens and lets you know all's well . . . it happens rarely. It happened last night."

"Our main problem," Sondheim said in Boston, "is that there is too much of everything. It's the biggest, most complicated musical ever, and we're just going to have to cut it down to size. It's an embarrassment of riches."

One of the musical's first priorities was finding a way to get Yvonne De Carlo's large solo number, "Can That Boy Foxtrot!" to work. ("Yvonne couldn't do it," Bennett says. "It needed someone dry like Elaine Stritch.") After much wasted time, Sondheim retreated to his hotel room and wrote her a replacement song, "I'm Still Here."

Another number that was dropped was "Uptown Downtown." "I quite honestly don't understand why Steve had to write 'Lucy and Jessie' for Alexis to replace the other number," Bennett says candidly. "I liked 'Uptown Downtown' so much better. It also lost me a phrase to hang her dance on. I was originally able to differentiate the character's two personalities by having half the phrase strutting up and the other half strutting down. It was terrific having just the backs of the chorus. When I lost the song, the number turned into merely a number about backs."

"One thing that we played around with a lot was the intermission," says James Goldman. "It was very damaging to the show because the show was not written to have an intermission. It was in and out and tried in two different places: after 'Too Many Mornings' for a while, and after 'Who's That Woman?' also. But we found that we scored better with the numbers that came after the intermission when there was no break. The whole show played better. Also, the piece was constructed to get you into the 'Loveland' sequence—further and further from reality. When you took everyone out to the lobby to have a cigarette you could not bring them back to the atmosphere we had created. It was a kind of accumulation of feelings that the show built to and when we interrupted that, it was damaging."

"A lot of our best ideas were never workable," Bennett admits. "I had a concept for 'Rain on the Roof,' 'Ah, Paris!' and 'Broadway Baby' that I couldn't do. I planned to have the numbers staged in silhouette, and it would have had the effect of seeing a movie montage . . . but it took the performers a week just to learn how to sing the ending and it took me three days just to explain to them what the number was going to be like. Finally I gave up. The only thing I switched in Boston was the order of the three numbers, moving 'Ah, Paris!' from last to second and 'Broadway Baby' to last. Fifi D'Orsay was very unhappy about being moved to second place but Ethel Shutta's number was the best and she did it brilliantly . . . you certainly couldn't top it with the other song. Fifi became very disruptive and she could have been much better than she was. I would not like to do a show with old people again. It's very hard."

"I thought it was a remarkable experience," says Gene Nelson. "Coming back to the stage after ten years to work with such geniuses as Hal and Michael. Michael has the most incredible sensitivities and knowledge for one so young. He thinks in terms of cause and effect, not of the steps you do but the emotions they create. And Hal's way of directing a show . . . we had major scenes that were played with people wandering all over the stage. There are old rules in staging that you never move on a joke line. . . . And you never move on a star's speech . . . these have been taboos for years. Well, Hal had ghosts going by and show girls crossing in front of you and everyone walked on his own lines—and it all worked!"

Bennett: "I spent a very long time staging Gene's number, 'The Right Girl,' which started out to be a tap. It wasn't like any kind of tapping you've ever seen. It was an extension of stamping your feet when you're angry. . . . The use of tap to show frustration and anger. It would have been terribly successful had Gene been able to stay on the beat. But since it was all built around rhythmic patterns . . . well, let's just say he couldn't do it. I finally had to take the tap shoes off and redo the number. It ended with him doing tricks which I absolutely hated, but it was the only way to make that number work, to get any kind of applause at all, and unfortunately, they each needed their big number . . . if they didn't have it they would have been very unhappy and it would have showed throughout the evening."

With cutting, clarification of staging and book, and the new numbers in and learned, *Follies* was scheduled to hit Broadway. All they needed was an opening that worked.

Bennett: "I restaged the opening six times . . . six completely different versions. The original opening was very scary and everybody was afraid that it would put the audience off. It had no music. It was done with the orchestra tuning up and it was raining and all the guests arrived with umbrellas and the ghosts started appearing. Steve did not want me to do a dance prologue, but I told him that it was my responsibility in the prologue to establish for the audience that they were going to watch the past and present all evening long. I remember calling a meeting in Boston where I asked to hear everybody's feelings about the opening. I listened and then I told them: 'Okay. I'm going to do this one more time and if it doesn't work I want you to bring in Ron Field to do the opening because I have only one left.' So I choreographed it using the music for a song called 'All Things Bright and Beautiful,' a number that was in the original *Girls Upstairs* that didn't work in our show. I staged it, it went in the last night out of town, I said good-bye, and left Boston that night. Personally,

I think the music and the orchestration of the opening are the best I've ever worked with in my entire career. When that curtain went up it was the most exciting thing ever . . . the most fabulous set, the most beautiful costumes, the most gorgeous chorus girls, the most brilliant lighting . . . it was just incredible!"

When the cast and crew arrived in New York to begin previews, they received the news that Gene Nelson's nine-year-old son had been hit by a truck in Los Angeles and was in a coma. Prince quickly had to make a decision; whether to preview and open on time or to call in the critics earlier in the week when he was sure to have Nelson still in town, in the role he was scheduled to perform for the press the following week. The Wednesday before opening, all the media were urged to see the show in preview. Then on Friday night, during his dance number, yet another crisis developed when Nelson tore the muscle from his hipbone and hemorrhaged. He was allowed to walk through performances but, under doctor's orders, was allowed no dancing during a subsequent three-week ultrasound treatment. (With Nelson's son in stable condition on the Coast, he continued in the show for the duration of its run.)

With as much diversity in opinion as *Company* received one year earlier, *Follies* opened at the Winter Garden on April 4, 1971, and precipitated

Alexis Smith performs "Could I Leave You?" in *Follies*, 1971. (MARTHA SWOPE)

all-out war. Although many were deeply taken by its theme, its characters, and its dazzling theatricalities, many more were bored and uninterested.

"*Follies* is a pastiche show so brilliant as to be breathtaking at times," said Douglas Watt in the *Daily News*. "It struck me as unlikely that the tools and resources of the Broadway musical theater had ever been used to more cunning effect than in this richly imaginative work."

"*Follies* is intermissionless and exhausting, an extravaganza that becomes tedious," wrote Walter Kerr in the Sunday *New York Times*.

"*Follies* is a brilliant show, wonderfully entertaining, extraordinarily intelligent, and having both a stunning direct appeal and a rare complexity of feeling and structure," raved Jack Kroll in *Newsweek*.

But Clive Barnes in the *New York Times* came in for the grand slam: "I think I enjoyed it better than the Sondheim/Prince last torn marriage manual *Company*, and obviously everyone concerned here is determined to treat the musical seriously as an art form, and such aspiration must be encouraged. Yet perhaps too many little old ladies are passing by just lately. . . . Mr. Sondheim's music comes in two flavors—nostalgic and cinematic. The nostalgic kind is for the pseudo-oldie numbers, and I must say that most of them sound like numbers that you have almost just forgotten, but with good reason. This non-hit parade of pastiche trades on camp, but fundamentally gives little in return. It has all the twists and turns of yesteryear, but none of the heart—and eventually the fun it makes of the past seems to lack something in affection. The cinematic music is a mixture of this and that, chiefly that. I doubt whether anyone will be parodying it in 30 or 40 years' time. . . . The lyrics are fresh as a daisy. I know of no better lyricist in show-business than Mr. Sondheim—his words are a joy to listen to, even when his music is sending shivers of indifference up your spine. The man is a Hart in search of a Rodgers, or even a Boito in search of a Verdi."

In answer to Barnes's and Kerr's scathing reviews of *Follies*, Martin Gottfried wrote in the Sunday *New York Times*: "Sondheim's qualities as a theater composer can hardly be overstated. He is constantly extending his vision, a composer applying a trained imagination to a stage he intimately understands. He works with, perhaps, the finest orchestrator in our theater's history, Jonathan Tunick, who uses ingenious and sympathetic instrumental combinations to bring out Sondheim's inner voices, his fresh turns of harmony, his inventive meters and surprising resolutions. Sondheim's music is modern even when it is nostalgic and Tunick understands this. Moreover, by writing his own, virtually perfect, lyrics, Sondheim matches the words to the (musical and intellectual) personality of his music as no partner lyricist could possibly do. . . . I am convinced that *Follies* is monumental theater. Not because I say so but because it is there for anybody to see."

Sondheim's twenty-two-song score for *Follies* contained "book" songs that dealt with character and "pastiche" numbers that re-created the era. For the latter, Sondheim says he intended to imitate the styles of the great songwriters of the times, and affectionately comment on them as well: "One More Kiss" (written in the tradition of Friml and Romberg), "The Story of Lucy and Jessie" (Cole Porter), "You're Gonna Love Tomorrow" and "Love Will See Us Through" (Jerome Kern and Burton Lane, with an Ira Gershwin–E. Y. Harburg lyric), "Beautiful Girls" (Irving Berlin), "Broadway Baby" (DeSylva, Brown, and Henderson), "Loveland" (Jerome Kern), and "Losing My Mind" (George Gershwin with a Dorothy Fields lyric).

Although *Follies* received a great deal of publicity (mostly from the celebrated Broadway musical debut of Alexis Smith, who managed to charm even the reviewers who hated the show), business was not terribly good. The production claimed the Drama Critics Award as Best Musical of the Year and seven Tony Awards (Sondheim for music and lyrics, Prince and Bennett for direction, Bennett for choreography, Boris Aronson for scenic design, Florence Klotz for costumes, Tharon Musser for lighting, and Alexis Smith as actress in a musical), but because the show's break-even was so unusually high, it closed after a year's run at a loss of its entire investment. Prince, however, sent the show out for an intended tour of large cities with its original Broadway cast. After opening in Los Angeles (to better reviews than the show received in New York) as the first attraction at the brand-new Shubert Theater in Century City—a theater that had not as yet made provisions for subscription service, which in Los Angeles is not only helpful but necessary to sustain any run—the show faltered quickly at the box office and was forced to end its tour there. (Although full-scale reincarnations of *Follies* never occurred, a new production is promised for London's West End—its first visit there—by producer Cameron MacKintosh for the spring of 1987.)

Prince: "I thought *Follies* was popular. Something nobody realized was that if *Follies* had had the break-even of *Company*, if it had run the extra six months, it would have paid off. But it cost too much. The profit was so minimal. I suppose I didn't produce it as well as the other things. On the other hand I couldn't imagine doing it for considerably less money. But it was one of the few times in the theater that I can remember anyone spending a lot of money and actually *seeing* every cent of it on the stage. That's exactly how the show *had* to be done."

Most of the criticism of *Follies* was directed at the book and its subject matter, which led to bad word of mouth among the theatergoing public who originally thought they were going to see a show with a lot of pretty girls kicking and dancing. "I think it probably made a lot of people very uncomfortable," theorizes James Goldman, "particularly older people. The younger people who saw the show and responded to it very vigorously had an advantage over those who were older because they could be of the mind that they're young enough to change their lives so that they were not in the position the characters themselves were in. Even if you're young and can't actually do anything about your life, you *think* you can. You say, 'That's not going to happen to me!' So they saw their parents up there and saw the anguishing but were sure *they* could escape it. It was a show they could respond to emotionally without being terribly distressed. Another reason for the show's rejection was that I don't believe people will go to the theater to cry, although they'll go to the movies and be torn apart."

Bennett: "It's really no secret that I did not like the book to *Follies*. Hal and I began fighting about it way back when we were rehearsing the show in the Bronx before we even left for Boston. But that's where co-directing is a mistake. Somebody has to be the boss, and in the case of *Follies*, with Hal being the producer and co-director, he was the boss. That would have been fine except that I disagreed about the book. Not as to what it was about, but the fact that I didn't think the audience understood what the book was about and as a result they stopped caring or trying to understand by the middle of the show.

"I never believed that the show would be successful. And I think that 80 percent of *Follies* was the greatest musical ever done. When we were in Boston I felt very strongly that we should go on to another city. I didn't care if we toured for three months. What's the point of coming into New York if the show wasn't ready? The concept and the musical numbers could not support the show . . . the musical numbers were more successful than the show. To tell the truth, I could not talk about *Follies* for a year after it opened, I was so bitter about its failure. So much of that show was better than anything I've ever seen or anything I've ever done."

Prince: "I think it was probably a better show book-wise than Michael

does. I don't hate the book at all. I would have liked some different things but I would not have liked the same kind of things he would have liked. The bone of contention was really the fact that Michael wanted to call in Neil Simon to fix the book. That's where we had our standoff battle. There is no question that we could have done things less naturalistically, but that has nothing to do with Neil Simon."

Goldman: "I think that Michael Bennett is a vastly talented guy. . . . I don't know whether it was because he was so young, but he's very anxious for the large hand . . . and the large hand is very helpful and very reassuring and very comforting. It often seems to assure you of success of some kind, and like all of us, he's very success-oriented, very ambitious —probably no more ambitious than I am, or any of us are . . . we are *all* a very ambitious bunch of people. He was not at a time in his life when he was interested in the kind of feelings that the show had to have or the risks that we simply had to take. I think if we had gone Michael's way the show might have run a long time. That's perfectly possible. But at the same time we would have disemboweled it, and I think Michael was perfectly willing to do just that and of course I wouldn't have wanted that to happen. You want something to succeed for being as close to what you wanted it to be, not something else. It wasn't my money, but I think it was worth it and we all should be very proud of what we did. I thought it was a first-class production. I thought that Hal and Michael did a wonderful job in staging it and I thought that the material—whatever Steve did and whatever I did—was displayed to its best advantage. It was just gorgeous. I thought we were fortunate in our casting . . . we had marvelous people to play the roles. And it failed at the box office. But not all good things are successful. It was never my expectation nor do I think anyone else's that the show would be controversial. As far as the possibility of its success, I myself was very much misled because I thought it was a serious show and a moving show, and I thought that if the audience didn't care for the people there was enough simple delight in it for them to have an enjoyable time and say, 'It was a good evening. To hell with the story, there were still lots of swell songs and dances.' That was a foolish mistake on my part. When that curtain went up and there was that great skeletal overhang, no matter how light some things were later on, you knew you were in some sort of graveyard."

Sondheim: "I think, in retrospect, that there were too many pastiche numbers in the show which hurt the book and subsequently hurt the show. Perhaps if we had used fewer songs and had more book the show would have been more successful."

Goldman: "No, there *weren't* too many songs. It was a music-heavy show and should have been . . . or at least I wanted it to be. The book-writing on the whole was very terse and very little was said that didn't have to be said. One of the things that always pleased me about the book was that somehow—I don't know how it happened—but somehow it seemed to survive the whole Follies section. . . . That when you came back to the characters for their final scene, after what must have been more than twenty minutes in Loveland, somehow or other the art of the piece survived.

"The final scene of the show has always bothered me, I must admit. There were all kinds of thoughts as to how we should have gone out at the end. I was pleased with the ending that Buddy and Sally had. I think

Ethel Shutta as Hattie Walker sings the show-stopping "Broadway Baby," as the ghost of her younger past mirrors her in the background in *Follies*, 1971. (VAN WILLIAMS)

"Loveland" sequence from *Follies*, 1971.
(VAN WILLIAMS)

it was honest and on target and about all you could do. I'm not so sure that if I had it to write over again that I would have had Ben and Phyllis together at the end. Marriage is a very difficult situation, but I don't think it's a bad one and I didn't want to write a show that was down on marriage. I wanted one of them, at least, to have hope in it, or at least the hope of something better. I'm not sure that that's honest. I very much wanted them to get together at the end and I feel now that that was very much imposed on them. I can believe it of Phyllis, I just don't believe it of Ben. I think his game is over. I don't think there is any kind of life left in him. It was bitter at the end when we found them but there was still great emotion for the man. But the man is finished . . . and *I* didn't want him to be. I wanted to leave the characters with a feeling that not everything is hopeless because, indeed, not everything *is* hopeless. Ben was a

SONDHEIM & CO.

very important character to Hal. It's a woman's show, I'm afraid. It depends on who you are and who you most identify with but I certainly don't think Ben was the central character around which the plot moved."

"I tend to agree with Hal," says Flora Roberts. "I think the most important character in the play *was* Ben. I think that Ben was too big a figure for a musical. I also think that Jim was done in by the sets and the costumes. If that show was to be a musical, it maybe should have had someone less talented than Jim writing it. He is a playwright, a magnificent playwright, and he's very musical. But I think on *Follies* he tried to be both a playwright and a librettist. And the only time Arthur Laurents ever did that was on *Anyone Can Whistle*. It's much too heavy."

"Quite honestly," offers David Merrick, "anyone who knocks *Follies* on the basis that Jim Goldman's writing is inferior is foolish. My theory was and still is that the general public is not interested in the problems of artists, because the general public cannot understand why an artist isn't living a beautiful, glamorous life . . . making a lot of money . . . being famous . . . traveling and seeing a lot of interesting people. . . . They can't understand *why* they should be having problems. It's simply a subject that doesn't interest anyone. I thought Hal Prince did a miracle job on *Follies. I* still found it boring but when they got to all the razzle-dazzle at the end, the cheap stuff, I was interested. I must say that since the show received some sensational reviews and made the covers of the big magazines, I thought it would have done better than it did. But the public vetoed the press. . . . It happens frequently these days."

The reunion of former showgirls in *Follies*, 1971. (VAN WILLIAMS)

ORCHESTRATION · · · 15

A N ASPECT of the musical theater that the majority of the theater-going public knows little or nothing about is the role the orchestrator plays in the preparation of a theater score. For three consecutive years, Sondheim was seen on national television picking up Tony Awards for his scores and giving special thanks to orchestrator Jonathan Tunick for his extraordinary contribution in a fairly thankless job.

"Few people who go to the theater even know what an orchestrator is!" Sondheim exclaims. "The contribution he makes to a show should not be ignored and his function should, by this time, no longer be such a mystery."

"An orchestrator is very important for the sound you hear in the theater," notes Ralph Burns, orchestrator of *Do I Hear a Waltz?* "That is, if he's not the usual Broadway hack—and there are loads of them around. But Steve's lucky. He's got one of the best, if not *the* best, working for him. Jonathan Tunick is simply superb."

Tunick, who orchestrated Broadway's *Promises, Promises,* worked on Sondheim's *Company, Follies, A Little Night Music, Pacific Overtures, Sweeney Todd, Merrily We Roll Along, The Frogs,* and *Stavisky,* and served as music coordinator and special arranger for the musical evening *Sondheim: A Musical Tribute.*

"Orchestration," Tunick explains, "is a way of enhancing a song—using the deviled-egg metaphor—by taking it, mashing it up, adding some ingredients, mixing it, and putting it back together again. By definition, orchestration is the craft of distributing to the various instruments of the orchestra their proper parts. In its own narrow definition, it does not include any other kind of arrangement, such as writing introductions or endings; but in a show, the orchestrator is called upon to do all these little extras, too, depending on the inclination of the songwriter.

"As the numbers are rehearsed and staged, they reach their final form. While they're being rehearsed, keys are being decided upon, cuts are made, and the music is tailored to fit the production. I spend a lot of time at rehearsals and I tape-record the practice sessions, copy the music and mark it up, see what the staging is like. Being at the rehearsals, I can see where the people are on the stage, so I know what they need to hear and how they need to be accompanied. Before you actually begin to work on a show, you must absorb the music and decide on what the general style of the score is. In the case of *Company*, it was a very contemporary, urban sound that's very influenced by pop music. It has a lot of city sounds, mechanical sounds. I always want the director and songwriter to describe what they want in metaphoric terms. *Follies* is not a re-creation of, but a glorification of, every Broadway pit band that ever played . . . and it's not what the pit band actually sounded like, it's what you *thought* the pit band sounded like, so it's a completely different approach. And *Follies* actually has two different scores, with some numbers being the book songs and others the pastiche score. The approach to the book songs is not so different from the approach to songs I took in *Company*.

"Orchestrating Steve's music is extremely difficult. *Company* was especially difficult because every song had to have a new style created for it. You could not pick a song and say this is the big ballad or this is the Twenties number. You cannot use gimmicks. Other arrangers that have orchestrated his music have not realized that because they don't understand the music." (Flora Roberts recalls that Don Walker, who orchestrated *Anyone Can Whistle*, complained that the score was much too complicated.)

"Working with Steve's music is different from working with anyone else's. A lot of people have complained that Steve's work can't be whistled. The next person that says he can't whistle Steve's songs, ask him to whistle 'Stardust.' Ask him if he thinks that's melodic. I think it is, but it's very difficult to whistle. Steve's songs have difficult intervals and sometimes he gets into some pretty tricky harmony, pretty dissonant harmony. But Steve tends to avoid stock patterns. People who are looking for something easy to listen to will look for those patterns, phrases that are even. They'll look for very simple, even rhythmic pulses. They'll look for very bland harmony that doesn't assault the ear. Now I can go into a whole thing about how we are living in an age that worships the amateur. Today a person calls himself a composer when he has no more business being called a composer than a person who calls himself a doctor because he knows how to apply a Band-Aid to a cut. Somebody buys a cigar-box guitar and plays a few chords, gets someone to write it down, and he's a composer. That may be an extreme example, but up until recently you were expected to know at least some of the language of musical notation. Can you imagine a novelist who doesn't know how to read or write?

"People complain that Steve's music isn't memorable. I know how to achieve that. How to make music memorable is to play it over and over again. The old masters knew this. See any old show and notice the number of reprises. But Steve does not like reprises. He doesn't use them much and they could be to his advantage.

"Steve's music is unique. Steve's music is also written with full piano accompaniment and what the orchestrator must do is listen to the way it sounds on the piano, reduce the notes to basic harmony, and then reconstruct it orchestrally. The notes on the orchestral score may be very different from the notes on the piano page and yet sound the same. There are profound differences between the piano and the orchestra, which is one reason why so few pianists can become good orchestrators. Most good orchestrators are players of orchestral instruments or conductors, simply because of the necessity of being familiar with the orchestra from the inside.

"I think it's also very important to be familiar with the lyric. I don't think the lyric is something different from the music. I try not to talk in musical terms with my collaborators. When I refer to a part of a song, I'll always go for the lyric rather than saying, 'Let's take bar four on the second beat.' I'll go for the lyric because that's what really expresses what's happening, more than the note, which is abstract. But in a good song, the lyrics and the music climax at the same time."

"Jonathan is also very aware of subtext," Sondheim points out. "In *Follies* there was a song called 'In Buddy's Eyes' which was Dorothy Collins's lie to the John McMartin character, in which she says that everything is just wonderful and she's having a terrific time at home, she's so happily married. Nothing in the lyric, not a word tells you that maybe it isn't true. Nothing in the music tells you, although there is something in the orchestration. The actress has to tell you, and if you had watched Dorothy Collins deliver that song with intense anger because she feels she has been had, because she had been jilted thirty years before, the whole song takes on a very peculiar quality. It isn't quite what it seems to be. Jonathan has orchestrated it so that every phrase in the song which refers to her husband is dry, all woodwinds. Whenever she refers to herself it's all strings again."

"At the climax of that song," Tunick says, "I added a very penetrating cold sound, which is a favorite of mine. It's a combination of muted trumpets and sometimes bells which give you that kind of icy buzzing sound. I used that a lot in *Company*, which was a show that called for a lot of penetrating, nasty stinging sounds.

" 'Another Hundred People' from that score was a song that suggested the restless energy, the drifting of rushed life, the endless progression of events that goes on in New York City. It's a figured piece rather than a rhythmic one. 'Another Hundred People' is a song that was orchestrated in several layers. The first was a very simple chord pattern which is based on Steve's own piano accompaniment, the keyboard pattern. Then as the song built in intensity, I brought in some of the jabbing sounds. When it reached the chorus it became very busy with lots of bells and woodwinds.

"The 'Company' number was probably the one that I was able to help the most on. The biggest problem with it was getting it to build momentum and the song was always in danger of becoming monotonous, so it needed help in pointing out where sections ended and where new sections began. I tried to bring in new rhythmic elements starting with a quarter-note pattern which, at a certain point, began to skip, then an eighth-note pattern would come in over it. It slowly built to the chorus which I think was very exciting.

"What makes me angriest about the Broadway musical theater is the attitude of directors, who seem to have reached the conclusion that, unlike children, orchestras should be heard and not seen, so they try and cover them up. The unfortunate result is that they are neither heard nor seen, so they try to remedy this with electronic equipment which takes the guts out of the music. The whole stage is wired and miked anyway, but they put monitors on the stage and you turn them on and the microphones onstage pick up the monitored sound, which results in horrible distortions. You turn the monitors down and the people onstage can't hear the music. But there is something far worse than this, when you put a roof over the pit. If there is no roof over the pit, the performers can not only hear the orchestra but see it as well. The orchestra is full of people and if the guy sitting there with his horn can hear the show and see it and know what's going on, then he knows that when he's blowing his horn in the pit he relates to a person singing on the stage. He's no dummy. He's an artist, too. Hiding the musicians makes hacks out of them. Nobody knows what's going on and I know this firsthand from playing in the orchestra.

"For instance, someone playing in the orchestra for *Follies*, who had never come to see the show from the audience, would never have any idea of what the show was about. Covering the pit not only causes terrible acoustical problems but takes all the humanity out of playing. The pits in Broadway theaters are disasters. If you go to any good opera house or any well-designed theater, you'll see an orchestra pit that's fairly shallow and extremely wide, which is very desirable because it allows the sound to rise through a large opening and become diffused in the air. I'm told that the Broadway theater owners decided at one time to put in rows of seats in the front of the house covering over about half the orchestra pit. They then dug out under the stage to make room. So in any Broadway house there is usually an opening of three feet and the rest of the orchestra is under the stage. The orchestra should not be under the stage, which is why, when you see a Broadway show, you wonder why a twenty-five-piece orchestra sounds like a circus band.

"It's very difficult, but one thing I try to do is to keep a standard of good taste and, believe me, you've got to fight for it. Hal's organization is very good about that. Hal Prince is one of the few producers who can discern between good quality and inferior quality work. I haven't encountered nearly the resistance with him that I have with some other people, who actually prefer the orchestra to sound trashy and encourage the players to play as though they were in a burlesque house. . . . I guess that's the way they think it should sound."

"There are all sorts of important contributions a good orchestrator can make," states Sid Ramin, co-orchestrator of *West Side Story* (with Leonard Bernstein and Irwin Kostal), *Gypsy* (with Robert Ginzler), and *A Funny Thing Happened on the Way to the Forum* (with Irwin Kostal). "The orchestrator, after discussing the tone of the show with the composer and the director, makes important decisions as to the style of the score and the kind of orchestra chosen. In *West Side* and *Gypsy* we didn't have any violas, only celli and violins. In *Forum*, we sold Steve on the idea of not using violins at all, and we used only violas and celli in the string section. Another specific contribution was when 'Everybody Ought to Have a

Maid' wasn't working and nobody was applauding this very funny number: I felt that the reason the song wasn't working was because it didn't have a ride-out, an ending. I asked if they'd mind if I made a suggestion and I sang the ending for them. We did it that way in the show and it was a showstopper."

Tunick: "The orchestrator must be very careful of claiming his resources with great economy because he is held down to a limited number of musicians. In opera, a chamber orchestra consists of thirty-five to forty pieces. In a Broadway show a huge orchestra is twenty-eight. *Follies* had those stage musicians. There were twenty-eight musicians on the payroll, but four of them were being used as scenery on the stage so I really only had twenty-four men. I could use only four violins, which really cut into my string arrangements. . . . There were an awful lot of things I couldn't do with the strings.

"In *Night Music*, the orchestra's rhythmic impulse is within the strings and the winds. It's based on a turn-of-the-century European style and is probably the first Broadway musical since the Twenties that doesn't have a rhythm section in the pit.

"I think that a rather good example of what an arranger can add to the music is the scale I put into 'Losing My Mind' in *Follies*. To someone who's really into music, it is something that is really suspense-building because I put in an A-flat major scale played by a harp and a celesta, and if you can hear enough ahead you know there aren't enough notes to get there, you know it's a note short and you wonder how that scale is going to end. So when it breaks chromatically, it's a great moment of relief. Another one of the things I added was in *Company* in 'Being Alive.' Steve composed it with a very confining pattern. On the lyric 'Someone to crowd me with love' I added the underscoring of 'Someone Is Waiting.' It was quite a liberty to take, the song was written out of town, it was rehearsed in the pit an hour before the show, and when it was played for the first time, I was half expecting Steve to say, 'Get that out.' He was on one aisle and I was on the other and I started walking toward him to tell him what I had done, when he got up and began walking toward me. He had this Charlie Brown grin on his face and he was nodding his head up and down. . . . He was *very* pleased."

THE GAME IS NEVER
OVER

ALTHOUGH one of Stephen Sondheim's favorite contentions is that he's one of the laziest people he's ever worked with, his view of himself is perhaps as hypercritical as is his view of others. And it is precisely this type of analytical judgment that keeps many of his acquaintances in constant fear of intimidation.

"The fact that a lot of people are afraid of Steve," says Arthur Laurents, "may be because he is very intelligent and will call people on their lack of intelligence. He doesn't have much patience. . . . Let's say, he doesn't suffer fools gladly."

"I think that Steve has a very thin coating," observed Burt Shevelove. "Steve is enormously sensitive, enormously warm, and he has a thin layer of, let's see, I won't say chicken fat—that would make him sound too Hebraic—a thin veneer of protective varnish that *does* make people afraid of him. But he likes to work and when he's not writing a show he often complains that no one ever calls to ask for his help on other projects for fear that he'll turn them down before they finish their question."

Although Sondheim's overbearing presence does send many people fleeing for fear of being pricked by a sharp-tongued quip, his ledger of friendships is quite extensive. And should anyone actually *believe* that he is all that lazy, it should be noted that by the late Seventies, in addition to his dozen Broadway musicals, Sondheim had found time over the years to write a Christmas carol for the play *I Know My Love* (1951), which starred the Lunts; the opening number for Ginger Rogers's nightclub act; music and lyrics for "Rag Me That Mendelssohn March," a song for the

Stephen Sondheim at home with his games, 1972. (FRIEDMAN–ABELES)

play *A Mighty Man Is He* (1955), which starred Claudette Colbert in Massachusetts and Nancy Kelly in New York (1960); the incidental music for the play *The Girls of Summer* (1956); the lyrics (after the opening of *Gypsy*) to Jule Styne's music for two songs for Tony Bennett called "Come Over Here" and "Home Is the Place" (the latter of which Bennett subsequently recorded); the incidental music for the play *Invitation to a March* (1961); the score for the minimusical *Passionella* (1962) as a segment of the New Jersey engagement of *The World of Jules Feiffer*, a production that starred Dorothy Loudon and Ronny Graham, with which Mike Nichols made his directing debut; the lyrics to Mary Rodgers's music for Judy Holliday's opening number, "Don't Laugh," for *Hot Spot* (1963), as well as the lyrics to her music for "The Boy From . . ." in *The Mad Show* (1966) under the pseudonym Esteban Ria Nido (a literal Spanish translation of his name); and to serve as musical adviser and lyricist to Manos Hadjidakis's music for an unsung song for Melina Mercouri in *Illya Darling* (1967); to create the diabolical crossword puzzles for *New York* magazine (1968) for a year and a half; to write the music to George Furth's lyrics for "Hollywood and Vine" sung by Sada Thompson in Furth's *Twigs* (1971); the incidental music for Arthur Laurents's play *The Enclave* (1973); the musical score for Alain Resnais's motion picture *Stavisky* (1974); to make his professional acting debut, opposite Jack Cassidy and Estelle Parsons, in the television revival of the George S. Kaufman–Ring Lardner play *June Moon* (1974) for WNET, under the direction of Burt Shevelove; to write the score for Shevelove's adaptation of Aristophanes's *The Frogs* (1974) starring Larry Blyden and featuring such chorus members as Meryl Streep, Christopher Durang, and Sigourney Weaver, staged by Shevelove in the Yale swimming pool as part of the Yale Repertory Theater season; and to write the music and lyrics for "I Never Do Anything Twice," sung by Regine in the Herbert Ross film *The Seven Percent Solution* (1976).

"One of the most extraordinary things about Steve," says Leonard Bernstein, "was that he swore on his honor that he would never write lyrics for anybody else's music again as long as he lived. Then he went and worked so terribly hard on the new production of *Candide* (1973), and along with Hal Prince and Hugh Wheeler made the show work after so many attempts that ended in failure. But that's an example of Steve's friendship and generosity. After *Company*, *Follies*, and *Night Music*, I guess he felt secure enough to take a little vacation from being a composer."

The Chelsea Theater Center's production of *Candide*, staged in the environmental setting of Eugene and Franne Lee's drawbridges, catwalks, platforms, and ramps, created a sensation when it opened in Brooklyn for a limited engagement. Hugh Wheeler's new book, based on Voltaire rather than Lillian Hellman's libretto from the original 1956 production, changed the characters from madcap adults to wide-eyed teenagers (although, as some critics pointed out, the musical *still* suffered from being a one-joke episodic show with the problem of diminishing comic returns inherent in the story).

"This version of *Candide* was exactly what I wanted it to be," says Bernstein. "It's exciting, swift, pungent, funny, and touching and it works just like sideshows at a fair. About half the score went in the process, I am sorry to say. We lost five songs that were on the original cast album, although what's on the record is not the full score by any means. [Goddard Lieberson's Broadway cast recording of the original production was responsible for making the show the best-known and most

Stephen Sondheim (left) making his acting debut with Jack Cassidy in the television revival of the 1929 George S. Kaufman–Ring Lardner *June Moon*, 1974. (WNET)

popular cult musical the theater has ever known, after its brief two-month legitimate run.] 'Eldorado,' 'Gavotte,' 'Quiet,' 'Mazurka,' and 'What's the Use?' are not in the new production. But there were other things that had been written for the show and never used. They found this music in old trunks and boxes and Steve wrote new lyrics to them. Steve's new songs are 'Life Is Happiness Indeed,' 'This World,' 'The Sheep Song,' and half of 'Auto Da Fé.' " (Sondheim used Bernstein's music for "Gavotte" to create "Life Is Happiness Indeed.")

"Actually," Sondheim admits, "Lenny had asked me to do the lyrics for *Candide* originally. He had been working on lyrics with John Latouche and then Latouche died. About that time we went to work on *West Side Story*, and Lenny asked me if I'd work with him on *Candide*, but I turned him down because it seemed at the time that Hal was going to produce a new musical called *The Last Resorts*, a show suggested by Cleveland Amory's book. So I began working on a score for that proposed show. I wrote three songs and Jean Kerr wrote a libretto . . . but the show was never done."

With the triumph of *Candide* in Brooklyn, Prince put up half the $450,000 budget to co-present the show with Ruth Mitchell and the Chelsea Theater on Broadway. The Lees, who only a season before had torn apart the Broadway Theatre to create the unusual setting for the disastrous musical *Dude*, were back in the same theater re-creating the environmental *Candide* set as it had appeared in Brooklyn only months before. (Since the theater was changed from a two-thousand-seat house to one that seated nine hundred and since Broadway costs are so high, the show broke even at $65,000 a week—almost as much as the larger-scale *A Little Night Music*, which was running simultaneously only a few blocks away, and which, for its day, was quite a hefty operating cost.)

With Sondheim's increasing extracurricular activities, he has had less time to work on his best of all possible hobbies: the creation of homemade puzzles and games, though his Turtle Bay townhouse (which he purchased after the movie sale of *Gypsy*) does not indicate a deficiency in its penny arcade–like ornamentation. The walls of the lower level of his home are covered with nineteenth-century game boards, and about the house are such artifacts as a skittle-pool table, obscure puzzles, a slot machine, jackpot games of various sizes, a gigantic chess set, antique ninepins, a ship's telegraph, a glass harmonica (an 1820s set of tuned glasses), and a bicycle (Sondheim's favorite form of transportation). Sondheim's penchant for games (not to mention word puzzles—he's reputedly one of the world's

Opposite: Larry Blyden as Dionysos fights off *The Frogs* in the Yale Repertory Theater production staged by Burt Shevelove in the University swimming pool, 1974. (WILLIAM BAKER)

Eugene and Franne Lee's renovated
Broadway Theatre setting for Harold
Prince's Chelsea Theater Center
production of *Candide*, 1974. (FRIEDMAN–
ABELES)

fastest anagram-crackers) inspired yet another friend, director Herbert Ross, to persuade Sondheim to turn a party entertainment, a murder game, into an original screenplay for one of the most mind-boggling motion pictures of 1973. (Playing this murder game in London and visiting Sondheim's home in New York inspired playwright Anthony Shaffer to write *Sleuth*—the original title of which was *Who's Afraid of Stephen Sondheim?*)

Ross's firsthand exposure to one of Sondheim's more elaborate creations occurred when he participated in a Hallowe'en treasure hunt devised by Sondheim and Anthony Perkins, which sent several teams of celebrities searching thirteen locations all over New York. Ross's team won.

"We'd know when we were in the right location," Ross told the *Los Angeles Times*, "when we saw a poster of a woman who was running for Congress. In one place on West 48th Street, we saw the poster and beside it was a woman who invited us upstairs. When we got there she served us cake and tea. If you put the slices of cake together, the icing spelled out the next clue. Lee Remick's team lost . . . they ate the cake."

But it was Sondheim's murder game that intrigued Ross enough to go to Warner Bros. suggesting that they commission Sondheim to develop a motion picture out of precisely such a puzzle.

"Steve started work on it," Perkins recalls, "but at one point he decided that he didn't want to try to do it all himself. He called me and said, 'Now I know this is ridiculous but would you like to collaborate with me on this project?' I had never written a word but he said, 'Look, it's not as though we have to do this. It's not as though we've accepted any money or anything. If you don't like what I write and if I don't like what you write, we'll just forget it.' So I said okay and then we circled it and circled it for three months and Steve finally said, 'I think we've got to start writing something. How should we start?' And I said, 'Let's take the first sequence. . . . I'll write one part and you write the other.' So I went home, put a piece of paper in the typewriter and typed 'Fade In' and just started writing."

The initial plotting for *The Last of Sheila*, set on a snowbound weekend in Long Island with a group of business associates, was immediately rejected by Ross, who felt that the situation wasn't glamorous and the people would not be game players, so the locale was changed to the more colorful one of a motion-picture producer's yacht in the Mediterranean.

Basically, the story deals with a rich, sadistic producer (James Coburn) obsessed with games, who invites a bunch of people with whom he works to spend a week on his yacht. The group: a glamorous actress (Raquel Welch) and her overly ambitious manager–husband (Ian McShane), a frustrated screenwriter (Richard Benjamin) married to a woman of considerable wealth (Joan Hackett), a sex barracuda Hollywood agent (Dyan Cannon), and a one-time great film director (James Mason). The producer announces a project he wants to start work on, namely a biography of his wife, Sheila, who was mysteriously killed one year before in a hit-and-run accident. . . . But in the meantime, during their shipboard holiday, they will play one of his games. Each is handed a slip of paper with a guilty secret that the others have to discover. They soon find that the secrets are true, not to the holder but to one of the other players, and on the second night the producer gets killed.

"From that point on it got tough," Perkins says, "Steve wasn't that interested in the scary elements. He was more interested in the puzzle and I was more interested in the atmosphere, so I let him take care of the puzzle and I took care of the scary stuff. It was difficult to write, mostly because we had very busy schedules. I was filming *Play It as It Lays* and Steve was writing *A Little Night Music* while we were writing *Sheila*. Steve would write scenes and send them to me for my opinion, and I would send scenes to him for his opinion, we'd edit them on the phone, Scotch-tape them together, and we had a movie. There were only two scenes in the entire picture that we wrote in the same room at the same time.

"The only thing we did wrong was write far too much. We have about a hundred pages that were never used. And it was a difficult script to cut, since it was an intricate puzzle and we had clues all the way through. We wanted the audience to be able to play along with the actors. . . . That was the fun of it."

From its outset, *The Last of Sheila* had its problems. Two weeks before rehearsals were to begin on board the *Marala*, a luxury yacht selected by Ross for on-board filming, the ship foundered near Mykonos in the Aegean. Ross immediately called motion-picture executive Sam Spiegel in Hollywood, who owned the *Marala*'s sister ship, the *Malahne*, and got an okay to use the near-identical craft. But the new ship was thirty-nine feet shorter than the original, which made the shooting of indoor cabin sequences impossible. Ken Adams, the production designer, unexpectedly had to order the building of sets for the interiors of the cabins at the nearby Studios La Victorine in Nice, and shooting of those sequences had to be postponed until the end of the film.

When rehearsals did start, Sondheim and Perkins arrived on the set and

walked through ten (of the fifty-four) Côte d'Azur locations with the director and the cast.

"One of the things I enjoyed most," Perkins says, "was spending time on the movie set watching Steve take pictures of the stars—that's a side of him that one might not expect to see. It really turned him on and it was beautiful."

When the two screenwriters left the south of France after Ross's rehearsals with the actors, the real problems began. After the first week's shooting, Ross was forced to fire his cinematographer, Ernest Day, scrapping all early unsatisfactory footage and putting the cast back into rehearsal until the replacement cameraman, Gerry Turpin, could arrive. When the

Authors Anthony Perkins (left) and Stephen Sondheim on the Cannes set of *The Last of Sheila*, 1973. (WARNER BROS.)

film finally got started, the weather turned cloudy and the water became too rough for the shots lined up, causing more delays in the shooting schedule.

The actors, "trapped" in one of the world's more luxurious resort areas, kept busy with their own games. Joan Hackett caused the biggest stir when she announced that she didn't want to say a number of her lines in the script. Ross contacted Lee Remick to see if she would be available to replace her, but the matter was resolved when Miss Hackett stayed on and performed her lines as written.

In the midst of delays and technical problems ("The film was more difficult than I ever imagined," Ross says), the word came during one long evening session while filming outside a hotel in Villefranche that the Arab Black September terrorist group planned to explode a bomb on the set unless filming ceased because, they claimed, there were too many Jewish people working on the film. Shooting was halted as French police set up roadblocks and searched everyone in the vicinity. No bombs were found, and shooting resumed.

After nearly three months of shooting, the film, over budget and over schedule, was drawing to completion when Raquel staged one of her celebrated publicity stunts. Claiming that Ross had attacked her, she fled to London. Later she returned, finished her scene, and issued a statement to the newspapers in London that she planned to sue Herbert Ross for assault and battery because of an incident in her dressing room on the French Riviera. James Mason told the press that Welch was the most inconsiderate actress he had ever worked with. Tempers flared and the film ended in a barrage of unnecessary hostility, though Ross did everything in his power to keep his actors cool.

One year later, back in port at Cannes, Warner Bros. previewed *The Last of Sheila* at the annual film festival, and Rex Reed reported in the Sunday *News*: "The crowning disaster of the festival was *The Last of Sheila*. . . . Sondheim is an acknowledged genius. Maybe he's too smart for the movies. Anyway, his first movie script requires a postgraduate degree in hieroglyphics to figure out. The film is so full of impossible situations, demented logic and clues that are undecipherable even while they are being explained, that the end result is one of total pretentiousness."

Some of the other reviews were comparatively better: "*The Last of Sheila*," wrote Stephen Farber in the Sunday *New York Times*, "is completely heartless, but it has a brain. It doesn't beg for sympathy for its unsavory characters; it stays ice cold, and it never insults the audience's

intelligence by going soft. Taken on its own terms, this is an honest and immensely gratifying movie. . . . The script by Stephen Sondheim and Anthony Perkins is a dazzling technical achievement."

The Last of Sheila, like many Sondheim projects, was for a select audience. And like all of Sondheim's puzzles, even if one realized that the solution could be found in the title of the film, it required a lot of thought, keen concentration, and a bit of arcane intellectual mind-probing.

It could drive a person crazy.

From left: James Coburn, Dyan Cannon, Ian McShane, Raquel Welch, James Mason, Joan Hackett, Richard Benjamin, in the film *The Last of Sheila*, 1973. (WARNER BROS.)

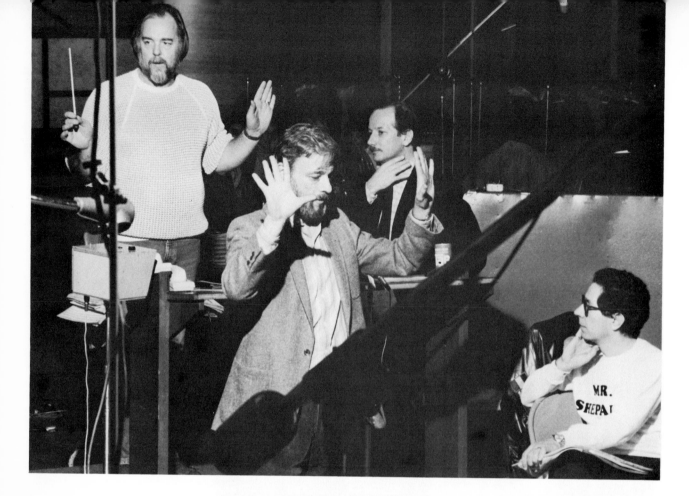

Above (from left): Musical director Paul Gemignani, composer-lyricist Stephen Sondheim, orchestrator Jonathan Tunick, and record producer Thomas Z. Shepard rehearse for the cast recording session of *Merrily We Roll Along*, 1981. (© HENRY GROSSMAN, RCA RECORDS)

Right: CBS Records Group president and Broadway cast album producer Goddard Lieberson (left), *Anyone Can Whistle* composer-lyricist Stephen Sondheim, 1964. (COLUMBIA RECORDS)

ORIGINAL CAST RECORDINGS

FORTUNATELY, for those who are fond of the Broadway musical, there is the original cast album, a tradition begun by Decca Records when it recorded *Oklahoma!* in 1943. Thereafter, Columbia Records, under the directorship of the late Goddard Lieberson, went on to become the industry leader of the cast album business which, according to Lieberson, "started slowly, rose to enormous proportions, and then fell back down again."

"I think," said Lieberson, "that I changed the quality and style of Broadway cast albums. I'd usually be with a show since its inception, I'd go out of town two or three times, and by the time it came for the recording session, I'd know it pretty well. I sometimes changed the arrangements and tempos for the record—not always pleasing the arranger—but the sound you write for in the theater is quite different from the sound you need on an album. I don't believe in monkeying around electronically—I hate that—and it's a trap that a lot of record makers fall into. Another thing I did away with was dialogue lead-ins for songs unless they were absolutely necessary. I would have to explain patiently to the librettist and the composer and lyricist that you could listen to a song on a record forty times, but to hear some banal, spoken introduction to the song drives you nuts after the third time."

Lieberson, president of Columbia Records from 1956 to 1966 and a longtime Sondheim admirer, produced the cast albums of *West Side Story*, *Gypsy, Anyone Can Whistle, Do I Hear a Waltz?* and *A Little Night Music.* (The *Whistle* cast album, produced *after* the show closed, was done by

Lieberson as a labor of love, and Sondheim dedicated the score to Lieberson as a sign of his gratitude.)

When Lieberson left his position as cast album director, moving upward on the executive trail, Thomas Z. Shepard took over his post as director of Masterworks and original cast recordings with equal dedication and adeptness. He began his tenure by producing the superb cast recording of *Company* in 1970. After completing the new cast album of *Candide* in 1976, Shepard left his position at Columbia to accept a post at RCA Records as vice-president in charge of Red Seal artists and repertoire and original cast recordings. (In 1986, Shepard joined MCA Records as vice-president of classical and theatrical recordings.)

"One virtue of cast albums," wrote John Rockwell in the *New York Times* in 1984, "is that they allow a purer concentration on what the composer has achieved musically, independent of the book and the razzle-dazzle of the show's production."

When all is said and done, the Stephen Sondheim legacy will be most remembered by the cast recordings of his shows. Thomas Z. Shepard's dedication to creating a catalogue of his work for RCA Records—which includes *Pacific Overtures, Side by Side by Sondheim, Sweeney Todd, Marry Me a Little, Merrily We Roll Along, A Stephen Sondheim Evening, Sunday in the Park with George, A Collector's Sondheim,* and *Follies in Concert*—is noteworthy in that it's a rare case of the record producer's talent matching that of his subject.

"All professional recording," Shepard explains, "is the creation of an illusion; it's not the actual representation of the show. I think it's necessary to find ways of making the studio experience have the emotional impact of the theatrical experience. As a recording producer, you must make awfully sure that the people in your cast are delivering through their voices, as actors, what they have previously depended on delivering visually as well. I never look at the performers as they record because it's a trap . . . you'll *see* much more than you'll *hear*. For those who saw the excellent *Company* recording session documentary by D. A. Pennebaker, Elaine Stritch looked absolutely fantastic during the tapings of 'Ladies Who Lunch,' as I learned when I saw the film. And I had to wonder myself why I didn't use one of those takes. But the reason became obvious later, by just listening to all the tapes from that day. Aurally it was not the perfect, definitive recording of that song. That's why we had to track her in a few days later.

"There are many cases where you must completely overhaul a number.

In 'The Little Things You Do Together' in *Company*, for the record we created a piece that is continuous, the music never stops. In the theater, the karate section of that number took place without music, then the song started and stopped, and they had more karate and then more song. So we actually redid this number for the record."

Whereas pop recordings can take weeks or months to make, cast album recordings are governed by theatrical unions, which restrict recording time from 10 A.M. to 6 P.M. and require that the actors be paid a week's salary for each day's session. As an added pressure, cast albums are usually made with the orchestra and singers working together. In pop music (and in the cases of Stephen Schwartz's original cast recording of *Pippin* as well as producer David Foster's recording of *Dreamgirls*, among others), the orchestra tracks are often recorded separately, and the performers sing to these as they are played through earphones. If a singer makes a mistake, he can try again without affecting the prerecorded orchestra track. In cast album recording, a mistake by any one person means that a section of the number, if not the entire number itself, must be started from scratch.

"It's very difficult to do a cast album," says Shepard, "because the strain of rehearsing a musical, playing out of town, previewing in New York, and then opening it, is difficult enough—but then, in most cases, at the end of the opening week, on their day off, the cast must come into a recording studio and create what will become the definitive, lasting performance. . . . It's very demanding.

"*Company* was one of the longest recording sessions we've ever done. We began at ten o'clock Sunday morning and eighteen and a half hours later, at four-thirty Monday morning, we concluded. It was a complicated show and it was too good to settle for anything less than perfection. I learned from Goddard Lieberson that the record company must be there to serve the theater and if it means a few extra hours, it's worth it. In a few years no one will remember the time we spent . . . you're not going to think that you ran a few thousand dollars over your estimated budget. You'll hear only what's on the album and there's no going back."

It's generally felt that producer Harold Prince made a mistake by giving the recording rights of *Follies* to Capitol Records, which, in order to squeeze the unusually long score onto one disc, mutilated the songs by condensing some and omitting others.

"Hal was sore at CBS," Lieberson said, "because he did a film with Hugh Wheeler called *Something for Everyone*. . . . It was shot for a company we owned called Cinema Center Films and it wasn't a success. I thought CBS was very nice to him, we spent a lot of money on it. But he didn't like the way we handled the movie so he wouldn't allow us to record *Follies*. Hal should hate Capitol. They loused up everything he's ever done with them . . . *Forum* was a terrible album. But he's stubborn and, in this particular case, he was irrational and he had to suffer the consequences."

"I would have loved to have recorded the original Broadway production of *Follies*," admits Shepard. (Shepard eventually produced the recording of *Follies in Concert* in 1985.) "I think the show presented enormous challenges to a recording producer—to try and capture the past and present on record, to separate them and juxtapose and intermingle them would have been a real challenge. It might have resulted in a great album. I think the way *Follies* emerged as a record album was irresponsible . . . to take a score of that scope and try to put it on one LP, to mangle the songs in order to do it, and then to do a rush job of it is shocking. A lot of people ask for two records when the subject of recording a show comes up and, frankly, I don't think most shows need it, but I don't see how they could have avoided it for *Follies*. There are a lot of recordings that are not 100 percent technically perfect but at least have the spirit and the flavor of the show. Forgetting that *Follies* is so terrible technically, the spirit and flavor are gone—if you didn't see the show you would have had no idea what it was about—and *that* alone makes it a monumental failure."

That incident was followed by another tense period for the Prince office. After being unable to sell the rights to what was considered initially a "noncommercial score," Goddard Lieberson stepped in during the opening week of *A Little Night Music*, made a deal for Columbia Records, and personally recorded the show himself in a dramatic return to the studio following his long absence from active record-producing. Soon afterward, Clive Davis was fired as president of Columbia Records and Lieberson was reinstated to his old position as head of the record company. Lieberson's highly acclaimed *Night Music* cast album, released simultaneously with a *Newsweek* cover story on Sondheim, proved more commercial than anyone had anticipated.

"Although directors have done wonderful realizations visually on stage," says Shepard, "I think one of the big reasons why Sondheim's records are so good—and unfortunately this has nothing whatsoever to do with me—is that the material is so self-contained. Each song is very often a scene in and of itself. And the addition of lights and sets and costumes, which are so necessary to make the show work, are not nearly as necessary in making the dramatic thrust work in a Sondheim score. There are, of course, exceptions, and there are things that Steve does that are entirely wedded to action . . . but these are more the exception than the rule.

"In the case of other composers," Shepard explains, "like Jerry Herman . . . who writes essentially wonderfully talented, well-crafted, neat songs . . . there is a strong contrast with a Steve Sondheim who writes scenes. Jerry is simpler but very gratifying to record. But a difference is that Jerry also thinks in terms of songs and their extractability and their other lives. And when he wrote 'The Best of Times' for *La Cage aux Folles*, he didn't just write a song to be sung in the show on stage by a character in a restaurant in St. Tropez. . . . He wrote it because he felt that this number could be the Bar Mitzvah and wedding standard for the rest of the twentieth century, and he may well be right. Now when Steve writes 'Finishing the Hat' for *Sunday in the Park with George*, he is more specifically writing for an artist in the middle of his personal and creative struggle . . . and not, at that moment, for anybody's present or future hit parade.

"It's really important that on records of shows, you eliminate the need to project, so that the performers can concentrate far more on characterization and less on declamation . . . even though I think that musicals are essentially a declamatory art form. And each record of each show has to have its own flavor.

"I thought of *Sweeney Todd*, to a large degree, as re-creating an old-time radio program. I thought of things like *Inner Sanctum*, but realized that in some respects *Sweeney* was a broader work and more informal. Having had a certain amount of experience with sound effects on *Porgy and Bess* I found *Sweeney* fun to do because of things like the squeaky door of the oven that Mrs. Lovett gets pushed into, or the wonderful effect created by my associate producer Jay Saks, of the sounds of bodies being murdered and then traveling down the chute, using three components—the chair from the theater, the slow wipe that stereophonically whooshes across the room, and the body plop. In fact, we had so much fun with it, the record album has one more killing than the show had."

One of Shepard's crowning achievements, his recording of *Sunday in the Park with George*, was reconceptualized especially for the album. "I wanted to turn it into a dramatic cantata rather than a collection of numbers . . . where dialogue would be abridged and used over music so that the thing ran as a continuous stream. And Steve and Jim leaped at the opportunity."

Sondheim and Lapine cut, pasted, transposed, and came up with a new ground plan for the recording.

"I also thought that we had to do in sound for the record what was done in pictures for the stage," Shepard explains. "We had to create an opening where the orchestra would grow, the way the stage filled with light—as George kept adding color. We used three different-sized orchestras. The regular pit orchestra was used for most of the score; the midsized orchestra—with twice as many strings—was used for more sweeping and romantic numbers like 'Move On'; and the biggest orchestra —with three times as many strings—was used for the finales of both acts. I wanted it so that, when you got to 'Sunday'—which was the realization of the actual painting—the sound would be more glowing and more burnished. I even recorded the voices further back from the microphones, with digital reverberation added later on. Here was the painting represented in its most idealized form. We were using music as the equivalent of color and light to establish a mood for the entire recording.

"But the real pleasure in doing *Sunday*, which was recorded digitally all the way through, is to hear the compact disc. . . . When you hear that arpeggio at the beginning, it comes out of an absolute eerie silence . . . and there's nothing like it. There is a tactility to *Sunday in the Park with George* that I have never achieved before."

One of the most successful records of 1985 was the all-new recording (on Deutsche Grammophon) of Leonard Bernstein conducting *West Side Story* with a cast of prominent opera stars. It stayed #1 on *Billboard*'s classical chart for a surprising twenty-eight weeks, but the resulting album was of questionable quality.

"I thought it was very impressive, all those opera people coming together," says Shepard, "all that seriousness of purpose . . . but it has little to do with *West Side Story*. I played it once and it's not a record I will ever listen to again. It has no real energy, and casting a wonderful singer with a Spanish accent to play the American is . . . incomprehensible. So we have the wonderful original cast recording and the new ponderous giant, and I think it's the end of *West Side Story* as far as ever being recorded again. I think now, unfortunately, the door is absolutely shut."

Sondheim's musicals through the years have received fourteen Grammy nominations for Best Cast Show Album. They have won six times, though Sondheim personally has only received four of those awards. In 1959, the year *Gypsy* won—tying with *Redhead*—the Recording Academy had designated the trophy to the album's star, Ethel Merman, and its musical director, Milton Rosenstock. It wasn't until two years later that the award was reassigned, more appropriately, to the songwriter and record producer. And in 1985, when the new edition of *West Side Story* grabbed the award, it went solely to record producer John McClure, since the composer and lyricist are included only if the recording is of a new score.

The popularity of recordings is measured primarily by *Billboard* magazine's weekly chart, listing the nation's two hundred best-selling albums. The movie soundtrack of *West Side Story*, released during the golden age of show music acceptance, holds the distinction as the all-time champ—the album that stayed #1 for the most weeks in the history of *Billboard*'s Top Pop Album Chart. Beginning May 5, 1962, *West Side Story* remained #1 for fifty-four weeks—seventeen weeks longer than Michael Jackson's *Thriller*, which holds second place.

Since musical motion-picture actors, unlike Broadway performers, are signed for their box-office appeal rather than their singing voices, over-dubbing long ago became a Hollywood tradition for movie soundtracks. In the film version of *West Side Story*, Natalie Wood was dubbed by Marni Nixon; Rita Moreno in "A Boy Like That" was dubbed by Betty Wand, and in "America" Moreno's voice was interspliced with Marni Nixon's; Richard Beymer was dubbed by Jim Bryant. In *Gypsy*, Natalie Wood was once again dubbed by Marni Nixon; and Rosalind Russell's songs were sung by Lisa Kirk. (In Goddard Lieberson's Broadway cast recording of *Gypsy*, Stephen Sondheim's voice was used as Rose's father in "Some People"—"You ain't gettin' eighty-eight cents from me, Rose.")

"I think that the albums have a lot to do with the acceptance and acknowledgment of Sondheim as a major composer worldwide," says Shepard. "They keep his music alive and available when the shows are not alive and available. Recording a stage show is essentially an adaptive process, but I believe that a record can also be an art form that works on its own terms."

From left: Glynis Johns, Judy Kahan,
Hermione Gingold, Stephen Sondheim
listen to the playback of the final take
of "The Glamorous Life" during the
recording session of *A Little Night
Music*, 1973. (COLUMBIA RECORDS)

IS HANS CHRISTIAN ANDERSEN EVER RISQUÉ?

WITH THE CLOSING of *Follies* at a loss of its entire $800,000 investment ("We sold more posters than tickets," says Annette Meyers) and the termination of its all-time long-run hit, *Fiddler on the Roof* (an eight-year meal ticket for the organization), the Harold Prince office found itself in a most unfortuitous position. They simply had to do a new show that would not only be as artistically acclaimed, adventurous, and tasteful as their previous ventures, but would also make some money.

In 1957 Sondheim and Arthur Laurents first suggested to Prince that they consider turning Jean Anouilh's *Ring Round the Moon* into a musical comedy. Prince attempted to secure the rights but was turned down. In 1971 Prince, still wanting to do a romantic musical, suggested to Sondheim that they attempt once again to acquire the rights. When they were turned down a second time, Sondheim, remembering the 1956 Ingmar Bergman film *Smiles of a Summer Night*, urged Prince to set up a screening. After seeing the movie and reading the published screenplay, Prince contacted Bergman, readily obtained the required permissions, brought in playwright Hugh Wheeler (author of Prince's film *Something for Everyone*), and began adapting the cinematic piece into a book for a stage musical.

"It was something that we always wanted to do," says Prince. "A musical that dealt with love and lovers and mismatched partners . . . love and foolishness, tying it all together with age."

The central characters in this lighthearted comedy are Désirée Armfeldt, a middle-aged actress who is busily trying to rid herself of one lover (Carl-Magnus, a pompous dragoon) in order to marry another (Fredrik

Egerman, a well-respected lawyer). Both men are already married: Carl-Magnus to his ever-faithful Charlotte and Fredrik to an eighteen-year-old child bride. To complicate matters, Fredrik's son, Henrik, a guilt-ridden Lutheran seminarian, is deeply but secretly in love with his virgin stepmother. Presiding over this madcap group is Madame Armfeldt, Désirée's mother, who at one time was herself a prominent courtesan.

Sondheim: "Our original concept was that of a fantasy-ridden musical. It was to take place over a weekend during which, in almost gamelike fashion, Désirée would have been the prime mover and would work the characters into different situations. The first time, everybody would get mixed up, and through farcical situations, would end up with the wrong partner. Then magically, the weekend would start again. The next time, everything worked out, but Henrik committed suicide. The third time, Désirée arranged everything right but this time when she was left alone with Fredrik, he put on his gloves and started to walk off the stage because she hadn't done anything to make him want her.

"The way all this worked was that Madame Armfeldt, who was like a witch figure, would reshuffle the pack of cards and time would revert and we'd be back at the beginning of the weekend again. The characters would then re-form, waltz again, and start over. It was all to be presented like a court masque with a music-box quality. But Hugh Wheeler finally gave up on it. He just couldn't make it work to his satisfaction. The show also began differently from the approach of the songs. I saw it as a *darker* Chekhovian musical. Hal didn't and admittedly it was a willful lack of communication on my part. I had already written six songs that were much bleaker, more reflective, almost out of Strindberg, and Hal finally persuaded me that instead of being as dark as Bergman, we should go entirely in reverse. And of course he was right. I usually love to write in dark colors about basic gut feelings, but Hal has a sense of audience that I sometimes lose when I'm writing. He wanted the darkness to peep through a whipped-cream surface. Whipped cream with knives. And, quite simply, I was writing for Bergman's film, not Hugh Wheeler's play."

For the new musical, Boris Aronson began creating a modern setting of six sliding panels made of transparent plastic painted over with birch trees, and Florence Klotz went to work creating an array of elegant turn-of-the-century costumes.

Sondheim began composing his score, now in a much lighter vein, in the style of Ravel, Rachmaninoff, and Brahms, constructing fughettos, canons, contrapuntal duets, trios, a quintet, a quartet, and a double quartet, all composed in three-quarter time and multiples thereof. "The score," Sondheim explains, "was made up mostly of inner monologue songs in which the characters described their deepest thoughts, almost never singing to one another."

Wheeler made some changes in the scope of the piece—enlarging the role of Madame Armfeldt and changing Désirée's four-year-old boy into a thirteen-year-old girl. Basically his book became a straightforward telling of Bergman's story, although Prince and Sondheim planned to treat the show as an operetta instead of a musical comedy.

Prince: "When Steve wrote the very first song he said that he brought in a *liebeslieder* group standing around a piano and I couldn't see why. Then I got the idea for a singing overture and the whole use of the lieder singers, who would represent the people in the show who aren't wasting time."

"Almost the bravest thing Steve did," said Burt Shevelove, "was after writing *Company* and *Follies*, which were in the New York idiom, to take a departure and do a musical set at the turn of the century in Sweden. Steve said at first, 'I don't know if I can write this . . . what do *I* know about Sweden at that time?' And I told him—and I always go to the top —'What did Shakespeare know about ancient Rome? Just do it. You're not writing a documentary. Just write what you're feeling about those people!'

"Steve limited himself on this show by doing it all, an entire score, in multiples of three-quarter time. He made an entity out of it. He had a point of view. Hal and Steve never said that they were going to retell the story of *Smiles of a Summer Night*. They decided to lyricize the various aspects of love. That was the intention. And there's a point of view to everything that's on that stage from the old lady to the maid in the grass."

Prince: "It was a very difficult show for us to discuss. We don't have famous family histories in Sweden. None of us related specifically to any of the characters on the stage. In *Follies* I put myself through a whole emotional crisis because I somehow or other got confused with the character of Ben. In this show, unlike most of the shows I've done, I had nothing to hang on to for my own Jewishness . . . or whatever it is that brings me close to the material."

Money, which hadn't been a problem for Prince in a very long time, was now his chief concern. "Some of Hal's big investors were dying," says Flora Roberts. "I thought he was joking when he told me that in the middle of a telephone conversation with one of his biggest investors, the man died of a stroke."

"I hate to admit it," says Prince, "but we nearly had to resort to backers' auditions . . . and I haven't had to have backers' auditions since *Pajama Game*!"

When new investors were brought in and the show was finally capitalized, Prince next had to decide on a title for their new musical. Sondheim suggested calling the production *A Little Night Music*, a direct translation of Mozart's *Eine kleine Nachtmusik* (a title not foreign to Sondheim, since he had earlier suggested it to ABC-TV in 1966 as an alternative title to *Evening Primrose*).

Casting *A Little Night Music* became a close race between Glynis Johns and Tammy Grimes for the principal role of Désirée. Miss Johns, whom Prince found to be the more vulnerable of the two, was eventually given the part. Len Cariou auditioned for the role of Carl-Magnus, Désirée's lover, but Prince saw him, instead, playing the role of Fredrik. The most difficult role to cast became that of the grandmother, Madame Armfeldt. Although Hermione Gingold was desperate to play the part, Prince was

Len Cariou (left) as Fredrik Egerman and Laurence Guittard as Carl-Magnus sing "It Would Have Been Wonderful" in *A Little Night Music*, 1973. (MARTHA SWOPE)

certain that she was all wrong for it. "I always thought of her as a comic," he says, "and I wanted the wit of the role to come from within the character."

"I heard they wanted Edith Evans," Hermione Gingold commented, "but I knew she wouldn't come over from England. She was too old to make the trip. So I rang and rang Hal's office and I told them the *least* they could do was allow me to audition. And *I* haven't auditioned in forty years! They finally said it would be all right and I went down and sang a song I remembered vaguely that I'd done on TV two or three times. I sang it and Steve said, 'Now would you sing something else . . . and don't speak it quite so much, sing it more.' And I said, 'I'm sorry, but I only know one song. I'll sing it again if you'd like.' And I did . . . and about ten days later I was told I had the part. I'd never been so nervous in years. I'd played for royalty, but Steve Sondheim and Hal Prince were too much for me. The only one who frightened me more was Noël Coward. Noël used to frighten me to death.

"The song Steve wrote for me, 'Liaisons,' is the most difficult song I know. It's very long and I can hardly ever remember which man I had when. It's a wonderful number and it requires a fairly intelligent audience to understand it. I thought that it would go over much better in London than here . . . *there* at least they know what a liaison is."

During the first days of rehearsals, two songs were immediately cut: "Two Fairy Tales" and "My Husband the Pig." There was greater tension, however, when the company realized that nearly half the score still hadn't been completed.

Prince: "Going into rehearsal with ten of our sixteen songs was sheer lunacy. It was maddening and I'll never allow it to happen again with anyone!"

Sondheim: "I'm very neurotic and very slow, as well as being hyper-critical of my own work. Some of my best ideas come after I get to see the actors rehearsing the material. For example, one day after seeing Glynis perform her second-act scene with Len in a different way, I got an idea, went home, and that night wrote 'Send in the Clowns' . . . which is pretty good for me, since it usually takes me a week to write a song.

"Late in rehearsal I also wrote the finale to the first act. All along, Hal had wanted a Gilbert-and-Sullivan-type operetta ending to the act in which he wanted to incorporate the entire cast. Finally, through our discussions, we decided that the one thing all the characters had in common was that they were going off for a weekend in the country. Hal and

Hugh outlined a series of events revolving around the invitation and I wrote the number 'A Weekend in the Country.' "

Having lost Michael Bennett to the ranks of director-choreographers, Prince signed Patricia Birch to choreograph *A Little Night Music* following the praise she received for staging the dances for *Grease.* "I was somewhat apprehensive about doing *Night Music*," Patricia Birch says. "I realized that the show was almost anti-choreographic. Here was a musical that was going to be built on all of Steve's beautiful waltzes, and I could hear myself saying that I don't ever want to break into 'The Grand Waltz' because I don't think that that is what Bergman is about, nor do I feel that that's what's written, nor was it going to be possible to start poking 'numbers' in.

" 'The Glamorous Life' always seemed to be a terrible problem to stage. Hal kept saying, 'I want the ending to swirl, swirl, swirl' and I kept trying to make it swirl, swirl, swirl. . . . It never quite swirled. But staging Sondheim songs is very different from staging any other kind of musical number. There are moments that are very frustrating. In 'A Weekend in the Country,' for instance, I had to *find* a place for movement . . . and it occurred every time they sang the lyric, 'A weekend in the country.' If you moved them at any other place during the song, the lyric would not have been heard and certainly the line was far more important than having a bunch of people going *cha-cung*.

"We also had to decide how much to allow Hermione to move. How could that lady who'd been sitting in a wheelchair all night suddenly get up and dance? In *Night Music* she *couldn't!* It's not the kind of show where you suddenly go crazy and some old lady gets up and looks adorable. None of us wanted a case of the cutes. At one point I had Hermione waving a cane around, doing a few jaunty steps, which she adored, but it was disgusting because it had nothing to do with the character. . . . It had to do with Pat milking a musical number.

"Another thing was trying to find out how to handle the lieder singers. We all had a *vague* idea and suddenly I found myself in a room with them and their material. There are many directors and choreographers that preplan, I'm sure, much more than I do."

"The show had a great deficiency in choreography," Flora Roberts says. "The first time I saw those lieder singers I became very impatient. I came in and said, 'Who are those klutzes?' Steve's original idea for them of having them all around the piano was fine but they just never worked out too well."

Opposite (from left): George Lee Andrews as Frid, Glynis Johns as Désirée, Hermione Gingold as Madame Armfeldt, in *A Little Night Music*, 1973. (VAN WILLIAMS)

Laurence Guittard sings "In Praise of Women" to Patricia Elliott in *A Little Night Music*, 1973. (MARTHA SWOPE)

A Little Night Music was greeted modestly in Boston. "It suffers," said Kevin Kelly in the *Boston Globe*, "from a kind of complicated simplicity that stirs admiration but not much feeling. . . . It's distinctive, charming, pleasurable, and remote. I appreciate all of its qualities, except its over-worked intricacies, and wish it had the power to make an impression on my emotions since it is a musical dedicated to the mystery of emotions. . . . I think it is a musical for a very special, very limited audience."

Elliot Norton in the *Boston Herald American* added: "It slows down in the end, saunters and dawdles when it should gallop apace, and loses some of its bright edge of irony. Even so, *A Little Night Music* is a lovely show, a civilized entertainment, elegant and amusing."

"You take things in priorities on the road," explains Flora Roberts. "Hal was busy working and you have to be careful not to throw the baby out with the bath water. Unfortunately, the show's biggest problem was that the first fifteen minutes were dull. But Hal was right to keep the piece simple and quiet."

"The whole time we worked on it in Boston," Prince acknowledges, "we didn't think it was going to be that popular. I really was quite convinced that it *couldn't* be. Mostly because of the beginning . . . it takes its own good time to get started. Everyone kept saying, 'Why don't we get started sooner?' and I felt that if we did, we should never have done the play. I said it's Chekhov in style, let's stick to Chekhov and they've got to go with us. The only reason for doing it was we wanted to do this kind of musical. If we gave them a wham-bam opening number so that they felt comfortable, we would, in the long run, fail. And we stuck to our guns and we *were* popular."

The only commotion that stirred out of town was the firing of Garn Stephens, the girl who played the role of Petra, the maid. "It was a big blow to me," says Patricia Birch. "I had never told them to get her, but from the time I first read the script I said, 'That's Garn.' She was in *Grease*, which I had just done, and Joanna Merlin spotted her and we finally signed her. But during rehearsals Steve wrote 'The Miller's Son' and, by God, Garn's acting was fabulous but she was simply having desperate trouble with the song. It was purely a vocal problem. Her firing was a terrible shock to the company."

"The crazy thing," says Len Cariou, "was that nobody was really working with Garn on the song. She was getting better gradually, but she maybe could have done it. She was earthy and very sexy and her replacement was obviously not that at all, although she sang the song well."

With the deletion of the song "Bang!" (replaced by "In Praise of Women") and the servant's only song, "Silly People," cut from the score, *Night Music* began previewing in New York. Everything went smoothly until its fifth preview, when Glynis Johns became ill with an intestinal virus and nervous exhaustion. And the Prince office immediately went about seeking a replacement.

Cariou: "Ten o'clock that morning they had spoken to Glynis and at twelve she was in an ambulance on her way to the hospital. Hal said, 'If that can happen in two hours, we've got to cover ourselves,' But by six o'clock that night Glynis was fine. . . . It really was a bitch of a thing to happen opening week."

In the February 21, 1973, edition of the *New York Post*, columnist Earl Wilson wrote: "Tammy Grimes was in the audience of *A Little Night Music* amid reports that she might replace hospitalized Glynis Johns if the latter's recovery is slow."

Three performances later Miss Johns returned to the show ("Nobody else is going to sing *my* songs!" she said) and the headline "*Night Music* Postpones Bow One Week" was changed the next day to "*Night Music* Goes Back to Original Date."

On February 25, 1973, *A Little Night Music* opened at the Shubert Theatre, and Clive Barnes of the *New York Times* more than made up for his vitriolic blasts at *Company* and *Follies*. "At last a new operetta," he exclaimed. "*A Little Night Music* is heady, civilized, sophisticated, and enchanting. It is Dom Perignon. It is supper at Lasserre. And it is more fun than any tango in a Parisian suburb. . . . Yet perhaps the real triumph belongs to Stephen Sondheim, who wrote the music and lyrics. The music is a celebration of ¾ time, an orgy of plaintively memorable waltzes, all talking of past loves and lost worlds. Then, of course, there are Mr. Sondheim's breathtaking lyrics. They have the kind of sassy, effortless poetry that Cole Porter mastered. . . . People have long been talking about Mr. Prince's conceptual musicals; now I feel I have actually seen one of the actual concepts. . . . Good God!—an adult musical!"

While most other critics shared Barnes's enthusiasm for the new production, some found the show to be lacking in emotion. "Yes, *A Little Night Music* is exquisite, all right," said Douglas Watt in the Sunday *Daily News*, "exquisite and rather lifeless. It is overrefined operetta, attractive to the intellect but cool to the touch . . . something special, remote, elegant and unable to reach the heart."

"I think Steve's score to *Night Music* is glorious," says James Goldman, "but I found the show too polite. I thought Hugh Wheeler's book was tastefully written and a fine piece of craftsmanship, but it lacks feeling and that's a pity. The abrasiveness that is part of Steve is what stimulates him most. On the other hand, he was dealing with musical styles that are very dear to him. . . . To have reference to all those styles was very rewarding to him. But I don't know why the show was as successful as it was . . . and I don't think they did either.

"I visited them in Boston and they didn't know what they had. The reception was polite, but not hysterical, not wildly enthusiastic, and Hal kept humorously referring to the show as his 'Gentile musical,' and at the same time wondering, quite honestly, what he was doing doing it. It seemed so well planned and so lacking in the kind of gut excitement that both Hal and Steve are generally drawn to. If it were more the show I would have written, it probably wouldn't have been as successful. The reason that it did so well at the box office was probably because of its neatness and placidity . . . there is nothing disturbing about it. The feelings those people have are very real—at least in my head they're real—but they're not as disturbing or real or foolish or anguishing in the production as I wish they had been.

"I recall that Pat Birch had a lot of trouble with it. I never thought their beginning worked. I never thought that the lieder singers singing the opening was an overture. . . . I thought it was the start of the show.

From left: Len Cariou as Fredrik, Victoria Mallory as Anne, Mark Lambert as Henrik in "Now," "Soon," and "Later," from *A Little Night Music,* 1973. (VAN WILLIAMS)

Then there was that dance. It always seemed to me that the show had two opening numbers, two opening scenes, and I really wanted to get into the story. Also, unless you knew the show, you wouldn't have a clue that those people who were dancing were characters in the show. The things they did in the dance had application to what came later but you didn't know that in the beginning. Unless I knew what Glynis Johns looked like —and lots of people don't—they could as well have been all chorus people dancing. I also don't think they realized soon enough what a good device the lieder singers would be. Out of town it was too late to do with them what might have been done had they realized their potential months earlier."

"An interesting thing about the book of *Night Music*," points out Harold Prince, "was that I once again utilized certain movie techniques as I did with *Company* and *Follies*. The last scene in *Night Music*, which takes place *everywhere* on the estate, appears to be happening only on the lawn. What no one else realizes is that the young wife and her stepson are running along a hall and down an alley and off to the country. Désirée is having her scene with her lover in her bedroom. The countess and Fredrik are having a conversation on the lawn, and so on . . . it's all over the place. It's actually a situation that can't be done on a stage, but I told Hugh Wheeler not to worry about it, to write it as though it were a movie. What I did was put it all on the landscape and I don't think the audience quarreled with it . . . or even asked where they were. I think people sense some things. I think people sense that *you* know where they are so they leave it alone. I think if they ever sense that you're unsure of what you're doing, that insecurity filters through the work.

"*Follies* is a great example of that. If we didn't know when those great big staircases were coming in and out and where each of those actors was at every given moment, the audience would have been nervous. But that was the essence of the best movies of the 1960s. That's why the Antonioni movies and the Fellini movies were so good. Insofar as they were abstract, *I* didn't always know where they were but I knew *they* did."

A Little Night Music added to its security a roster of trophies: the Drama Critics' Award as Best Musical of the Year, the Tony Award as Best Musical of the Year, and Tonys for Best Music and Lyrics (Stephen Sondheim, his third consecutive award), Best Book (Hugh Wheeler), Best Costumes (Florence Klotz), Best Actress in a Musical (Glynis Johns), and Best Supporting Actress in a Musical (Patricia Elliott). Within six months

Above: *A Little Night Music*'s lieder singers "Remember?" in 1973. (VAN WILLIAMS)

Left: Glynis Johns amuses Len Cariou prior to singing "Send in the Clowns" in *A Little Night Music*, 1973. (MARTHA SWOPE)

Stephen Sondheim listens to Glynis Johns record "Send in the Clowns" at the studio session for *A Little Night Music,* 1973. (COLUMBIA RECORDS)

not only had the new musical paid back its investment but Prince had already begun receiving offers for European productions of the show.

Although the ads for *A Little Night Music* exploited the show as being "sinful" when business began to fall off, it was not that at all. Rather, it was a good-natured fairy tale and, as Sondheim himself wrote in one of the song's lyrics, "Is Hans Christian Andersen ever risqué?"

"No, the show didn't really treat sex in a bawdy manner," Sondheim admitted at the time. "We were very polite about it. *Night Music* was a show that gave me pleasure for different reasons than the other musicals I've written. I like writing elegant stuff sometimes, although I generally like to write shows that are more openly emotional because they are more satisfying to me personally. I also don't think the show was as great a departure for me as some have said it was. It's all of a fabric—just another segment of my work. It's in a different style, an operetta style, and it's got a trio, a fugue, and the finale of the first act has all that ensemble singing.

"The reason that it was more successful than the last two shows? Probably because it had less tension . . . it made an audience *feel* easier. And it had a truly happy ending. What I really think is that *whatever* the last show would have been, they would have liked it more than the first two. They're just getting used to our stuff . . . I suppose I'm finally wearing them down."

Three years after *A Little Night Music* opened on Broadway, Harold Prince began shooting the motion-picture version. With a screenplay by Hugh Wheeler based on his stage libretto, Prince set out to create a lighter, less Chekhovian piece as a vehicle for Elizabeth Taylor, who would be singing for the first time on film.

"It's going to be a very romantic movie full of good-looking women and elegant costumes," Prince said in an interview in the *San Francisco Examiner*. "I think that's what people want to see again, as in the old days of the movie musical. . . . It's now a more buoyant, extroverted musical . . . [it] has quite a different rhythm from the stage version."

With major delays due to lack of financing, the production switched locations from Sweden to Vienna, with newly infused Austrian and German tax-shelter financing to the tune of $7.5 million. With a cast that included Diana Rigg, Hermione Gingold, and the fragile star, who was plagued by injuries and illness, the film ran into leading-man difficulties right from the start.

Peter Finch, the first actor announced to appear opposite Elizabeth Taylor, quit early on. He was replaced by Robert Stephens, who in turn was fired by Prince during rehearsals, amidst allegations that he behaved rudely toward Taylor.

Although *Variety,* on August 18, 1976, reported that Prince claimed sole responsibility and cited "private reasons" for Stephens's dismissal, the newspaper stated that "Taylor was quoted as saying the 'chemistry' wasn't right between herself and Stephens, but Stephens told the British press, 'Chemistry? Chemistry? We're actors, not bloody pharmacists.' " (Later Stephens wrote a letter to the editor of *Variety*, denying that he had "behaved rudely." And added, "As to Hal Prince's reasons for dispensing with my services—he says they are 'private'—may they remain so since he has never communicated them to me.")

"Elliott Kastner, the producer, was pushing Hal to get someone like Cary Grant," says Len Cariou, "and Hal told him, 'Look, I love Cary Grant, but give me a break. I can't have him in this film.' "

Prince's last-minute call to Cariou was one of desperation. They were due to start filming and needed someone in a hurry. Cariou, thrilled at the opportunity to re-create his stage role for the film, took the next flight to England.

"They were all in London prerecording the soundtrack," Cariou says, "and Elizabeth happened to be there as well because she was doing the 'Send in the Clowns' track. So Stephen had this great idea that I should jump into a limo and come over to the recording studio and meet her.

"Well, I got there and the poor woman is sitting there and the London Symphony Orchestra is sitting out there and Paul Gemignani is waving at me and I was ushered into the booth—I probably slept two hours in the last twenty-four—and I was introduced to her. It was very tense, because Elizabeth wasn't exactly sure what a measure of music was . . . she didn't know when to start singing and she would always miss it by about half a beat. And it just didn't work. So I said to her, 'Okay, every time there is an entrance, I'll squeeze your shoulder when we sing together, then I'll tap you on the shoulder and I'll point to myself when I sing, and I'll point to you when you sing.' And she said, 'Well, okay, that sounds good' and we set it down on tape. Although she seemed scared, she was thrilled with how it turned out."

"I was nervous and petrified," Taylor said in an interview in the *San Diego Union.* " 'Send in the Clowns' is one of my favorite songs. But everyone in the world has recorded it and here comes dumbbell to sing it. They put me in a little glass box with earphones on and I felt like a prisoner of war, like it was me against the world."

"It was an interesting experience," says Hugh Wheeler. "Elizabeth is such a complicated personality. She could easily drive you crazy. You fall madly in love with her, then you want to kill her, and then you fall madly in love with her all over again."

The film was stalled for three months when locations were shifted, and Patricia Birch, who had already committed to stage a national tour of *Grease,* was then unable to remain in Vienna for the filming.

"I was so heartsick that I couldn't stay," says Birch. "I was just able to go over for three weeks of rehearsal with Elizabeth, who was not in great shape. You see, prior to starting the picture, she had fallen off a motorcycle and had taken a big gouge out of her leg. It was pretty nasty. So for the first day of rehearsal, she was carried down in a chair for the reading. A bit later, she could move around a little, but she was hurting. But she was certainly willing . . . she was a good egg."

From left: Len Cariou, Elizabeth Taylor, Stephen Sondheim, Harold Prince, and Hugh Wheeler at a party for the movie of *A Little Night Music*, 1978. (© HENRY GROSSMAN)

Larry Fuller, filling in after Birch's departure, served as Birch's assistant and helped to put her work on film.

Fuller: "It wasn't easy. Elizabeth really couldn't walk until the second week of the three-week rehearsal period. But then she learned four or five segments rather quickly. Then on the second day of the third week, she was doing a movement where she had to run toward Len, and she stubbed her toe on a little crack in the floor of the stage and the next day we got a report that she had cracked a bone in her toe. So we were beside ourselves. . . . We had to start filming in the theater and we had to be out by a certain date no matter what, and you start to wonder what you are going to do if you can't get her on film. So we ended up having Elizabeth do basically most of what she learned—but in closeup—and everything else we cheated and shot with a double."

Cariou: "Later in the shooting, we did the dance sequence on the lawn and it was at night and cold and damp. And I said to Hal, 'This woman is going to catch pneumonia—and you know it. I mean she has absolutely no resistance to anything whatsoever . . . it's universal knowledge.' And there she was in a gown with that beautiful bosom bared to the night air and I could only imagine her hacking and coughing in the morning. . . . And indeed she was. I think they had to reschedule a week's shooting while she recovered."

Filming of *Night Music* concluded in November 1976, and poor word-of-mouth soon began spreading after private screenings of a rough cut were shown.

"The latest on the fate of *A Little Night Music*," reported the *New York Post*'s Page Six column on July 27, 1977, "is that it may be sold directly to a TV network without benefit of a theatrical release. Eight months after the film was completed there's still no sign of a distributor and the producers are getting nervous."

Finally, on March 8, 1978, Roger Corman, through his New World Pictures, released the Sascha-Wien Film very briefly to movie theaters and received an avalanche of some of the worst reviews in motion-picture history.

"This picture has been made as if Harold Prince had never *seen* a movie," wrote Pauline Kael in the *New Yorker*.

"A wizard of stagecraft, he seems to freeze behind the camera," said Frank Rich, then the film critic for *Time*.

David Ansen said in *Newsweek*: "Taylor's robust proportions may be historically appropriate to a story set at the turn of the century, but the audience is likely to respond to her overblown presence as if she were a character out of Al Capp."

Kathleen Carroll observed in the *Daily News*: "With her performance fluctuating as wildly as her weight (at one point, Prince tries to conceal her double chin by photographing her in shadows, while moments later she seems to be mysteriously slimmed down), Elizabeth Taylor plays the worldly, sophisticated Désirée as if she were an overeager schoolgirl."

"I know people who openly loathe it," wrote Rex Reed in the *Daily News*, "and I am at a loss to understand why. I find it quite the most consistently stylish, intelligent and enchanting movie musical since *Gigi*."

But Vincent Canby in the *New York Times* declared: "It's something more than a shock that the film adaptation of the Broadway show not only fails to raise the spirits; it also tramples on them. The more kindly disposed will leave the theater depressed, a lot of others may be in a rage. Though it's possible to fail with intelligence and grace, the movie pursues disaster in the manner of someone who, with mindless self-confidence, saws off the limb he's sitting on . . . it looks like a publicly posted suicide pact. . . . Mr. Prince appears to have made every decision that could sabotage the music and the lyrics. He has cast the film with people who don't sing very well and then staged almost every number in such a way that we can't respond to the lyrics. . . . There's no reason Miss Taylor should be photographed so unflatteringly. . . . He often photographs singers in those blandly uninformative close-ups that force us to consider hairlines, necklines and lip-sync techniques."

Prince: "It was just ridiculous. There were too many cooks, that's all. It could have been a good movie, but you just have to disregard all those people that were around. At the same time, the 'Weekend in the Country' segment was just wonderful. It's just as good as you can get . . . but the whole movie could have been like that."

Sondheim: "I never wanted the movie made because I didn't think it would translate well onto the screen. And I tried to persuade Hal and Hugh but they wanted to make it anyway, so I wrote the new songs."

For the movie, Sondheim wrote a new opening number and a new "Glamorous Life," and deleted from the stage score "The Miller's Son" and "Liaisons."

It was nominated for two Academy Awards—Florence Klotz for costume design and Jonathan Tunick for Adaptation Score—and Tunick actually took home an award on Oscar night.

In an interview on April 8, 1977, Harold Prince discussed his newly completed film, many months before its premiere. "In the movie, we've had a chance to fix things that didn't work on stage," he said. "The movie is much more romantic, much more open, less neurotic. The emotions and the comedy are more on the surface. I like the movie better."

But for Stephen Sondheim, the well-made motion-picture adaptation of one of his stage shows—perhaps temporarily—still eludes him.

At the afternoon runthrough for
Sondheim: A Musical Tribute, Nancy
Walker rehearses "I'm Still Here," a
Sondheim song originally sung by
Yvonne De Carlo in *Follies*, 1973. (VAN
WILLIAMS)

FOR WHOSE BENEFIT? ... 19

THE PRODUCTION of a full-scale theatrical benefit for one evening is a monumental endeavor, mostly because one must depend entirely on goodwill and performer dedication. Union regulations prohibit the signing of performer contracts, and there is the constant fear that illness will strike or that a cast member will accept a lucrative job offer that will take him off to Tangiers for a motion-picture role. Rehearsal time is extremely limited, but in most cases, it is hoped, the performers are familiar with their material. A few weeks before the show, the performers agree to rehearse with the choreographer (should there be more than simple stage movement planned) and to rehearse with the musical director and the orchestra. But it is usually not until the very day of the performance that the entire cast, orchestra, and production crew meet at the same time, at the same place, in order to bring some semblance of continuity to the event.

Preparation for *Sondheim: A Musical Tribute* began a full five months prior to the performance, when the American Musical and Dramatic Academy and the National Hemophilia Foundation first proposed a fundraising event to honor Harold Prince. When he refused the distinction, Stephen Sondheim was chosen in Prince's stead. Although Sondheim assented, thinking the affair would be "merely a dinner," it developed into a thirty-three performer, thirty-piece orchestra musical production.

The evening, under the direction of Burt Shevelove, was planned to be a seemingly informal gathering of every performer available who at one time or another appeared in a Sondheim musical, to be staged on Boris

Director Burt Shevelove stages "Your Eyes Are Blue," a cutout song from *A Funny Thing Happened on the Way to the Forum*, for Pamela Hall to sing at *Sondheim: A Musical Tribute*, 1973. (VAN WILLIAMS)

Aronson's country-garden set from *A Little Night Music* (which was to open at the Shubert Theatre two weeks preceding the benefit).

Shevelove routined the show into four sections: Sondheim as a lyricist, songs that were cut out of his shows on the road, a segment featuring comedy numbers, and a climactic line-up of songs for women.

Ethel Merman was asked to appear—for several reasons. Primarily, she was the biggest Broadway star to have appeared in a Sondheim musical. In addition to performing her numbers from *Gypsy*, it was hoped that she would sing "I'm Still Here" from *Follies*. And most important from the production standpoint, she was one of the three names that Columbia Records wanted guaranteed before they would agree to record an original cast album of the evening. The other two were Zero Mostel and Phil Silvers.

"Ethel Merman notified those arranging the musical salute to Stephen

In rehearsal, Alexis Smith re-creates "Could I Leave You?" from *Follies*, 1973. (VAN WILLIAMS)

Sondheim March 11 she'll be away on vacation otherwise she'd be there singing. . . ." Earl Wilson reported in the *New York Post*.

Zero Mostel wanted to do the show . . . *all* of it.

And Phil Silvers was still recovering from the stroke that put him out of action and closed the Broadway revival of *A Funny Thing Happened on the Way to the Forum*.

Columbia was off the record.

Others who never made it to the theater that evening were Carol Lawrence, who wanted her hairdresser flown in from Los Angeles and put up in a first-class hotel; Gene Nelson, who suffered a hernia; Elaine Stritch, who was opening the day after the *Tribute* in the London edition of Tennessee Williams's *Small Craft Warnings*; Sergio Franchi, who attempted to extricate himself from a West Coast nightclub engagement; Lee Remick, who wasn't sure whether her shooting schedule for a film in

From left: Beth Howland, Harvey Evans, Pamela Hall, Jack Cassidy, Angela Lansbury, Larry Blyden, Mary McCarty, Tony Stevens, Chita Rivera, Teri Ralston performing "Comedy Tonight" from *Forum* during the comedy section of *Sondheim: A Musical Tribute*, 1973. (VAN WILLIAMS)

London would free her for the weekend of the show (as indeed it didn't); and Elizabeth Allen, who first *insisted* that she be included in the night's proceedings and then, at the last minute, decided that she needed the time in a health spa to prepare for an upcoming role.

Some of those who did perform that evening were Larry Blyden, Len Cariou, Jack Cassidy, Dorothy Collins, Hermione Gingold, Ron Holgate, Glynis Johns, Larry Kert, Angela Lansbury, Chita Rivera, Alexis Smith, and Nancy Walker—a cast exciting enough for Warner Bros. to record a live two-album set, which, according to *Playbill*, was the first time "a Broadway benefit performance has been recorded as a show album to be sold."

"*Sondheim: A Musical Tribute* was presented at the Shubert Theatre and all of Broadway turned up to pay homage," reported Clive Barnes in the *New York Times*. "Those who were not on the stage seemed to be in the audience. It was an impressive celebration of the talents of the composer-lyricist, and an equally impressive demonstration of the way Broadway feels about him."

New York magazine's music critic, Alan Rich, was one of those in the audience and has these reminiscences:

"There were any number of reasons for wanting to be at the Shubert Theatre on that warm, muggy night of March 11, 1973. One was to be a part of the kind of crowd that you don't often see at a Broadway theater these nights—Broadway being for the most part a rather sad area nowadays. Another might be to hear a lush and lavish concert of the best songs that anyone has written for the theater in the past, say, fifteen years. A third—and this is actually the reason that ties all other reasons into one neat bundle—was to pay homage to the man who, all by himself, has restored the quality and the self-respect to the American musical theater that could have made such a crowd *want* to be at the Shubert that night: that small, shaggy, enigmatic genius, Stephen Sondheim.

"There were times when Broadway used to put on this kind of tribute

Seated at the piano, Stephen Sondheim is joined in the finale of *Sondheim: A Musical Tribute* by (from left) John McMartin, Alexis Smith, Larry Kert, Angela Lansbury, Glynis Johns, Len Cariou, Hermione Gingold, Nancy Walker, Jack Cassidy, Dorothy Collins, and Ron Holgate, 1973. (VAN WILLIAMS)

fairly regularly, and with just cause. They followed the same basic pattern: a lot of good material, interspersed with a lot of sentimental speeches from celebrities who would come up on stage and talk about the particular evening's hero as 'a man without whom . . . etc.' People made this kind of speech at the Sondheim tribute, too: Leonard Bernstein, Tony Perkins, Harold Prince, Sheldon Harnick, Jule Styne . . . big people, whose words always carry weight. Only this time the words didn't ring hollow, as so many tributes do. Broadway doesn't have many heroes to pay tribute to these days, and the box-office returns bear sad testimonial to that fact. Sondheim stands alone. In his hands, and only in his, rests the splendid tradition of the American musical, probably the only truly indigenous art form this country has ever produced . . . Sondheim has raised this art to a new plateau of greatness.

"Thirty-three performers paraded across the stage that memorable evening, in a program that listed 42 separate songs, ran for over three hours and seemed to have lasted just about eighteen seconds. Most of the cast had been associated with Sondheim one way or another, even though some of them, like many of the songs, had never reached an opening night. (Jack Cassidy, for example, had been earmarked for a show called *Saturday Night*, which was to have been Sondheim's first, but which died in manuscript in the early '50s; he sang two songs that night from the show that never was.) Part of the show was pure nostalgia: great familiar moments revisited. Wonderful old Ethel Shutta stopped it all for a time with her 'Broadway Baby' number, as she had in *Follies* night after night. Chita Rivera and Larry Kert did their 'America' and 'Something's Coming' from *West Side Story*, and Steve's words and Lenny's music worked like some subtle time machine to roll us all back to those nights in 1957. Angela Lansbury, who had made her musical debut in the ill-fated *Anyone Can Whistle*, came on with further proof that the show had just been too good for Broadway in its time.

"But the time-machine element was only part of the story that night. Much of it was brand new, and in a very special way. This element consisted of songs that were written for various of the great Sondheim shows, and then dropped. Anyone who knows the way the theater works knows why songs sometimes don't make it: matters of length, or better second thoughts, of simply being the wrong thing for the wrong person. . . . There is no real point, however, in trying to catalog every various device this Sondheim program contained for turning on both the mind and the gut.

"Everybody is writing about Sondheim now, about the phenomenal, steel-trap mind of his, out of which comes that inexhaustible string of rhymes and verbal dances that turn the whole English language into one colossal word game—and I defy you to second-guess any one line of text to some song you may not have heard before, from the one preceding—or the fabulous inventive originality of his music, which gets under your skin and stays there for reasons almost impossible to translate on the printed page.

"His songs are not, of course, only designed as a learning experience. And yet, the ultimate genius of every song heard during *Sondheim: A Musical Tribute* was that you constantly found yourself *thinking*—about words, about music, about great singers singing great songs. It's not such a bad thing, now, is it—being treated in the theater as if you just might be a grownup with a grownup's intelligence? Thank you, Steve Sondheim, above all for that."

Leonard Bernstein (right) congratulates Stephen Sondheim following the performance of *Sondheim: A Musical Tribute*, 1973. (RON GALELLA)

Yuki Shimoda as Lord Aba in authentic
Kabuki makeup in *Pacific Overtures*,
1976. (MARTHA SWOPE)

EAST SIDE STORY · · · 20

SHORTLY after *A Little Night Music* settled into its Broadway run, John Weidman, a young law student and fledgling playwright who had majored in East Asian history when he was in college, went to Harold Prince with an idea for a new play he thought Prince might be interested in directing.

John, son of novelist and playwright Jerome Weidman (the Pulitzer Prize–winning author of *Fiorello!* and *I Can Get It for You Wholesale*), had written a first draft by the time he met with Prince, who then advised him to rewrite the play from a different point of view—as if a Japanese playwright had created it.

On January 6, 1974, the *New York Times*'s "News of the Stage" column announced that Prince had taken an option on a new play he planned to produce and direct on Broadway in the fall. This untitled piece was by a new playwright, in his third year of law school at Yale University, and its leading character was Commodore Matthew Perry, the American naval officer who in 1852 was sent to Japan by President Millard Fillmore to establish diplomatic and trade relations.

"I thought it was fascinating," Prince says. "I knew nothing about Commodore Perry. I did not know that we had sent four warships on a 'peaceful' mission to a country that had been isolated from the world for 250 years. And I didn't know that we insisted on their establishing trade relations with us, thereby destroying their isolation and their peace."

"We were a long way down the road," Weidman says. "It was three drafts later and I had come into New York from New Haven for the play's final casting session when Hal asked me to meet him at his office. He said that he was feeling uncomfortable about doing this piece as a straight play and thought it needed to be musicalized. And I was stunned more than anything else. I said, 'Isn't it a little late in the game to come to this conclusion?' I left his office and bought myself a drink. But as soon as Hal told me that Steve Sondheim was interested, and we started talking to him, I became very excited about the idea of reshaping the material.''

''Last January, Harold Prince picked up an option on an untitled play by John Weidman,'' read the ''News of the Stage'' on June 16, 1974. ''Now Mr. Prince has decided to turn it into a musical bearing the title *Pacific Overtures.* . . . Stephen Sondheim has been commissioned to provide the score.''

Sondheim: ''At first I thought it could never work. I liked the play but I didn't see how music would fit.''

Prince: ''Steve really thought I was crazy. I thought, maybe we could do this strange, hybrid, musical revue, with a story, but not particularly linear characters . . . the story of America and Japan.''

Sondheim: ''What we actually did was to create a mythical Japanese playwright in our heads, who has come to New York, seen a couple of Broadway shows, and then goes back home and writes a musical about Commodore Perry's visit to Japan. It's this premise that helped to give us tone and style for the show.''

Pacific Overtures also tells the story of a friendship between Kayama Yasaemon, a minor samurai and a traditionalist who, over a period of fifteen years, becomes the progressive, Westernized governor of Uraga, and Manjiro, a shipwrecked fisherman who returns from the United States full of excitement at the coming of a new age, but who in the same period of time becomes a reactionary samurai intent on turning the invaders out.

Prince: ''When we first started, we were going to do a revue that told this nonlinear story by examining every acting style: part Kabuki, part French farce, part Shakespeare, part agitprop, part musical, part opera, part nonmusical. And then we realized, as we started, that the Kabuki was so strong, it was overwhelming. So the minute we put Japan and Kabuki together, we were stuck with Kabuki and that's where our concentration centered: we were going to do our own American Kabuki.''

Sondheim: ''It's interesting how you can become hooked on something. When I first considered this show I couldn't have been less interested in politics or this particular kind of theater, Japanese theater, which I'd always found just silly and screaming and endless and slow and boring.

But as usually happens, the more you get into something, the more in love with it you become, and by the time I was three months into it, I thought it was just the best idea in the world."

Sondheim's approach to the show was to attack the musical aspect first, to try to find the kind of sound that would not violate the spirit of Japanese theater and would at the same time be neither pretentious nor coy. For a month he researched Japanese music and discovered that the Japanese pentatonic scale, which is unlike the Chinese pentatonic scale, has a "minor modal feeling."

"Japanese music is not tonally like ours at all," Sondheim explains. "There aren't the same frequencies in the notes and they're not hit dead on. That's what makes them sound so 'twangy.' The instruments are not well tempered the way they are in Western music cultures; and they have approximate pitches, so you can't blend them gracefully in any way, shape, or form with Western orchestras or with Western voices.

"I was searching for a Western equivalent, and one day I hit on the correlation between the Japanese scale and the music of Manuel de Falla, a composer whose work I admire a lot. So I just started to imitate him. I took the pentatonic scale and bunched the chords together until they resembled that terrific guitar sound. And I was able to relate to it because suddenly it had a Spanish Western feeling and at the same time an Eastern feeling. It seldom occurs to me to write in minor keys, but because I had to have the feeling of Japanese tonality this afforded me the opportunity to do it."

Designer Boris Aronson displays his scenic concept for *Pacific Overtures*, 1976. (MARTHA SWOPE)

Aronson's scenic production of *Pacific Overtures* fully realized on the stage of the Winter Garden Theater, 1976.
(MARTHA SWOPE)

Finding the lyric style was much less difficult than he thought it would be: the use of parable sentences, very simple language with very simple subject–predicate structure, and very little rhyme. "I tried to keep the lyrics haiku-like, and I tried to avoid all words with Latin roots . . . Romance language roots, to keep it simple but to prevent it from being poesy, as opposed to poetic. Japanese haiku, when translated into English, trembles on the verge of parody: so you have to be very careful about it. And then as the score progresses, the language becomes more Western— as does the music—after the invasion.

"The only heavily rhymed songs in the show are 'Chrysanthemum Tea' and the admirals' song, 'Please Hello,' which is all about foreign powers. Structuring a lyric obviously takes a very long time, and I find it useful to write a general outline of the lyrics before doing it. When I did the admirals' number, I wrote down on a separate piece of paper for each

S O N D H E I M   &   C O.

admiral what had to be accomplished with that admiral. I knew what the order had to be because I wanted to give a history lesson as well as write a funny number. Then I thought, all right, now how do I make all these into one song instead of five separate songs? That took a long time to do, but because I knew what each one had to accomplish, it made it a little easier.

"My main concern was that I wanted the audience not to feel as I had, the first time I went to the Kabuki . . . either frightened or bored right away. I didn't want the music to feel strange. I wanted it to have a flavor —but a flavor from within another flavor."

Prince wanted to use many authentic conventions of the Japanese Kabuki, Bunraku, and Noh theater traditions. Scenically, Boris Aronson's sets employed screens and a *hanamichi*—a Japanese runway used primarily for ceremonial processions and the entrances and exits of important characters. Stagehands, dressed in black (which, according to Japanese tradition, means they are invisible), changed the sets in full view of the audience. A "Reciter" (played by Mako) observed, participated in, and commented on the play; and male actors played the female as well as the male parts until the finale, the Westernization of Japan, where women actually appeared.

Although the songs were developing inevitably into a score, it became clear early on that there were certain book problems that needed to be dealt with immediately.

Weidman: "When I finished the first draft of the book to the musical, there were problems with it. . . . I was sort of stuck. Hal said, 'I would like to show the script to Hugh Wheeler to see if he could help,' and I said that that was fine. It was, I think for both of us, a slightly uncomfortable relationship, but we both made the best of it."

Prince: "Yes, a lot of scenes got rewritten. We asked Hugh to come in and help. He did. But John primarily was the author. And he was terrific. Most assuredly, John wrote that show."

Wheeler: "I was brought in because it really needed somebody to write it. I mean, it was more like a treatise than a dramatic thing. And I thought I brought as much as I could to the piece under the rather restrictive circumstances. I would suggest doing certain scenes in a particular way and every now and then Hal would say, 'Hugh, please write that particular scene rather than both of you doing it together.' It was all just made up as we went along. After I came in, the whole second act was just thrown out and a new one was put in.

"Hal's whole concept was indeed daring, but it restricted me to a certain extent. I wanted to give more humanity to the characters, in my old professional way. But that wasn't Hal's idea. He kept saying, 'This is not about people. This is a musical about the clash of two cultures, which means do not emphasize the human aspects of it.' That was his decision, so that's how one worked. But my feeling as a writer and as an audience was that I terribly wanted to be interested in the people."

Sondheim: "Hugh actually went off and wrote a whole new book, assiduously (and perversely, I think) avoiding everything of John's. It didn't have anything usable. We then went back to John's book and Hugh did some patch work."

When the book was done, Weidman received sole credit in the program, and Hugh Wheeler received a special credit for "additional material."

Heading toward rehearsal, *Pacific Overtures* proved to be an almost uncastable show. Joanna Merlin, Prince's casting director, explained that at the Actors Equity principal interviews, not one Asian walked through the door. In searching for actors, she made contact with the Asian community and theater groups, Asian newspapers, and the State Department. Adding to their general state of concern, more specifically, the musical required nineteen actors to play the sixty-one roles in the script.

"At one point," Merlin told the *New York Times*, "we had found six

Mako as the Shogun in the "Chrysanthemum Tea" number of *Pacific Overtures*, 1976. (MARTHA SWOPE)

214 . . .

actors to audition when ordinarily we would have had six hundred. With sixty-one roles to be filled, we expected some doubling up, but we wouldn't have done as much if we had had more actors."

"We were so desperate for casting," says Prince's assistant Annette Meyers, "that whenever we saw somebody who looked Asian, on the subway, on the street, at the supermarket—anywhere—we wanted to go over to him and say, 'Can you act?' "

"It took a year and a half," says Prince, "and three different people making seven trips to the West Coast just to hold auditions, to get the company together."

Although most of the roles were filled on the West Coast and in New York, nearly a third were cast with nonprofessionals of various nationalities, including American-born and naturalized Japanese, Chinese, Filipinos, Hawaiians, Burmese, and Koreans.

When rehearsals finally began, Prince's creative team enthusiastically but apprehensively leaped into production. "My first reaction was, 'Wait a second, what am I doing here?' says choreographer Patricia Birch. "I didn't want to fool with Oriental forms and make a mess. But then when Hal said that it was our own Kabuki, I started a month of research— watching all sorts of classical forms of Japanese dancing, running around in my kimono with my fan—I mean I absolutely drowned myself in films of Kabuki and I felt more reassured. Then I realized that my background with Martha Graham was really helpful: there was a definite Oriental influence in a lot of the stuff that she had done."

Birch hired Kabuki dancer Haruki Fujimoto as an assistant, and he guided her through her paces. "After a while I told him, 'Okay, enough,' because I couldn't absorb any more. I said to Haruki, 'If I'm vulgarizing anything, let me know, otherwise leave me alone.' When Hal said he wanted to close the first act with a lion dance, I started more traditionally and ended with an American cakewalk, to make a statement. My image was General MacArthur saying, 'We shall return.' And once I got through that, I was fairly comfortable because I began to be able to adapt it.

"I remember one of my favorite things that I did was the suicide. That came out of knowing a certain amount of real Kabuki hand moves—birds flying, leaves falling—and then taking it and making it pretty much my own.

"The opening number, 'The Advantages of Floating in the Middle of the Sea,' was interesting. In the middle of it, there was a little puddle of people moving straight at us. And I had always had the image from the minute I started that these were the people on the island of Japan. Of course, the thing with Steve's numbers is that he gives you so many images to work from, so you're not just building something for the sake of building something."

Birch's biggest staging problem was to make the finale work. In the show there was an enormous jump in time from the old Japan to the new. And there was confusion as the tone radically changed.

"A lot of rehearsal time was devoted to working on the ending," Weidman acknowledges. "We went into rehearsal with an as yet unwritten but fairly well-defined ending, which was very different from what we wound up with on Broadway. It was very long, almost a travelogue of Japanese history from 1865 right up to the present. And it was going to be done with puppets and with snips of scenes. Finally, what we decided was that it would be more effective to do that with just one bold stroke —which is what we finally wound up with at the end of the show."

"The last song was called 'Next,' " Birch explains, "and I kept asking, 'What do you mean next? Who's next? What's next? What are we saying here?' We never did deal that much with the war. I knew it was about the industrialization of Japan . . . a kind of rape. But I'm not sure that by skipping over the events of the forties and hurdling from the old to the new . . . we really made an enormous jump there. I don't think the number was ever intended to be a song song. It had all those statistics in it. I thought, well, maybe the image I ought to use here is literally a trade show . . . and then try to keep the lion image going, which I did, but it was hard to find the build in it."

One of Sondheim's most affecting numbers in the show was "A Bowler Hat," sung by Kayama, one of the central characters who was Governor of Uraga. Interspersed with a series of letters, the song moves almost cinematically through ten years, illustrating the character's growing affluence and Westernization. ("In a few minutes, and with the use of only a few details," Frank Rich later wrote of the song in the *New York Times*, "Mr. Sondheim transforms a character's trivial autobiographical chronicle into a paradigm of an entire civilization's declining values.") "It's my favorite number," Prince reveals. "It's just everything I would love to have happen in a musical, and occasionally does: that kind of moment where in one number you can accomplish something on so many levels theatrically and emotionally. I asked for that and Steve delivered it and it was perfect."

Mako as the Reciter in the "Advantages of Floating in the Middle of the Sea" number of *Pacific Overtures*, 1976.
(MARTHA SWOPE)

While Jonathan Tunick was preparing the show's orchestrations, musical director Paul Gemignani was coping with the intricacies of the score with the orchestra and the cast.

"Rhythm was a problem for everybody," Gemignani remembers. "We decided to use three Japanese musicians in addition to the pit orchestra, and they were on the side of the stage and only one of them spoke English. We put them together and I had to develop a whole new language code so that I could communicate with them. One musician didn't read music and the other two read only in their own fashion. What exists now in the script as underscoring is literally what we improvised at the time. For instance, when they would accompany the swordfights, that was all improvisation just the way it would have been done in the Kabuki theater."

"There were odd things," Prince says. "Certain readjustments that we had to make. Like, you'd go backstage a half-hour prior to a performance to give notes to the cast . . . very standard procedure. But it was too late, because they needed the half-hour to meditate. So there they were, many single people, all sitting around in dressing rooms or on the stage, sitting in deep silence. So whenever I wanted to give notes on the show I had to get to the theater very early."

Pacific Overtures opened in Boston on November 11, 1975, to some devastatingly bad reviews. "Kevin Kelly in the *Boston Globe* gave the show the worst review for anything I've ever read," says Prince.

"It would probably be a lot better," wrote Kelly, "if *Pacific Overtures* were done totally in Japanese. Then giving it the benefit of the linguistic doubt, we could all say we didn't understand it. . . . Mr. Sondheim's score is schematically admirable, sometimes propulsive, sometimes gentle, always complex and extremely wearisome . . . nearly everything goes in one ear and stays there, like a plug. . . . As far as I'm concerned, *Pacific Overtures* sank on opening night."

But *Variety* was much more supportive and encouraging: "Whether or not it becomes a Broadway smash . . . *Pacific Overtures* may prove to be a step forward in American musical theater creativity . . . [it] is unlike any musical in memory."

"The show opened badly," says Prince. "It was more difficult than any show I've done other than *Merrily We Roll Along.* But we just worked every day, a little bit, a little bit, and each day it got better."

Pacific Overtures, historically, was Harold Prince's last collaboration with Boris Aronson, the brilliant set designer who worked so closely with Prince for over ten years. "What Boris did on each show," explains Annette Meyers, "was to come up with the essence of the piece—the concept —what the show would look like. But he couldn't do it on this show. He had real problems with it. He said afterward that he could never figure out what the show was about . . . and because of that, Hal was very confused about how to direct it."

For Sondheim, a modest amount of rewriting took place. A song called "Prayers," which was actually the basis of the whole score, was no longer in it. Three versions of the opening number were written, and "Chrysanthemum Tea" was thrown out and replaced by an entirely new version out of town. Another rewrite was a second version of "Welcome to Kanagawa," a number that "could have been better," Prince admits. "It isn't as good a piece of material as the rest and we didn't do it as well."

After two weeks in Boston and five weeks in Washington, D.C., *Pacific Overtures* began previews at the Winter Garden on Broadway, under certain unfortunate circumstances.

Prince: "Some shows are lucky and some are not. This show was not lucky. One night early in previews, there was a bomb threat and we had to empty the theater. It hurt us. The next night—because earlier that day they had read about the bomb threat the night before—a mouse got caught in a chandelier and ran around and little bits of plaster started to drop into the auditorium, and someone screamed 'Bomb!' The audience became hysterical and the theater emptied out again. It was quite bad.

"And then one day, Howard Haines, who was the general manager, and I stood on the street in front of the theater and he said, 'Do you know what the biggest problem with this show is? They don't know it's an American musical. Look at it.' And we looked at the front of the Winter Garden, which was gorgeous, but it looked like the Grand Kabuki was touring America. It looked as though it was a limited engagement of a Japanese show. And I said, 'How can we fix it? They're not Caucasians, they're Asians. It's the subject. It's the stage set. It's Kabuki, American Kabuki. What do we do?' And he said, 'I don't know.' "

Pacific Overtures officially opened on January 11, 1976, to radically divergent critical response. Rex Reed wrote in the Sunday *Daily News*: "It breaks new ground in the theater and leaves the audience shaken and breathless with excitement and beauty. . . . The result is a revolutionary musical of wit, perception, insight and shining brilliance. . . . [It's] not a show for all. It is likely to bore many. But it is different, courageous, gorgeous and jolting."

"*Pacific Overtures* is a pretty bore," wrote Douglas Watt in the *Daily News*.

"*Pacific Overtures* is an irritating bore," wrote Richard Watts in the *New York Post*.

"Producer-director Harold Prince refuses to play it safe," wrote Jack Kroll in *Newsweek*. "Unlike other Broadway big shots, you don't find him maiming old Mames or dolling up old Dollys. . . . No other team in the American theater could have achieved this show's integration of elements, its harmony of form, color, sound and movement."

T. E. Kalem, in *Time*, said: "*Pacific Overtures* might be called Prince and Sondheim's moonwalk musical. They land, but the dramatic terrain proves to be as arid and airless as the moon."

Howard Kissel in *Women's Wear Daily* exclaimed that the show was "a landmark musical . . . a triumph of sophistication, taste and craft . . . the most original, profound, the most theatrically ambitious of the Prince-Sondheim collaborations. It is also, for this viewer, the production in which the team that sets Broadway's highest standards most fully meets the astonishing objectives they set themselves."

"It is a very serious, almost inordinately ambitious musical," reported Clive Barnes in the *New York Times*, "and as such is deserving of equally serious attention. . . . Mr. Sondheim's music is in a style that might be called Japonaiserie (Leonard Bernstein quite often seems to be trysting with Madame Butterfly in the orchestra pit). . . . Musically there is a disparity between Mr. Sondheim's operettalike elegance and ethnic overlay, but even this succeeds with all its carefully applied patina of pastiche —that on demand can embrace Sullivan or Offenbach. . . . The form of the musical itself is perhaps not up to the seriousness with which it is presented . . . at times it seems as though we are well and truly in the world of Suzie Wong. . . . There are generic and stylistic discrepancies in the musical that are not easily overlooked—but the attempt is so bold and the achievement so fascinating, that its obvious faults demand to be

From left: Patrick Kinser-Lau, Timm Fujii, and Mark Hsu Syers sing "Pretty Lady" to Freddy Mao in *Pacific Overtures*, 1976. (MARTHA SWOPE)

overlooked. It tries to soar—sometimes it only floats, sometimes it actually sinks—but it tries to soar. And the music and lyrics are as pretty and as well-formed as a bonsai tree. *Pacific Overtures* is very, very different."

A certain number of the show's overly negative reviews appeared to have been heavily influenced by a seemingly pompous interview with Sondheim that appeared in the Sunday *New York Times* a week before opening, where Sondheim was portrayed as arrogantly bad-mouthing the Broadway community.

"It was a shocking article," Sondheim says. "It was written by Clive Hirschhorn, theater critic of the Sunday *Express* in London. I think he was angry because I was not as enthusiastic about certain shows as he was, so I think he decided to make me pay for it. For example, he started the piece by saying that I had a Japanese servant, which is not true. It seemed that the article was meant to damage, and meant to wound, and that's what it did. I think it was entirely an act of malice . . . as well as being inaccurate; and Hal and I both thought it definitely hurt us with some critics who actually quoted from the article in their reviews."

Prince: "The most seriously damaging review was Clive Barnes's. He didn't get the show—but he never gets anything. He didn't get *Follies*. He didn't get *Company*. When his review of *Pacific Overtures* came out I wrote him a letter. I'd never done it before and I've never done it since. I said, 'You've just closed the show and you will regret it someday.' And I sent it over by messenger. Well, of course, they never regret these things. But my heart was in this show. It's not the kind of show you do to make money."

Pacific Overtures was nominated for ten Tony Awards, winning only two: Best Scenic Design for Boris Aronson and Best Costume Design for Florence Klotz. (The show lost the rest of its awards to the big winner that year: *A Chorus Line*.) It closed at the Winter Garden on June 26, 1976, after 193 performances and a loss of its entire $650,000 investment. (The show was videotaped before it shuttered for a presentation on the Nippon Educational Television Network in Japan, making it the first telecast of an American stage musical in that country.)

Eight years later, Fran Soeder, a new, up-and-coming young director (who worked as a production assistant on *Sweeney Todd*), found himself directing a litany of Sondheim musicals in Cleveland, and then off-off-Broadway for the York Theatre Company. His most recent production had been a revival of *Pacific Overtures*. Bernard Jacobs and Gerald Schoenfeld of the Shubert Organization, together with Elizabeth McCann and

Nelle Nugent, felt the production was too good to pass up and moved it to the Promenade Theatre, a 370-seat off-Broadway house on New York's Upper West Side. It had its debut on October 25, 1984, and the show's authors were elated.

"From my point of view," Weidman says, "the revival gave me an opportunity to do some rewriting, to make some cuts and to add some material, primarily for clarity, but also to focus some of the scenes."

Sondheim: "When a couple of the intermittent scenes were cut, it became more of a personal story about two men. What made it less so on Broadway was that we tried a scrapbook technique in which the personal story would be interrupted with scenes of what was going on politically in the country and then we'd return to the personal story. Although the score remained the same, except for some lyric changes, the cuts and rewriting of the book made the difference.

"Although I loved the Broadway production, I also liked the off-Broadway production because with the intimacy of the theater, you could focus on the characters more. And close up you could get to know the people better. The audience tends, with a kind of ethnic blindness, to think of all Orientals as alike: 'You can't tell one from another.' You can't train an audience out of its prejudice and when you're sitting in the Winter Garden and they are thirty to eighty feet away from you, and you have that prejudice, it's hard to get involved with the story because you feel slightly hostile and confused. That was never true off-Broadway, because you were close enough to see the faces and to see the differences in character . . . in everything from bone structure to the look in their eyes. And so the prejudicial walls are broken down."

"Another factor," Weidman points out, "is that in the last decade, people in America have become so much more familiar with Japan and the Japanese, and with things Japanese. This time they weren't entering alien territory. I don't know in 1976 if you would have seen sushi bars as readily in New York City."

"What I basically did," Fran Soeder explains, "was to tone down the severity of the Asian theater techniques. I felt that they had a tendency sometimes to alienate and confuse and slow down the production. Since we had the intimacy of the theater, I worked much more at fleshing out characters. One of my idols was Walt Disney, and I always saw the show as more of an animated feature. It helped me to conceptualize it . . . I was able to find a connection. And the more we fleshed it out, the better it played.

Opposite (above): "Please Hello" by the original Broadway cast of *Pacific Overtures*, 1976. (MARTHA SWOPE)

Opposite (below): Cast of off-Broadway revival of *Pacific Overtures* performs "Please Hello," 1984. (MARTHA SWOPE)

"One example of how some small changes made a big difference was when we put in a new speech that was written to go before 'Chrysanthemum Tea.' It was like night and day, the difference it made to how that number played."

When *Pacific Overtures* began its second life, the critics were particularly pointed with their comparisons to the original production.

"Both on Broadway in 1976 and off-Broadway now, in its loving revival at the Promenade," wrote Frank Rich in the *New York Times*, "*Pacific Overtures* is a one-of-a-kind experiment in the annals of the musical the-

ater. . . . But if [the show] is never going to be anyone's favorite Sondheim musical, it is a far more forceful and enjoyable evening at the Promenade than it was eight years ago at the Winter Garden."

Soeder: "There were theories that the size of the original production overwhelmed the material. I only remember seeing the original show that Hal created and being in a state of wonderment. I think it was a breathtaking show on every level.

"What was awkward for me was that *Pacific Overtures* was, I think, Hal's favorite show, and he had always wanted to revive it. The original set of reviews we got were almost a detailed comparison of the productions. And I think that that was a very embarrassing experience for Hal. I don't think the reviewers were very kind to him. I just don't understand why they were so specific about making comparisons. It was rough. And I spoke with Steve about it and he felt that Hal had had some shows back to back that didn't work and it was just bad timing."

Prince: "I was relatively pissed off when the off-Broadway production was praised for its modesty. That's not what Kabuki is. The idea was to do Kabuki. It's bold painting—it's not subtle theater. I conscientiously didn't see the other production. I knew that it was very much influenced by my direction . . . the whole way it was directed was mine. A popular thing to say is that the original show was overproduced by Boris and me. That's not true."

Birch: "It was our show. I saw it and I thought, well, the structure was exactly the same but it was on a smaller stage. I got very angry about it. . . . Hal was livid. I took a look at it and I said, wait a second. Nobody has taken this and reconceptualized it. It was Hal's concept and my concept."

"I thought it was a much better production than the original," says Bernard Jacobs. "Unfortunately, the audience did not agree with me. I was ultimately not surprised it did not do better because it's a very special kind of theater. We also made a major mistake. We kind of concluded the Upper West Side was Sondheim country and there would be a big local audience for the show. We did not get that audience and the West Side of New York is not the kind of place that people from Brooklyn will go to. So although the Promenade was a very fine theater for the show, we made a major miscalculation. I think if we had done it in one of the off-Broadway theaters in the Village or Midtown area it would have done better."

Pacific Overtures in revival lost its entire budget of nearly half a million dollars, and closed on January 27, 1985, after 109 performances—84 less than the original.

The show, in both of its incarnations, inspired much controversy. Many rejected its moral of guilt, and others found the show boring. Still, some felt it was a landmark in the musical theater. The score also managed to confuse the Broadway audience, many of whom found it simply atonal. But the extraordinary craftsmanship of Sondheim's work produced an enchanting score that included what Sondheim feels is the best song he's ever written: "Someone in a Tree," the Rashomon-like telling and retelling, from several different perspectives, of what might have happened at the treaty house where the first Americans met with the Japanese.

"Steve told me that when all was said and done," John Weidman explains, "the show probably still felt like an assignment. There was still the feeling that it was hard work. Still the feeling that you couldn't go and sort of take your shoes off and relax into it. It was something that you 'ought to' see. And I think it probably never really escaped that stigma."

Stephen Sondheim in the music room of
his Turtle Bay townhouse in New York
City, 1972. (FRIEDMAN–ABELES)

SONGWRITING · · · 21

NEW YORK TIMES music critic John S. Wilson perhaps best described Sondheim's lyric-writing contribution to the theater in his review of the *Night Music* cast album: "The coincidence, early in March 1973 shortly after *Night Music* opened, of a 'tribute' to Sondheim —an evening of his songs stretching back over a period of two decades to his first, unproduced score for *Saturday Night*—brought home in vivid fashion the unusual level of lyric writing that he has maintained throughout his career.

"It is a body of work that has depth, range and consistency far beyond that of any previous lyric writer for the Broadway theater. Earlier lyricists may have been noted for their cleverness—Cole Porter, Lorenz Hart, Noël Coward, Ira Gershwin—or their inspirational sentiments (Oscar Hammerstein II, from whom Sondheim learned the basics of the art). But, after almost 20 years, there is no readily identifiable Sondheim lyric writing style, as there is for Porter or for Hammerstein. Each Sondheim song has an individual completeness within itself that goes beyond the superficialities of style (although Sondheim often deliberately and brilliantly uses a whole panorama of styles as elements in his writing).

"He is, in effect, a summation and an elevation of all the lyric writing that has gone before him. To have this made clear in an evening's program of 40 songs covering 20 years is impressive. But to find this point being made with equal clarity in a single score is an indication of the creative level at which Sondheim has arrived."

Collaborator Arthur Laurents reflects: "Without question, Steve is the best Broadway lyricist, past or present. Any lyric he has written can be quoted to illustrate this contention. Steve is the only lyricist who writes a lyric that could only be sung by the character for which it was designed, who never pads with unnecessary fillers, who never sacrifices meaning or intention for a clever rhyme, and who knows that a lyric is the shortest of one-act plays, with a beginning, a middle, and an end. Moreover, he knows how the words must sit on a musical phrase. His approach to writing for the musical theater is nothing less than remarkable."

"I used to write on both sides of the page," Sondheim explained once in a talk, "and Leonard Bernstein got annoyed because he would be constantly trying to find lyrics and turning the pages over and over, so I don't do that anymore. I find it very useful to use a separate pad for each section of the song.

"I'm a lazy writer. My idea of heaven is not writing. On the other hand, I'm obviously compulsive about it. And I don't really look for properties. I'm usually dragged in kicking and screaming by somebody. The closer a show gets to rehearsal, the more I'm writing. I end up working seventeen hours a day, because I'm a procrastinator. It's my own fault. I don't write nine-to-five. I'm disciplined in the work but not disciplined in work habits. Once in rehearsal it becomes very hectic, because you spend half your time coaching (I'm going to have a lot of halves in this sentence), half your time attending rehearsals and giving advice, half your time rewriting, and half your time writing new songs. I don't happen to like rehearsals a lot, so I think I try unconsciously to keep as far behind as possible so I have to stay home.

"I do lots of recopying—that's like pencil-sharpening. I get a quatrain that's *almost* right, so I tear off the sheet and start at the top on a clear one with my nice little quatrain which I know isn't right—but this makes me feel I've accomplished something. I use a rhyming dictionary, the Clement Wood, which is the only one I would recommend because it's the only one with lists of words where the eye goes up and down the columns. You don't use a dictionary for trick rhymes, of course, you won't find them in there. I also use a thesaurus, and I find *The Dictionary of American Slang* very useful in writing contemporary stuff.

"I use soft lead pencils, very soft. Supposedly that makes the writing easier on your wrist, but what it really does is allow you to sharpen them every five minutes. I am very undisciplined, though most of the writers I've worked with have been disciplined. I have to have somebody pushing me constantly to get it in by Tuesday, and then Monday night I start to work on it. . . .

"Obviously, all the principles of writing apply to lyrics. Grace, affinity for words, a feeling for the weight of words, resonances, and tone. The basic differences between lyric writing and all other forms are two principles which dictate what you have to do as a lyric writer. First, lyrics exist in time—as opposed to poetry. You can read a poem at your own speed, but on the stage, as the lyrics come at you, you hear them only once. If there's a reprise you hear them twice, if there are two reprises you hear them three times. The music is a relentless engine and keeps the lyrics going.

"Second, lyrics go with music, and music is very rich, in my opinion the richest form of art. It's also abstract and does very strange things to your emotions, so not only do you have that going but you also have lights, costumes, scenery, characters, performers. There's a great deal to hear and get. Lyrics therefore have to be underwritten. They have to be very simple in essence. That doesn't mean you can't do convoluted lyrics, but essentially the thought is what counts and you have to stretch out enough so that the listener has a fair chance to get it. Many lyrics suffer from being much too packed.

"I've always thought of lyric writing as a craft rather than an art. It's so small. I'm tending to write long songs these days, but the average lyric has maybe sixty to eighty words, so each word counts for a great deal. Any writer takes as many pains as he can over each individual word, but the words are more important in a lyric, more important even than to a playwright because each line is practically a scene in itself. The rigidity of lyric writing is like that of sonnets, and onstage this rigidity makes creating characters difficult, because characters, if they are to be alive, don't tend to talk in well-rounded phrases. But on the other hand, the power that is packed into the rigid form can give it enormous punch and make the characters splat out at you. One example is 'The Ladies Who Lunch,' which is so packed that it exudes ferocity, mainly because I chose a fairly rigid form, full of inner rhymes and with the lines in the music almost square—not that it's sung square, I mean the lyrics are very formed. . . .

"Many lyric writers don't understand the difference between rhymes and identities. In a rhyme, the vowel sound is the same but the initial consonant is different, as in 'way' and 'day.' In an identity, both the vowel and the consonant that precedes the vowel sound are exactly alike, as in 'consternation' and 'procrastination.' That's not a rhyme, it's an identity. It's not that identities are outlawed, it's just that they don't prick the ear the way rhymes do. They don't point up the words, so if you're going to use an identity you have to use it carefully. They can be monochromatic but very useful. Oscar [Hammerstein] not only liked to use identities, he liked to repeat words where ordinarily you might rhyme, as in 'Younger than springtime am I/Gayer than laughter am I,' using the exact word as a little refrain. I did it, in 'There's a place for us/Somewhere a place for us.'

"You try to make your rhyming seem fresh but inevitable, and you try for surprise but not so wrenchingly that the listener loses the sense of the line. Larry Hart is full of that kind of wrenching, that's why I'm often down on him. The true function of the rhyme is to point up the word that rhymes—if you don't want that word to be the most important in the line, don't rhyme it. Also, rhyme helps shape the music, it helps the listener hear what the shape of the music is. Inner rhymes, which are fun to work out if you have a puzzle mind, have one function, which is to speed the line along. I used it a lot in 'The Ladies Who Lunch,' where the inner rhymes are hidden to give the lines a tautness so the listener would feel what the lady is feeling. 'Here's to the girls who play wife—/Aren't they too much?/Keeping house but clutching a copy of *Life*/Just to keep in touch.' The 'clutch' is hidden, there's no musical pause there, no way of pointing it up, but it's there to help make the line terse, the way the character is.

"As for alliteration, my counterpoint book had a phrase: 'the refuge of the destitute.' That's my attitude toward alliteration in a lyric. Get suspicious. For example, when you hear 'I Feel Pretty' and she sings 'I feel fizzy and funny and fine,' somebody doesn't have something to say. On the other hand, I used a line very much like it in *Gypsy* in the song 'Small World,' where she sings 'Small and funny and fine.' Well, here the alliteration is accidental, but it's okay because 'funny' is the song's key word. It starts out 'Funny, you're a stranger who's come here.' 'Funny' works as the theme of the song, so 'Small and funny and fine' is quite different. But I would have been a fool if I had used an 'f' word in place of 'small'; it would have killed the lyric with alliteration. Ideally, the third word shouldn't have an 'f' in it either, it should be 'Small and funny and nice,' maybe, because the almost-alliteration hurts the line. Of course if you use alliteration subtly, it can be terrific. It's a great aid at times in speeding the line along.

"One function of rhyme is that it shows intelligence and a controlled state of mind. The run-on sections of the bride number, 'Getting Married Today,' in *Company* were purposely without rhyme. If they did contain rhyme, she would not have been hysterical and would have been in greater control. For the songs for the character of Fredrik, the lawyer in *A Little Night Music*, however, I used heavy rhyming because he is a man who rationalizes everything and does a lot of thinking.

"Incidentally, it would also be easier if audiences would concentrate more on lyrics. Nobody listens in the theater any more, and it's because everybody is so used to miked sound that they don't have to concentrate. Since they don't have to concentrate, they not only talk among themselves but they are not into the play. . . .

"Once the lyric starts to take shape, I don't want it to get too far ahead of the music, and vice versa. Then it's a matter of developing both simultaneously. I generally do it section by section. But it is just a matter of shaping a little bit at a time, like doing a jigsaw puzzle. It gradually closes in until it's all there.

"Music writing and lyric writing are very different skills. Music writing utilizes many techniques on which you have to spend a number of years of training in order to know what you're doing; otherwise you're at the mercy of insufficient tools. Many composers write with no tools at their disposal and their music is dull. I've never used lead sheets [vocal lines only, with chord indications] and neither has any self-respecting composer with any training. Give me a melodic line and I'll harmonize it one way, you may harmonize it another way. It's an entirely different song, even though it's got the same melodic line. Music is made up of a number of elements, and it is the putting together of all those elements that gives the song its flavor, character, quality, weight, texture, everything else. Lead sheets have nothing to do with anything as far as I'm concerned. If you leave it up to the orchestrator to fill in the textural details in the orchestra, it becomes essentially the arranger's score. That's what the word 'arranger' really means: somebody who takes a lead sheet and chords and makes an arrangement of a tune. For my money that's the composer's job, otherwise he's not composing. A lot of people aren't trained to do that and need arrangers, but not any of the composers whose work I respect.

"I try to work away from the piano as much as possible, because if you work at the piano you get limited by your own technique. I have fairly decent technique, but fingers tend to fall into favorite patterns. . . .

"When music and lyrics are done by different people, the best way for the lyricist to collaborate with the composer is in the same room whenever possible. Close collaboration is the best. First, you must talk very clearly about what the number is to accomplish emotionally, in terms of plot, in terms of character. I mean, *overtalk* it so you are sure that you are both writing the same song. Then there's more chance that you'll be able to work together, to give each other enough kind of supple space within which to invent and not be restricted.

"Obviously, the hardest kind of lyric in the world to set is often the best kind to read. Iambic pentameter is wonderful to read and terrible to set. I learned from Oscar and Cole Porter: as you're writing a lyric, get a rhythm even if you don't have a tune in your head. Maybe make up a tune. Hammerstein almost always wrote to well-known tunes. He just wouldn't tell Rodgers what they were. He would take operatic arias or whatever. He was not a composer, he couldn't think up melodies, so he used other people's.

"Porter, who was able to think up melodies, said he always wrote knowing exactly what the rhythmic structure of the melody was, even if he didn't know the notes. That's generally what I do when I'm working on a lyric, whether it's with somebody else or when I'm doing the music myself. If I have a musical atmosphere, I don't worry so much about the melodic line until I start to get the melodic rhythm of a lyric, so that the two will go together. *Then* you start filling in the actual vocal line and let the vocal line expand, because you don't want it to be lagging behind the lyric. It's very useful to have an absolute rhythm in your head.

"In a couple of instances, with Jule Styne and Dick Rodgers, I gave them a lyric written on music paper, with the exact rhythms marked so they would have something to follow. They may have made some variations on it, but they knew exactly what I had in mind. . . .

"Reprises. I find the notion that the same lyric can apply in the first act and the second act *very* suspect. Most of the time the character has moved beyond, particularly if you're telling a story of any weight or density. *Company* was a show where we could have used reprises, because it was about a fellow who stayed exactly the same; but I didn't want him to be the essential singing character, so I decided not to. In the case of *Forum*, we did a reprise of a song for comic intent. That is to say, you heard the song again, but in an entirely different context, and in fact with a different lyric.

"Maybe there are instances where it *does* happen, but even if you are using the same musical material it seems to me something has progressed, and the lyric can't be the same. Also, satisfying as it is for an audience to hear a tune that they've heard before, I think it is more satisfying that they follow and be excited by and intrigued by the story and the characters. It's nice to be able to combine the two if you can find an instance. I have found places where the music could be reprised, but I've never found one where the lyric could be reprised.

"I'm not downgrading reprises, I'm saying it's very difficult to find a way that is honest for the evening and therefore doesn't break the audience's concentration and doesn't remind them that they are in a Broadway theater listening to a reprise of a song that still maintains the mood and yet is a reprise. I just think it's very hard. I remember when we were writing *Do I Hear a Waltz?* Dick Rodgers wanted a reprise of 'Take the Moment.' I asked why. He said, 'I want them to hear the tune again.' For me, that isn't enough reason.

"As for humor in lyric writing, it's always better to be funny than clever—and a lot harder. There are very few times when you laugh out loud in the theater at a lyric joke. One laugh per score is a lot for me, and I think most of my shows have one laugh. In *West Side* there's the section in 'Gee, Officer Krupke' which uses a favorite technique of mine, parallel lines where you just make a list:

My father is a bastard,
My ma's an S.O.B.
My grandpa's always plastered,
My grandma pushes tea.
My sister wears a mustache.
My brother wears a dress.
Goodness gracious, that's why I'm a mess!

"That's not exceptionally funny on its own, but it brought down the house every night because the form helps make it funny. It was a genuine piece of humor because it depended not on cleverness but on the kids' attitudes, and that's what humor is about: character, not cleverness. There's one big laugh in *Gypsy* where Rose, who's trying to book her act, changes from fierce one second to smiling good nature the next when she finds out that the act is finally booked, and she sings, 'Have an egg roll, Mr. Goldstone.' The trouble with that song is that once that line was started and there was a big laugh, it was all over, there was nothing else to say, and I had to fill out two or three minutes of plays on words. If you could stop that song after the first line it would have brought down the house.

"The funniest line in *Forum* is 'I am a parade,' the only direct translation from Plautus in the whole show. In *Company*, the funniest lyric line isn't even rhymed, it's just shoved in there during the scene where Bobby is in bed with the stewardess. All the wives are singing 'Poor Baby,' knocking the girl he's in bed with, and Elaine Stritch comments, 'She's tall enough to be your mother.' It doesn't rhyme, it's not rhythmically like anything else, but it is again a character observation and that's what makes it funny and it consistently got a laugh.

"The problem with the one-joke song is that as the song goes on and on the joke becomes less funny. Yvonne's [De Carlo] cut number from *Follies*, 'Can That Boy Foxtrot!' was supposed to be done by a lady standing at the piano with a drink in her hand. One chorus and off. I wasted some time trying to build the number in Boston, and Yvonne did it very well, she has a very large register. The number always started up slam bang and ended with a nice hand, which was why we replaced it with 'I'm Still Here' in Boston. And curiously enough, some of the best songs are written out of town, because pressure is good for all writers. Writers respond very well to that kind of pressure and certainly I find it almost necessary.

"Although one can't underestimate the importance of the songs, it's the book that the musical theater is all about, not the songs, and I'm not being modest. It annoyed me deeply when the reviews of *Follies* said the show was good 'in spite of the book.' The show is good *because* of the book. A book is not only the dialogue, it's the scheme of the show, the way the songs and the dialogue work together, the style of the show. I don't know of a musical since the 1930s that is good or successful in spite of its book, which is the seed from which the collaboration grows. Any bookwriter I work with knows I'm going to steal from him and I try to help him out whenever I can, too. That's the only way you make a piece, make a texture. I keep hearing about people who write books and then give them to composers or composers who write scores and then get a bookwriter. I don't understand how that works. The piece can't have a texture unless it's all blended. The interrogation scene in *Anyone Can Whistle*, the long section called 'Simple'—Arthur wrote some paradoxical sketches, I wrote some lyric syllogisms. We sat together at a piano and sort of ad-libbed our way through it because we knew this mixture of dialogue and song was going to go on for twelve minutes. It had better sound as though one writer wrote it or it would be terrible.

"The important thing about the book is the characters, the essence of what dramatic songwriting is about. Wilson Mizner said: 'People beat scenery.' That's what the musical theater is about. When you are writing songs for a dramatic piece you must ask yourself always, 'Why are the songs necessary to the play?' Not why are they enhancing, or fun, but why are they necessary? Is the play a poorer thing without them? James Goldman once said in a lecture that when he goes out of town with a play, he posts a piece of paper on his dresser or bathroom mirror so he can see it every morning. It says, 'What is this play about?' so that in all the terrible rewriting, where you suddenly have to write for the actress to make a costume change, you don't lose the point. I find it useful to write at the top of the page a couple of sentences of what the song is to be about, no matter how flimsy.

"I go about starting a song first with the collaborators, sometimes just with the bookwriter, sometimes with the director. We have long discussions and I take notes, just general notes, and then we decide what the song will be about, and I try to make a title. If I am writing the music as well as the lyric, I sometimes try to get a vamp first, a musical atmosphere, an accompaniment, a pulse, a melodic idea, but usually the tone comes from the accompaniment figure, and I find the more specific the task, the easier. If somebody says write a song about a lady in a red dress crying at the end of a bar, that's a lot easier than somebody saying write a song about a lady who's sorry. Then I usually make a list of useful rhymes related to the song's topic, sometimes useful phrases, a list of ideas that pop into my head.

"I find it useful to write backward, and I think most lyric writers probably do, too, when they have a climax, a twist, a punch, a joke. You start at the bottom of the page, you preserve your best joke for the last, the ideas should be paced in ascending order of punch. And another thing, the last word ought to be singable. It's best to end with an 'ow' or 'ah'— open sounds that the singer can go with. Two of the most useful words in the language are 'me' and 'be,' but unfortunately they have pinched sounds. I tried desperately to fix the end of 'The Road You Didn't Take' in *Follies*. The line I wanted to use was 'The Ben I'll never be, who remembers him?' but 'him' is a terrible sound for a singer to hold and expect to get any kind of applause. It's also the job of the lyric writer for the theater to consider the singer's problems, to be careful of consonants.

Some very odd things happen when you string words together with music, because actors can't play with rhythm an awful lot.

"In the genesis of a song, a principle that I've always believed in is: content dictates form. Looking back over the first page of notes I ever made about *Company*, I see that we sat around and talked about how we could turn these one-act plays into a musical. We talked about the central character, and Hal said it would be nice to have a number called 'Company.' Well, 'company' is a word you can't rhyme—except Larry Hart rhymed it with 'bump a knee,' which isn't my kind of rhyme—so it would be a little hard to do it as a title refrain. Then Hal said, 'I would also like it to introduce the various styles of the show, the way we are going to cut back and forth and I also would like it to use the set. . . .' So I replied in my usual grudging way, 'Well, I'm not sure if I can . . . well, let me see if I can do it . . . maybe I can write the score . . . I don't know . . .'

"It's also useful to work with a director, because he has a sense of the way things look, and I think it's useful when you're writing songs to know exactly what the stage looks like. I didn't start one note of *Company* (I was just doing my usual procrastination number) until the entire set had been designed, a model built, and a picture of the model shown to me. The opening number of *Company* is about the set. I wrote it to present the cast and the set to the audience and also to tell them what the evening's about. I could never have written it without actually seeing the set and knowing there were five distinct playing areas where the couples could be.

"On my sketch sheets I put down: 'Everybody loves Robert (Bob, Bobby). . . .' The idea of nicknames had already occurred to me. Then I had Robert say, 'I've got the best friends in the world,' and the lines occurred to me, 'You I love and you I love and you I love,' and then, talking about marriage, 'A country I've never been to,' and 'Who wants vine-covered cottages, marriage is for children.' It's all Bob's attitude: 'Companion for life, who wants that?' And then he says, 'I've got company, love is company, three is company, friends are company,' and I started a list of what's company. Then I started to expand the lines: 'Love is what you need is company. What I've got is friends is company. Good friends, weird friends, married friends, days go, years go, full of company.' I started to spin free associations and I got to 'Phones ring, bells buzz, door clicks, company, call back, get a bite,' and the whole notion of short phrases, staccato phrases, occurred to me. By the time I got through just listing general thoughts, I had a smell of the rhythm of the vocal line, so that when I was able to turn to the next page and start expanding it, I got into whole lists of things: 'No ties, small lies. So much, too much. Easy, comfy, hearts pour, the nets descend, private jokes,' all short phrases—but what came out of it eventually was the form of that song, which worked out better than I had expected.

"I learned this from Jerome Robbins: those of us who write songs should stage each number within an inch of its life in our own heads when we write. We should be able to tell the director and the choreographer, 'All right, now when he starts to sing the song he's sitting down in a chair. Now around the second quatrain he gets up and crosses to the fireplace and throws her note in the fireplace. Then he sings the third quatrain directly to the audience, then he goes back and shoots himself and sings the fourth quatrain.' I mean, *really* plot everything in detail, because directors and choreographers hate nothing so much (and I can't blame them) as being presented with a song and a notation: 'And then, during the song, the seasons change.' Well, that's what the song's supposed to accomplish—the season change. But you should plot it out for them: 'Now at this point he's looking at the tree and the leaves are red. Then when it gets to the line about the grass, he turns around, the leaves are green.'

"Now, your plot may be impossible to put on the stage; that isn't the point. The point is, you have it choreographed in your own head, then they take off from it. They may not use anything in your blueprint at all, but they have something to work on, something to build from. And so you're collaborating with them.

"In the opening number of *Company*, I wanted to pick a moment when the elevator would work. It had an elaborate set of glass and chrome, and there was a workable elevator on the stage. That's a moment you don't want to throw away, you want to stun an audience with that. So I had to figure: where in the opening number am I going to use that elevator, and what justifies it being used? I built the number to the moment where the elevator goes, and I thought, now, wait a minute. It's going to take quite a while to get those people off those levels, some of them down in the elevator, some down on the stairs; to get them down to the central level for the last chorus. I called Boris Aronson and asked, 'How long do you think it will take somebody to get from the top level to the floor, down the stairs, the longest way?' He said, 'Oh, about fifteen seconds.' I thought, all right, I've got to have something going on for fifteen seconds.

I ended up with just having a sustained note on the word 'love,' the key word of the song. That is not just a held note, it was timed to fit Boris's set so that when Michael Bennett got to working on the musical numbers he wouldn't be stuck for another eight bars to get the performers down off the set . . . I knew where Bobby was standing. I knew in my head where all the people were. This had nothing to do with what Michael eventually did with it, except that he was delighted to receive a general blueprint which helped him over certain hurdles. He was able to invent freely because he never felt he would be hung up the next day in rehearsal by having to wonder what to do about a blank space.

"If you don't do that, suddenly not only is the choreographer stuck, but also your structure has to be changed. Supposing you didn't allow for that, and he says, 'I need eight bars.' Suddenly there's this hole in the middle of the song where everybody just holds a chord or a note, or there's some dance music or something like that. If you want your piece to be closely structured, allow for every single thing that should happen on the stage—a *very* important lesson and I think not a widely known one. The way I learned it was the first time Jerry Robbins heard 'Maria,' and he said, 'Now what happens there?'

"I said, 'Well, you know, he is standing outside her house and, you know, he senses that she's going to appear on the balcony.'

"He said, 'Yeah, but what is he doing?'

"I said, 'Oh, he's standing there and singing a song.'

"He said, 'What is he doing?'

"I said, 'Well, he sings, "Maria, Maria, I just met a girl named Maria and suddenly that name will never be the same to me." '

"He said, 'And then what happens?'

"I said, 'Then he sings . . .'

" 'You mean,' he said, 'he just stands looking at the audience?'

"I said, 'Well, yes.'

"He said, '*You* stage it.'

"I knew exactly what he meant. He was being grumpy, but what he was saying was, 'Give me something to play so the audience will be *interested*.' After all, it's not an art song, it's part of a dramatic action. There are certain kinds of shows which are presentational. You just get out there and sing the song. But that's not *West Side Story.* It's supposed to be an integrated musical. It's supposed to be full of action. It's supposed to carry you forward in the story, which means that every second should carry you forward in some way. Well, it's up to the songwriter to think those things up before you put the show in the director's lap. If you don't, you get clumsy staging or static songs and you end up throwing lots of things out on the road because they don't work. They work wonderfully in a living room, but they don't work on the stage because nobody thought about what should be happening. And in fact you sometimes find that you've written a song where nothing *can* happen. To avoid that static moment, plot and plan within an inch of its life every bar that you can.

"In certain cases what you preplan doesn't always work. 'Who's That Woman?' in *Follies* was a number designed for a lady named Stella Deems who hasn't performed the number in thirty years. The six girls who used to perform the number with her are all thirty years older except for one who is dead. The number was to be for Stella Deems and five girls with a hole in the line. I thought that would be macabre and touching. The number ended with a challenge dance between the two leading ladies who were at the ends of the line—I had the whole thing worked out carefully in my head, including tap dance sections. Here was an instance where Michael came along and threw the whole idea out and changed it entirely to what the number became on the stage, which I think was, in terms of staging, the most brilliant musical number I have ever seen in the theater."

From left: Angela Lansbury, Stephen Sondheim, and Len Cariou during the recording session of *Sweeney Todd*, 1979. (© HENRY GROSSMAN, RCA RECORDS)

MURDER, HE WROTE · · · 22

I N 1973, Stephen Sondheim was in London rehearsing for the West End production of *Gypsy* starring Angela Lansbury. He found himself with an evening free and attended a performance of a new version of the English classic, *Sweeney Todd, The Demon Barber of Fleet Street*, written by a thirty-two-year-old Liverpool playwright named Christopher Bond. Its performances at Joan Littlewood's Stratford East Theatre had created a stir, and Sondheim himself responded with great enthusiasm.

"The show was playing in this wonderful East End theater," remembers Flora Roberts, "and they had a piano player in the lobby and people drinking beer and eating meat pies. . . . It was such a fun atmosphere, very colorful. And I immediately saw why Steve was excited."

The original *Sweeney Todd* was written in 1847, and it has been constantly rewritten over the past 140 years. One of the most popular plays in the history of British theater, the show was almost never put on in London but often performed in the provinces.

"I had heard it was Grand Guignol, and it was something that just knocked me out," Sondheim says. "Bond's new version was a tiny play, still a melodrama, but also a legend, elegantly written, part in blank verse —which I didn't even recognize until I read the script. It had a weight to it, but I couldn't figure out how the language was so rich and thick without being fruity. He also infused into it plot elements from Jacobean tragedy and *The Count of Monte Cristo.* He was able to take all these disparate elements that had been in existence rather dully for a hundred and some-odd years and make them into a first-rate play. It's the other side of farce. It's as cleverly plotted as *Forum*, but not as intricate, and it does have a couple of surprises that are terrific. It struck me as a piece that sings.''

Sweeney Todd is the tale of a barber named Benjamin Barker, a victim of society who is imprisoned and exiled after being unjustly sentenced by a lecherous judge who takes his wife and child from him. Fifteen years later, he escapes and returns to London, under a new identity—Sweeney Todd —to avenge his ruined life. He meets up with Nellie Lovett, a woman who bakes and sells meat pies; and before long there is a strange relationship between the customers who fall prey to Sweeney's razor and the fillings that find their way into Mrs. Lovett's pies.

Sondheim inquired into the rights and found that the producing team of Richard Barr and Charles Woodward were in negotiations to present the show in New York as a straight play with some interlude songs. Barr and Woodward agreed not only to team up with Sondheim to turn the play into a full musical, but to postpone their plans until after he had completed his imminent commitment: writing the score for *Pacific Overtures*.

Eugene Lee's reconstruction of a Rhode Island iron foundry setting for *Sweeney Todd*, 1979. (MARTHA SWOPE)

When Sondheim brought the idea of the show to Harold Prince, Prince was bewildered and rather uninterested. "*Sweeney* was the one show I was reluctant about," says Prince. "I really did not know what that play was. I said, 'Steve, there's a little bit of send-up here. Are you really going to write that? 'Cause if you are, I'm the wrong guy to direct it. Are we going to serve meat pies at intermission?' . . . I really couldn't see beyond Sherlock Holmes. I wasn't comfortable here. I couldn't find what the motor of the show would be."

"This show was the first time I sort of dragged Hal into sharing my vision," Sondheim acknowledges. "But Hal is not the fan of melodrama and farce that I am. . . . I think they are my favorite forms of theater."

"It was only when I realized that the show was about revenge," Prince says, "that I knew how to do it. And then came the factory, and the class struggle—the terrible struggle to move out of the class in which you're born, and suddenly it became about the Industrial Age and the incursions of machinery on the spirit . . . that was very important. It made it possible for me to conceive it."

Sondheim: "For me, what the show is really about is obsession. I was using the story as a metaphor for any kind of obsession. Todd is a tragic hero in the classic sense that Oedipus is. He dies in the end because of a certain kind of fatal knowledge: he realizes what he has been doing. I find it terribly satisfying—much more so than any kind of accidental death, which often occurs in flimsy forms of melodrama."

Prince: "I suppose people who are collaborating should be after the same thing, but Steve and I were obviously not with respect to *Sweeney*. I think it's also about impotence, and that's quite a different matter. The reason that the ensemble is used the way it is, the unifying emotion for the entire company, is shared impotence. Obviously, Sweeney's is the most dramatic, to justify all those murders. Impotence creates rage and rage is what is expressed most by Sweeney's behavior."

The creation of *Sweeney Todd* was stalled until *Pacific Overtures* opened on Broadway. Then on August 27, 1976, a first announcement appeared in the *New York Times* acknowledging that *Sweeney* was moving forward and would open in California in the spring, and in New York either summer or fall of 1977. Co-producer Charles Woodward described the show as "very high comedy—it does not try to scare you. It's a comic musical." And it was announced that Sondheim would write the music, the lyrics, and the book.

Almost a year later, there was no production materializing, but there was another distraction: Sondheim was adapting old songs and writing new ones for the movie version of *A Little Night Music*, which began filming in September 1976. Then on September 16, 1977, another *New York Times* announcement appeared: "Stephen Sondheim will not do the book for *Sweeney Todd*, but Hugh Wheeler will." (Sondheim didn't actually start writing the score until the summer of 1977.)

Sondheim: "I started it, trying to write everything myself because it was really all going to be sung . . . it was going to be virtually an opera. I did the first twenty minutes and I realized I was only on page five of Bond's script. So at that rate, the show would possibly have been nine hours long. And I realized I didn't know how to cut it, so Hal suggested I call Hugh because he had written mysteries and he was British and he would understand the tradition of the play."

Wheeler: "It's a wonderful story and I thought Bond's version was slightly better than the others, but from my point of view, even his version was that absolutely unreal, old melodrama where you boo the villain . . . whenever Sweeney would come in, the audience would hiss and throw hot dogs. The version we wanted to do was a whole tone that was so difficult to get. We wanted to make it as nearly as we could into a sort of tragedy. I wrote it as a play, but I encouraged Steve to cannibalize it and make it nearly all music.

"The hardest thing of all was how to take these two really disgusting people and write them in such a way that the audience can rather love them. And I think people did love Mrs. Lovett—yet she doesn't have a single redeeming feature."

"What I wanted to write," Sondheim says, "was a horror movie. The whole point of the thing is that it's a background score for a horror film, which is what I intended to do and what it is. All those chords, and that whole kind of harmonic structure . . . the use of electronic sounds and the loud crashing organ had a wonderful Gothic feeling. It had to be unsettling, scary, and very romantic. In fact, there's a chord I kept using throughout, which is sort of a personal joke, because it's a chord that occurred in every Bernard Herrmann score."

Very few moments in the show were performed without music; and those that were, were brief scenes that had to do with exposition. "I figured the only way to tell a horror story," Sondheim explains, "is to keep musical texture going, because in most horror films what really scares you, apart from the lighting and makeup, is the music. You know you don't have to see a single shark's tooth in *Jaws*: the minute the lights go

down and that score starts and you hear all those double basses, you get frightened right away.

One of the ways of making things creepy is to sing softly with very dry lyrics against a kind of rumble of 'Gee, what's going on? They're not saying terrible things on the stage, so why do I feel uncomfortable?' It's because something is *promised.* Hitchcock and all of the people who've ever done suspense used music in that way. Music is what holds it together. That's why so much of *Sweeney Todd* is sung and underscored—

The *Sweeney Todd* nineteenth-century factory setting in full operation, 1979. (MARTHA SWOPE)

not because I wanted to do an opera, but because I realized that the only way to sustain tension was to use music continually, not to let the heat out, so that even if they're talking, there's music going on in the pit." (Another scare device Prince employed for the show was the use of a shrill factory whistle, which screamed out every time a murder occurred or an ominous moment arrived.)

In composing the score for the show, which Sondheim subtitled, "A Musical Thriller," he used the Dies Irae, the Mass of the Dead of the Roman Catholic Church, as the basis for the music of a man in love with death. "I always found the Dies Irae moving and scary at the same time," says Sondheim. "One song, 'My Friends,' was influenced by it . . . it was the inversion of the opening of the Dies Irae. And although it was never actually quoted in the show, the first release of 'The Ballad of Sweeney Todd' was a sequence of the Dies Irae—up a third, which changed the harmonic relationship of the melodic notes to each other."

"Immediately, the good news," reported the "Broadway" column in the December 23, 1977, issue of the *New York Times.* "Angela Lansbury is coming back in a musical. It will be *Sweeney Todd* in which she will co-star with Len Cariou, but which unfortunately will not get here until next season. . . . [The show] is to open in Boston next October and come into New York in November."

"The first time I heard about it, I was standing in my kitchen in my house in Ireland when I received a wire," Angela Lansbury remembers. "I didn't know the original play at that time, but one grows up knowing the name Sweeney Todd and one is immediately frightened."

Lansbury's first concern was that she obviously wasn't going to play Todd, so how did Mrs. Lovett fit into it and not just appear as a subsidiary character?

"It became clear to me," Lansbury says, "that the part was a key role and it also represented the only relief in the whole piece. It had the kind of comedic moments which appealed to me because I knew I understood the background of the piece really well."

Lansbury soon found herself meeting with Sondheim at his home to hear the little of the score that he had completed. "The first song he wrote," Lansbury recalls, "was 'By the Sea,' and he said 'Angie, I've written you a song in which you have no time to breathe whatsoever.' Steve always took some kind of delight in doing that and presenting one with that kind of challenge and then saying, 'Well, yes, but you can catch a breath here and you can catch a breath there.' And, of course, most of us who have performed his work find that, indeed, there are places to breathe.

"Much later, he played me 'The Worst Pies in London'—another song that has absolutely no place to breathe. I'll never forget the first time he sang it and made all the noises and banged the dough and exhaled his breath and did all those things. . . . I mean, we were really screaming hysterically on the floor."

Sondheim: "When I wrote the song, the first thing I thought of was: it's fun flicking the dirt off the pies. And then I thought: why isn't the whole shop alive with roaches and flies and dust? It would be fun to punctuate the song with her constantly wiping her greasy hands on her apron and blowing things off the pies and slapping cockroaches. So the song is filled with little punctuated moments which give it a rhythmic vitality and also give the actress various bits of business to do, so the piece could become a tour de force.

"Also the audience has just gone through five to ten minutes of intense and very brooding and creepy atmospheric stuff, and I wanted the contrast to be sudden and sharp, just the way the contrast between the two characters is sudden and sharp—Todd, the brooding, totally involved, obsessive man and Mrs. Lovett, the cheerful, totally amoral, practical, chatty lady."

Len Cariou had been sent the script for *Sweeney* early on and at first thought that Sondheim and Prince "had gone over the edge. . . . I thought, they've been working together so long they've lost their minds completely." But after reading the script several times, Cariou imagined how the show would play with a romantic score and became very excited.

"The score was everything I had hoped it would be," Cariou says. "There were some things that threw me, though. I was a little shocked, I must admit, at the end of my opening number when the character sings about the world 'filled with people who are filled with shit.' I mean, theatrically speaking, I thought it was superb . . . but I thought, 'Well, we aren't endearing them to us, are we?' "

The romanticism of certain songs, juxtaposed with what was actually transpiring in the story, was equally riveting—and extremely disturbing. Two of Sondheim's most heartfelt melodies were "My Friends," which, instead of being a poignant ballad sung to a loved one, was sung by Sweeney to his gleaming razors; and the equally rhapsodic "Pretty

Angela Lansbury looks on as Len Cariou sings "My Friends" in *Sweeney Todd*, 1979. (MARTHA SWOPE)

Women," a seemingly innocent yet passionate anthem to the virtues of womanhood, which was sung as a lyrical distraction while Sweeney prepared the judge's throat to be slit.

A song that took a month for Sondheim to write was "Epiphany," a full-blown play-within-one-musical-number, where Todd's mind cracks and the audience sees his motivation to become a mass murderer. "Epiphany" is the turning point of the musical, for all subsequent action depends on the audience believing this moment.

As with the other Prince-Sondheim shows, several readings were scheduled to test the material prior to rehearsal to see if the writing was on track. The first reading occurred when Sondheim had written five songs and Hugh Wheeler had a first draft of the book. It became clear that some of the material was heavy and relentless, and more humor was needed.

Sondheim's plan for the score was that the main characters would each have a basic musical theme, to serve as the starting point for their songs. Each of their songs would depend on the previous one, until the end, when the themes would collide.

Sondheim: "The notion of using motifs is to pique the audience's memory, to remind them that this theme represents that idea or emotion.

They're guideposts along the way. In a sustained piece you have to do that. Most audiences are used to it in movies. Most movie scores use a few motifs over and over again. When the motif comes on, no matter what the guise, the audience has a subconscious—and sometimes a conscious—emotional response. Most audiences are more comfortable with music that is more familiar. In *Sweeney Todd,* instead of using reprises of whole songs, I use reprises of motifs. By the time the second act rolls around, the audience is familiar with almost all the musical material. There is some new musical material in the second act but there is nothing in the show that is not reused at least once. I had a better time writing the last twenty minutes of *Sweeney Todd* than anything I've done since the background music of *Stavisky.* It was just a matter of, 'Okay, let's scare them.' "

Not content to let the piece merely evolve as a narrative, Sondheim included a musical clue in the show for mystery fans. "The beggar woman is in disguise," he explains, "and the audience is supposed to be surprised in the end when they find out who she is. A few, very alert people caught on right away though, and knew that the beggar woman was Sweeney's wife, because when the young wife appears and is raped, the minuet

Sarah Rice as Johanna, and Victor Garber as Anthony, are the young lovers in *Sweeney Todd,* 1979. (MARTHA SWOPE)

they're playing is the beggar woman's theme in a different guise. The justification for this is that the lady's gone crazy because of the rape and the symbol of that rape is the music which is always playing in her mind."

The original design concept was to do the show in a *Candide*-like environment, to keep the show close to the audience with smoke and streetlamps and fog rising from the floor "and somebody would pop up beside you and scare you to death," Sondheim adds. "But the writing process took so long that the Shuberts couldn't keep the Broadway Theatre in the environmental surroundings after *Candide* closed." So the concept became different; it became larger, rather than more intimate. Prince and set designer Eugene Lee acquired an actual Rhode Island iron foundry and reconstructed it to resemble the play's nineteenth-century factory setting.

The producing team of Richard Barr and Charles Woodward was joined by Robert Fryer, Mary Lea Johnson, and Martin Richards in association with Dean and Judy Manos, and the financing began through the unusual route of placing an ad in the *New York Times*, which netted $225,000 from investors from dozens of states and several foreign countries. Eventually, 271 investors contributed the $900,000 plus 10 percent budgeted for cost overruns. "That's a huge number of backers for a legit production," reported *Variety*, "especially in the present-day climate in which larger institutional investments are common. It's thought to be a record number of backers for a Broadway show." *Sweeney* was noteworthy also because it marked the first Prince-Sondheim musical that Prince did not produce himself.

Rehearsals were rough because of the complexities of the physical production and the volume of Sondheim's score: twenty-five songs in all. But this time, Sondheim went into rehearsal with only one song—plus the twenty-minute finale—yet to be written. Since the production was so overwhelming, it became impossible even to contemplate a Boston run; they would preview in New York and open at the Uris (now renamed the Gershwin) Theatre, nearly five years after Sondheim originally committed to write the show.

"The hardest thing to work out was the chorus," says musical director Paul Gemignani, "because it was so complicated and they were on the stage every five minutes. My biggest job was to try to get variety in who was singing . . . in harmonization. I literally memorized the color in everybody's voice and then when I came up to another section of the 'Ballad of Sweeney Todd,' I'd completely turn it upside down and we never used the same person twice for solo lines. So over the course of the evening, the same tune sounded just a little different each time you heard it."

"One of the things I learned more about, with this show, was choral writing," Sondheim says. "The first choral stuff I wrote was for *Anyone Can Whistle*, and it was fairly rudimentary. I learned more when I did *The Frogs* at Yale several years later. But in *Company*, the opening number was my breakthrough in choral writing. This show was the next stage."

"Needless to say it was a very depressing piece to play," comments Gemignani. "It was very difficult from the standpoint of being so concentrated. The first month I did that show, I thought I was going to die. I'd get to the end of the first act and think, 'I can't do the second act. I haven't got the energy for it.' I don't think any of us realized how intense it was going to be until we started performances. One of the things I really feel about Steve's work is that, as you go on, it's getting harder and harder. It isn't only the music itself, but the intensity and the concentration levels of the characters and the score are getting greater."

Angela Lansbury performs "By the Sea" for Len Cariou in *Sweeney Todd*, 1979. (MARTHA SWOPE)

Before previews began, Prince had his usual "invited friends run-through" of the show, and he was surprised and relieved. "I didn't know whether it was working or not," Prince admits. "I mean, the entire show was on its feet and we had this run-through and that was the first day that I realized it was working. I had no particular conviction whether it was good or not. Then we did it in front of people and they were sobbing. So there's no relationship between my enthusiasm and cocksuredness and how good the work is . . . I sometimes back into my best projects."

"Hal is a very organized person," Lansbury says. "You can rely on him, which is terrific on the one hand. He certainly had a great job to do, to place this huge canvas on that stage, and I think he did an extraordinary job. But it took me a while to get used to his style of working. I was always looking for a director who was going to help me with my actual performance. And Hal does not want to do that. He wants to leave that to the individual actor. He doesn't want to talk about character motivations. Nothing is ever said. You learn your lines, you come out, you deliver your lines. And to me, that's just the very beginning . . . then the work begins. But the work never began and I realized I had to do it myself. Whereas Arthur Laurents would talk until the cows came home about how you should play a scene, or how you were going to arrive at a result, with Hal it was a different approach."

The first preview in New York was a very difficult night, with the show running too long, the audience being sometimes unresponsive and sometimes shocked, and the cast trying to catch their bearings.

"I felt it was going to be a very unique, rare piece of theater," acknowledges Angela Lansbury. "We sensed that Steve was breaking new ground that nobody'd ever scratched. I certainly approached it with a good deal of seriousness of purpose, realizing that to be very funny, you sometimes have to be frightfully serious. But I never, ever realized how put off people would be by the blood—and I'm a very squeamish person. I guess I never addressed myself to what was really happening on stage. But from the very first of the previews, the gasps and the general reaction of the audience was stunning. They didn't like it. I think they were awed by the presentation, which fascinated and interested them, but they didn't like what they were being asked to stomach."

Cariou: "I think most of our time was spent discovering just how to walk that tightrope between broad farce and melodrama. I was mostly thankful that I had done Shakespeare because I needed that kind of energy for my performance."

"Previewing in New York is pretty horrifying," Lansbury says. "When I started working in front of an audience, I'm not sure that Hal may not have felt that my tendency to go for the comedic at times was ill thought out. I think he was afraid of my going too far when previews began, but, of course, as time went on it became apparent that it was necessary to give the audience that relief. But we had to do it under the evil eye of the sternest critics, the New York preview audience."

Sondheim: "It was awful. I hated it because all the professional bitches come to the first preview and tell their friends how terrible it is . . . it's discouraging and it upsets the morale of the cast and it irritates me because we are there to work and improve it. But no preview experience in New York is ever good. They're all terrible."

The first *Sweeney Todd* preview was especially trying because of last-minute, unforeseen problems.

Lansbury: "The caravan that the Italian barber arrived in was made out of old wood that Eugene Lee had gotten from some junk yard: I think he had bought an old barn or something. Well, it was full of the biggest wood lice you've ever seen. And they were crawling all over the stage and all over us at the first performance.

"Then my costume, which was that very raggedy sort of woolly pullover that is full of holes and everything was considered incomplete . . . they decided it wasn't dirty enough. So Franne Lee, the designer, took my costume down to the basement of the theater, took a plate of spaghetti, and slammed it onto the front. So right before I went on the stage, the sweater came up to me, all dried up and stinking of romano cheese and tomato sauce and old meat. And I nearly threw up. I couldn't believe she'd done this to me. I was absolutely outraged. I had to do that performance with that smell—but she was a refugee from *Saturday Night Live*, and if you needed a result, you just used any means." Thereafter, chemicals were used to give that look of the stained clothing.

Column items began running tales of other preview difficulties. "The big problem is—how to make the blood spout properly from the victims' freshly slit throats," reported the "Page Six" gossip column in the *New York Post* on February 19, 1979. "Angela Lansbury and Len Cariou are feeling lucky. They barely escaped getting hit and possibly injured when a heavy bridge fell inches from them on stage," reported Earl Wilson in the February 26, 1979, edition of the same paper. (Ironically, Lansbury was singing the line, "Nothing's gonna harm you, not while I'm around" as the bridge hit the stage.)

"A lot of the 'troubles' were simply not an issue," Prince explains. "We were working. We were on schedule. Every day we would do more and more, aiming toward the opening night."

Most shows in preview, no matter how well planned, usually require additional musical material, which then requires additional orchestration, which then makes for expensive orchestra rehearsals.

"I think the show may hold a Broadway record," Sondheim says. "It was in such good shape musically from the first preview that we never had an orchestra call. Every show, including *West Side Story*—which had opened in great, great shape—had one. Except for *Sweeney*."

But there was a problem in deciding what to cut. Since 80 percent of the first act is sung, and the book was economically constructed, ten minutes needed to be cut from the songs. Two sections that seemed overlong were excised from the Italian barber's number, and the judge's song was dropped entirely.

"The judge's song is a number that I didn't like," Prince says. "I thought the song was dangerous. Steve thinks the reason we took it out was that there were so many other things to do that we couldn't take the time to address it, but I think there's more to it than that. Steve wrote that song for the judge to whip himself . . . while he's presumably watching Johanna, his charge, through a keyhole. I didn't know how to stage it because it was so explicit: at the end of the number he has an orgasm. I thought it was pretty gruesome." The song was later incorporated into the New York City Opera production of *Sweeney* and was reinstated, along with the other musical cuts, for the original Broadway cast recording of the show.

Sweeney Todd opened at the Uris Theatre on March 1, 1979, and received mostly enthusiastic reviews. Certain critics concerned themselves with the question of whether the piece was a Broadway musical or an opera; others quarreled about the morality—or immorality—implicit in the play; but nearly all agreed that the score was Sondheim's most romantic and the production was a triumph of Prince's directing skills.

"*Sweeney Todd* is a staggering theater spectacle and more fun than a graveyard on the night of the annual skeleton's ball," wrote Douglas Watt in the *Daily News*. "Practically everybody connected with this wonderful enterprise [is] operating at the top of their form. . . . This is Sondheim's most playful score. . . . Harold Prince has staged the piece dazzlingly. . . . Lansbury is an endless delight as first the slatternly, then gaudily splendid Mrs. Lovett. She is the grandest, funniest, most bewitching

Opposite: Angela Lansbury sings "The Worst Pies in London" at *Sweeney Todd* recording session, 1979. (© HENRY GROSSMAN, RCA RECORDS)

SONDHEIM & CO.

witch of a fairy tale fright you're ever likely to encounter. And Cariou, hair parted in the middle and with visage of deathly pallor, is a magnificently obsessed Todd. . . . So joy to the world, dear children! *Sweeney Todd* is here to enrich your nightmares. A triumphant occasion, indeed."

Jack Kroll wrote in *Newsweek:* "In sheer ambition and size, there's never been a bigger musical on Broadway. . . . *Sweeney Todd* is brilliant, even sensationally so, but its effect is very much a barrage of brilliancies, like flares fired aloft that dazzle and fade into something cold and dark. . . . [It] slashes at the jugular instead of touching the heart. . . . Sondheim has been inching closer and closer to pure opera and *Sweeney Todd* is the closest he's come yet. . . . The problem is one of concept and unity: *Sweeney Todd* wants to make the same fusion of popular and high culture that Brecht and Weill made in *The Threepenny Opera.* But the fusion is never really made. . . . Nevertheless as an exhibition of sheer theatrical talent, *Sweeney Todd* must be seen by anyone who cares about the gifts and risks of Broadway at its best."

"I thought it was simply great," reviewed Clive Barnes in the *New York Post.* "The story is totally crazy but, in its macabre way, absolutely compelling, and the musical has been put together with unusual love, taste and style. Sondheim's score—the most distinguished to grace Broadway in years—owes more to Mahler, Alban Berg and Benjamin Britten than Weill."

Walter Kerr, in a *New York Times* think piece, was less impressed. "I am afraid that what *Sweeney Todd* most wants to be is impressive. It succeeds in that. . . . We are plainly in the hands of intelligent and talented people possessed of a complex, macabre, assiduously offbeat vision. Unhappily, that vision remains a private and personal one. We haven't been lured into sharing it."

"*Sweeney Todd* is one giant step for vegetarianism," extolled T. E. Kalem in *Time.*

Hobe in *Variety* was particularly negative: "Pehaps the idea was to dazzle the eye and thereby obscure the dearth of engaging entertainment. . . . There are few melodic tunes or hummable themes. . . . As a box-office prospect, the venture seems dubious."

But Richard Eder, briefly the principal theater critic for the *New York Times,* reviewed the show with controlled enthusiasm. "There is more of artistic energy, creative personality and plain excitement in *Sweeney Todd* than in a dozen average musicals. . . . Mr. Sondheim has composed an endlessly inventive, highly expressive score that works indivisibly from

Opposite (above): Angela Lansbury as Mrs. Lovett, and Len Cariou as Sweeney Todd, perform "A Little Priest" in *Sweeney Todd,* 1979. (MARTHA SWOPE)

Opposite (below): The ensemble sings "The Ballad of Sweeney Todd," 1979. (MARTHA SWOPE)

his brilliant and abrasive lyrics. . . . What keeps all its brilliance from coming together as a major work of art is a kind of confusion of purpose. . . . The music, beautiful as it is, succeeds, in a sense, in making an intensity that is unacceptable. Furthermore, the effort to fuse this Grand Guignol with a Brechtian style of sardonic social commentary doesn't work. There is, in fact, no serious social message in *Sweeney*; and at the end, when the cast lines up on stage and points to us, singing that there are Sweeneys all about, the point is unproven. . . . These are defects; vital ones; but they are the failures of an extraordinary, fascinating, and often ravishingly lovely effort."

After settling in for its Broadway run, the show went on to win eight out of its nine nominated Tony Awards, including Best Musical, Best Score, Best Book, and Best Direction.

In May 1979, all was calm just prior to the awards, until a major billing dispute arose between the *Sweeney Todd* producers and Christopher Bond's London agent. "Blanche Marvin, a British author's agent, asserts that her client has received his contractual billing only after bitter wrangling with the *Sweeney* management," reported *Variety*, "including the threat of a lawsuit. Richard Barr, a co-producer . . . concedes that Bond's billing has been improved since the show opened."

Business picked up and all bad press disappeared after the awards were presented, and the large weekend houses of the cavernous Uris made up for the weeknight losses. A year into the run, Lansbury and Cariou left and were replaced by Dorothy Loudon and George Hearn, who received equally glowing reviews; but the show never really recovered and closed on June 19, 1980. Several days later the London edition, presented by the Robert Stigwood Organization, opened to very mixed reviews and closed four months later.

A national tour was mounted with Angela Lansbury and George Hearn, which culminated in Los Angeles with a now-historic videotaped performance of the show, but it performed rather weakly on the road. Later *Sweeney* entered the New York City Opera repertoire, through the perseverance of NYCO director Beverly Sills.

With all its success, after a sixteen-month run on Broadway, *Sweeney Todd* still only repaid 59 percent of its investment. "I think if we were doing the show right now, we'd have a devil of a time getting it done on Broadway," Harold Prince admits. "Now, mind you, there is Steve and there is me, and maybe some good-hearted person would be willing to lose money. But it did lose money. It may have won every award in the book but it didn't pay back."

"It was very interesting," says Angela Lansbury. "Audiences had been uncertain, but once they got the word from the critics that it was okay to like the show, then there was an avalanche of affirmation. And even people who didn't understand it went around saying, 'Oh, yes, wasn't it extraordinary!'

"I actually thought it would be less of a hit," she admits. "I thought it would be sort of a collector's item again . . . another classic failure. I was amazed when it took off and ran as long as it did. But the critics got behind it. The thinking theater people loved it. They realized what an extraordinary piece of work it was. It had a magnetic effect on people. And the New York audiences who had come to previews and didn't particularly like it, suddenly were told to pull up their socks, open their eyes and their ears, and receive this extraordinary piece of work and give it the attention it deserved. And thank goodness they did . . . because, you know, sometimes you just have to educate an audience."

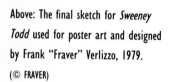

Above: The final sketch for *Sweeney Todd* used for poster art and designed by Frank "Fraver" Verlizzo, 1979. (© FRAVER)

Right: Frank "Fraver" Verlizzo's rejected preliminary sketch of a three-dimensional painted sign which was then to be photographed as the poster art for *Sweeney Todd*, 1979. (© FRAVER)

POSTER ART · · · 23

"**I**T'S AMAZING," says graphic artist Frank Verlizzo. "There are some producers who really think that poster art is a throwaway and nobody ever pays attention to it. And that's really mind-boggling because when you think of an individual show, it's the thing you remember."

Verlizzo, who signs his artwork "Fraver" (part Frank, part Verlizzo), is best known for designing posters of Sondheim's *Sweeney Todd, Sunday in the Park with George,* and the off-Broadway revival of *Pacific Overtures.* He is part of a small group of designers who are urging Broadway to treat a show's artwork as seriously and as meticulously as each of the components that end up on the stage.

"Many producers will just use type and no image," explains Fraver. "Others use a photo of the star with some horrible handwritten type that's hard to read, and others will use a cast photo which, nine times out of ten, is blurry and you can't make out anybody's faces. Then there are those who start out with a good piece of art and in midstream—and for no apparent reason—change it to something else. They've just spent a lot of money burning an image into the public's mind and then it's changed."

The key to penetrating the broadest audience is making certain that the same art, once it is chosen, is used consistently for the poster, in all forms of print advertising, and on the album cover.

Oddly enough, poster artists get relatively little input before they are asked to submit a sketch. Sometimes the producer or director may give a little talk about the show's tone; other times, scripts are circulated. But in most cases, the artist must work merely from the title and his own imagination.

"It is of the utmost importance," Fraver explains, "that the art be effective in a small newspaper ad. Generally, if it works small and in black and white, it will work really well large and in color. It's imperative that it be a very bold, distinctive image. Once that image is clear to me, I think about what I want the poster to look like and what colors to use to get that image across. The poster is always the audience's first impression of the show. Even if you don't tell them exactly what the show is, it should convey the energy and excitement of the show.

"On *Sweeney Todd*, I started working with the producers almost nine months before they went into rehearsal. Without any input from Hal or Steve, I did a three-dimensional wooden sign, like a tavern sign, that had a rough sort of painterly portrait of Angela in one oval and Len in another oval. The lettering was very sloshy on the curve and the two side panels looked like barber poles. But the one on the right had blood dripping from the last red stripe. Hal said it looked like *Destry Rides Again* . . . sort of a Western look. He thought it was completely wrong. So we started over again and came up with the image that eventually was used. Actually, until the last minute it was a tossup as to whether they would use the caricatures that I had done or another image someone else designed of two silhouetted figures with no heads."

When Prince left to do *Evita* in London, Sondheim met with Fraver to fine-tune the poster. "It's pretty unusual to have the composer involved in poster art," he says, "but Steve's pretty much involved in everything that's going on, which is great. The advertising agency was concerned that there was too much blood and it would turn people off. But Steve felt pretty strongly that that's what the show was about and there was no reason to hide it. So we added blood to Mrs. Lovett's apron and blood on Sweeney's hands where originally it had just been on the razor."

With *Sunday in the Park with George*, Fraver had little information. He was told that the first act was about Georges Seurat and his painting *A Sunday Afternoon on the Island of La Grande Jatte* and took place in 1884, and that the second act was set in 1984. The top half of the poster he designed was a simulation of the two characters right out of Seurat's painting, and the bottom half—which was separated from the top with a jagged tear along the center—matched the same two people in contemporary clothing. In one glance, the vision of the show was summed up

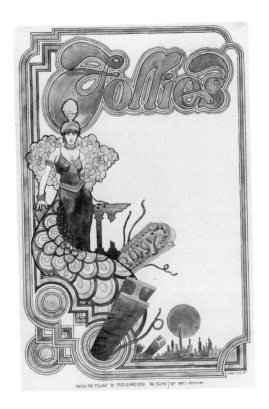

Above: The final artwork for *Follies* designed by David Edward Byrd, 1970. (© DAVID BYRD)

Left: David Edward Byrd's original first sketch for *Follies* based on the image of Gloria Swanson standing in the rubble of the Roxy Theatre, 1970. (© DAVID BYRD, COLLECTION OF CRAIG ZADAN)

vividly. And the poster he initially designed was almost never changed, with the exception of the background color going from turquoise to orange, and the positioning of the woman's legs going from a dance pose to a strolling walk.

Fraver began his career studying with a talented artist, David Edward Byrd, who achieved perhaps his greatest celebrity designing the original poster art for the Broadway production of *Follies*. "David's posters were unique," says Fraver, "because they were actual pieces of artwork. It wasn't something that you saw very often at that time. He definitely started the movement to get more attractive posters."

"I almost never got to do *Follies*," Byrd says. "The advertising agency was already paying eleven artists for sketches, so I said I would do it for free. Since I had not read a script and knew nothing of the show, I had to work only with Steve and Hal's concept that it was based on the Gloria Swanson photo of her standing in a gown in the ruins of the Roxy Theatre. So I drew my first sketch of the Follies girl at the top of the staircase, very period, in this rubble with the New York skyline. It was kind of melancholy. I got a call back from the advertising agency that they liked the sketch but that the woman was too butch—that's the word they used—and they wanted me to give her blond hair and big tits . . . which had nothing to do with the Follies. The style of the period was to be boyish, to have your chest bound. They weren't into voluptuousness. I got very pissed off, but I went home and did it. I looked at it and I thought, God, I don't want this to be seen by the public.

"But then I still had in my mind that I wanted to do posters that had big images because the Broadway poster at that time was so ditzy. I was so sick of those posters where you had a logo and a little cartoony man would be leaping out of the *o*. It made me crazy. So I got mad at this big-tits thing. I don't think the public is that stupid. So I immediately started looking through all my old photographs and I found a photo of Marlene Dietrich from the *Empress of Shanghai*. That face and the whole way it looked gave me the idea for this Follies lady with the headdress being the logo, and the only way I could transfer the rubble without drawing the rubble was by putting the crack in the face. A couple of days later, Hal called me to say that it was chosen as the poster, and on opening night of the show, Alexis Smith came up to me and said she knew that the face in the poster was hers. I never told her it was Dietrich.

"Poster art is a tricky business. I think that Hal and Steve always wanted the concept of the show to be perfect, right down to the art. I think what Joe Papp did with all the Paul Davis posters from the New York Shakespeare Festival—foregoing all billing—was a great thing. It was very brave.

"I'll never forget, though, years ago, I did some sketches for David Merrick for *Hello, Dolly!* They were quite good, but he didn't like any of them. He looked at me and said, 'I'll tell you what my idea of a great poster is: first of all, it's all red.' David, of course, has a red named after him. Every poster Merrick has ever had for any of his shows has been red . . . and it's the same color red . . . so it became known as David Merrick Red. So he says to me, 'Here is the poster concept: CAROL over CHANNING over HELLO over DOLLY!' And that was it. And what could you say? For him, that was enough. But that's not a poster, it's not a piece of art. It's an announcement. And there is a difference."

Stephen Sondheim and Harold Prince,
surrounded by their production team,
discuss a scene from their new musical
at the first rehearsal of *Merrily We Roll
Along*, 1981. (MARTHA SWOPE)

"IT'S STILL ··· 24
BACKWARDS"

"**T**HIS TIME, Hal Prince is giving his wife, Judy, much of the credit," reported the *New York Times* "Broadway" column of October 31, 1980.

The announcement explained that Mrs. Prince had been "nagging" her husband for years to do a musical about teenagers. And then one morning, while he was shaving, Prince remembered a play that was one of his favorites when *he* was a teenager: *Merrily We Roll Along*, by Moss Hart and George S. Kaufman. (The original production featured Prince's late and beloved producing partner, Robert Griffith.)

Prince called Sondheim immediately ("It was the first time he ever said yes on the phone," Prince exclaimed in the *New York Times*), and next called librettist George Furth to round out the trio that had worked together so successfully on *Company*.

Another reteaming came with the announcement that Ron Field would join the group as choreographer. In earlier days, Field was responsible for the critically acclaimed dances and musical staging in Prince's *Cabaret* and *Zorbá!*, before becoming the Tony Award–winning director-choreographer for *Applause*.

"I wanted to work with the master," Ron Field says. "I had helmed a lot of productions and I really wanted to improve my skills as a theater director. To my mind, working with Hal as the show's choreographer was like a refresher course, because of my admiration for the body of work he had contributed to the theater. I had also done an Israeli opera with him a few years previously, called *Ashmedai*, and it was so much fun.

"I was, of course, a huge fan of Sondheim's, and Hal kept saying, 'This is the perfect show for you, it's a musical comedy . . . it's nothing intellectual, nothing esoteric. This is right up your alley.' He said it was going to be the biggest dancing show of their careers. It was going to be *Gypsy*. So I thought, great, Steve Sondheim's first musical comedy in years and I get to do it."

The story, which concerns a group of successful theater people in 1980, moves backward in time during the course of the musical to the idealistic and hopeful days of their youth. The plot tells of Franklin Shepard, a composer; Charley Kringas, a lyricist; and Mary Flynn, a promising writer friend of both—how they meet and change as the composer corrupts himself and tramples friendships during his hungry ascension to success. By the final scene, where they meet for the first time and watch for Sputnik in 1957, the threesome sing of an optimistic future.

Since *Merrily We Roll Along* was a show about friendships, Sondheim chose to focus the attention of his score on the relationship of Frank, Mary, and Charley, by having their songs interconnected through chunks of melody, rhythm, and accompaniment.

"It's not whimsical," Sondheim points out. "The songs are all based on the interrelationships of the three of them and the things they have in common get fragmented and distorted over a period of years, the way aspects of our friendships do.

"The idea of the score was that it was built in modular blocks, and the blocks were shifted around instead of having transitions from number to number or interweaving themes the way the songs functioned in *Sweeney Todd*. You take a release from one song and you make that a verse for a different song, and then you take a chorus from a song and make that a release for another song, and then you take an accompaniment from yet a different song and make that a verse in another song. . . . It's like modular furniture that you rearrange in a room: two chairs become a couch, two couches at an angle become a banquette."

So musically, the release in "Rich and Happy" became the refrain in "Our Time"; the melody of "Old Friends" became the accompaniment for "Opening Doors"; and the chorus for "Like It Was" became the interlude for "Old Friends." And all of Franklin Shepard's songs were based on the same tune; "The Hills of Tomorrow" develops into "Opening Doors" and emerges into "Good Thing Going."

"What the tone of the show is supposed to be," Sondheim says, "is just musical comedy in a most traditional way, only with contemporary harmonies—but real, thirty-two-bar songs."

In writing the score, Sondheim made a decision from the start not to try to re-create the musical styles of the years that he was writing about. "If it was a show that took place in three decades—like the Sixties, Seventies, and Eighties—then I think I would have done that," he says, "but you can't really make a point about changes in music, for instance, between 1964 and 1968; the music didn't really change enough between those segments. As an example, when we got to 1968, our original scene was a homecoming party for Charley, who had been jailed for draft-card burning; so you're in your folk-song protest period. But then how do you differentiate that section musically from '66 and '69? That's the problem. So I wrote in a consistent musical-comedy style for the whole show. In fact, if the score is listened to in reverse order—although it wasn't written that way—it develops traditionally."

From its initial conception, *Merrily* would be cast, according to Prince, with teenagers instead of adults.

"I got a job as a gofer on *Pacific Overtures* when I was fifteen," explains Lonny Price, who eventually landed the role of Charley Kringas. "I worked for Hal for about a year and then someone in his office fired me because—I was told—I asked too many questions, like 'What was the breakeven on *Pacific Overtures?*'—which, for some reason, was an enormous secret." After performing in some showcases, off-Broadway shows, and

From left: Lonny Price as Charley, James Weissenbach as the original Franklin, and Ann Morrison as Mary in a preview shot of *Merrily We Roll Along*, 1981. (MARTHA SWOPE)

studying acting with Prince's casting director, Joanna Merlin, he was asked to appear in a reading of *Merrily*. "Hal wanted to do these readings to see if kids could pull off George Furth's sort of New York banter. So we did it and it was successful. And Steve played—I'll never forget—he played 'Old Friends' and I remember thinking, after *Sweeney Todd*, he's writing such young, vibrant, exciting music—sort of more in the tradition of *Company* and *Whistle*—in a vein that he hadn't written in for quite a while."

The actor signed to play Franklin Shepard was James Weissenbach, a son of one of Prince's old college friends. "I had a meeting with Hal because I was a theater student who was interested in producing and directing," Weissenbach says. "I asked him if I could be his assistant and he said that I was a little young, but that he was doing a show about kids and would I be interested in auditioning for this reading they were going to do? And I thought 'Interested? I'd sweep the floors.' Then Steve asked me if I could sing, which was kind of a loaded question. So I said, 'Sure.' I mean, everyone sings. While I was very much involved in the musical theater department at Syracuse, I was more in the directing end, behind the scenes. But I sang for Hal and Steve and they told me I had the part. And just when I was coming off the ceiling, they told me the show was postponed because Steve had to finish the score."

With the delay of nine months, the cast spent much of its time socializing and even published a *Merrily* newsletter. Ron Field, in the meantime, held dance classes in anticipation of the upcoming rehearsal period.

Rehearsals for *Merrily*, with Lonny Price, James Weissenbach, Ann Morrison, and a young cast of actors (including Prince's own daughter Daisy), finally began in September 1981, and there was great enthusiasm and optimism. John Corry reported on the first day of rehearsal in a *New York Times* article, with Hal Prince stating that the show was about a lot of serious things but he didn't think it would be an especially serious evening. "It's about corruption, the antihero, friendship and the years from 1980 to 1955," Prince explained. The original *Merrily* covered the years 1934 to 1916, with its protagonist a playwright. Produced in 1934, it ran only 155 performances.

"One reason the original didn't work," Prince told the assembled group, "was that he was an antihero. He sold out. He became rich." His contention was that in the 1930s the antihero was not a sympathetic figure. In 1981, it's a different story.

"When Mr. Sondheim finished singing what might be a song intended to stop the show," Corry reported, "everyone burst into applause. There did not seem to be a soul in the room who did not think they had a hit."

"It was not too exciting for me," admits Ron Field, "because I couldn't understand the show. I was listening, with question marks coming out of my ears, my eyes, my heart, and my brain. It didn't seem possible that this was going to work—this thing that was backwards. I just couldn't understand it. The lazy part of me kept saying, 'You'll get it . . . it'll come to you.'

"I was so perplexed. I would look at the set and it didn't seem attractive or make any sense to me. Then I would look at the people who were cast who couldn't sing, certainly couldn't dance, were clearly unattractive, and most had never been in a show before. They were amateurs. But that was the concept. And I went, 'Oh, well, if that's the concept let's pick the homeliest and awkwardest, and put them on this funny set. And then they're going to wear what? Wigs? Gray wigs? And they're going to wear clothing, like from their mother's closets, and they're going to pencil in moustaches and sideburns. . . . Well, this will be interesting. How come I don't get it? So there I was in an office filled with people who clearly had gone further in school than I had and had a lot more Tonys than I had, and I was the only one who seemed to have reservations. Strong ones. But at that time I was very covert about my feelings."

The producers decided that economically it was not feasible to test *Merrily* out of town. It was also decided not to make many changes in the show until it began previewing at the Alvin, giving the inexperienced actors a chance to work into their material.

"I think there was a lot of conflict," says Weissenbach. "Both Hal and Ron seemed to have different feelings as to whether or not it was going to be a dance show. The first couple of weeks were filled with Ron staging a number of dances and Hal coming in and saying, 'No, that's not what I want,' and then Ron restaging them and Hal coming back and saying, 'No, that's not what I want.' So it was kind of strange for all of us because we were saying, 'Gee, aren't they talking to one another?'

"Even so, during rehearsals we thought we had the biggest hit. Until the run-through. Then I knew, for the first time, that we had problems. When I came out for my first entrance, the audience laughed at a line that was somewhat serious. . . . They were just not laughing at the right spots."

From left: Ann Morrison, Lonny Price, and Jim Walton as the new Franklin, who replaced James Weissenbach during previews of *Merrily We Roll Along*, 1981. (MARTHA SWOPE)

The first major alert to cast and crew that their new musical had significant problems was the dress rehearsal where Prince threw out all the costumes.

"I remember sitting in the theater as we were rehearsing," says Lonny Price, "and just looking at the set and thinking, 'Why is it so ugly?' It was horrifying. And they had made these really original, very strange, very witty costumes at great expense. And I had suits and wigs. I had like twelve hairpieces. During the Sixties sequence, I looked like John Lennon. So we were doing the dress parade and there were these fifteen-year-old girls who had beaded dresses on, looking like Ann-Margret. We all looked like we were in *Bugsy Malone*.

"And Hal stood up and said, 'Look, we've made a mistake here and I want you to take everything off and we're going to put you all in jeans and sweatshirts.' And I thought it was the bravest thing I'd ever seen. He said, 'I'm sorry. The whole concept doesn't work, I'm sorry.'"

Prince: "I had never gotten into such trouble before. I had no idea of what the show should look like beyond a very initial instinct. Earlier on, I called everyone together and I said the only way I see this show is with no scenery whatsoever. Back to *Our Town*. And Steve said, 'Follow your instincts.' But everyone else said, 'You can't do that and charge thirty dollars. You can't do that on Broadway. If you want to do that, you've got to go off-Broadway, otherwise forget it.' So I was persuaded. So we tried to find scenery that didn't look like scenery and we got into terrible trouble on the costumes. We tried to make the set look like it wasn't there; instead it was there and it was awful."

Sondheim: "It's true those problems were never solved. It was oppressive and depressing and wasn't at all what Hal wanted, although he takes full responsibility for it. It was an attempt and a mistake. But you have to get practical when something doesn't work."

Merrily We Roll Along began previews at the Alvin Theatre (the home of *Company*) on October 8, 1981, and confusion reigned. The evening was forty minutes too long, and with no out-of-town tryout, the show was incoherent, the backward structure was unclear, the performances were weak, the leading man wasn't coming across, the dances were not working, and some of the worst word-of-mouth gossip ever began circulating through the theater community.

On October 18, Liz Smith reported in the Sunday *Daily News*: "The walkouts from the new Hal Prince–Steve Sondheim musical are almost epidemic. There were about 140 people who left after the intermission at a recent performance. 'Terrible' and 'tacky' are the words most often being used in the milling disarray at previews."

"We could always tell that the audience was not liking the show," says Weissenbach. "First of all, you could always look up to the balcony during the performance and see the flickering exit signs. They were always flickering because of the heads passing by as they were filing out of the theater. The other way you could tell was in the section of the show right after the Kennedy number was performed. I had a line . . . something to the effect of, 'We were a little off tonight.' And there was always somebody in the audience who would make some sarcastic remark like, 'Tonight? What about every night.' It got to the point where I would get to that line at every performance and I'd hold my breath."

On October 21, in the *New York Times*, came the announcement: "*Merrily We Roll Along*, a musical in preview at the Alvin Theatre, has changed its leading man and postponed its opening from November 1 to November 8. On Monday night on a trial basis, Jim Walton [who was playing a smaller role in the show] replaced James Weissenbach as the composer who becomes a movie producer. The change became permanent yesterday. A spokesman for the production said that as changes occurred during rehearsals and previews, Mr. Walton seemed to be better for the role."

"You see, Hal and I liked Weissenbach very much," Sondheim says. "But we bowed to the feelings of a lot of other people who didn't like him. We thought, in fact, that he was perfect."

"Hal was really quite down on *me* personally," says Lonny Price. "I was the one that I thought would get fired, so letting Jim go was a surprise. It seemed that Hal loved what Jim was doing. On the other hand, Hal would say things to me like, 'You're pulling my focus. Being good is not the idea of this show. You have to be raw.' But, personally, I was going crazy because I didn't have my big song, 'Franklin Shepard, Inc.,' until three days before previews. So for five weeks of rehearsals, they would say, 'Now Lonny sings his song' and my entire character was in that song, so I was having trouble playing the rest of the show not knowing what exactly that breakdown was going to be. But the truth of the matter is that the show worked better in the rehearsal room than it ever worked on the stage. . . . It was really touching.

"And just at that time, things were getting more and more tense with Ron Field. He was being less patient with these kids who were not chorus dancers. Ron also had an assistant who was just a horror, who then got hepatitis and we all had to get shots."

Field: "What I did in *Cabaret* and *Zorbá!* was work organically. But with this show, Hal wanted it amateurishly staged and awkward. Nothing could seem as if there was a professional touch to it. I'm not saying that there were two or three kids that I had to bury behind the good ones. If I'd buried the bad ones, you'd have been looking at the set.

"Look, Hal is a cerebral, intellectually gifted, architecturally brilliant person. Here, he was in trouble and he was not ready to admit that he was wrong, especially because he had just done *Evita*.

Cast of Broadway production of *Merrily We Roll Along* performs "Rich and Happy," 1981. (MARTHA SWOPE)

"I couldn't stage one number right in the show. Not one. I did three or four versions of everything and I couldn't stop apologizing for not pleasing him. The last thing I wanted to do was to fail him. It wasn't like I said, 'Fuck him.' I was with the master and my name was as big as his in the program.

"At the previews it was astounding how many people refused to come back. Astounding! And that seemed not to be recognized by anybody. And I kept hearing how great the show was. I was in so much pain. . . . My mind would no longer allow me to be just a faithful servant and I couldn't believe that they were so unfair as not to collaborate. Maybe at that point they thought I was such a fool . . . maybe they didn't want to be with me.

"They didn't want to listen. Hal didn't even want to talk. I finally said, 'You know, Hal, I'm very good at fixing things and I'm real fast.

You know how I went in and worked on *Peter Pan*. I can see mistakes, give me something to do.' And he looked at me as if he didn't know what I was talking about. I'll never forget the look on his face when he said, 'Ron, we're not in trouble.' And I thought that *that* was unconscionable. That for all our years of friendship and the fact that I had given up my opinions and judgments and surrendered to him, he wouldn't let me in at that point was very hurtful and I thought very stupid.

"And of course their way of fixing the show was to come to the conclusion that the lead had to go. *Why* did he have to go? Because he had more lines than anyone else. This was a guy who walked into Hal's office, the son of a schoolmate, and he wanted to be a gofer on this production and wound up with the lead. The lead! The one the whole show pivoted around. This person who had never acted or sung . . . who couldn't move!

"It was like summer stock. And I went crazy. If someone says they saw Ron about that time and he was a crazy man, they were right. I felt like I was among traitors. That was my first experience of no one telling the emperor. . . . I looked around at the staff and I thought, 'How can you love this man and take his money every week and not want to support him and tell him the truth? I can't believe you don't know what I know.'

"So I pleaded with him to give me an appointment to see him at his office. He never called. So I finally went over to the theater and when he came in I handed him a paper I had written out with a list of suggestions. And he said, 'What is this?' and I told him, 'Clearly you don't want to see me contribute to this thing.' And he said, 'Ron, we're doing fine. The show is working.' And I said, 'It is hurting me more than anything that you don't want to discuss this with me. What have you put on that stage?' And he called me self-indulgent and walked away. And then something came out of my mouth and he stopped and said, 'What did you say?' And I said it again. And then he asked me to leave the theater. And I said, 'Thanks. Thanks.' "

The headline in the October 24 edition of the *New York Times* read: "Ron Field has been replaced by Larry Fuller as the choreographer of the new musical currently in previews at the Alvin. Mr. Field and the producers of the show said he left the production because of artistic differences."

On October 27, the *New York Times* reported: "*Merrily* Is Postponed Second Time to November 16 . . . to give Larry Fuller additional time to work on the dances."

Fuller: "I felt that I could fix them—make them better, anyway. Basically, I said I wanted to start at the top and redo them all. It was almost like doing summer stock . . . make a decision and do one a day.

"My point of view was to try to make the numbers more behavioral from the character's point of view, and less plain musical staging. Although it was a lot more musical comedy—and that was what they wanted —than *Sweeney* was. There seemed to be a lot of extraneous moving around that didn't have a point of view. There were very distinct limitations. I know one number, 'Old Friends,' I did about five versions of. We were desperately trying to make it stop the show, like a number with Judy Garland, Mickey Rooney, and Donald O'Connor. Only we didn't have Judy, Mickey, or Donald."

Merrily We Roll Along finally opened on Broadway on November 16, 1981, to crushingly bad reviews.

"I'm afraid the news this morning is glum," wrote Douglas Watt in the *Daily News*. "The new Stephen Sondheim musical which came to the Alvin last night is a dud. . . . The production looks like it cost all of $28. . . . *Merrily We Roll Along* is kid stuff in more than one sense, and a severe letdown for at least one Sondheim admirer."

"*Merrily* was a blunder," Brendan Gill wrote in the *New Yorker*, "all the more mysterious because it was carried out by some of the least blunder-prone people on Broadway. The mercy of memory is its selectivity; this *Merrily* has already joined its predecessor in those dim recesses of my mind that I reserve for the failed efforts of people I admire."

Howard Kissel, in *Women's Wear Daily*, said: "The problem through much of the evening is George Furth's book, which is short on character, short on motivation, long only on bitchiness. But it is sad to report that [it] is also Sondheim's thinnest score. He has written several beautiful ballads. . . . But many of the numbers merely sound like echoes of earlier, stronger work and lack their predecessors' conviction."

Clive Barnes, surprisingly, wrote a rather positive review. (He even liked Eugene Lee's set and Judith Dolan's costumes.) "Whatever you may have heard about it—go and see it for yourselves. It is far too good a musical to be judged by those twin kangaroo courts of word of mouth and critical consensus."

"As we all should probably have learned by now," Frank Rich said in the *New York Times*, "to be a Stephen Sondheim fan is to have one's heart broken at regular intervals. Usually, the heartbreak comes from Mr. Sondheim's songs—for his music can tear through us with an emotional force

Ann Morrison and Jim Walton lead the company in "Now You Know" in *Merrily We Roll Along*, 1981. (MARTHA SWOPE)

as moving as Gershwin's. And sometimes the pain is compounded by another factor—for some of Mr. Sondheim's most powerful work turns up in shows that fail. Suffice it to say that both kinds of pain are abundant in *Merrily We Roll Along*. . . . Mr. Sondheim has given this evening a half-dozen songs that are crushing and beautiful—that soar and linger and hurt. But the show that contains them is a shambles . . . the book's tone often seems as empty as the characters. . . . what's really being wasted here is Mr. Sondheim's talent. And that's why we watch *Merrily We Roll Along* with an ever-mounting—and finally upsetting—sense of regret."

Prince: "We really worked hard during previews. We kept each other's spirits up. And we just kept working. And by the time we were through, not only were they not walking out in droves, but many were sitting there and cheering. But it was too god-damned late. We had destroyed ourselves during those three weeks preceding the opening, in terms of gossip. It was the gossip columns that told us we had committed a major crime against society. And, of course, if you had tickets for a show and you walked in having read that, the show didn't get much of a chance.

"It's all economic . . . that's why we didn't go out of town. Everything is totally economic. And very dangerous. Because each economic stricture, each imposition, affects the form, the quality of what you're doing. And because I had such a successful experience with *Sweeney Todd*, where we previewed in New York and opened cold to great results, I got seduced and thought it could work again. But it happens very rarely and it's not something to count on. The time out on the road, away from New York, is crucial."

Prince explained that *Merrily* had the most changes of intrinsic material he had ever experienced in the theater. He also admitted to a *New York Times* interviewer, the day before opening, that he had been charmed by the rawness of the twenty-six young actors, all in their late teens or early twenties. "I was charmed by the beginnings of their artistry, the roughness of their craft, their inexperience. . . . But we realized other people were not as charmed. We took away some of the things that the twenty-six actors were contributing as a group and settled pretty much on the six major characters for clarity. We did this after we realized that the audience was getting confused in the previews, and when an audience gets confused, it gets hostile. They pay their way and they have a right to follow what we're doing."

Sondheim: "It's a swell idea to do a show for teenagers, but teenagers, like Asian Americans, aren't that experienced on the stage, and you are charging $35 a seat . . . and maybe you should have done it in a smaller theater that suits that kind of ambience, or it should have been done, not

The cast of *Merrily We Roll Along* recording the album the morning after the show closed on Broadway, 1981. (© HENRY GROSSMAN, RCA RECORDS)

with teenagers, but as it was done in 1934 with adults—actors portraying themselves at forty and at eighteen . . . which is the way we eventually did it in revival in California."

"I worried that the reason the play didn't work originally might hurt the musical as well," says Flora Roberts. "And when they began to realize some of their errors, they never had time to change them. The concept had to be rethought. So it really should have been tried out in Boston."

Sondheim: "A lot of people found the central character unlikable. The idea is, of course, that he is unlikable, but you get to like him better as the evening goes on. A lot of people turned off and didn't come back. But you know, maybe that's why the play failed when Kaufman and Hart did it, because it got very good reviews. It wasn't a big failure, but it just wasn't the success that it was supposed to be."

When it became clear that the show wasn't going to run, RCA Records decided to pull out of its recording commitment for the cast album. But Sondheim's music publisher, Tommy Valando, and RCA Records vice-president Thomas Z. Shepard went to Bob Summer, the president of the record division at that time, and pleaded with him to take the plunge. They talked about their "family" relationship and how RCA will always have Sondheim's catalog. Summer relented, and the day after the show folded on Broadway, the cast of *Merrily We Roll Along* assembled in the recording studio to document, and sing for one last time, the score to their newly defunct musical.

"It was a difficult album to record," explains Shepard. "It took a very long time. I didn't want the album to sound the way the show looked. . . . The show looked like a school show and I didn't want it to sound like a school album. I wanted to make sure that it sounded elegant and polished. We spared no expense to prove that no matter what the show was like, it was a fabulous recording. The material is very precise, very crisp, and I had this image in my head that it should sound sort of like *Company* . . . it should have that kind of sparkle."

After *Merrily* closed on Broadway, George Furth sent the script and tape of the show to director-playwright James Lapine. It was after the Los Angeles opening of Lapine's much-heralded off-Broadway musical *March of the Falsettos*, and Furth was knocked out by Lapine's staging. He had hoped to rework *Merrily* and initiate a new production with Lapine as director.

"I thought the material George sent me was fantastic," recalls James Lapine, who had never seen the Broadway production. "I believe George was unhappy with his work on the book. I think he wanted to give it another shot. But when I mentioned it to Steve, he seemed reluctant to have *Merrily* done again at that point. Since we were starting a new relationship—and we really had just met—Steve felt that it was more important for him to write something new with me. So *Merrily* stayed on the back burner."

In 1985, after the successful collaboration with Sondheim on their prize-winning *Sunday in the Park with George*, Lapine was approached by Des McAnuff, an old friend, who asked him to direct a production for McAnuff's first season as head of the La Jolla Playhouse in California. Lapine suggested *Merrily We Roll Along.*

"Steve, by that time, said, 'What the hell,' " Lapine remembers. "So I became very excited. I first went back and read the original Kaufman and Hart script, which blew me away. I just thought that it was so brilliant. But it's a very tough show—as I learned when we did it in La Jolla."

With a cast considerably older than that of the Broadway production, led by John Rubinstein, Heather MacRae, and Chip Zien, *Merrily* opened at the La Jolla Playhouse on June 16, 1985.

Lapine: "When I read it, there were no stage directions that said it should be played by young people. In fact, it wouldn't have dawned on me to do it that way in the first place. But one of the problems that I had with this show exists in a lot of plays. It's called the cipher in the middle. You have a Frank Shepard, and he's mostly defined by the people around him. That's difficult. And he is a hard character to like."

For the La Jolla production, George Furth greatly revised the book scenes and deleted both the opening and the closing graduation sequences. The score was clarified by the replacement of "Rich and Happy" with the new song "That Frank," the addition of another new song, "Growing Up," and a change of lyrics in "Now You Know."

With the La Jolla cast, the characters seemed somewhat better defined, and with the use of slide projections, the passing of the years became much clearer. But still not clear enough. "To my amazement, people still didn't get that the play was going in reverse," says Lapine, "which astounded me. I did everything but have a calendar with pages flying off."

"Stephen Sondheim and George Furth have revised their 1981 Broadway flop . . . to see if the show merits another roll of the commercial dice. The verdict is in—roll 'em!" exclaimed *Variety.*

And Jack Viertel in the *Los Angeles Herald Examiner* was overwhelmed with the improved production: "*Merrily We Roll Along* now appears to be what it set out to be in the first place—a gripping evocation of friendship under fire from the demands of success . . . Sondheim, Furth and Lapine have located the show everyone hoped was inside the wreckage of the Broadway version, and La Jolla Playhouse has given them the space to do the creative work necessary to make it come alive. From the ashes of one of the unhappiest of Broadway failures has come a musical that can stand among the finest works the genre has ever offered."

But Sylvie Drake, in the *Los Angeles Times*, was less impressed: "*Merrily* at La Jolla is an improvement over *Merrily* on Broadway, but is that saying a lot?"

Although the production was made possible by a subsidy from the Shubert Organization, Bernard Jacobs was not anxious to take the show back to New York. "It was better," Jacobs admits, "but most of the essential faults from the original work were still there. The audience sat there in bewilderment until far into the play. Whether that was due to the problems of the La Jolla production or whether it was due to the way it was rewritten, I don't know, but I didn't think it had improved enough to take it any further."

Lapine: "When I left after the show opened, I was feeling very good about it. But when I went back to see *Merrily* at the end of its four-week

From left: Old friends John Rubinstein as Franklin, Heather MacRae as Mary, and Chip Zien as Charley toast to their future in the La Jolla revival of *Merrily We Roll Along*, 1985. (MICHA LANGER/ LA JOLLA PLAYHOUSE)

run, I was sort of disappointed. I felt we had done such good work on it, but as I looked at it more objectively, I saw how much more work I thought needed to be done.

"I think for Steve and me, it just really became about, do we want to take the time to work on it again or do we do a new show? And I think it became clear, particularly for Steve, that it was time for us to move on."

Merrily We Roll Along, in its initial incarnation, may be remembered as the shortest-running Sondheim musical on Broadway (sixteen performances) since *Anyone Can Whistle* (nine), with a rising tide of sentiment that has already placed it in *Whistle*'s cult classic category. It was also, historically, the last of a succession of Harold Prince–Stephen Sondheim collaborations—at least for the time being.

Many believe that its insurmountable quest was clearly making the basic concept lucid to an audience. Ron Field points to his own initial fear that the piece could never work. "I remember running into Michael Bennett one night while we were previewing on Broadway," Field recalls. "He said to me, 'How's the show going?' And I shrugged and I said in bewilderment, 'How good could it be? It's *still* backwards.' "

From left: Choreographer Larry Fuller (who replaced Ron Field), librettist George Furth, Stephen Sondheim, and Harold Prince at the premiere of the Broadway production of *Merrily We Roll Along*, 1981. (VAN WILLIAMS)

POP RECORDINGS · · · 25

"STEVE SONDHEIM is, without a doubt, a classy composer and lyricist," says Frank Sinatra. "However, he could make me a lot happier if he'd write more songs for saloon singers like me."

Sinatra's feelings notwithstanding, Sondheim has devoted his career to creating songs that fit ineradicably into the fiber and texture of his shows, which is why he has less exposure in the pop market than one might expect of such a top songwriter.

In 1959, Johnny Mathis had a Top Twenty success with "Small World" from *Gypsy*, which generated for Sondheim and Jule Styne a Grammy nomination for Song of the Year (it lost to Jimmy Driftwood's "Battle of New Orleans"). Sondheim's highest charting single came two years later when Ferrante and Teicher had a Top Ten record with, ironically, a piano instrumental of "Tonight" from *West Side Story*.

In 1973, the year *A Little Night Music* opened on Broadway, Frank Sinatra picked up "Send in the Clowns" and recorded it on his *Ol' Blue Eyes Is Back* album. But the major breakthrough for the song occurred in 1975 when Judy Collins released a single of "Clowns," establishing a popularity for Sondheim on records that had always eluded him.

"The 'Clowns' single, from Judy's *Judith* album, hit the charts and peaked at #36," reports Paul Grein, *Billboard* magazine's music and chart expert. "More than two years later, in September 1977, it was re-released and climbed to #19. It was re-released because of a hot radio phenomenon at the time termed 'passive research.' That's when radio stations sought to determine, through call-out polling, which songs their 'passive' listeners (those who don't phone in requests or buy singles) want to hear."

Opposite: Barbra Streisand and Stephen Sondheim collaborate on *The Broadway Album*, 1985. (MARK SENNET/COLUMBIA RECORDS)

And so, sixteen years after his first Song of the Year nomination, Sondheim was nominated again in the same category. "With the popularity of the Collins version of the song and the release of the London original cast recording—which was also nominated that year—'Send in the Clowns' won the Grammy for Song of the Year," Grein says. "It was a great triumph because it beat such #1 hits as 'Love Will Keep Us Together' and 'Rhinestone Cowboy.' And it's one of only three Broadway songs in history to win the Song of the Year Grammy, along with 'What Kind of Fool Am I?' from *Stop the World* . . . and 'Hello, Dolly!' "

With her earlier success still within memory, Judy Collins recorded a version of "Green Finch and Linnet Bird" from *Sweeney Todd* on her 1980 album *Running for My Life*. And in 1981, timed to the opening of *Merrily We Roll Along*, Frank Sinatra included "Good Thing Going" on his *She Shot Me Down* album, and Carly Simon sang "Not a Day Goes by" on her *Torch* album. But none of the albums had nearly the impact of a much celebrated record, simply titled *The Broadway Album*, recorded by Barbra Streisand and released for Christmas of 1985: a record that became—surprisingly, but encouragingly—one of the biggest selling albums of the year.

"Barbra Streisand . . . has just released what may be the album of a lifetime," exclaimed Stephen Holden in the *New York Times* of November 10, 1985. "[It] soars with full-bodied, tender bel canto renditions of ballads . . . that stand among the most thrilling performances of her 23-year recording career. . . . Miss Streisand's return to a style of music she abandoned 15 years ago as uncommercial is a career coup that has surprised Columbia Records. . . . It is also something of a historic milestone in that Miss Streisand persuaded Stephen Sondheim, who is represented by six songs (eight counting two lyrics for *West Side Story*) to re-write three songs for the project, including 'Send in the Clowns.' "

"It's interesting that I hadn't sung any of Stephen's songs before," says Barbra Streisand. (Years before, she had recorded "There Won't Be Trumpets" from *Anyone Can Whistle*, but it was never released.) "My repertoire in the early years was much older than that: old Rodgers and Hart, early Harold Arlen. I think there were also simpler lyrics in some of the songs I recorded, but I now appreciate the complexity. Some people accuse Stephen of being too intellectual or too sophisticated . . . but that's what I think is so extraordinary about him. For instance, I didn't understand 'Send in the Clowns' when I first heard it, which is why I didn't sing it years ago. I thought it was the most gorgeous melody but I didn't understand that kind of irony yet . . . the kind of cynicism that is inherent in the lyric. I wasn't mature enough to sing it. It's like growing into a part like *Medea* or *Hedda Gabler*; it's not good when you're twenty. You need to be older."

When Streisand first contemplated doing an album of Broadway songs, after thinking about it for several years, she decided to team up again with Peter Matz, who did the orchestrations for most of her early albums. With Matz as her co-producer on the majority of songs, and Richard Baskin and David Foster handling the production on other cuts, she began marathon listening sessions to find a blend of obscure songs and standards. She found herself discarding many of the songs with simpler lyrics in favor of Sondheim's more intricate and adventurous material. Attracted to a particular number, "Putting It Together" from *Sunday in the Park with George*, she called Sondheim, whom she hardly knew, and asked if he would make a slight change in one of the lyrics.

"I told him of my conversation with my record company," Streisand remembers, "where I told them I didn't want to do another pop album at this time, that I wanted to do an album of Broadway songs. And they were very resistant and unhappy, and they said, 'Barbra, you can't do a record like this. It's not commercial. This is like your old records. Nobody's going to buy it.' Every word they said only encouraged me. I wanted to put all their comments into this song. And I thought, 'What a great way to open this album.' "

Sondheim: "She wanted to make it relevant to the music business, so she asked me if I could just fix one word to replace 'lasers,' and I said, 'Why don't you say "vinyl" instead?' and she leaped at it and thought that was wonderful. And I said, 'Let me look at the rest of the lyric, if you want to personalize it. I'm sure I can make it more record-oriented and less art-related, which is what it was in the context of the show.' Once you get into it, then it becomes fun to do, and that's why I did it. I figured, why do it half-assed—there's no point in making it confusing. So it started with her asking for a word to be changed and I ended up rewriting half the song. The way it turned out, I think it's terrific."

Streisand: "I would talk to him for hours. I felt I couldn't ignore the truth . . . you don't hide it; you use it. So I told him, 'Here I am, a very successful recording star and yet I have to fight for everything I believe in. I'm still auditioning after twenty-three years.' I asked him if he could encompass that thought and he wrote, 'Even though you get the recognition / Everything you do you still audition.' You see what I mean? It took a month to work on one song, which is what I love about singing this kind of material."

One disagreement that Sondheim had with Streisand was over an image in the song that he was reluctant to change. "There's a line in the show," Streisand says, " 'A vision's just a vision / If it's only in your head / If no one gets to see it / It's as good as dead' and I wanted him to change it to 'If no one gets to *hear* it,' and we had a wonderful argument. He said, 'You can't hear a vision . . . that's a visual thing. It's a vision, right?' And I said, 'No, no, I *hear* a vision. In other words, I hear the album done . . . so it's a vision of it. It's an audio vision.' And he gave in to me because he said, 'The rules are that whoever is the most passionate about something, wins.' In other words, if you could live with it either way, leave it the way it was.

"But this was one of the most exciting collaborations I've ever had, because we both talk fast, we think fast; so it was like shorthand half the time . . . we practically didn't have to finish sentences. It was so exhilarating, there were moments I was screaming with joy over the phone."

Sondheim spent several weeks in Los Angeles working in the recording studio with Streisand as she tested the newly revised material. "I didn't know if he trusted me when he first met me," she recalls. "Was I going to hurt the songs in some way? But I think, as he thought about it, he got excited by the ideas. He didn't close his mind to the experience of having something changed. He was fabulous to work with and fabulous to argue with."

In making a final selection of songs, Streisand considered singing "Rose's Turn" from *Gypsy*, but couldn't find a way to make it work for this album. "A few years ago, Jule Styne approached me about playing the mother in *Gypsy*," Streisand says. "I re-read the script and I just heard Ethel Merman all over again. It seemed impossible even to attempt it. I did, however, want to record songs from the show. I worked on 'Rose's Turn' for quite a while for this album, but I couldn't quite solve it. I even asked Stephen to try and figure a way of integrating it with 'Some People,' but it didn't work. I was also considering doing several other songs from *Sunday in the Park with George*, like 'Move On' and 'Finishing the Hat' and 'Children and Art.' But I'll probably get to those songs in *Volume Two*, which I'm already thinking about."

For *The Broadway Album* Streisand recorded, in addition to "Putting It Together" and "Send in the Clowns," "Somewhere" and "Something's Coming" (from *West Side Story*), "Being Alive" (from *Company*), a coupling of "Pretty Women" (from *Sweeney Todd*) and "Ladies Who Lunch" (from *Company*), and "Not While I'm Around" (from *Sweeney Todd*).

Streisand: "The song that was a surprise—how deeply it appealed to people—was 'Not While I'm Around.' I fell in love with it when I saw the show. It was in my head for years. I thought it was one of the great lyrics and melodies—everyone can understand it and relate to it. We produced two versions of it. The first was too lush and grand: the arrangement was too big for the song and overpowered the delicacy of it. The second one, which was what we used, was more fitting to the size of the song . . . it had more of a quiet intensity . . . and my interpretation changed. The first time I was singing it as a lover to her lover. The second time I sang it, I was more of a mother singing to my son. My character changed.

"You see, when you sing theater songs that have a kind of built-in story, you instinctively operate more as an actress. When you sing a pop song, who are you? I guess you are yourself. But when you sing a song from the theater, somehow you become more of a character . . . it's not just you."

One of the most surprising changes for the album was Sondheim's lyric revision of "Send in the Clowns," his most successful and widely sung song.

"It was a tiny little throwaway song for a little voice," Sondheim says. "I didn't know it was going to be popular. And so it never had a so-called second chorus. And I even thought of writing one for the movie of *A Little Night Music*, and I thought, 'Oh, it's not worth it,' because by that time it had become a popular song. And then when Barbra said that she didn't get the emotional transition in it, I said, 'Well, it's because there is no emotional transition—there's a missing scene in there.'

"The last eight bars weren't written as a chorus but as a reprise. In the show, something happens between the chorus and that reprise to give the character an entire change of attitude, and that is what confused her. But she was absolutely right: there was no transition between the first chorus and what other people have been singing for the last eight bars . . . and there's no way you can make that work as an actress, because it's a whole other scene. So I said, 'You're right, I'll make a transition for you.' "

"I adored the melody of the bridge," Streisand says, "and I wanted to repeat it. . . . But I thought to myself, 'Do I dare ask him to write a new lyric for a song that was already standard?' So I squeamishly brought it up, and he agreed to write it."

One of Streisand's favorite songs, "Pretty Women," posed a problem for her. How could she sing it, since it was written from a man's point of view? "That's when I thought, 'Why don't I put it together with 'Ladies Who Lunch'?" Streisand says. "I could make something out of the opposing viewpoint. 'Ladies Who Lunch' is a very cynical song, putting down a certain kind of woman. 'Pretty Women,' on the surface, is adoring of women. And I thought it might be like the way I had sung 'Happy Days Are Here Again,' cynically. My attitude in my performance of it was, 'Are they *really* happy days?'

"So I looked at 'Pretty Women' from a more questioning point of view. Who are these women who are so pretty? In a way I envy them, they have no ambition, they're not obsessed by their work. Their work is to be pretty, to adorn a man. They get everything bought for them, they get taken care of completely, they have massages, work out at the gym, buy clothes . . . and they live long, they have no stress. So these women *became* the ladies who lunch."

Streisand asked Sondheim to write some lyrics to connect the songs, but they finally ended up cutting the new material when she realized all that she needed to do to make the transition was to hum. She did get him to supply a new ending with a number of short phrases that put a theatrical cap on the piece, and integrated the two songs.

"Steve seemed very pleased with the working process," says Richard Baskin, "because he had been mainly used to the experience of being in the studio with Broadway cast recording sessions, where everything is done so quickly in a highly pressurized setting. With this album, there was a proper amount of time for collaboration and experimentation, until all the elements came together and we were all quite happy with the results."

The Broadway Album, to everyone's surprise, reached #1 on the *Billboard* chart and remained there for three weeks without the help of the now mandatory Top Ten single and heavy radio airplay. (The album's first released single of "Somewhere" only reached #43.) With the album selling over three million copies, Sondheim's songs reached an enormous audience of record buyers, many of whom had never seen one of his shows or heard any of his cast albums.

"It's all about Barbra," Sondheim says. "If anyone else had recorded the exact same set of songs and sung them very well, it might not have sold. But she's got one of the best voices on the planet. And it's not just her voice, it's her intensity, her passion, her control. Although every moment has been thought out, you don't see all the sweat and decisions that went into the work. It is as though she just stepped out of the shower and began singing at you."

"I thought the album would do respectably," Streisand admits. "I never thought it would be such a big hit. But to have a #1 album of these songs . . . well, it really renews my faith in the public, wanting to hear this kind of material. And although I'd never sung any of Stephen's songs before, I guess with this album, I was making up for lost time."

Composer-lyricist Stephen Sondheim and
writer-director James Lapine during
dress rehearsal of *Sunday in the Park
with George*, 1984. (MARTHA SWOPE)

ART ISN'T EASY ... 26

AFTER THE ABRUPT CLOSING of *Merrily We Roll Along*, Sondheim became depressed and pessimistic. He gave an interview in which he said that he was going to give up writing for the theater and, instead, perhaps work on some mystery novels.

"I just didn't feel like going back to work," Sondheim says. "It was so discouraging because I felt the hatred on Broadway that was directed at Hal and me. I really don't like that whole aspect of show business, and I wish it could go away."

And then an unexpected phone call came from producer Lewis Allen, in June 1982. He was inquiring about Sondheim's disposition toward collaborating on a new musical based on the Nathanael West novella *A Cool Million.* The show was to have book and direction by a young off-Broadway writer-director, James Lapine, who had staged the hit musical *March of the Falsettos* and had written and directed *Table Settings*, as well as a piece that Sondheim had seen at the New York Shakespeare Festival, *Twelve Dreams.*

"I was knocked out by both the writing and directing [of *Twelve Dreams*]," Sondheim says, "and at the time I thought, 'Gee, I wonder if that man would like to write a musical? I bet he could.' But I was too shy to ask, so I just let it go."

So the call from Allen a few months later was coincidental and fortuitous—and Sondheim jumped at the chance for the meeting. "I thought that something might come of it," he remembers. "After licking my wounds for four or five months, I thought, 'I've really got to earn a living, there are bills coming in. . . . I should get back to work.' "

Upon re-reading the West book, Sondheim realized that it was a pastiche of *Candide*—with exactly the same plot—set in the West during the Depression. Although he wasn't interested in working on it, the meeting went well and he and Lapine agreed to pursue other ideas.

"I really didn't know much about Steve," James Lapine admits. "In fact, the very first Broadway musical I had ever seen was *Sweeney Todd*—which knocked me out so much I saw it three times. But I hadn't really been interested in Broadway, particularly Broadway musicals. Once we started working, though, Steve made me tapes of all the shows he had ever done and then I spent literally two years of my life listening to everything he ever wrote. And *then* I was blown away—and I was crushed that I didn't get to see those great musicals on stage. I wasn't a culture vulture in the past. I was a photographer and a designer and I just never went to the theater until the late Seventies. And I was more into the avant-garde stuff . . . the visual theater, not stuff that was reliant on a text."

Sondheim and Lapine met once a week to talk through some ideas. They became interested in the notion of a show made up of a theme and variations, rather than one with a linear story. "One evening," Sondheim recalls, "I showed Jim a French graphics magazine of the Fifties and Sixties called *Bizarre*, and one issue was devoted entirely to a couple hundred pages of every conceivable variation of the *Mona Lisa* . . . both visually and verbally. And Jim told me that he had, at one time, directed a piece by Gertrude Stein called *Photograph*. It was a poem which he staged with famous images as the centerpiece of the show . . . it had a lot of photographs of paintings in it . . ."

Lapine: "So I brought him a bunch of photographs of people and we just sort of sat and placed them all on the floor and looked at them and thought, 'Wouldn't it be interesting to see this person next to that person?' And then we thought about finding an existing image . . ."

Sondheim: ". . . and Jim said, 'Do you know Seurat's painting *A Sunday Afternoon on the Island of La Grande Jatte?*' And we realized that that painting was the setting of a play. All the people in that painting . . . when you start speculating on why none of them are looking at each other . . . and maybe there's a reason for that . . . maybe someone was having an affair with another one, or one was related to someone else. And then Jim said, 'Of course, the main character's missing.' And I said,

'Who?' And he said, 'The artist.' And once he said that, I knew there was a real play there. Once you get the idea that the artist has manipulated these people into this farcical afternoon they're having in which they're all pretending to be all pulled together, strolling apart, when actually all their passions are all over the place. . . ."

Born in 1859 in a middle-class Parisian home, Georges Seurat discovered the pleasures of painting as a teenager. In 1884 he began his most famous painting, *Sunday Afternoon on the Island of La Grande Jatte*, which used the dotlike technique of pointillism, which he made famous. While painting *The Sideshow*, which is on view at the Metropolitan Museum, Seurat met Madeleine Knobloch at a carnival booth, and she became his mistress and gave birth to their child about a year later. A short time after that, Seurat developed a persistent sore throat and choked to death in 1891; less than two weeks later, his son, Pierre, died of the same strange illness.

Sondheim: "As we researched Seurat's life, we became more and more excited. Here was this marvelous, mysterious genius who died of some strange disease, probably a rare form of meningitis. He led a double life —on the one hand, almost every night he'd stroll over to his mother's house for dinner . . . yet only a few weeks before he died, she discovered he'd kept a mistress and had had a baby by her."

Lapine quickly wrote a first act, abandoning the notion of a nonlinear work. He determined that some kind of story line from the first act must be carried to the second act, or there would be no focus. And so, using the painter's life as inspiration, he wrote an entirely fictitious work.

The first act follows Seurat, an obsessive artist, who is doing a painting of a group of people who are relaxing on their days off in the park of La Grande Jatte. With little time for personal relationships, he ignores Dot, his mistress, who subsequently goes off with a pastry baker to start a new life in America, leaving the artist alone with his work. The first act begins with a blank canvas and ends with a tableau of the creation of his masterpiece. The second act jumps one hundred years: Seurat's great-grandson, George, an American sculptor of light machines, is struggling in the contemporary art world and is unable to unblock his creative path. The show ends when he visits the island of La Grande Jatte, where Dot reappears, helping the new George to put his life together and to "move on."

While Lapine wrote, Sondheim waited.

"I was really dubious," Lapine recalls. "I thought, 'Why isn't he ever writing any music?' I write very skeletally and very quickly. I sketch it in and then fill it out. Steve is very different: I mean, Steve tends to complete and polish a song before he ever wants anybody to hear it. And I tend to just sort of put anything out there.''

Lapine contacted Playwrights Horizons, an off-Broadway nonprofit organization dedicated to supporting the work of promising playwrights. Earlier, Lapine had directed *March of the Falsettos* for them, and at that time was the recipient of a commission for a new work that he owed them. *Sunday in the Park with George* would fulfill that obligation.

To allow Sondheim a chance to find the tone for the score, a small group of actors was hired and a reading of Lapine's first act was scheduled.

"The reading was very helpful,'' says Andre Bishop, artistic director of Playwrights Horizons, "because Lapine writes in a very elliptical way. . . . I think a lot of his plays are really blueprints for what they're going to be on stage. He's the only writer I know who really should direct his own work. Things that seem to be very simple and almost naïve and crude on paper, seem extremely evocative and also very funny on stage. And I

Mandy Patinkin as Georges finishes the hat in *Sunday in the Park with George*, 1984. (MARTHA SWOPE)

think the reading was very helpful for Steve. I think he suddenly figured out what the score should sound like."

Later, as the work developed further, there was another reading, only this time there were two acts and five songs. It was at that point that they decided they were ready for a full workshop; Sondheim's first foray into the off-Broadway experimental arena.

Lapine suggested Mandy Patinkin for the part of George; but since Sondheim was writing the role for a baritone, he was somewhat dubious. Then Lapine brought Patinkin in to audition and had him sing one of the songs for Seurat, and Sondheim was overwhelmed. He happily adjusted the songs to suit Patinkin's voice. "Mandy has a wide tessitura, both top and bottom," Sondheim says. "It's an extraordinary voice with a working two-octave range."

Lapine: "When it came to casting Dot, I thought of Bernadette Peters and I never in a million years thought she would do it because we had only a sketch to show her. I mean, it was just thirty pages of the first act with one song. I was shocked that she said yes immediately, but she just loved the material."

"What is going to be the hottest ticket in town this summer?" queried the "Broadway" column in the *New York Times* of June 17, 1983. "The obvious answer is *Cats*. But not during the three-week period from July 9 to 30. That is when *Sunday in the Park with George* will make a fleeting appearance at Playwrights Horizons. The musical, which has a cast led by Bernadette Peters and Mandy Patinkin, will be staged as a workshop and is supposed to be open to subscribers only. But inevitably there will be outstanding displays of creativity as others devise ingenious schemes to get in. . . . 'This is not a way station to Broadway,' says Sondheim. . . . 'It is a work in progress. We want to take a look at it and let it determine its own future course.' "

With the announcement of the new production came a barrage of gossip regarding Sondheim's apparent "breakup" with his longtime collaborator Harold Prince. The talk centered around "irrevocable damage" to their working relationship due to the monumental failure of *Merrily We Roll Along*.

Sondheim: "Public perception is difficult because there's nothing you can do about it. The fact that Hal's worked with dozens of other people never seems to cross people's minds. Suddenly, I do a show with somebody else, and everybody says, 'What is that?' "

Lapine: "I feel for Steve and Hal . . . that people were making such a big deal of it, because I don't know that *they* made such a big deal of it. I don't think it was—from what I could tell—such a major thing for them. I think Hal obviously has always worked with other people. And Stephen hasn't, but then Stephen hasn't written that much.

"We're in a business where they love nothing more than to build you up and tear you down. I think Hal suffered unfortunately from that. I mean the man has made such a contribution to the theater and won such acclaim and been so successful that I think it's too much for some people and they have to strike back. I'm quite sure Steve and Hal will work together again and I think probably successfully. I don't think it's a bad thing at all that they took a break from each other. They're still extremely close and very supportive of each other."

The new collaboration took a little time to settle into, since Lapine's working relationship with Sondheim was so dissimilar to the one Sondheim enjoyed with Prince.

Sondheim: "The main difference between Jim and Hal is generational. So not only are the methodologies different, but also the temperaments. Hal is my age, we've had a more than thirty-five-year collaboration, and it's something of a marriage. Hal is ebullient, outgoing. Jim is twenty years younger and quiet, soft-spoken. He comes from an off-Broadway background where there is a different way of working and there's more of a community feeling; everybody feels much more like a family—closer, actually, to the experience you have in a school play. And Jim was a photographer and an artist who became a writer and a director, and Hal was a stage manager who became a producer and then a director. They are from different disciplines."

Lapine: "I think probably one of the biggest shocks for Steve working with me, as opposed to working with Hal, is I'm so laid back. . . . I'm not enthusiastic. I mean I am, but I'm not effusive in any way. Actually, it's gotten in the way sometimes as a director because I'm not one who bounds on the stage and screams, 'Fantastic!'

"In the beginning, Stephen would tell me a lot about how he and Hal worked. A lot of times, I just didn't have the same work habits. But the primary difference, of course, is that I'm the author as well as the director."

As he wrote—slowly—Sondheim attempted to keep his music open and pure, the way the painting was; he wanted it to shimmer. "I was also fiddling with chord clusters," Sondheim says, "because there seemed to me some kind of analogue to Seurat's close juxtaposition of different-colored dots. Another aural equivalent of Seurat's color scheme was repeating motifs and certain key words and phrases. The way the score was constructed was based on the relationship of the two central characters. Theirs is a continuous and continuing love song that isn't completed until the end of the show. In the song 'Sunday in the Park with George,' Dot, in one section, begins a lyrical theme, which is her affection and her love for George. This is picked up later in 'Color and Light,' and it develops and starts to reach a climax, and just at that point, they break off and they speak. Then in 'We Do Not Belong Together' it's picked up and further developed as if it's almost where they left off, and ends with an unrhymed line where she sings, 'I have to move on.' And when their love is finally consummated, which is the end of the second act, it all comes together and becomes a completed song in 'Move On.' 'Move On' is a

Bernadette Peters as Dot sings "Sunday in the Park with George" to her lover, George, 1984. (MARTHA SWOPE)

combination of all the themes involving their relationship, including every harmony and every accompaniment; it's where everything culminates. Only it's over a period of four major scenes covering a hundred years. It's one way of threading the theme through time.

"In its use of motifs, it's actually halfway between *Sweeney* and *Merrily*, in that it's partly developed and partly modular blocks. I made parallels between the two acts: like the whole 'Day Off' sequence, which is in the middle of the first act, parallels the sequence in the art museum in the second act, which becomes the theme in 'Putting It Together.' The theme in 'Putting It Together' is the same tune as 'Finishing the Hat.' So the attempt is to re-use sections of songs to tie both the two centuries and their relationship together."

In writing the score, Sondheim realized that Seurat's specific kind of painting style translated wonderfully into rhythmic music. "The more I found out about him, the more I realized, 'My God, this is all about music.' Seurat experimented with the color wheel the way one experiments with a scale. He used complementary color exactly the way one uses dominant and tonic harmony. When you start thinking about it, there are all kinds of analogues. It seemed effective to use rhythm to reflect putting dots on the canvas, to show his distraction as well as his concentration. But that, of course, becomes motivic, that rhythmic idea. There are two basic rhythms, actually: there's the arpeggiated rolling rhythm that is set up right in the opening arpeggios and eventually becomes 'Finishing the Hat' and the kind of rolling vamp in 'Sunday in the Park with George'; then there's the painter's theme, which is sharp and staccato and jabbed. That, combined with the rolling vamp, becomes 'Move On.' "

Sunday in the Park with George began its first of twenty-five performances at Playwrights Horizons with an incomplete first act. It was only at the end of the second week of its four-week run that Sondheim completed all of his first-act songs. And even then, several of the numbers required rethinking. There were many alterations in "The Day Off" sequence, and a new song, "Gotta Keep 'Em Humming"—which was in the second act for the last three performances at Playwrights—was replaced and eventually turned into a new number, "Putting It Together." A song called "Soldiers and Girls" was cut and replaced by just a fragment, because it appeared to be too big a song for the character of the soldier.

"The original idea was for all the secondary characters to have songs," says Lapine. "What we discovered in the workshop was that people weren't interested in them. They were interested in George and Dot, and we realized that it was very hard to write a 'little' song, because then it became very unsatisfying. So we ended up paring down a lot of the songs in the workshop and making them more like little sketches, as opposed to full-blown moments for the characters, and then putting all our focus on developing the relationship of our two leads."

Lapine wishes in retrospect that the second act had been finished prior to the workshop. "Steve and I were working so closely together and suddenly, because I was the director, I had to leave and go direct the show, and I wasn't able to stay as involved with what he was doing because I was too busy. And it's not that he went off track, but certain things might have been helped if we'd finished all of our work before we started any production of the show."

Bishop: "I think that I should have been more forceful in getting Act Two done because I remember months later, Steve and I were talking and he said, 'Well, you know in musicals, the second act's never as good as the first because people spend more time on the first than the second.' It made me realize that if that work had been done earlier, the show wouldn't have fallen together so late in the game. But we were very much in awe of Steve. I was much more reverential and deferential than I normally am with most of the writers here, and in retrospect, I wonder whether I did the right thing, because Steve wanted to be treated like everyone else. But I was very concerned about not pushing them too hard and allowing them to work together under reasonably nonpressured circumstances."

With the show fairly incomplete and insubstantial, the rehearsal period was fraught with emotional outbursts—especially from Mandy Patinkin.

"We had many conflicts in the beginning," says Patinkin. "I was very testy because I wasn't used to any kind of workshop atmosphere. So I was working for five weeks and sitting on the side, with not many things to sing and not enough of my part written for me to figure out what it was going to be, and getting more and more impatient, and right before we opened to the public, I quit."

Lapine hurriedly called Patinkin and asked him to do the performance that night, urging him to have his wife and his agent in the audience. "He said, 'If they think you should quit,' says Patinkin, 'then go ahead.' And I did what he asked and we went out to dinner afterward and my friends all told me that I should stay. And I said, 'Okay, okay, I'm just crazy and nervous, but I'll stay with it.' And my relationship with Jim went from thinking that he didn't know a thing about what he was doing in the beginning to the point where I thought he was one of the best directors I had ever worked with.

"But you have to understand that a few days later, Steve wrote 'Finishing the Hat.' How did I know he'd come up with a song like that? I was standing around, waiting for a song to be written and going absolutely crazy. I didn't know what the hell the guy was going to do. It was very frustrating. But once that happened, I started to recognize, okay, this is the way this guy works—he takes his time, he needs the pressure, but he's going to come up with some amazing stuff . . . and I'll just shut up and serve him as best I can."

At another workshop performance where Patinkin as George was doing a scene with his mother, he was so pent up and frustrated that he broke down and cried. "It was where Steve had written only her half of our duet called 'Beautiful.' And we had people coming to see this very unfinished piece and I hadn't yet given in to the idea that we were doing a workshop with people paying money. . . . It seemed a little incongruous to me. And I blew off some steam and Steve came up to me and said, 'I'm getting ready to start writing your part of the song, could I pick your brain a little . . . can I call you?' And I said, 'Sure.' And he did, and we talked for two or three hours . . . and it had to do with a lot of feelings that we shared, having to do with people that you love, things you'd like to say to them, ideal states of when you can communicate and when that communication can never take place again. It was one of the most incredible conversations I had ever had with anybody. And four days later, he came in with this conversation turned into a poem called 'Beautiful,' set to this simple, gorgeous music."

Reproducing Seurat's *Bathing at Asnieres*, Tony Straiges's scenic design included a combination of painting and live actors, 1984. (MARTHA SWOPE)

Although only the first act was being performed, the second act of the play was written in skeletal form. An early version followed incidents in the painting's history as it moved from France to the Art Institute in Chicago, where it is currently on view. Other ideas included a second act in which different aspects of art would be explored in the style of a musical revue. Both were rejected early on.

Sondheim: "Before the workshop was over, we did the last three performances with the second act of the book and two songs. The shape of the second act was exactly what we ended up with later on. The one difference was that at Playwrights, George was not a light sculptor (working with

Mary D'Arcy as Celeste #2, Robert Westenberg as the Soldier, Melanie Vaughn as Celeste #1 and the cardboard pop-up of the Soldier, display Tony Straiges's design concept of combining live actors with inanimate pieces of art, 1984. (MARTHA SWOPE)

projections and lasers), he was a performance artist; and that was scream-
ingly funny, but we worried about it making him out to be a fool. So we
changed that. Also, at one point we were going to go back to the Fifties.
We even had a little boy in the cast to play George in 1953, but we never
put that in."

Lapine: "Part of the problem was the wealth of things we wanted to
say. When I saw the show up on the stage, I thought that it was about
too many things. We were trying to say too much. . . . We needed to
cut it way down."

Because there was a limited budget, the show became part of the regular
Playwrights workshop series, so each night subscriber audiences got to see
it in progress.

Lapine: "I had originally thought, 'Oh, well, it will be a lot of ladies
from Queens—just a lot of regular people.' But usually half of the 150
people were all the taste makers of New York, who managed to get tickets
. . . which is not the audience you want to face in this rough state."

Meanwhile, an ongoing and persistent debate raged: should the first act
be expanded and there be no second act? Or, if there was to be a second
half, how organic and relevant would it be to the first half?

"A lot of people felt that the first act was a perfect evening," says Andre
Bishop. "Some felt that they shouldn't bother with Act Two. I even think
the two of them were a little nervous. What they tried to do was very
hard—to start all over again in the second act with a new hero—and how
much could we care about him and his problems when you've only got
fifty minutes to do it? But I was very much pushing for Act Two, because
I felt emotionally the appeal of the show was in the second half, more
than in the first."

Lapine: "We had a bad rap. A lot of people were pooh-poohing the
second act. I love the second act and I think you wouldn't like the first
act as much ultimately if you didn't see the second, because it puts it in
an even stronger perspective. We really wanted the first act to be about
the making of a painting and the second act to be about the life of a
painting.

"After the workshop, a few people who saw both acts said, 'Why don't
you just do the first act stuff and expand it or put a Follies number in it?'
But that wasn't the show we wanted to write. I'm sure a lot of people
would have been happier if we did."

Six months after the close of the workshop, after much discussion, it
was decided that *Sunday* would indeed move on. The *New York Times*

"Broadway" column of January 13, 1984, announced the plans: "When *Sunday in the Park with George* was being developed last summer in a top-secret workshop at Playwrights Horizons, there was little doubt that the show would turn up on Broadway this season. It was just a question of when and where. All that has now been answered . . . [the show] will open April 22 at the Booth Theatre. . . . The producers are the Shubert Organization, Emanuel Azenberg and Playwrights Horizons."

Although there was originally much speculation that the show might move to an off-Broadway house, the producers could not figure out a way to make it sustain itself financially in such an arrangement. But whether the show would be able to make it financially at a small Broadway house and whether it was the kind of show Broadway audiences would flock to remained to be seen.

"I was quite nervous about going to Broadway, I have to admit," says Andre Bishop. "It was not clear what would happen. We were very mixed because we felt it was a very special show."

With some additional time to prepare for his role, Patinkin took classes at the Art Students League, watched documentaries, read books, and even flew to Chicago twice to see the original painting, where he spent a total of seven hours staring at Seurat's masterpiece. "I talked to it," says Patinkin, "and I listened to people talking about it. I got up on a chair and looked to see the red and the blue and the hat and I tried to see where the yellow flecks were, so that I could create it on stage correctly. I also did the whole first act of the play in front of it, talking to the different people in the painting. I felt I was him . . . or his ghost."

"I think the actors were very vocal in pushing for more exploration of the characters," says Ira Weitzman, musical theater program director of Playwrights Horizons. "After the workshop, it was clear that Bernadette would not go on with the show without that exploration—which is not to say that they wouldn't have written it anyway, but I think a lot of it —with Bernadette and Mandy questioning Jim and Steve so much— influenced the writing quite a bit."

"When we were in rehearsals for the Broadway production," recalls Bernadette Peters, "I had many concerns. I thought that the character of Dot wasn't strong enough. If George was such a defined character and if they had this very deep connection in their relationship, then she needed to be a much stronger person. 'We Do Not Belong Together' was originally more of a duet, but Steve realized that this was a mistake: you didn't hear enough of the woman's point of view in this relationship, otherwise

she would just be one of those other women that he sings about in 'Finishing the Hat.' So the number was refocused to carry Dot's emotions. The song, even more strongly, shows how Dot makes a decision and resolves within herself that they do not belong together, even though they *do* belong together."

Sondheim found himself, for the first time, without the contributions of his brilliant orchestrator Jonathan Tunick, who was then devoting himself to composing. Michael Starobin, the talented orchestrator of

Mandy Patinkin as the contemporary George and Bernadette Peters as Dot in *Sunday in the Park with George*, 1984. (MARTHA SWOPE)

March of the Falsettos, which Lapine had directed, and who first worked with Sondheim as one of the three musicians playing for the workshop of *Sunday*, inherited Tunick's role as orchestrator.

"Steve had definite ideas of what his music was about and how it should be presented," Starobin says. "There are some songwriters you work with where the songs need some help and you're sometimes even changing accompaniment figures or the structure. Steve, on the contrary, writes his own accompaniment figures, so he's asking you to support the ideas that he's already put down.

"The only number that I had trouble with was the opening number, because it was more musical theater than a lot of the rest of the show and I didn't know what to make of it. But he said that that was exactly what he was trying to do, that it was supposed to be musical comedy to warm the audience up, so they're not nervous, thinking they're in for a heavy artistic piece . . . that there was going to be humor in the show and there was going to be melody."

Musical director Paul Gemignani faced many frustrations in "casting" his pit musicians. "It's a very difficult score," says Gemignani. "There were eleven pieces in the orchestra and I had six or seven people coming in and looking at the parts and deciding they didn't want to play it. It was too difficult for them. I mean, every turn of the page was more complicated. It is rhythmically intense and there's less left to the imagination, in the sense that everything is written out. It's a puzzle. For instance, the opening sequence is a son of a bitch because the chords have to come on the movement of the trees in the set."

The Shuberts, anxious to accommodate Sondheim's requirements, ripped out a row of seats in the Booth Theatre to get at the orchestra pit. A wall was torn down to accommodate the moving of a grand piano into the pit, and the stage had to be plowed under for Tony Straiges's dazzling set, which used "pop-ups" of scenic elements that came up through the stage floor.

At the first preview on Broadway the first act ran an hour and forty-four minutes, and Lapine immediately trimmed twenty minutes out of it with shaping and pacing. Even then, the show had many other problems and the audience was extremely impatient.

Lapine: "My biggest shock was the Broadway theatergoing audience. When you go to an off-Broadway show, you almost expect something different. Broadway people, I found—particularly theater parties going to musicals—were expecting opening numbers and dance numbers and that kind of tits-and-ass stuff that now is very much what Broadway musicals are all about. So after the first few performances, where the stalwarts came and went, the theater parties came and hated it. They'd sit there stone-faced and start getting up and walking out and talking and I was in a state of shock. I couldn't believe it . . . because I thought it was going fine. I knew what the show needed—and we were working on it— but I had no sense of any danger in that regard. The actors began to get discouraged, and I was fighting to just let everybody know that this was still the show we wanted to do and we weren't going to tailor it to the taste of these people."

Sondheim: "For the audience, it's wonderful to be intrigued in the theater, but it's just awful to feel baffled. It's finding that line where everything isn't exactly explained, and yet it doesn't rouse hostility in the audience because they're confused."

Bishop: "The preview period was terrible, with so many theater parties booked in, and they were just hideous and hateful and should all have been shot. It was very hard sitting there watching them all stream down the aisles. And they're usually people who don't like the theater anyway, much less something like this."

The *New York Times*, April 10, 1984, reported that *Sunday* had postponed its opening from April 23 to May 2 because Stephen Sondheim was writing some new material.

"There were two missing songs," says Sondheim, "and I knew what they were going to be about but I just couldn't write them. I had a lot of trouble . . . and no one would believe what a big difference it would make to the show, except for Jim."

Patinkin: "Many of us felt, let's just do the first act. On the other hand, when we talked about the second act, I would write essays to both Steve and Jim about what I thought was needed . . . and no one ever disagreed. It was awful because I knew that by the middle of the second act we didn't have a show—and that was coloring my whole first act. The show was deteriorating as we went on and I just couldn't deal with that. So I not only performed an incomplete second act, but I didn't feel I did a very good job in the first act because I didn't have the life. My spirit was dying.

"One night in the dressing room, I said to Steve, 'Please, I beg you, just write the songs, write anything for these two places, even if it's shit.' And I was trying to read his thoughts and I felt that he was saying, 'I have to do it my way, and if it's going to take time, and if I don't get it

Mandy Patinkin and Bernadette Peters perform "Move On" during the recording session of *Sunday in the Park with George*, 1984 (PETER CUNNINGHAM/ RCA RECORDS)

done, then I won't get it done.' But he appreciated the fact that I was having a nervous breakdown. And then he went away and wrote 'Lesson #8' and 'Children and Art' and the whole thing came together . . . it was unbelievable. A dramatic change? That's an understatement. I mean, the whole piece, the spirit of the company—it was like a magic trick."

Lapine: " 'Children and Art' went in on a Friday and the critics started coming on Monday. The first night it went in it was electric. That song is so moving and is so much what the show was about. The piece was 99 percent there and it was that final 1 percent that made it all work . . . it just yanked the whole show together."

After two years of painstaking work, *Sunday in the Park with George* opened at the Booth Theatre on May 2, 1984, to divided reviews.

"Personally I was nonplussed, unplussed, and disappointed," wrote Clive Barnes in the *New York Post*. "The difficulty with the show is that —despite the almost superman efforts of its two splendid stars—it simply doesn't sing. . . . But when all is said and sung, the spectacle appreciated, and the performances admired, it might be better to go to the park with anyone than to spend it boringly in the theater with George."

Julius Novick in the *Village Voice* asked, "Is it worth sitting through the eye-filling but boring first hour or so to enjoy the moving despairs and affirmations that then supervene? It was for me. It will not be for everyone."

"*Sunday* is pretty," reported Douglas Watt in the New York *Daily News*. "Trouble is, you can't simply pass on to the next gallery after a bit and take in another show . . . [it] doesn't bear looking at or listening to for very long."

Jack Kroll in *Newsweek* heralded, "Sondheim's score is original even for him. . . . The new collaboration with Lapine may be a promise of exciting things to come. . . . To say that this show breaks new ground is not enough; it also breaks new sky, new water, new flesh and new spirit. . . . That harmless sounding title masks more daring and surprise than the American musical stage has seen in a long time."

And Frank Rich in the *New York Times* declared: "Stephen Sondheim and James Lapine demand that an audience radically change its whole way of looking at the Broadway musical . . . [they] have created an audacious, haunting and in its own personal way, touching work. . . . This protagonist is possibly a double for Mr. Sondheim at his most self-doubting. . . . In keeping with his setting, Mr. Sondheim has written a lovely, wildly inventive score that sometimes remakes the modern French composers whose revolution in music paralleled the post-Impressionists' in art. . . . Look closely at that canvas—or at *Sunday in the Park* itself—and you'll get lost in a sea of floating dots. Stand back and you'll see that this evening's two theater artists, Mr. Sondheim and Mr. Lapine, have woven all those imaginative possibilities into a finished picture with a startling new glow."

Later, Rich, in a *New York Times* Magazine piece, further proclaimed: "*Sunday* is at once a culmination of past musical theater innovations and a rejection of them. . . . *Sunday* is a watershed event."

Lapine: "When all the reviews said that the show was so inventive for Broadway, I was shocked. Because I thought, 'My God, if this was done at the Public Theatre nobody would blink an eye.' I thought, 'This is odd, because I didn't feel I'd done anything that I wouldn't have done anywhere else I would work.'

"After we opened, people still walked out. But we found an audience.

A lot of people who come to Broadway come not to work. They come to forget. And that's not what *Sunday* is about. If you just sit back and watch, you're probably going to get bored. You have to really listen. And you have to think. Not a lot, but you can't let it wash over you like certain other shows.

"I don't read reviews generally, but when the Shuberts told me that there were so many pans, I was in a state of shock. I thought, 'Okay if they have mixed feelings about it, but pans?' I do think the show is hard to get the first time. It has a lot of layers and we labored over every moment of it. Stephen and I choose our words very carefully. It wasn't banged out."

With the majority of reviews on the negative side, *Sunday* still had a rather successful run because of the all-out support of the *New York Times*. Recognizing its quality, the newspaper adopted the show and covered it extensively. "Sondheimania Grips *N.Y. Times*; *Sunday* Plugs Keep on

The cast of *Sunday in the Park with George* during the first-act finale "Sunday," 1984. (MARTHA SWOPE)

Coming," read the headline in *Variety*, pinpointing a slew of *Times* features and articles. (Broadway competitors, quite bitter about the abundant coverage, cynically dubbed the show *Sunday in the Times with George.*)

Sunday received ten Tony nominations that year, losing all but two—for Tony Straiges's set and Richard Nelson's lighting. The big winner was *La Cage aux Folles.* The ceremony took on an unusually acrimonious tone when it became a battle for recognition between two different styles of musicals, contrasted by the work of Stephen Sondheim and that of Jerry Herman.

"This award," Herman declared, accepting his trophy for Best Score, "forever shatters a myth about the musical theater. There's been a rumor around for a couple of years, that the simple, hummable show tune was no longer welcome on Broadway. Well, it's alive and well at the Palace!"

"One of the most frustrating evenings of my life," says Bernard Jacobs, co-producer of *Sunday*, "was the night of the Tony Awards, when the *La Cage aux Folles* people got up and talked about hummable music . . . like Steve's music's not hummable. Steve is not only melodious, but he understands word structure in a way that nobody does. . . . He is one of the great poets in the history of the English language."

Although the show did not do well at the Tonys, in April 1985 *Sunday* received the coveted Pulitzer Prize for Drama.

"Winning the Pulitzer Prize was wonderful, but it normally has little impact on theater business," says Jacobs. "Had it won the Tony Award, it would still be running. And it's kind of a disgrace that it lost the Tony to a show that's nowhere its equal. Unfortunately the show only got a few great reviews. Had the other critics been intelligent enough to understand what *Sunday* was about, it would have helped enormously. But there was not enough cumulative support from the critical community for the show other than the *New York Times* and a few others, largely due to the fact that the critics don't have sufficient taste or intelligence.

"I think there is a reflection between Seurat's acceptance and Steve's. . . . I think it's part of the reason he did that piece. My guess is that it's his reflection of his own place in the world. In my opinion, there's going to be a bigger audience for Sondheim fifty years from now than there is today. It may be his work is for its time, but the number of people who appreciate it will always be limited."

Bishop: "I took my aunt to see the show about two months before it closed. And she's not a theatergoer, but she's sensitive. And she loves art, but she doesn't know very much about it. And at the end of the first act she burst into tears and she said, 'I don't know why I'm crying, but there's something about it, the beauty of it, and the coming together of life in this beautiful way, that is very meaningful to me.'

"I found a lot of younger people identified with the show. They related to the guy who was sort of lost and not knowing what to do with his life."

Lapine: "What I really love in the theater is for the audience to put it together themselves. And, of course, this gets criticized a lot. Each member of the audience sees what he wants to see. A good example was when Michael Bennett said to me, 'Gee, I always assumed George was dying all through the first act and that's why he behaves the way he does.' Now I never wrote it that way, but when he said that, I thought, 'God, that's really an interesting way to look at it.' It makes sense when you suddenly hear in the second act that he died at thirty-one; you say, 'Well, I see. That's why he pushed her away, because he knew he was dying.' "

"I always knew the show would be limited," says Bernard Jacobs; "that's why we did it in the Booth and not the Majestic. We negotiated a unique economic formula for the show so that had its audiences been broader, it would have been successful in the smaller Broadway theater, and it would have paid back. As it was, I think for the kind of show it was, it did reasonably well."

"I never thought it would fail, but I always wondered who the audience would be for it and who would relate to it," says Ira Weitzman. "I think, in some cases, musical theater is moving in the direction that plays have always been going—a more personal expression on the part of the writers. There may be less mass appeal, but I think this show's typical of this new kind of expression."

Sunday in the Park with George closed on Broadway after 540 performances, losing one-fourth of its $2.4 million investment. It was a unique theatrical effort that introduced Sondheim to a brand-new team of collaborators and an entirely different style of working in the theater. Many believe it was also a major emotional breakthrough in his writing.

Jacobs: "I think it was a wonderful experience for Steve. . . . I think he was a much more emancipated, creative person on this show. That doesn't mean that Steve should not work with Hal again. It just means that the idea of working in a different atmosphere, I think, helped Steve grow enormously."

"I care a lot about art and the artist," admits Sondheim. "The major thing I wanted to do in the show was to enable anyone who is not an artist to understand what hard work art is. You can't tell why a show is success-

ful or not. But I think one of the reasons this one did fairly well was that it created a world. . . . You just wanted to live in that park forever and ever, which is part of the point of the play. It became mesmeric . . . so the audience success had to do with a willingness to know that it was all going to be a little strange, and then realizing they'd fallen into an enchanted world. *Sunday* was a world on a stage."

George Seurat observes his finished masterpiece, *A Sunday Afternoon on the Island of La Grande Jatte*, in *Sunday in the Park with George*, 1984. (MARTHA SWOPE)

Above (from left): *Follies in Concert* director Herbert Ross, musical director Paul Gemignani, pianist Paul Ford, Carol Burnett, and Stephen Sondheim at rehearsal, 1985. (DON PERDUE)

Right: Elaine Stritch rehearses "Broadway Baby" while Liliane Montevecchi looks on during preparation for *Follies in Concert*, 1985. (DON PERDUE)

ONE LAST LOOK AT · · · 27
WHERE IT ALL BEGAN

THE IMPULSE started with Theodore Chapin, the managing director for the Rodgers and Hammerstein office, who was trying to figure out a plan to justify the re-recording of *Follies*. (Chapin was an observer on the original *Follies*.) One day Chapin suggested to Thomas Z. Shepard at RCA Records that they put together a new studio recording.

Along with throngs of theater enthusiasts, Shepard had always been disheartened that the original Broadway cast recording was incoherently compressed onto one disc, poorly produced, with some songs abridged and others cut entirely. Although he had always dreamed of re-recording *Follies*, and was trying to figure out a plan himself, he felt that the lack of rehearsal time and the prohibitive cost of the budget would make a studio recording virtually impossible. Instead, Shepard suggested that they throw a benefit concert, on the order of *Sondheim: A Musical Tribute,* and perhaps include the New York Philharmonic.

With Sondheim's approval and encouragement, Shepard and Chapin went to the Philharmonic with a proposal to include them in the recording of a live concert event. The plan was accepted and casting immediately began, with Shepard himself serving as producer.

From the start, Sondheim requested Barbara Cook, Lee Remick, Mandy Patinkin, and George Hearn for the four leads. He also suggested getting Arthur Rubin, an ex-Broadway tenor and current vice-president of the Nederlander Organization, to sing "Beautiful Girls." Elaine Stritch was considered for one of several numbers, including "I'm Still Here" and

George Hearn performs "Live, Laugh, Love" as Daisy Prince looks on during *Follies in Concert* rehearsal, 1985. (DON PERDUE)

"Who's That Woman?" before she was chosen to perform "Broadway Baby." Carol Burnett was asked to do "I'm Still Here."

After first accepting, Barbara Cook at one point withdrew. "She had constructed a one-woman show," says Shepard, "and she had a firm booking that she could not work around. And what finally brought her back to us was that somehow that firm booking fell out, and, at the time, we had not been successful in replacing her. If we hadn't had her it would have been our greatest disappointment. There is still only one Barbara Cook. And she brought something to this concert that is inexpressible."

Soon, the rest of the cast began to fall into place: Betty Comden and Adolph Green would sing "Rain on the Roof," Liliane Montevecchi would do "Ah, Paree!" and Phyllis Newman would perform "Who's That Woman?" An inspired and moving addition to the company was Licia Albanese, a former Met star for twenty-seven seasons, who joined Erie Mills, a soprano who starred in the New York City Opera's revival of *Candide*, to sing "One More Kiss." With Jim Walton, Howard McGillin, Liz Callaway, and Daisy Prince filling in the younger roles, the production —with its renowned cast from the worlds of theater, movies, television, and opera—began moving forward with great momentum.

But not without its share of confusion.

"I got a letter from Stephen," says Carol Burnett, "asking if I would do the 'recording' of *Follies* and I immediately fired back a yes. And there was a while when a lot of my correspondence from Tom Shepard's office with further details of the session was at my agent's office being held for me. One evening I was having dinner in New York with Beverly Sills, and she said, 'Oh, I'm going to come see you when you do *Follies*.' And I said, 'Oh?' And I pictured her coming into a recording booth. I believed that the plan was to go into a studio for two days and record the album. And she said, 'Dear, it's a concert.' And I said, 'Pardon me? You mean, in front of people? A performance?' And I got really frantic. I was a wreck. I just hadn't realized we were going to do it live in front of an audience."

A decision needed to be reached about the presentation of the concert, which prompted a discussion about the kind of person who would best be able to stage it. "We didn't approach any director for the show until late in the game," says Shepard. "I was unclear as to what degree this show ought to be staged. My original feeling was that people would basically enter and exit and that the material would carry it. But as we got closer to the concert it seemed more and more imperative that this needed some kind of really professional stage director. And Steve said—and he was right—that we needed somebody with enough clout that when you got this group of stars together they would listen to him.

"Steve went to Michael Bennett and he agreed to stage the show. Michael had some extremely interesting concepts, but I think he was a bit frustrated because some of the things that he wanted to do were

Director Herbert Ross teaches Lee Remick her dance routine for "The Story of Lucy and Jessie," *Follies in Concert*, 1985. (DON PERDUE)

considered almost unaffordable or unmanageable, given the amount of time and money we had."

Sondheim: "Michael's plans were so elaborate and at the time, with his plans to direct *Chess* pressing in on him, he decided it was just too much. And he didn't want to do something simple because that would not have been fun for him."

With Bennett's departure, Sondheim discussed *Follies in Concert* with Herbert Ross while he was in Los Angeles working on *The Broadway Album* with Barbra Streisand.

"He sent me the material," says Ross, "and what I did was sort of give it some form. Steve did all the continuity for the musical sequences, which followed the narrative. And I edited the book way, way down so that Jim Goldman could write the minimal amount of narration and dialogue necessary to convey the dramatic ideas behind the songs.

"I wanted to use the impresario, the Weismann character [played by André Gregory] as a hook to start the evening. And then I asked Steve to change the ending. I never liked the kind of hopelessness of the show's finale. . . . I think you never really believed that the death of the theater was a sort of symbol for the death of these people's lives. My view of it was that this was a celebration, and the original ending was too downbeat and not appropriate for this event."

Ross next engaged the services of choreographer Danny Daniels, who had choreographed his film *Pennies from Heaven*, to create a tap sequence for "Who's That Woman?" and to stage the women's entrances in "Beautiful Girls."

The moment the tickets for *Follies in Concert* went on sale, there was an unexpected uproar at the box office. Samuel G. Freedman reflected in the *New York Times* on September 1, 1985: "All this activity suggests that both critics and audiences are catching up to Mr. Sondheim, changing his status from an innovator with a cult following to a more mainstream, if still uncompromising, artist. The commercial response to the *Follies* concert indicates as much: all 5,500 tickets sold out in two hours and fifty-one minutes."

Ross: "I had no idea that there would be that much interest in the material and that the score was as celebrated as it was. I also didn't know there was this cult that absolutely worshiped the show. But I was very divorced from the play. It was all about trying to celebrate the music.

"My main concern was that we were limited in terms of staging. We had to keep it visually interesting to accommodate the needs of the spec-

Betty Comden and Adolph Green perform "Rain on the Roof" at the concert performance of *Follies*, 1985. (MARTHA SWOPE)

tator and we had to observe a system of microphoning in order that it be recorded properly."

In the midst of the elation, a chilling turn of events transpired that threw a damper on the proceedings. Harry Haun, in the *Daily News* of August 15, 1985, revealed: "RCA Records decided, on second thought, *not* to record the all-star New York Philharmonic concert version of *Follies*. Seems the box set of Sondheim the company released last spring [*A Collector's Sondheim*] hasn't been selling all that well, and that little fact prompted the pull out."

Trims were made in the concert's budget, and Shepard agreed to waive his entire advance in favor of a higher royalty rate, but the record company still resisted. (A *month* after its subsequent release the album was already in profit.)

"I reached a point," says Shepard, who was not only producer of the pending album but producer of the entire event, "where it became clear that although RCA would fire me if I made this record for another company, I knew the record had to be made no matter what. I was shocked, I felt my credibility in the business—as a man who could deliver—had been absolutely destroyed. There was a feeling of embarrassment. It was an unavoidable conclusion that this concert was going to be a landmark. And Tommy Valando [Sondheim's music publisher] and I took an active role in persuading everyone to reconsider this decision."

Three weeks before the concert, Shepard had a showdown, putting his job on the line, and his record company relented. "It didn't belong at another record company," he says. "It belonged at RCA. It was against the best interests of my company *not* to have this show. In the end, Bob Summer understood and agreed, and he was absolutely delighted because he saw how much it meant to me. He saw that I knew I had something worth fighting for, and he admired that, so it had a very happy ending for everyone concerned." (Soon after the release of the album, Shepard resigned and went to MCA Records.)

The rehearsal period for *Follies in Concert* was nerve-racking and intense, fraught with constant difficulties and anxieties.

"The time was very short," says Paul Gemignani, "and the orchestra was fairly unfamiliar with this kind of stuff. I had to work quickly and hard to get them to play at the level that we all know they can play at."

"The *Follies* songs are not rangy and difficult like the songs from *Anyone Can Whistle*," explained Lee Remick, "but 'Could I Leave You?' is an acting song, so it was difficult to find a balance. 'Lucy and Jessie' was difficult because of the words, the puzzle of trying to find a way to commit them to memory; because if you get lost with one word, you've had it. I think it was the most nervous I've ever been. But we were all joined at the hip by the end of it. Everybody wanted to take it on the road."

"I have such admiration for Lee Remick," says Paul Lazarus, who served as assistant director. "The first day of rehearsal, I thought she wasn't going to make it. I thought we were in desperate trouble and that she was miscast. I really didn't think she had enough singing skill, but she worked with a vocal coach for nearly four hours a day, and with Herbert helping her with some physical things, she managed to pull it off wonderfully."

Mandy Patinkin, who was rehearsing for the concert and concurrently starring in *Sunday in the Park with George*, had great difficulty making "Buddy's Blues" work.

Mandy Patinkin in a tour de force vaudeville turn performs "Buddy's Blues" during *Follies in Concert*, 1985. (DON PERDUE)

Carol Burnett sings "I'm Still Here" during *Follies in Concert*, 1985. (MARTHA SWOPE)

Opposite: Barbara Cook sings "Losing My Mind" at the performance of *Follies in Concert*, 1985. (DON PERDUE)

Patinkin: "I had tried the song out at different occasions with many different people playing the two women in the number, and it never was good enough. Then one day when I was working on it at home, I was performing it in front of the mirror and I was imitating the girls singing it with me—and suddenly it dawned on me, 'Wait a minute, the women are supposed to be in his head, why don't I do them all and play all the parts?' So I decided to pull out all the stops and make it a total vaudeville. And I told Paul Gemignani, 'If they don't like this they're going to have to get somebody else to sing it because this is the only way I can make it work.' And we were petrified. But we auditioned it for Steve and Herb and they loved it."

Ross: "I had wanted Carol Burnett and Elaine Stritch to do the number with him, but when I saw what he had done with it I almost fell over."

Patinkin: "But then Herb had Danny Daniels help me clean it up, and I was so busy trying to make it better, it made me unable to do the number at all. Herb came up to me and said, 'You've ruined it. What are you doing? Just do the number like before . . . do it like you used to do it.' And then I thought I wouldn't ever be able to do it again. I had a major anxiety attack . . . but it all came back to me."

"The cast was so wonderful to work with," says Paul Lazarus. "And Elaine Stritch, in particular, was so funny. She has such a large personality, she can overwhelm you. We were rehearsing one day in this very tight little chorus room at the Philharmonic. Herb and I were literally right up to the performer's faces while they were singing, and everybody else was crammed in at the sides. And I looked around and the chorus people were laughing, and Phyllis Newman and Lee Remick were just hysterical . . . which made no sense, because in the middle of the room, Barbara Cook and George Hearn were passionately singing 'Too Many Mornings.' And I couldn't figure out what was going on. Well, what was happening was, at the other end of the room, Elaine Stritch was taking off all her clothes and putting on her tights . . . her number was coming up and she wanted to be able to dance. So there she was running around

Barbara Cook (left) and Lee Remick sing "Waiting for the Girls Upstairs" at the *Follies in Concert* performance, 1985. (MARTHA SWOPE)

bare ass. And believe me, with Elaine Stritch, the phrase 'letting it all hang out' has new meaning."

One of the most anticipated performances of the concert was that of Barbara Cook, back to singing a theater score again after many years of touring in clubs and concert halls. Performing a song that was considered a throwaway in the original *Follies*, Cook turned "In Buddy's Eyes" into a harrowing performance that was not only a surprise but one of the concert's highlights.

"Doing 'In Buddy's Eyes' was a great experience. In a way this song is a lie. The character is trying to convince herself that all this idyllic stuff that she is singing about is really true, though she doesn't really believe it. But I decided to perform the song as if she meant every word of it . . . from the bottom of her heart."

"Barbara Cook is the most extraordinary artist," says Ross. "It was the most perfect marriage of her particular vocal quality and the demands of the song. I'll never forget the first time she did it—however good it was

Phyllis Newman (center) flanked by (from left) Liliane Montevecchi, Betty Comden, Elaine Stritch, Lee Remick, and Barbara Cook in the *Follies* production number "Who's That Woman?" in 1985. (MARTHA SWOPE)

Another reunion occurred at the *Follies in Concert* gala benefit: the show's original co-directors Michael Bennett and Harold Prince, 1985. (© HENRY GROSSMAN)

in concert, it was never better than the first day that I heard it in rehearsal."

Cook: "The concert was a very important thing for me to have done personally. It was a very emotional experience . . . it opened us up to a lot of feelings. And it was also so wonderful getting the opportunity to work with Herb again. We were really like children starting out together. We worked together a lot in the past and we've known each other through all the years, and all the ups and downs. We have lots of memories together. And we hadn't seen each other for a long time until the first day of rehearsal. And at one point we had stopped, and we were sitting around waiting for the rehearsal to continue, and Herb and I were sitting directly across from one another in the rehearsal hall and we just stared at one another. . . . I had been thinking about the old days and all that has happened. And he was looking at me, and I knew he was thinking about those years—and we just started crying. We didn't say a word, we each knew what the other was thinking . . . and we walked over and hugged each other and cried, and then we sat down and continued with the rehearsal."

"Herb Ross was quite terrific taking into consideration that this was primarily a recording session," says Shepard. "His staging had to acknowledge that constantly. The performers really had to stay close and swallow the mikes. We couldn't crank them open too far or else we'd get too much orchestra into them. The sound turned out so well it's hard to believe it's a live event.

"In the dress rehearsals I got all the codas without applause and all intros without dialogue lead-ins. As luck would have it, there turned out to be large stretches of performance from that dress rehearsal which wound up in the final recording, so it's a goddamn good thing that we had it.

"I had always had in mind to treat the record as if I had gone into a recording studio with no applause. But when the orchestra came in and the women came down the stairs, the house exploded . . . the roof came off—and that's when my thinking changed. For me to have left that out of the recording would have negated the event. It became like Judy

Stephen Sondheim is congratulated by Jule Styne after the benefit performance of *Follies in Concert*, 1985. (© HENRY GROSSMAN)

Garland at Carnegie Hall. There was a magic to what happened with that audience. So then I really didn't know what the hell I was going to do. Then I thought maybe I'd put applause at the end of each side break. . . . So we created a semi-consistency: we would use applause after every Follies number, but we would not use applause after most of the expository songs."

At the end of rehearsals, and following the tense dress rehearsal, Ross got an emergency call to return to California. "The truth is that my wife [Nora Kaye] became really ill," says Ross, "and she had to go into the hospital. I thought she would be well enough to join me, but, in fact, she took a turn for the worse. The doctor said it looked serious, and he asked me to come home immediately."

Regretful of missing both concert performances, Ross departed after the dress rehearsal, leaving Paul Lazarus and Danny Daniels to oversee last-minute finishing touches.

On the night of September 7, *Follies in Concert* had its first of two performances at Avery Fisher Hall at Lincoln Center, and the audience reaction was explosive. On stage (and backstage) the individual performers were scared to death.

"When the orchestra started that overture," says George Hearn, "you just wanted to run and hide. It was so terrifying. But then that audience was so loving, it was thrilling."

"The first night we were all so nervous," says Barbara Cook, "I think I did the whole show in a slight daze."

"It was quite a shock," says Mandy Patinkin. "We were backstage and we didn't know what was going on. . . . No one expected anything like that audience reaction. It was just so out of reality."

"When we got to the performance," admits Carol Burnett, "I asked for cue cards because 'I'm Still Here' was such a hard song to learn. But they ended up putting them upstage, so I never could see them anyway. It just made me feel better to know they were there. I don't know if I have ever been so nervous in my life. I was just so happy I didn't blow a lyric. That's all I cared about."

Although the evening ran pretty much as hoped for, there were some performance glitches. Liliane Montevecchi was way ahead of the orchestra in singing "Ah Paree!" and Mandy Patinkin lost his way, singing "The Right Girl," and stopped the orchestra and began over again.

Lazarus: "I don't know what happened with Mandy. He was the last person I expected to go up, since he was the most prepared. Something

From left: Stephen Sondheim, Elaine Stritch, and Barbara Cook appear at a record-breaking album-signing party at Barnes & Noble after the release of the *Follies in Concert* live album, 1985. (© HENRY GROSSMAN)

happened and he got off and he realized there was no recovering, so he stopped."

"I was nervous," Patinkin explains, "and I couldn't figure out a way to relax. So I went out to sing 'The Right Girl' and I went blank. I spooked myself into believing that I'd never be good enough for this house. I figured that in a couple of minutes the guys in the white jackets would come and take me away. So I stopped the orchestra and I apologized to the audience, and they applauded, and then I was the most relaxed I can ever remember being . . . and I never had a better time. But I was devastated the minute it was over. I went into shock. It was so intense and then it was gone."

"The Broadway musical theater put on its top hat, white tie and tails," wrote *Variety*, "and took over Avery Fisher Hall for a pair of concert performances of *Follies* that will rank as milestones in the current Era of Sondheim."

Frank Rich reviewed in the *New York Times*: "The thrilling—and possibly historic—New York Philharmonic concert version of *Follies* was also a reunion of sorts, albeit one with a happier ending. . . . It was impossible to separate the fictional show-biz reunion dramatized in *Follies* from the real one unfolding on stage. The audience, more than willing to let the distinction slide, simply erupted into pandemonium. The cheering rarely subsided thereafter, and not without reason. [The] performance made the case that this Broadway musical, like such other initial commercial failures as *Porgy and Bess* and *Candide*, can take its place among our musical theater's very finest achievements."

In a subsequent think piece in the "Arts and Leisure" section of the *New York Times* of September 15, 1985, Rich added: "The emotions that *Follies* touched in its audience last weekend may say as much about how Broadway has changed since 1971 as it does about the merits of the piece. . . . The theater people at Avery Fisher Hall were not unaware of how time and history had at last caught up to the perceptions of *Follies*. The cheering went on and on—in part to honor a restored musical treasure, in part to postpone that painful moment when the visiting ghosts of a glamorous old Broadway would once again disperse."

After filming three rehearsals, one dress rehearsal, and one of its two performances, *Follies in Concert* became a television special for PBS and the BBC, airing on American television on March 14, 1986. While most of the television show consisted of behind-the-scenes documentary footage of the rehearsals, the concert performance itself was relegated to excerpts—creating great unhappiness and criticism.

"Unfortunately on television," wrote Mel Gussow in the *New York Times* of March 9, 1986, "the concert was incomplete . . . reduced to highlights. The cast record of the original Broadway production was criticized for its brevity; a similar charge would be made against the television adaptation. One regret is that the concert did not lead to a complete version on television."

Sondheim: "The problem was that the television broadcast should have been called something that let you know that it wasn't going to be the whole concert. But somehow the labeling led everyone to believe they were going to see the entire thing, so they were all disappointed and outraged. Unfairly, too—if PBS or the BBC could have afforded to shoot the entire concert, they would have."

Follies in Concert, a much-acclaimed album, proved to be a dream come true for Tom Shepard, and for musical-theater enthusiasts. And, after many ups and downs along the way, after fourteen years since its original recording, Stephen Sondheim's wish for a "definitive" *Follies* album became a triumphant reality.

Opposite: At the finale of *Follies in Concert*, Stephen Sondheim joins his illustrious cast for a final bow, 1985. (© HENRY GROSSMAN)

David Kernan (center), with Millicent
Martin (right) and Julie N. McKenzie
(left). Ned Sherrin (far left) directs and
narrates *Side by Side by Sondheim*,
1977. (MARTHA SWOPE)

PERPETUAL ANTICIPATION

28

JEFFREY LONOFF, in his liner notes for a collection of Sondheim's work on RCA Records, declares: "Once an unknown, then a newcomer, he grew to cult figure, to star, to legend. Now he is even more. He's an adjective. Other works are often described as being 'Sondheimesque' or not. His work is the barometer against which everyone else's is measured."

Over the last decade that work has taken many varied and exciting forms. Although today Sondheim has achieved greater popular acceptance than ever before, it is still within a relatively limited arena. And although he is still battling some criticism of coldness in his work, the tide actually began to turn in 1975 in, of all unlikely places, a tiny theater in England (just at the time he was becoming widely known as "songwriter of the year" for Judy Collins's hit record "Send in the Clowns").

It started with David Kernan, then playing Carl-Magnus in the London production of *A Little Night Music*, who was getting bored with his long run and was seeking an extracurricular activity. One day he received a call from Cleo Laine and her husband, John Dankworth, who were looking to book a show in Wavendon as a benefit performance to help raise money for their little country theater. Kernan contacted Ned Sherrin, a frequent collaborator, and suggested to him that they do a revue of the songs of Stephen Sondheim.

"When I wrote to Stephen," says Kernan, "telling him that we wanted to do a compilation of his work, I received a telegram back saying, 'By all means try, but I can't think of anything more boring except possibly the Book of Kells.' "

Late in the summer of 1975, with a cast of Millicent Martin, Julie McKenzie, Kernan, and Ned Sherrin, who narrated and directed the evening, *Side by Side by Sondheim* had its first public performance. It was such a success that it played four additional Sunday dates. Cameron Mackintosh, a young English producer, agreed that the show must go on and decided to present it at the Mermaid Theatre on May 4, 1976; Sondheim agreed to come over and work with the cast.

"What Steve did," says Kernan, "was direct the show, and without a doubt, he's the finest director I've ever had . . . and the cast agreed."

The show ran for eight weeks at capacity and then moved on July 3, 1976, to the larger but still intimate Wyndham Theatre, where it ran for three years.

"Everyone in London was talking about Sondheim," says Kernan. "I think the songs are extraordinary because they are all little one-act plays anyway. They stood on their own, and I think, in a way, they were more palatable in this revue format."

On opening night at the Mermaid, Harold Prince agreed, conditionally, to produce the show on Broadway. "I was very valuable in the most important way," says Prince. "I was able to persuade Actors Equity to let the British people come—and I'm not sure anyone else could have. I had never made an appearance in front of the committee, I don't ask favors, so they'd never seen me in that capacity. I told them that there was no point in bringing this show over unless the British were allowed to come, because the show was American material viewed by another society. I persuaded them by telling them that if it worked, think of the employment it would create throughout the country. If they hadn't agreed I would not have produced it. It needed that glamor. And speaking of glamor, that's the other thing I did. I brought in Florence Klotz. We did new costumes and redesigned it. It did not look good enough in England. It needed that extra component and we gave it that."

But during the course of the move from London to Broadway, Prince and Sondheim had some reservations about the content of the show. "I remember them saying, you really can't sing 'Could I Leave You?' " says Kernan. "Which is a number I made into a sort of homosexual song . . . I gave it that angle. They said that there was no way we could get away with that in New York. Hal also made the point that two people singing 'A Boy Like That' would not work. I was going to bow to their judgment, but I did say, 'Please, you did buy the show as it was done in London and

I would love to try it as it was done, before we make any changes.' And absolutely none were made because it worked like a gem."

The show opened at the Music Box on April 18, 1977, and the critics were boisterous.

"A ravishing musical retrospective," reviewed Douglas Watt in the *Daily News.*

Clive Barnes, in the *New York Times*, proclaimed: "Here is a tiny, multi-faceted gem that lights up Broadway. . . . It is Stephen Sondheim revealed as Stephen Sondheim has never been revealed before. . . . This is a dream of a show . . . happy, funny, witty, and so compassionate. It makes you feel good. Turn cartwheels to the box office for this British celebration of a rare American."

"The one quibble," said Howard Kissel in *Women's Wear Daily*, "was with Sherrin's use of his only male singer, David Kernan, who does several songs expressly written for women, accompanied by subtle, albeit fey, gestures—the first time it works, then it wears. . . . [But] *Side by Side* is enormously entertaining because the English cast is so expert and the material itself is such great theater."

Each of the performers was nominated for a Tony in the featured categories, and the show itself was nominated as Best Musical.

A few months later, the British cast was phased out and replaced by Nancy Dussault, Larry Kert, and Georgia Brown—with Hermione Gingold replacing Ned Sherrin as the narrator. Gingold, in addition to serving as master of ceremonies, sang "I Never Do Anything Twice," the madame's song from the film *The Seven Percent Solution.* On February 22, 1978, the show moved up the block to the now demolished Morosco Theatre and was hosted by Burr Tilstrom and Kukla, Fran, and Ollie; but it closed soon afterward, on March 19, 1978, after a combined total of 384 performances.

As Prince promised Actors Equity, the show spawned many other companies, and many performers appeared in it (including Cyril Ritchard, who opened the Chicago company and collapsed during one matinee and died.)

The success of this musical revue was a turning point in Sondheim's acceptance beyond his cult status. The reviews were almost unanimously favorable. Even those critics who had never shown that much enthusiasm for his work suddenly loved the songs out of context, citing romantic, melodic, hummable tunes.

"It did okay," says Prince, "but that's because it's this hybrid form and people are not into revues very much in the United States. I think it certainly called attention to his music. I think ultimately the show made people look more clearly at his astonishing body of work."

On February 14, 1980, a Broadway revival of *West Side Story*—to some minds long overdue—opened at the Minskoff Theatre. It was directed and choreographed by Jerome Robbins, with the book scenes co-directed by Gerald Freedman, and the reaction was mixed. The production was perceived as soft, the book seemed muted, the performers—with the exception of Debbie Allen—were bland, and the dancing cleaner and less fierce than the original. But this time around Sondheim was not, predictably, ignored the way he was in 1957.

"It was very hard to cast," says Sondheim. "And the result was that the actors came across as clean rather than gritty. There was also the datedness of the social situation that didn't help."

"Among the key actors," said T. E. Kalem in *Time*, "Josie de Guzman brings a radiant innocence to Maria that is quite affecting. Ken Marshall's handsome Tony is more wood than flame, and the incendiary performance is given by Debbie Allen as Bernardo's girlfriend Anita. This woman sizzles like a severed power line. When she dances, sings, and blasts her way through 'America,' the roof of the theater starts to buckle."

John Simon commented in *New York* magazine: "The score by Leonard Bernstein and Stephen Sondheim remains one of the best in musical comedy, arguably the best. With the possible exception of 'Something's Coming,' somewhat conventional and didactic, there is no second-rate number in the entire show, and Bernstein and Sondheim have the advantage of a more sophisticated vocabulary, musical and verbal, than any other composer-lyricist team's in Broadway history."

"An air of quaintness has begun to overtake *West Side Story*," wrote Douglas Watt in the *Daily News*.

"[It] is useful largely as a documentation of how our musical theater has disintegrated in 20-odd years," reviewed Howard Kissel in *Women's Wear Daily*. "All that is lacking are menace and guts. . . . This then is a routine revival."

And Walter Kerr, at that time briefly reviewing theater on a daily basis again for the *New York Times*, theorized: "By some odd metamorphosis, *West Side Story* seems to have grown younger, more innocent, more endearing over the years. Perhaps that's a strange thing to say about a

Above: Debbie Allen as Anita performs "America" in the Broadway revival of *West Side Story*, 1980. (MARTHA SWOPE)

Left: Ken Marshall as Tony and Josie de Guzman as Maria in the Broadway revival of *West Side Story*, 1980. (MARTHA SWOPE)

musical that prides itself on toughness. . . . You'd swear [the characters]
were harmless if Mr. Laurents's libretto didn't tell you otherwise."

The revival of *West Side Story*, with its faithfully re-created Oliver Smith
sets, Irene Sharaff costumes, and Jean Rosenthal lighting, ran 333 performances and recovered only 25 percent of its $800,000 investment. It
received three Tony nominations: one for Best Reproduction of a Play or
Musical, and two for the Best Featured Actress in a Musical—for Josie de
Guzman and for Debbie Allen, who was acclaimed as a major new star.

Although Sondheim's only film scoring experience had been Alain Resnais's *Stavisky*, he agreed to take on another motion picture when a call
came in one day in 1980 from Warren Beatty, asking him to score *Reds*.

"Warren had asked me to contribute some music to *Heaven Can Wait*," Sondheim recalls, "but essentially all he wanted was a theme, and I didn't want to do that. Later, when he told me the idea for *Reds*, I just thought it was so wonderful, I wanted to be a part of it. Originally he wanted very little music, but later there was a little extra to do. The trouble was that *Merrily* began previews just at that time. He waited patiently for me, but who knew we'd get into so much trouble with the show? I finally had to tell him I wouldn't be available. He could not have been nicer or more understanding, and he got Dave Grusin to write some extra music for the film."

In late 1980, Craig Lucas, a chorus member (and subsequent meat pie) in *Sweeney Todd*, was working at being a promising playwright and waiting to have one of his efforts presented by The Production Company, when he was asked to create a late-night entertainment for them.

Lucas got the idea of putting together an evening of Sondheim's unperformed and unpublished material, and sent the request to him on a post card. Sondheim's immediate response: "Well, I think it's a terrible idea, but go ahead."

Lucas: "Our limitation was that we had to use The Production Company's existing set for a play that was already running called *Single Room Occupancy*. Norman René (the director) came up with the idea of two people—myself and Suzanne Henry—in the same apartment at different times. Then I thought, why not have it be two different people in two different apartments at the same time? We thought it would be interesting to show people who didn't have a lot of physical resources living in their shabby first New York apartments but having this rich fantasy life.

"Steve was really up to his ears writing *Merrily*, so we didn't really get to see him until run-throughs at the end, and he had a lot of helpful suggestions. Mostly the problem was that I was not really good in the show. He pulled me aside one day and said, 'What are you going to do ultimately? Write or perform? Because frankly you're a mediocre performer but you're a terrific writer'—which was very hard for me to hear at the time. But it eventually helped me give up performing and become a full-time writer."

Presented as a one-hour late-night entertainment, *Marry Me a Little* opened at The Production Company on October 29, 1980. John S. Wilson, in the *New York Times*, declared the show "an unusually moving evening."

It sold out for its entire off-off-Broadway run and moved for a commercial run off-Broadway on March 12, 1981, at the Actor's Playhouse. "There," says Lucas, "it was not successful and not a very happy experience. We added some things, which were not really appropriate. We took a theater which we hated and which did not preserve the intimacy of the show and tended to highlight its slightness."

Mel Gussow, in a follow-up review of the show in the *New York Times*, was less than impressed: "Unfortunately the caliber of the songs and the ingenuity of the theatrical approach are not matched by the expertise of the execution. . . . Faced with the disappointment and the discoveries of *Marry Me a Little*, one can only be, to borrow a line from a Sondheim lyric, 'sorry-grateful.' "

Lucas: "We originally got great reviews . . . you couldn't have asked for better notices. Norman and I thought that the producers should just take an ad and open the show, but they were overly confident and the newer notices were lukewarm. Then the resulting ad campaign was loathsome. The show, I'm certain, can really work . . . but it certainly wasn't produced brilliantly."

It all happened at the last minute. In 1982 Terry Hughes, a British director with seventeen years of experience with the BBC, went to Sondheim on behalf of the RKO–Nederlander organization to discuss his approach to adapting *Sweeney Todd* for television. Time was short, and with only ten days to prepare, Hughes made hurried arrangements to shoot the touring production starring Angela Lansbury and George Hearn, a short time before it was due to close in Los Angeles.

"We shot for four days," says Hughes, "one of which was an actual live performance. The rest of the taping was quite different. You see, most taping of shows is done with fixed cameras, sitting in various positions in the theater, aimed at the stage for two or three live performances, and then the tapes are edited together. What you'd get would be a very static presentation because there was no movement, no choice of angles, everything was very flat, very one-dimensional.

"With *Sweeney*, I was conscious that Hal's approach to it—consciously or unconsciously—was very filmic. There was a lot of parallel action and cross-cutting between conversations. So seeing this I realized I had to do it in stops and starts, with cameras that were able to give me range, that could go up on the stage, be hand-held, give me much more in-depth, intimate shots of characters. I brought in a huge crane camera, which I've

Opposite: Producer-director Harold Prince and composer-lyricist Stephen Sondheim adapt *Sweeney Todd* for the New York City Opera, 1984. (MARTHA SWOPE)

never seen used before in that kind of thing. We took out seats, we built rostrums and put cameras on them. We literally turned the theater into a studio. We had to, of course, turn it back into a theater again every night. And we edited the show like a film.

"In terms of Angela and George, what you are seeing mostly are large television performances rather than small theater performances. And everything was recorded live, except for the opening of Act Two, 'More Hot Pies' and the 'Johanna' walk-around, because we couldn't have matched it with the cutting otherwise."

The breakneck schedule was very difficult on the actors—taping all day and doing their regular theater performances each night. "I don't know how we got through it," says George Hearn. "We were just hanging on the ropes by the second day. I told Angie, 'I am reaching down into my boots for those high notes.' And she said, 'Baby, we're pumping iron!' "

"I think the show worked so well on television," says Lansbury, "because Steve had always told us that he originally had envisioned the show done intimately. And the video certainly focused your attention on the details of the characters; there was no question about where your attention should be. I think the way it turned out is a miracle and thank goodness it's preserved so beautifully for posterity."

Sweeney Todd was nominated for five Emmys, winning for Best Director, Best Editing, and Best Performance for George Hearn. It was first telecast September 12, 1982, on The Entertainment Channel.

City Opera premiered Harold Prince's production of *Candide* on October 13, 1982, a version that incorporated most of the music ever composed for the show—far more than had been used in any of its previous incarnations.

"This production has signaled a dramatic turnaround in the fortunes of City Opera," reviewed Bill Zakariasen in the *Daily News*.

Donal Henahan, in the *New York Times*, exclaimed: "*Candide* was performed so brilliantly that one would have thought it had been running for months rather than being mounted as part of the opera company's usual hectic schedule."

"You could not get a seat for *Candide*," says Beverly Sills, general director of New York City Opera. "It was pandemonium at the box office."

The success of *Candide* led the way to the subsequent presentation of *Sweeney Todd* and other musical-theater productions at City Opera by helping insure the company's fiscal strength and its audience's new willingness to support such endeavors. "I have to tell you, it's still a learning process for us," admits Sills. "We're in uncharted territory in the sense that we're doing these pieces in a theater that seats three thousand people. But I think we're going to be okay."

The operatic version of *Sweeney Todd*, directed by Harold Prince, was first presented by the Houston Grand Opera on June 14, 1984. With some of the same cast and exactly the same production, it opened at New York City Opera a few months later, on October 11, 1984.

"I thought *Sweeney* held up well in the opera house, and in my opinion, better than it did on Broadway," said Sills. "It just lends itself beautifully to the audience of an opera house. I think we didn't even need to amplify it as much as we did. Now when we do *Candide*, we don't amplify it, so even Hal is coming around to not needing as much artificial sound as he felt he needed when he first came here."

Except for the inclusion of "Johanna," the judge's controversial flagellation song which was cut from the Broadway version, and a lullaby for the beggar woman that was added to the London production, the score remained unchanged, but the reviews were mixed and the run was not nearly as successful as *Candide*'s.

Reviewed by Donal Henahan in the *New York Times* on October 12, 1984: "The operatic setting served chiefly to focus more attention on Mr. Sondheim's sing-song score than was good for it."

Peter G. Davis in *New York* magazine didn't like it either: "*Sweeney Todd* contains considerably more music than *Tosca*, and is at least as carefully composed. . . . Such razzle-dazzle technique is fine, of course, but that hardly guarantees artistic substance. For all its crafty mechanical efficiency, I find *Sweeney Todd* about as appealing, appetizing, and nourishing as the meat pies Mrs. Lovett makes from Sweeney's human victims. . . . The main problem is the drab, crabbed, and short-winded melodic invention that throws such a mean spirit, brittle veneer, and stifling gray shroud over every Sondheim show I've seen. . . . The musical content is so impoverished that I fail to see why the special resources of an opera company should be wasted on it."

"When I first saw *Sweeney*, I told Steve he had written an opera," says Sills. "Now I'm urging him to write an opera especially for us—and I think eventually he will. I think Steve is looking for more tryout time . . . he doesn't like the idea that an opera is reviewed on its opening night. But I think something could be arranged for him."

"I literally think it's impossible for people to write new operas that are any good at all," says Sondheim. "Critics as well as opera buffs are constantly deploring the fact that so few new American operas are any good. I bet there would be a lot of good ones if you could work the bugs out, but it's impossible if you've got five performances in a season and they're all spread apart. The important thing about musical theater is that it needs to play constantly, with the same cast, in front of audiences, day after day, before you can even begin to judge whether it's you, the actor, the music, the lighting, or whether it's just too long. Otherwise you're constantly throwing the baby out with the bath.

"*Sweeney* is not an opera, it's an operetta, so I didn't know how I'd feel about it at the opera house. It turned out better than I thought. I was worried that they would cast it entirely with heavy operatic voices and they didn't. The one show that might benefit from operatic voices, curiously enough, is *Pacific Overtures,* because of its declamatory style." (The English National Opera began workshops in late 1985 for a production of *Pacific Overtures* to enter their repertory in the 1987–88 season. Sondheim and John Weidman worked with the company on it in June 1986 and were "exhilarated.")

"I think that the people in opera have become more humanized to Steve," says Sills. "I think years ago, when he was talking about his stodgy concept of opera, you were dealing with a whole different kind of opera singer and I think that's a stereotype that's been long gone. I mean, there are no more big fat ladies coming out with horns on their heads. The new generation consists of singing actors and acting singers. I think he was absolutely astonished at the flexibility and the versatility and the talent of these young singers. I think any aversion he had to opera is gone, because we have young, beautiful American talent and these kids can do anything. That's why we began to incorporate musical theater pieces into the repertory. We have the talent, so why not use it? And I really think the day will come when I will get an original opera out of Steve Sondheim if I keep nagging him enough."

While president of the Dramatists Guild (1973–1981; currently on the executive committee), Sondheim became intrigued by the Young Writers Festival of the Royal Court in London. There, on a visit in 1980, he attended the festival and came back to the United States so excited by the concept that he initiated the Young Playwrights Festival under the aegis of the Dramatists Guild in 1982.

Opposite: Rosalind Elias as Mrs. Lovett sings "By the Sea" to a distracted Sweeney Todd, played by Timothy Nolan, in the New York City Opera production of *Sweeney Todd,* 1974. (MARTHA SWOPE)

From left: Stephen Sondheim, Angela Lansbury, George Hearn, Victoria Mallory, and Judy Kaye appear in *A Stephen Sondheim Evening*, the Whitney Museum concert presented at Sotheby Parke Bernet Galleries, 1983. (RCA RECORDS)

"The festival is open to anyone under the age of nineteen," says Peggy Hansen, producing director. "Every year, about seven hundred plays are received from around the country, and they are evaluated by a body of theater people. These entries are reduced to between twenty-five and thirty semifinalists, which are then given to a main committee of ten theater professionals, of which Sondheim serves as chairman."

From the semifinalists, the committee chooses approximately ten to be performed as readings. From those selected, several are picked to be fully produced and performed in one evening. In addition, some of the plays may be performed on a separate program of staged readings.

Some of the playwrights already discovered have gone on to other successes, including a TV production in Boston, an after-school special for network television, and even one play that was commissioned by the Royal Court in London. Ironically, the festival does not include musicals.

"This is a very important project to me," says Sondheim, who is currently involved in fundraising for the program as well as reading many of the submissions. "We donated half of the proceeds from the *Follies* concerts to benefit the group. I'm involved because it's imperative that we encourage new writers in this country."

On March 3, 1983, the Whitney Museum presented at Sotheby's, as part of its Composer's Showcase, a concert titled *A Stephen Sondheim Evening*, which consisted entirely of songs for which Sondheim had written both music and lyrics, spanning nearly thirty years of his career.

Six songs were receiving their New York premieres: "Invocation and Instructions to the Audience" and "Fear No More" (with text by William Shakespeare from *Cymbeline*) from *The Frogs*; "The House of Marcus Lycus" and "There's Something About a War," cut from *A Funny Thing Happened on the Way to the Forum*; and "This Is Nice, Isn't It?" and "What More Do I Need?" from the unproduced musical *Saturday Night*.

"I wanted to focus on the more emotional material," says Paul Lazarus, who produced and directed the two-concert evening. "I wanted to put together a program that would really counter all the criticism that his material is cold. And we realized that it would probably be most fun if we got a company of singers together to perform the whole evening— which is what we did."

With a cast of Liz Callaway, Cris Groenendaal, Bob Gunton, George Hearn, Steven Jacob, Judy Kaye, and Victoria Mallory, the evening had a surprise finale as Angela Lansbury walked out, unannounced, bringing her own "accompanist," Stephen Sondheim, and performed "Send in the Clowns."

Thomas Z. Shepard was on hand to record the evening live—a two-record set of the proceedings was released. Much of the same material was reissued later on Shepard's *A Collector's Sondheim* four-disc set in 1985. Included in the *Collector's* compilation was some material that had been recorded at Broadway cast recording sessions that didn't make it onto their respective albums: "It's a Hit!" from *Merrily We Roll Along*, "Can That Boy Foxtrot!" from *Marry Me a Little*, "Night Waltz II" from *A Little Night Music*, and Lee Remick's rendition of "There Won't Be Trumpets" from *Anyone Can Whistle*. Also included as an oddity was the disco version of "The Ballad of Sweeney Todd." The cut of "Old Friends" included from the *Stephen Sondheim Evening* was of particular interest, because it featured Stephen Sondheim singing the opening lines of the song.

At about the same time, Book-of-the-Month Club Records released *Sondheim*, a three-record Sondheim collection. This time, however, it was not an anthology, but an all-new set of recordings supervised by Sondheim especially for this album. Included was the world premiere of a twenty-seven-minute "Suite of Dances from *Pacific Overtures*" for which Sondheim rearranged six musical sections from the show's score. Another selection never before heard, performed by Mary D'Arcy (an original cast member of *Sunday in the Park with George*), was "Goodbye for Now," the first vocal rendition of Sondheim's theme for *Reds*.

In 1983, Stephen Sondheim was voted a member of the American Academy and Institute of Arts and Letters—an organization whose function is to "foster, assist and sustain an interest in Literature, Music and the Fine Arts . . . by singling out and encouraging individual artists and their work."

Considered the highest formal recognition of artistic merit in this country, the organization, which was chartered by Congress, consists of a mere 250 individuals. Since these are lifetime memberships, a vacancy occurs only upon the death of one of its members.

In addition to Sondheim's induction into the general membership of the organization, he became chairman of the Richard Rodgers Production Award committee, whose purpose, according to Margaret Mills, Executive Director of the Academy, "is to encourage young people in the musical theater by subsidizing off-Broadway productions of their work as well as bestowing development grants for professional readings of other new works."

Returning to his love of mysteries and puzzles, in 1984 Sondheim teamed up again with Anthony Perkins to create a mystery story called *Crime and Variations*, being developed by Motown Productions for potential presentation on Home Box Office. Sondheim and Perkins wrote a seventy-five-page treatment with all the scenes, stories, and clues laid out, although the scripts themselves were being written by another writer. It was scheduled for six hours of television viewing in a miniseries format.

"It's a fairly intricate murder investigation," says Perkins, who was writing again with Sondheim after collaborating with him on the screenplay for *The Last of Sheila* and the unproduced film treatment *The Chorus Girl Murder Case*. "We follow the same crime puzzle through the eyes of different people investigating it, and it's set in the New York socialite world."

Asked to provide a show that could engage viewers over successive nights, Perkins says, "We wanted to do something that would be cumulative in its interest rather than just a series. . . . We wanted something that wouldn't depend on prior viewership. Audiences seem to be very into whodunits these days, which is clearly confirmed by the success of *Murder, She Wrote* and other such dramas."

The collaborators had fewer limitations than had been imposed upon them for *The Last of Sheila*, so more time was spent dreaming up what they were actually going to write.

"It was characterized for the most part," says Perkins, "by Steve coming up with brilliant ideas and my saying, 'Well, couldn't she have put the pencil in the blue wig after the elevator man got out?' And he'd say, 'But that's crazy. I don't even see how you could have said that, because the wig wouldn't have been dyed until Thursday. Although, wait a minute.' . . . So I sort of aggravate him into a condition of impatience where, in trying to straighten me out on how ridiculous my idea is, maybe there's just a tiny grain in what I've come up with that can be incorporated. So I'm sort of a catalyst. And it is fun, although you have to be prepared to have your ideas looked at skeptically and sometimes with a bit of impatience."

In 1985 Terry Hughes, who had shot *Sweeney Todd* so spectacularly, had a good but less successful experience translating *Sunday in the Park with George* to the television screen for broadcast on Showtime and PBS. The program aired March 3, 1985.

Hughes: "*Sunday* is—because of what it is about—a painting and a very one-dimensional, flat piece. It works well only in terms of width, and television works better in depth. *Sweeney* also had an incredible power and narrative drive . . . it's a story that unfolds. *Sunday* is much more vague, much more cerebral and poetic in every sense than *Sweeney*. The piece is observed through George's eyes, and that was the trickiest part for me.

"What James Lapine was less happy about in my first cut was that he didn't think we were seeing it *enough* through George's eyes. My first cut had fewer wide shots that showed the whole stage picture. I tended to use closeups on people like the soldier. James felt they were secondary characters and therefore one should stay wide, so you don't treat them with the importance of the principal characters. I'm not sure I agree with that. Since they're using up air time, once they're on the screen, they deserve the same kind of closeups. But to be honest, I think James wanted more the Lincoln Center archive approach to it, which was fine because, after all, it's his creation."

Sunday was captured on tape by shooting most of one live performance and four additional days of camera work. One major problem was that Bernadette Peters, who was starring in *Song and Dance* at the time of the taping, was ill and had vocal problems when they began, so she had to revoice two and a half songs later in the studio.

"I think it turned out pretty well," Sondheim says. "The problem was that you want constantly to be looking at that picture frame filling up, and it's hard to do on a television screen. Nevertheless, I think it's swell and there is at least a recording of it, and I think it's important that there be a record of theater pieces."

Writer-director James Lapine (left) and composer-lyricist Stephen Sondheim discuss their new musical *Into the Woods*, 1986. (PETER CUNNINGHAM)

Soon after *Sunday in the Park with George* began running, Sondheim and Lapine sat around and chatted about working together on a new show. As they bounced around ideas Sondheim suggested that they invent a fairy tale that they might turn into a musical.

"What became clear," says James Lapine, "is that fairy tales are very simplistic . . . there's a complexity to them, but the characters are so clearly drawn, they're not shaded. Somebody is good. Somebody is bad. Somebody is naïve. They're not real, full people. Then I thought, 'Well, this is so dumb, because there are only four million of them already.' And that's when I hit upon the idea of bringing fairy-tale characters together. I thought it would be interesting and exciting to see how people react to stories they already know—but told from a different angle."

Sondheim was very excited at the prospect of doing a show that was dream-like, and Lapine was anxious to write a farce, "something that was fun and nonintellectual, yet packed a punch. It is so rare to go to the theater and be delighted by what you're seeing."

The new project is titled *Into the Woods* (though Lapine admits to having liked an earlier title, *Fee Fi Fo Fum*, as well). The story tells of a baker and his wife, a childless couple, who live under a curse cast by a wicked witch. In order to lift the curse, they must bring the witch four objects: a cow as white as milk, a cape as red as blood, hair as yellow as corn, and a slipper as pure as gold.

"So what they have to do," says Sondheim, "is go in and screw up everybody's else's fairy story. They've got to get Little Red Riding Hood's cape, Cinderella's slipper, Jack and the Beanstalk's cow, and Rapunzel's hair."

At the end of the first act, the witch gets the four objects (for reasons that only then are revealed), everybody gets what they want, and they all expect to live happily ever after.

Sondheim: "But the idea is that in order to get what they wanted, they each had to cheat a little, or lie a little, or huckster a little. The final image of the first act is a second beanstalk sweeping up to the sky, and the second act is about the giant's widow coming down for retribution. So when the second-act curtain goes up, the trees and the houses are smashed and the story becomes one of how the characters have to band together and make amends for what they did. Among other things, the show is about community responsibility . . . you can't just go and chop down trees and tease princes and pretend that beans are worth more than they are. Everybody has to pay for that. So they all have to get together and get rid of the giant."

Lapine: "The second act is just a parallel act that takes place a year later. It's about the consequences of the first act. So it's a lot of setting up things that don't necessarily seem important in the first half, that become incredibly important in the second. It's about the progression of these fairy-tale characters. I wanted to write a really heavy-plot show. It will be much more of an ensemble piece. I think every actor will play at least two roles, so there'll be a lot of doubling and tripling, which I think will be fun, because there are about thirty characters."

In writing the score, Sondheim has attempted to compose a lot of small songs. "What I'm trying to do with the score," he says, "is to sprinkle it with ditties: I'm trying to do little sixteen-, thirty-two-, and eight-bar tunes, almost cartoonish except in a sort of contemporary style. Morals, and traveling songs. And these little tunes start to go strange in the second act. You see, the first act is fast and funny and light and the second act is less goofy and a bit darker, so I would like the score to reflect that.

"The structure of the score is in a sense like *Merrily* in that it's modular again. In terms of style, the songs are more like *Forum* than anything else, because it's farce and full of surprises and incidents and mistaken identities and stumbling on things. . . . The whole prologue is a series of sixteen vignettes, each of which has a musical structure. And then there's one tune that keeps popping up, which becomes the major theme of the evening."

"It's a very exciting show," says Ira Weitzman of Playwrights Horizons, the organization that will present the workshop of the show, as they did with *Sunday in the Park with George*. "And my reaction to the first reading we did was actually even stronger than it was to *Sunday*. In a sense, I tend to think of Jim as a great director who writes. In this show that has changed. His writing is very, very strong and wonderful and a step forward for him. He and Steve had been reading Bruno Bettelheim's *Uses of Enchantment*, a great book about the psychology of fairy tales. I think this show is so accessible to an audience and it's amazing how Jim tied the show to a contemporary world and a contemporary consciousness."

As of publication time, a production of *Into the Woods* was being planned for early 1987 at a regional theater (on the order of *Merrily We Roll Along* at the La Jolla Playhouse and *Sunday in the Park with George* at Playwrights Horizons), with future Broadway plans left open until the authors had an opportunity to see the work staged in front of an audience.

Sondheim has gone through many physical changes during the past decade. During the summer of 1975, when he was writing *Pacific Overtures*, he went through a lazy period and stopped shaving. "And then I realized," he says, "that I looked better with the beard, so I kept it."

A year later, he stopped smoking. But in 1979, soon after the recording session of *Sweeney Todd*, he had a heart attack in the middle of the night.

The *New York Times* reported on April 7, 1979: "Resting comfortably in New York Hospital, Stephen Sondheim said: 'My heart attack was mild and the doctors say there was no permanent damage. I'll be able to go home in a week.' Mr. Sondheim was stricken late in the night of March 27, just five days after his 49th birthday."

Sondheim: "It happened at one o'clock in the morning. I just broke into a terrible sweat and had terrible pain . . . excruciating pain smack in the center of my chest, and I had enough sense to call an ambulance. I thought I was awfully young to be having a heart attack, which I was, but I thought, 'Don't screw around.' And I've been fine ever since, thank God. The experience also caused me to lose thirty pounds. And it's not easy because I tend toward fat. But the doctor urged me to stay thin and to exercise, and now I am as careful about it as possible."

"The heart attack was quite a scare," acknowledges Flora Roberts. "I remember telling Steve, 'Well, it was a *minor* heart attack.' And he said, 'There's no such thing as a minor heart attack.' And I thought, well, yes, he's right, of course. But look at how he came out of it. Look at how many of the great artists have been drunks . . . so self-destructive. And that a talent as huge as Sondheim's manages to be so disciplined, the fact that he is working so hard to stay alive is most affirmative. And his new look, with the beard and the weight loss and the exercise. . . . I must tell you, a friend of mine, who shall remain nameless, perhaps summed it up best. He said, 'Gee, a sloppy guy has turned into a sex symbol.' "

29

WITH SO LITTLE TO
BE SURE OF

"THE STATE of the Broadway theater now is a precarious one," said Arthur Laurents several years ago. "The critics in the old days had enormous power. They still do today, but at least *then* there was an audience to kill off. People were interested. The plays were exciting. I think the so-called 'new theater' and the touting of it is one of the things that is largely responsible for killing off the audience. There are a lot of plays that get ecstatic reviews on the grounds that they are unconventional, but they are really slob-city in my opinion. . . . They seemed to have been hurled up on the stage, they get great reviews, and the public goes and says, 'What is this?' and they don't come back again. I think that's bad for the theater . . . the superficial touting of things because they seem to be different. I think it was Jean Kerr who said, 'In the old days, the *New York Times* used to be the difference between life and death. Now it's the difference between death and death.'

"I will never do a show with anyone who is a creator as well as the producer because I think you are placing the final decision where it shouldn't be. . . . That's why I won't work with Hal Prince as a producer-director. I also think that for my personal taste, the shows that Hal and Steve have done together are all cold. Whatever may be wrong with what I do, it's not cold, and I am not interested at this stage in battling people for something warm and emotional. Hal comes up with concepts that I think are very good, very theatrical, but that's where they end. In *Follies*, you have a concept of the past always following you around. It's stated so brilliantly in the first few minutes. Where did it go from there?

Opposite: Stephen Sondheim, 1986.
(© HENRY GROSSMAN)

No place. And I thought, if I have to see one more restatement, I'm going to go out of my mind . . . or out of the theater. You have to *develop* a concept. I think *Follies* could have been improved by cutting songs and having a longer book . . . some way to get interested in those people. I don't mean jokes, I mean fleshing them out. The more book they cut, the more those people suffered, so finally the lines were song cues and since they were song cues for uninteresting people, none of it was terribly interesting.

"The only moment I cared about in *Follies*, besides the opening, was when Alexis Smith sang 'Could I Leave You?' That's real sophistication. But I'm afraid that that isn't enough for a show. In the old days the book didn't matter. There would be a silly story, what they considered 'nice tunes,' and the show was a success. But when you take someone like Steve, whose music is directly related to the texture and meaning and character of the story, if that story is deficient, the score is not going to make the show work. You cannot write emotional music for unemotional characters. The reason that I don't think *Follies* is viable is that it's the story of the second chance. If those people didn't take the chance the first time, they are pretty dreary, and if they don't like their lives, their lives are dreary. . . . So you're not interested in them before, during, or after.

"I can only point to the shows that Steve and Hal have done together and say that they are all cold . . . which may be their aim. But I've never liked the theory of alienation. I think it's an intellectual conceit. The gloss and technical excellence of those shows should have made you care. The one moment I really cared about in *Company* was when Bobby had nobody to tap with in 'Side by Side by Side.' That was emotional, it was visual, it was theater, it was what musical theater should be. It's very curious that from what the creators intended, the exact opposite came out. Most people took that show as a diatribe against marriage. Consequently, you got to a point at the end when a woman gets up and sings about being drunk—God knows why—and then the central character gets up and says, 'Oh. I see it all. It's better to have somebody. It's being alive.' And I do a mental double take and I don't understand it. And 'Being Alive,' which I think is an extremely good song, I listened to in the theater as a very good song . . . and I remained untouched because it came from no place.

"I'm not against fragmentation or using music that way, but I think it starts ass-backwards. What you needed to start with was an interesting character. If Bobby were interesting, fine. Now, why wasn't Bobby married? Because Bobby doesn't exist. Let's say, truth was not considered when Bobby was written. Mind you, I'm not saying that Bobby *had* to be homosexual, but he had to have something in him, particularly in the culture we live in, to explain why a man of that age was not married. It's not easy, but if you are writing a musical about a man who is not married and is the delight of all his friends, it's perfectly interesting, viable, if he is. It seemed to me that the reason he wasn't married was so they could do a show.

"Let me give another example. There's a song in *Company* called 'Another Hundred People.' Just think if you knew the girl who was singing that song . . . a girl who'd come to New York with all those desires and nothing happened to her. She was in all those singles bars night after night . . . and I don't mean to write a whole play about her, but if you knew her a little. As good as that song was and as much impact as that song had, it would have had a thousand times more impact. You would have cared. This way, they had a girl with a terribly good voice who looked like she just got off a motorcycle singing this marvelous song. It was like a revue, and in a revue you get a point to each sketch which is why they're not done much anymore, they're very hard to do. In a show you have to care even if you hate the character, you must have some strong reaction wanting them to succeed, or wanting them to be done in, but *something*.

"The only character I cared anything about was in *Night Music*. I thought Glynis Johns was wonderful. I think the show was very stylish and lovely to look at but, again, all the music in the world . . .'"

In an interview in the *Los Angeles Times* in 1984, Laurents commented on yet another Sondheim musical; this time, the collaboration with James Lapine. "Let's take *Sunday in the Park with George*," Laurents suggests. "For me, the show misses completely the value of people in one's life. It says if you are not an artist you are inferior. It says we must be shown how to look at *art*. But what about looking at *people?*"

"I like the direction Steve is headed," says Herbert Ross. "I think the major change for Steve, in terms of his public acceptance, is that the audience has become more familiar with his style . . . the harmonics, the rhythms. You can now sort of tell if it's a Sondheim song, whereas in the beginning that wasn't true. I also like that his work is moving more and more to the opera and growing less dependent on prose to carry it.

"I do think the shows that Hal and Steve did together should have been more human. . . . But the shows were extraordinarily done, they were quite special—and being special was both their limitation and their distinction."

"Yes, I think our shows were cool," admits Harold Prince. "But I think that is not something that generated from the relationship between Steve and myself. I felt that *Cabaret*—which Steve had nothing to do with—was cool, and I felt that *Anyone Can Whistle*—which I had nothing to do with—was cool, too. I think it has to do with your definition of what excites you in the theater and I think, essentially, Steve and I were excited by theatrics, by tension, by conflict . . . our whole idea was to give people a good time in the theater—to surprise, to astonish. I want to go to the theater to stay awake. I want the theater to be a place where people can be passionate.

"The whole label that was put on our shows, the whole notion of the 'concept' musical, was one that I really resent. I never wished it on myself. It caused a backlash and animosity towards the shows and us. I think for a lot of people it was like waving the red goddamn flag. And I kept hearing, 'We're sick of the goddamn concept musical.' And I kept thinking, 'Leave me alone . . . I never called it that.' It's called a 'unified' show, an 'integrated' show. But out of that came a lot of resentment.

"But look what's happened to the theater community. Look what happened at the Tony Awards with that hostile contest between *La Cage aux Folles* and *Sunday in the Park with George* . . . with all that nonsense about 'popular songs being alive and well.' You just sat there and you thought, 'What is all this bullshit and why does it have to be this ugly and counterproductive? Why can't there be a sense of community in the theater?' Why is that so naive? There wasn't that in the past. And one of the reasons for it is that there isn't numerically the theater community that there once was. I mean, you look back at the list of all the composers and directors and librettists who were working when Steve and I first came into the theater. It was incredible. And now look. So maybe that sense of crisis is making people less generous. And that's very dangerous. It's unnecessary. The sense of community is absent, and one of the reasons is that no one is secure. Security makes people generous. Insecurity makes people competitive and hostile.

"And you have to be nurtured. That's all a part of this. You don't get to be Steve Sondheim without that support. You don't get through the difficulty of his earlier days . . . those years of disappointment and non-reviews . . . you don't get through that unless you keep getting produced on the stage. And it's damn difficult today. I don't think there is a lack of talented people around, but there is a lack of opportunity for them to learn, to get produced, where they can make their mistakes.

"The way the theater is operating these days is cause for great concern. Even Steve's work . . . Steve's shows don't run very long. And it must drive him crazy. It sort of happened again with *Sunday in the Park with George*. It must be annoying to be the best in the world today and have that happen. But maybe that's what happens to the best in the world."

"Hal's talent," said Sondheim a few years ago, "is his ability to handle unconventional material in terms of truly popular theater. The reason I like to work with him is that we have the same point of view although we're abrasive with each other. We see the large and small parts exactly the same, but it's the middle ground where we disagree violently and it causes a lot of good work to be done.

"A lot of people have spoken of the work that Hal and I have done as being 'daring.' Hal and I are not knights—we've just been trying to stretch the musical and have some fun with it. We would be bored to take a viable successful piece, add songs to it, and put it on the stage. That does not preclude our doing adaptations, but adaptations on the musical stage, if they need be done, should not be done straightforwardly. They should be changed and new life should be breathed into them. It's also true that at least half of my songs deal with ambivalence, feeling two things at once. I tend to like neurotic people . . . people who are troubled. . . . I like to hear rumblings beneath the surface. I'm not a great traveler and, at base, I'm interested in the society I live in. I learned a long time ago to write what I care about and what I want to see, so of course there's always the danger that not everyone is going to agree with our shows or even like them."

A charge that has been leveled against Sondheim since he began composing is probably best summed up by actor Keith Baxter, who jokingly theorized: "It seems to me that when Steve composes a song, whenever he hears a melody creeping in, he slams his foot down and stomps on it!"

"I'm old enough to be Steve's father," Jule Styne said ten years ago. "I adore him. I really like him personally, not like other people who get to know him for his intellectual prowess and all that shit. I like him as a person. But I wonder what Steve's reference is. Does he use Lenny as a reference? If he does, he's in a lot of trouble. Is he trying to impress with a lot of chords? Chords don't make it. People aren't listening to chords.

And dissonances are marvelous—but they don't belong in the musical theater. Steve needs to write some hits. If he doesn't, those shows of his are not going to make it."

In a recent interview, published in 1985, Styne was much more appreciative of Sondheim's compositional work. "I think the most unbelievable job of music writing," he said, "and I say this with deep reverence and envy, the most brilliant job of music writing ever in my life, is *Sweeney Todd*. Only a long time from now will people say that."

"I know, some have said that Steve's music is unmelodic," said Leonard Bernstein a number of years ago, "and it's not . . . not anything like it. Steve does have a certain inhibitedness about the old word *self-expression*, which is operable in his life, detectable in day-to-day existence with him. He is in a way a product of a twentieth-century phenomenon, which takes different forms but which can best be expressed by the term *neoclassicism*, the main form that poetry and music took for so many decades to save itself from direct expression. I may be saying this because it's very much on my mind since a number of lectures I did at Harvard were about this, especially with Stravinsky and T. S. Eliot. If you just think about the tendencies in music and language in our century with these two great masters as the prototypes, I think you'll see what I mean. That indirection, allusion, obliquity, objectivism . . . the avoidance of the direct subjective *I love you*, is germane to the twentieth century. It has to do with fear, insecurity—I'm not talking about Steve in particular now, this has to do with all of us. We're all children of this century which has been a century of death. . . . We are all living with the threat of extermination all the time and have been, through the whole century. If you go back to Mahler in the opening years of the century, you'll know what I mean. Now how does all of this relate to Steve? It relates to him—and I'm not saying he's T. S. Eliot and his music is certainly not Stravinsky—but these qualities of allusion, of reference to the past or to others, of indirection through irony, through humor, and through the play of words and notes, are related to neoclassicism in the sense that it avoids the direct expression. It's self-protection in a way and that's what inhibitions are formed of. There are schools of psychiatry that call this a neurotic defense mechanism and there are other schools that call it inhibition for other reasons. In Steve's case, it's particularly pronounced because he is a perfectionist; he is very hard on himself in his private life, and on other people. He's extremely critical, very sour, and it's an image of himself that he's built up. Some people are terrified of his opinion, of whether he will approve or not, but he's hardest of all on himself. Anybody who is that critical and that frightening to other people is usually a person who is most frightened of himself, is hardest of all on himself, and that's where it comes from. Nothing's ever good enough, that's part of his perfectionism. Nothing must be straight out subjectively because it's dangerous, because it reveals your real insides. The fear usually takes the form of the fear of corniness, or being platitudinous, or whatever. Steve has very strong feelings and therefore must invent correspondingly strong defenses to guard those feelings. That accounts in part for his reluctance to let himself make a direct subjective statement. If he were freer in that department, which I think he will be as he gains more security, either through his psychoanalysis or through self-knowledge, or by simply growing up, I think that the directness of expression will become increasingly apparent and the more apparent it becomes, the more beautiful his music can be. He's always been a little bit afraid of the word *beautiful,* except as it can be reinterpreted as charming, decorative, odd, sweet, touching—touching in some oblique way, in some around the corner way. He did come close in *Follies* in 'Too Many Mornings,' where he really did try to make a direct statement. I don't know if it quite came off because he was still a little too self-conscious about it. In *Night Music* you begin to sniff a personal language. Of course he has a very artificial situation there which enables him to be a little freer in his expression. Whereas in *Company,* where people were saying what they really felt, people of today, not protected by a period, a bygone period, not protected by a Bergman movie from which it's derived, *he's* not protected so he protects his *statements* by making them indirect, objectifying them . . . as did T. S. Eliot and as did Stravinsky. I'm not saying that this is necessarily bad or that it prevents him from writing first-class stuff at all, but his breakthrough, I'm convinced, is going to come when he is able to break through his inhibitions. In *Night Music* I think that the 'Clowns' song really breaks your heart in the middle of all that. That's a real piece of poetry both musically and verbally. . . .

"More often than not [writing for the musical theater has] become the attempt to achieve the 'Broadway sound'—a sound I cannot bear. It's the sound when the overture begins that's supposed to get the audience excited. When I walk into a musical, which I rarely do anymore, I can't bear the phony vitality of musicals . . . getting down to the footlights and baring your teeth and wiggling your ass, all that phony energy which, when it isn't phony, is great, but it's always phony now because it's trying to recapture something that isn't there. The musical went backwards, it regressed. It went back to the sure-fire hit, the commercial musical. I haven't seen any real experiments tried. The closest thing was *Hair*, which was not much of an experiment. I think Rodgers and Hammerstein made great experiments. *South Pacific* was a very great show and I think *Carousel* was, too. *South Pacific* brought the American musical theater, at the time, to a peak because it's not a formula show. Those double soliloquies are not formula things. They are beautiful examples of music as theater. Of course there were formula numbers in it. There were formula things in *West Side*, too. 'Cool' develops into a much larger thing, but the song itself is a song about being cool. It turns out to be a big choreographic thing with a twelve-tone fugue and God knows what else but it's basically a formula, cued song.

"*Company, Follies,* and *Night Music* tried to avoid that kind of song. Conceptually, they were very interesting and imaginative. What they lacked, I think, was that direct musical expression that Steve, as of *Night Music*, is beginning to be able to achieve. . . .

"Steve is a very sophisticated musician, and that sophistication is something that very often gets in his way. It also has tremendous positive results because it doesn't limit him to being a songwriter. He writes songs by his own say-so, but it's not in that old thirty-two-bar sense that Cole Porter and other people would do, writing songs and going away and leaving it to somebody else to integrate them and make them work in the show . . . songs that very often were cued in by shoehorn methods. That's why a Sondheim score is so different."

"I think Steve's work has become more daring, more innovative," says Anthony Perkins. "Also, the variety of interests that he has now is probably greater than when he was in his forties. And it would no longer be a fair criticism to say that his music is lacking in personal emotion.

"I don't think comfort is a condition that Steve has ever sought in his work. Discomfort is perhaps more fruitful ground for sitting back and writing. I mean, obviously, Steve has never just sat back and written the easy songs.

"He's so determined to not settle down and permit himself to be a revered icon. This is one of the things that keeps him working so feverishly now. He doesn't want to become the grand young-old-man of the American musical theater. The *Follies* concert was an event about which, I think, he had mixed emotions. It was tremendously gratifying for him to see and hear the music performed as excellently as it was. But the accolades and the sort of reverence that went along with it was something that he was sensitive to and somewhat resistant to. He's too sharp to let himself become a figure and an object of veneration. All this is anathema to him. He just wants to keep writing."

"Over the years," said Sondheim recently, "my work has at times been considered cold. I find that people sometimes mistake sentimentality for feeling. I believe in sentiment, but not sentimentality. Of course, what's sentimental is often in the ear of the beholder. I also think people don't understand the difference between passion and sentimentality. Maybe it has to do with certain subject matters we've chosen. I don't understand it entirely. Quite often the stuff I write is not simple. I think I'm getting more and more accepted, but sometimes my work is too unexpected to sustain itself very firmly in the commercial theater.

"The only shows of mine since *West Side Story* and *Gypsy* that paid back their investments and went into profits on Broadway were *A Funny Thing Happened on the Way to the Forum, Company,* and *A Little Night Music.* It would be nice to have a smash. But I'm always stunned that a show of mine gets on at all.

"One of the continuing problems plaguing the theater is the obvious split between popular and theatrical music. It has widened over the last twenty years because the notion of popular music, which has to do with relentlessness, electric amplification, and a kind of insistence that is, I think, anti-theatrical; anti-dramatic, to be a little more accurate. I don't think that kind of music can ever define character, because it's essentially always the same, and it must be the same, because that's its quality. It's also a performer's medium; it's the singer, not the song. In trying to cultivate a young audience, how can I tell them the musical theater is just a different way of looking at things? They haven't been exposed to it, so it seems wishy-washy and unsatisfying to them because it's not what they require from music.

"I must admit that the state the theater is in today worries me a lot. The theater is dying economically. Unions make it more and more difficult for producers to get shows on, but the biggest problem is that theater has always been a luxury art and the only way for it to flourish is for it to be subsidized.

"The theater just cannot support itself. How can it? You can only play to a limited number of people a night. If it weren't for subsidy there would be no dramatic literature in the world whatsoever. Nor would there be any music. Mozart could not have lived on the fees he got from performing. But there's no cultural tradition in America—we're too young. You go to much poorer countries and in every city in Europe part of the taxpayers' money goes for subsidy of the culture. . . . But not in the United States, the richest country in the world.

"For the first time, I get the feeling that art might die because art depends on communication. It frightens me a lot. People ask me why I continue writing for the stage. The answer is simple: the theater is the only dramatic medium that acknowledges the presence of an audience. Movies do not. If you boo at a movie screen, they go right on acting. If you laugh, they won't stop for you. You have no effect on them and you know it from the minute you sit down. In the theater you're aware that the community experience exists between the stage and you. And that's what's unique about it.

"The theater is a place where I really love to work," Sondheim soberly admits. "It's a place where I hope to work until Broadway packs up and goes away, should that ever happen. The biggest challenge for me is the opportunity to constantly try new things. I believe it's the writer's job to educate the audience . . . to bring them things they would never have expected to see. It's not easy, but writing never has been. Creating art is hard work. Every time, it's like squeezing toothpaste out of an empty tube. One more drop, just one more drop. Probably one of the most frightening things in the world is staring at a blank sheet of paper wondering how you're going to fill it. . . . But somehow you do."

APPENDIX A: SONDHEIM · · · PRODUCTIONS

I. BROADWAY

West Side Story

Music by Leonard Bernstein
Lyrics by Stephen Sondheim
Book by Arthur Laurents
    (Based on a Conception of Jerome Robbins)
Produced by Robert E. Griffith and Harold S. Prince
    (By Arrangement with Roger L. Stevens)
Directed and Choreographed by Jerome Robbins
Co-Choreographer: Peter Gennaro
Scenic Production by Oliver Smith
Costumes by Irene Sharaff
Lighting by Jean Rosenthal
Musical Direction by Max Goberman
Orchestrations by Leonard Bernstein with Sid Ramin and Irwin Kostal
Opened: Winter Garden, September 26, 1957
Performances: 732, initial engagement; 249, return engagement

Musical Numbers:
"Jet Song," "Something's Coming,"
"The Dance at the Gym," "Maria," "Tonight," "America," "Cool," "One Hand, One Heart," "Tonight Quintet," "The Rumble," "I Feel Pretty," "Somewhere," "Gee, Officer Krupke," "A Boy Like That," "I Have a Love," Finale

Tony Award Nominations:
Best Musical, *Best Choreographer (Jerome Robbins), *Best Scenic Designer (Oliver Smith)

Cast:
The Jets
Riff (The Leader)........Mickey Calin
Tony (His Friend)........Larry Kert
Action........Eddie Roll
A-Rab........Tony Mordente
Baby John........David Winters
Snowboy........Grover Dale
Big Deal........Martin Charnin
Diesel........Hank Brunjes
Gee-Tar........Tommy Abbott
Mouthpiece........Frank Green
Tiger........Lowell Harris

Their Girls
Graziella........Wilma Curley
Velma........Carole D'Andrea

*denotes winner

Minnie........Nanette Rosen
Clarice........Marilyn D'Honau
Pauline........Julie Oser
Anybodys........Lee Becker

The Sharks
Bernardo (The Leader)........Ken Le Roy
Maria (His Sister)........Carol Lawrence
Anita (His Girl)........Chita Rivera
Chino (His Friend)........Jamie Sanchez
Pepe........George Marcy
Indio........Noel Schwartz
Luis........Al De Sio
Anxious........Gene Gavin
Nibbles........Ronnie Lee
Juano........Jay Norman
Toro........Erne Castaldo
Moose........Jack Murray

Their Girls
Rosalia........Marilyn Cooper
Consuelo........Reri Grist
Teresita........Carmen Guiterrez
Francisca........Elizabeth Taylor
Estella........Lynn Ross
Margarita........Liane Plane

The Adults
Doc........Art Smith
Schrank........Arch Johnson
Krupke........William Bramley
Glad Hand........John Harkins

Gypsy

Music by Jule Styne
Lyrics by Stephen Sondheim
Book by Arthur Laurents
Suggested by the Memoirs of Gypsy Rose
    Lee
Produced by David Merrick and Leland
    Hayward
Directed and Choreographed by Jerome
    Robbins
Settings and Lighting by Jo Mielziner
Costumes Designed by Raoul Pène du
    Bois
Dance Music Arranged by John Kander

Musical Direction by Milton Rosenstock
Orchestrations by Sid Ramin with
    Robert Ginzler
Opened: Broadway Theatre, May 21,
    1959
Performances: 702

Musical Numbers:
Overture, "May We Entertain You,"
    "Some People," "Small World,"
    "Baby June and Her Newsboys," "Mr.
    Goldstone, I Love You," "Little
    Lamb," "You'll Never Get Away
    From Me," "Dainty June and Her
    Farmboys," "If Momma Was
    Married," "All I Need Is the Girl,"
    "Everything's Coming Up Roses,"
    "Madame Rose's Toreadorables,"
    "Together, Wherever We Go," "You
    Gotta Get a Gimmick," "Let Me
    Entertain You," "Rose's Turn"

Musical Numbers Deleted Prior to New
    York Opening:
"Momma's Talkin' Soft," "Smile, Girls,"
    "Three Wishes for Christmas," "Who
    Needs Him?"

Tony Award Nominations:
Best Musical, Best Director—Musical
    (Jerome Robbins), Best Actress—
    Musical (Ethel Merman), Best Actor,
    Supporting or Featured—Musical
    (Jack Klugman), Best Actress,
    Supporting or Featured—Musical
    (Sandra Church), Best Conductor and
    Musical Director (Milton Rosenstock),
    Best Scenic Designer—Musical (Jo
    Mielziner), Best Costume Designer
    (Raoul Pène du Bois)

Cast:
Uncle Jocko........Mort Marshall
George........Willy Sumner
Arnold (and his guitar)........John Borden
Balloon Girl........Jody Lane
Baby Louise........Karen Moore
Baby June........Jacqueline Mayro
Rose........Ethel Merman
Pop........Erv Harmon

Newsboys........Bobby Brownell, Gene Castle, Steve Curry, Billy Harris
Weber........Joe Silver
Herbie........Jack Klugman
Louise........Sandra Church
June........Lane Bradbury
Tulsa........Paul Wallace
Yonkers........David Winters
Angie........Ian Tucker
L.A.........Michael Parks
Kringelein........Loney Lewis
Mr. Goldstone........Mort Marshall
Farm Boys........Marvin Arnold, Ricky Coll, Don Emmons, Michael Parks, Ian Tucker, Paul Wallace, David Winters
Miss Cratchitt........Peg Murray

Hollywood Blondes
Agnes........Marilyn Cooper
Marjorie May........Patsy Bruder
Delores........Marilyn D'Honau
Thelma........Merle Letowt
Edna........Joan Petlak
Gail........Imelda De Martin
Pastey........Richard Porter

Tessie Tura........Maria Karnilova
Mazeppa........Faith Dane
Cigar........Loney Lewis
Electra........Chotzi Foley
Show Girls........Kathryn Albertson, Gloria Kristy, Denise McLaglen, Barbara London, Theda Nelson, Carroll Jo Towers, Marie Wallace
Maid........Marsha Rivers
Phil........Joe Silver
Bougeron-Cochon........George Zima
Cow........Willy Sumner and George Zima

A Funny Thing Happened on the Way to the Forum

Music and Lyrics by Stephen Sondheim
Book by Burt Shevelove and Larry Gelbart
Based on the Plays of Plautus
Produced by Harold Prince

Directed by George Abbott
Choreography and Musical Staging by Jack Cole
Settings and Costumes by Tony Walton
Lighting by Jean Rosenthal
Dance Arrangements by Hal Schaefer
Musical Direction by Harold Hastings
Orchestrations by Irwin Kostal and Sid Ramin
Opened: Alvin Theatre, May 8, 1962
Performances: 964

Musical Numbers:
Overture, "Comedy Tonight," "Love, I Hear," "Free," "The House of Marcus Lycus," "Lovely," "Pretty Little Picture," "Everybody Ought to Have a Maid," "I'm Calm," "Impossible," "Bring Me My Bride," "That Dirty Old Man," "That'll Show Him," "Lovely" (reprise), Funeral Dirge, Finale

Musical Numbers Deleted Prior to New York Opening:
"Love Is in the Air," "Love Story" ("Your Eyes Are Blue"), "Echo Song," "I Do Like You"

Tony Award Nominations:
*Best Musical, *Best Producer (Harold Prince), *Best Book (Burt Shevelove and Larry Gelbart), *Best Director (George Abbott), *Best Actor—Musical (Zero Mostel), *Best Supporting Actor—Musical (David Burns), Best Actress, Supporting or Featured—Musical (Ruth Kobart)

Cast:
Prologus........Zero Mostel
The Proteans........Eddie Phillips, George Reeder, David Evans
Senex, a citizen of Rome........David Burns
Domina, his wife........Ruth Kobart
Hero, his son........Brian Davies
Hysterium, slave to Senex and Domina........Jack Gilford

Lycus, a dealer in courtesans........John Carradine
Pseudolus, slave to Hero........Zero Mostel
Tintinnabula........Roberta Keith
Panacea........Lucienne Bridou
The Geminae........Lisa James, Judy Alexander
Vibrata........Myrna White
Gymnasia........Gloria Kristy
Philia........Preshy Marker
Erronius, a citizen of Rome ....Raymond Walburn
Miles Gloriosus, a warrior........Ronald Holgate

Anyone Can Whistle

Music and Lyrics by Stephen Sondheim
Book by Arthur Laurents
Produced by Kermit Bloomgarden and Diana Krasny
Directed by Arthur Laurents
Dances and Musical Numbers Staged by Herbert Ross
Scenery Designed by William and Jean Eckart
Costumes Designed by Theoni V. Aldredge
Lighting Designed by Jules Fisher
Dance Music Arrangements by Betty Walberg
Musical Direction and Vocal Arrangements by Herbert Greene
Orchestrations by Don Walker
Opened: Majestic Theatre, April 4, 1964
Performances: 9

Musical Numbers:
"I'm Like the Bluebird," "Me and My Town," "Miracle Song," "Simple," "A-1 March," "Come Play Wiz Me," "Anyone Can Whistle," "A Parade in Town," "Everybody Says Don't," "I've Got You to Lean On," "See What It Gets You," "With So Little to Be Sure Of," Finale

Musical Numbers Deleted Prior to New York Opening:
"There Won't Be Trumpets," "There's Always a Woman"

Tony Award Nominations:
Best Choreographer (Herbert Ross)

Cast:
Sandwich Man........Jeff Killion
Baby Joan........Jeanne Tanzy
Mrs. Schroeder........Peg Murray
Treasurer Cooley........Arnold Soboloff
Chief Magruder........James Frawley
Comptroller Schub........Gabriel Dell
Cora Hoover Hooper........Angela Lansbury
The Boys........Sterling Clark, Harvey Evans, Larry Roquemore, Tucker Smith
Fay Apple........Lee Remick
J. Bowden Hapgood........Harry Guardino
Dr. Detmold........Don Doherty
George........Larry Roquemore
June........Janet Hayes
John........Harvey Evans
Martin........Lester Wilson
Old Lady........Eleonore Treiber
Telegraph Boy........Alan Johnson
Osgood........Georgia Creighton
Cookies, Nurses, Deputies, Townspeople, Pilgrims, Tourists: Susan Borree, Georgia Creighton, Janet Hayes, Bettye Jenkins, Patricia Kelly, Barbara Lang, Paula Lloyd, Barbara Monte, Odette Phillips, Hanne-Marie Reiner, Eleonore Treiber, Sterling Clark, Eugene Edwards, Harvey Evans, Dick Ensslen, Loren Hightower, Alan Johnson, Jeff Killion, Jack Murray, William Reilly, Larry Roquemore, Tucker Smith, Don Stewart, Lester Wilson

Do I Hear a Waltz?

Music by Richard Rodgers
Lyrics by Stephen Sondheim

Book by Arthur Laurents
Based on the Play *The Time of the Cuckoo*
   by Arthur Laurents
Produced by Richard Rodgers
Directed by John Dexter
Choreography by Herbert Ross
Choreographic Associate: Wakefield
   Poole
Scenery and Costumes by Beni Montresor
Lighting by Jules Fisher
Dance Music Arranged by Richard de
   Benedictis
Musical Direction by Frederick Dvonch
Orchestrations by Ralph Burns
Opened: 46th Street Theatre, March 18,
   1965
Performances: 220

Musical Numbers:
Overture, "Someone Woke Up," "This
   Week Americans," "What Do We
   Do? We Fly!" "Someone Like You,"
   "Bargaining," "Here We Are Again,"
   "Thinking," "No Understand," "Take
   the Moment," "Moon in My
   Window," "We're Gonna Be All
   Right," "Do I Hear a Waltz?" "Stay,"
   "Perfectly Lovely Couple," "Thank
   You So Much," Finale

Musical Numbers Deleted Prior to New
   York Opening:
"Perhaps," "Two by Two,"
   "Philadelphia," "Everybody Loves
   Leona"

Tony Award Nominations:
Best Music and Lyrics (Richard Rodgers
   and Stephen Sondheim), Best Actress
   —Musical (Elizabeth Allen), Best
   Scenic Design (Beni Montresor)

Cast:
Leona Samish........Elizabeth Allen
Mauro........Christopher Votos
Signora Fioria........Carol Bruce
Eddie Yaeger........Stuart Damon
Jennifer Yaeger........Julienne Marie
Mrs. McIlhenny........Madeleine
   Sherwood

Mr. McIlhenny........Jack Manning
Giovanna........Fleury D'Antonakis
Vito........James Dybas
Renato Di Rossi........Sergio Franchi
Man on Bridge........Michael Lamont
Mrs. Victoria Haslam........Helon Blount
Singers: Darrel Askey, Sydnee Balaber,
   Bill Berrian, Helon Blount, Rudy
   Challenger, Pat Kelly, Liz Lamkin,
   Michael Lamont, James Luisi, Jack
   Murray, Carl Nicholas, Candida Pilla,
   Casper Roos, Bernice Saunders, Liza
   Stuart
Dancers: Jere Admire, Bob Bishop,
   Wayne De Rammelaere, Steve Jacobs,
   Sandy Leeds, Joe Nelson, Janice Peta,
   Walter Stratton, Nancy Van Rijn,
   Mary Zahn

Company

Music and Lyrics by Stephen Sondheim
Book by George Furth
Produced by Harold Prince
In Association with Ruth Mitchell
Directed by Harold Prince
Musical Numbers Staged by Michael
   Bennett
Sets and Projections by Boris Aronson
Costumes by D. D. Ryan
Lighting by Robert Ornbo
Dance Music Arranged by Wally Harper
Musical Direction by Harold Hastings
Orchestrations by Jonathan Tunick
Opened: Alvin Theatre, April 26, 1970
Performances: 690

Musical Numbers:
"Company," "The Little Things You Do
   Together," "Sorry-Grateful," "You
   Could Drive a Person Crazy," "Have I
   Got a Girl for You?" "Someone Is
   Waiting," "Another Hundred
   People," "Getting Married Today,"
   "Side by Side by Side," "What Would
   We Do Without You?" "Poor Baby,"
   "Tick, Tock," "Barcelona," "The
   Ladies Who Lunch," "Being Alive"

Musical Number Deleted Prior to New York Opening:
"Happily Ever After"

Tony Award Nominations:
*Best Musical, *Best Music (Stephen Sondheim), *Best Lyrics (Stephen Sondheim), *Best Book (George Furth), *Best Director (Harold Prince), *Best Scenic Design (Boris Aronson), Best Actor—Musical (Larry Kert), Best Actress—Musical (Susan Browning), Best Actor, Supporting or Featured—Musical (Charles Kimbrough), Best Actress, Supporting or Featured—Musical (Barbara Barrie), Best Choreographer (Michael Bennett), Best Lighting Design (Robert Ornbo)

Winner: New York Drama Critics' Circle Award for Best Musical

Cast:
Robert........Dean Jones
Sarah........Barbara Barrie
Harry........Charles Kimbrough
Susan........Merle Louise
Peter........John Cunningham
Jenny........Teri Ralston
David........George Coe
Amy........Beth Howland
Paul........Steve Elmore
Joanne........Elaine Stritch
Larry........Charles Braswell
Marta........Pamela Myers
Kathy........Donna McKechnie
April........Susan Browning
The Vocal Minority........Cathy Corkill, Carol Gelfand, Marilyn Saunders, Dona D. Vaughn

Follies

Music and Lyrics by Stephen Sondheim
Book by James Goldman
Produced by Harold Prince
In Association with Ruth Mitchell
Directed by Harold Prince and Michael Bennett
Choreography by Michael Bennett
Scenic Production Designed by Boris Aronson
Costumes by Florence Klotz
Lighting by Tharon Musser
Dance Music Arranged by John Berkman
Musical Direction by Harold Hastings
Orchestrations by Jonathan Tunick
Opened: Winter Garden, April 4, 1971
Performances: 522

Musical Numbers:
Prologue, "Beautiful Girls," "Don't Look at Me," "Waiting for the Girls Upstairs," "Rain on the Roof," "Ah, Paris!" "Broadway Baby," "The Road You Didn't Take," "In Buddy's Eyes," "Bolero d'Amour," "Who's That Woman?" "I'm Still Here," "Too Many Mornings," "The Right Girl," "One More Kiss," "Could I Leave You?" "Loveland," "You're Gonna Love Tomorrow," "Love Will See Us Through," "The God-Why-Don't-You-Love-Me Blues," "Losing My Mind," "The Story of Lucy and Jessie," "Live, Laugh, Love"

Musical Numbers Deleted Prior to New York Opening:
"Can That Boy Foxtrot!" "Uptown Downtown"

Tony Award Nominations:
Best Musical, Best Book—Musical (James Goldman), *Best Music and Lyrics (Stephen Sondheim), *Best Director (Harold Prince and Michael Bennett), *Best Choreographer (Michael Bennett), *Best Scenic Design (Boris Aronson), *Best Costumes (Florence Klotz), *Best Lighting (Tharon Musser), *Best Actress—Musical (Alexis Smith), Best Actress—Musical (Dorothy Collins), Best Actor, Supporting or Featured—Musical (Gene Nelson)

Winner: New York Drama Critics' Circle
Award for Best Musical

Cast:
Major-Domo........Dick Latessa
Sally Durant Plummer........Dorothy
    Collins
Young Sally........Marti Rolph
Christine Donovan........Ethel Barrymore
    Colt
Willy Wheeler........Fred Kelly
Stella Deems........Mary McCarty
Max Deems........John J. Martin
Heidi Schiller........Justine Johnston
Chauffeur........John Grigas
Meredith Lane........Sheila Smith
Roscoe........Michael Bartlett
Deedee West........Helon Blount
Hattie Walker........Ethel Shutta
Emily Whitman........Marcie Stringer
Theodore Whitman........Charles Welch
Vincent........Victor Griffin
Vanessa........Jayne Turner
Young Vincent........Michael Misita
Young Vanessa........Graciela Daniele
Solange LaFitte........Fifi D'Orsay
Carlotta Campion........Yvonne De Carlo
Phyllis Rogers Stone........Alexis Smith
Benjamin Stone........John McMartin
Young Phyllis........Virginia Sandifur
Young Ben........Kurt Peterson
Buddy Plummer........Gene Nelson
Young Buddy........Harvey Evans
Dimitri Weismann........Arnold Moss
Kevin........Ralph Nelson
Young Stella........Julie Pars
Young Heidi........Victoria Mallory
Party Musicians........Taft Jordan, Aaron
    Bell, Charles Spies, Robert Curtis
Show Girls: Suzanne Briggs, Trudy
    Carson, Kathie Dalton, Ursula
    Maschmeyer, Linda Perkins, Margot
    Travers
Singers, Dancers: Graciela Daniele, Mary
    Jane Houdina, Sonja Levkova, Rita
    O'Connor, Julie Pars, Suzanne Rogers,
    Roy Barry, Steve Boockvor, Michael
    Misita, Joseph Nelson, Ralph Nelson,

Ken Urmston, Peter Walker, Donald
    Weissmuller
The Singers and Dancers appear as
    Guests, Waiters, Waitresses,
    Photographers, Chorus Girls, Chorus
    Boys, etc.

A Little Night Music

Music and Lyrics by Stephen Sondheim
Book by Hugh Wheeler
Suggested by a Film by Ingmar Bergman
Produced by Harold Prince
In Association with Ruth Mitchell
Directed by Harold Prince
Choreography by Patricia Birch
Scenic Production Designed by Boris
    Aronson
Costumes Designed by Florence Klotz
Lighting Designed by Tharon Musser
Musical Direction by Harold Hastings
Orchestrations by Jonathan Tunick
Opened: Shubert Theatre, February 25,
    1973
Performances: 601

Musical Numbers:
Vocal Overture, "Night Waltz,"
    "Now," "Later," "Soon," "The
    Glamorous Life," "Remember?" "You
    Must Meet My Wife," "Liaisons," "In
    Praise of Women," "Every Day a
    Little Death," "A Weekend in the
    Country," "The Sun Won't Set," "It
    Would Have Been Wonderful,"
    "Perpetual Anticipation," "Send in
    the Clowns," "The Miller's Son,"
    Finale

Musical Numbers Deleted Prior to New
    York Opening:
"Bang!" "Silly People"

Tony Award Nominations:
*Best Musical, *Best Music and Lyrics
    (Stephen Sondheim), *Best Book
    (Hugh Wheeler), Best Costumes
    (Florence Klotz), *Best Actress—
    Musical (Glynis Johns), *Best

Supporting Actress—Musical (Patricia
Elliott), Best Director—Musical
(Harold Prince), Best Actor—Musical
(Len Cariou), Best Actor, Supporting
or Featured—Musical (Laurence
Guittard), Best Actress, Supporting or
Featured—Musical (Hermione
Gingold), Best Scenic Design (Boris
Aronson), Best Lighting Design
(Tharon Musser)

Winner: New York Drama Critics' Circle
Award for Best Musical

Cast:
Mr. Lindquist........Benjamin Rayson
Mrs. Nordstrom........Teri Ralston
Mrs. Anderssen........Barbara Lang
Mr. Erlanson........Gene Varrone
Mrs. Segstrom........Beth Fowler
Fredrika Armfeldt........Judy Kahan
Madame Armfeldt........Hermione
    Gingold
Frid, her butler........George Lee
    Andrews
Henrik Egerman........Mark Lambert
Anne Egerman........Victoria Mallory
Fredrik Egerman........Len Cariou
Petra........D. Jamin-Bartlett
Désirée Armfeldt........Glynis Johns
Malla, her maid........Despo
Bertrand, a page........Will Sharpe
    Marshall
Count Carl-Magnus Malcolm
    ....Laurence Guittard
Countess Charlotte Malcolm........Patricia
    Elliott
Osa........Sherry Mathis

Pacific Overtures

Music and Lyrics by Stephen Sondheim
Book by John Weidman
Additional Material by Hugh Wheeler
Produced by Harold Prince
In Association with Ruth Mitchell
Directed by Harold Prince
Choreography by Patricia Birch
Scenic Production Designed by Boris
    Aronson
Costumes Designed by Florence Klotz
Lighting Designed by Tharon Musser
Kabuki Consultant: Haruki Fujimoto
Makeup and Wigs Designed by Richard
    Allen
Masks and Dolls by E. J. Taylor
Dance Music by Daniel Troob
Musical Direction by Paul Gemignani
Orchestrations by Jonathan Tunick
Opened: Winter Garden, January 11,
    1976
Performances: 193

Musical Numbers:
"The Advantages of Floating in the
    Middle of the Sea," "There Is No
    Other Way," "Four Black Dragons,"
    "Chrysanthemum Tea," "Poems,"
    "Welcome to Kanagawa," "Someone
    in a Tree," "Lion Dance," "Please
    Hello," "A Bowler Hat," "Pretty
    Lady," "Next"

Musical Numbers Deleted Prior to New
    York Opening:
"Prayers"

Tony Award Nominations:
Best Musical, Best Score (Stephen
    Sondheim), Best Director—Musical
    (Harold Prince), Best Book—Musical
    (John Weidman), Best Actor—
    Musical (Mako), Best Actor—
    Featured Role—Musical (Isao Sato),
    Best Lighting Designer (Tharon
    Musser), Best Choreographer (Pat
    Birch), *Best Costume Design
    (Florence Klotz), *Best Scenic Design
    (Boris Aronson)

Winner: New York Drama Critics' Circle
Award for Best Musical

Cast:
Reciter........Mako

Abe, First Councillor........Yuki Shimoda
Manjiro........Sab Shimono
Second Councillor........James Dybas
Shogun's Mother........Alvin Ing
Third Councillor........Freddy Mao
Kayama........Isao Sato
Tamate, Samurai, Storyteller,
    Swordsman........Soon-Teck Oh
Samurai........Ernest Abuba, Mark Hsu
    Syers
Servant........Haruki Fujimoto
Observers........Alvin Ing, Ricardo Tobia
Fisherman........Jae Woo Lee
Merchant........Alvin Ing
Son........Timm Fujii
Grandmother........Conrad Yama
Thief........Mark Hsu Syers
Adams........Ernest Abuba
Williams........Larry Hama
Commodore Perry........Haruki Fujimoto
Shogun's Wife........Freda Foh Shen
Physician........Ernest Harada
Priests........Timm Fujii, Gedde
    Watanabe
Soothsayer........Mark Hsu Syers
Sumo Wrestlers........Conrad Yama, Jae
    Woo Lee
Shogun's Companion........Patrick
    Kinser-Lau
Shogun........Mako
Madam........Ernest Harada
Girls........Timm Fujii, Patrick Kinser-
    Lau, Gedde Watanabe, Leslie
    Watanabe
Old Man........James Dybas
Boy........Gedde Watanabe
Warrior........Mark Hsu Syers
Imperial Priest........Tom Matsusaka
Nobles........Ernest Abuba, Timm Fujii
American Admiral........Alvin Ing
British Admiral........Ernest Harada
Dutch Admiral........Patrick Kinser-Lau
Russian Admiral........Mark Hsu Syers
French Admiral........James Dybas
Lords of the South........Larry Hama, Jae
    Woo Lee
Jonathan Goble........Mako
Japanese Merchant........Conrad Yama

Samurai's Daughter........Freddy Mao
British Sailors........Timm Fujii, Patrick
    Kinser-Lau, Mark Hsu Syers
Proscenium Servants, Sailors, and
    Townspeople........Susan Kikuchi,
    Diane Lam, Kim Miyori, Freda Foh
    Shen, Kenneth S. Eiland, Timm
    Fujii, Joey Ginza, Patrick Kinser-Lau,
    Tony Marinyo, Kevin Maung, Dingo
    Secretario, Mark Hsu Syers, Ricardo
    Tobia, Gedde Watanabe, Leslie
    Watanabe
Musicians........Fusako Yoshida
    (Shamisen), Genji Ito (Percussion)

Side by Side by Sondheim

Music and Lyrics by Stephen Sondheim
And Music by Leonard Bernstein, Mary
    Rodgers, Richard Rodgers, Jule Styne
Produced by Harold Prince
In Association with Ruth Mitchell
By Arrangement with The InComes
    Company, Ltd.
Directed by Ned Sherrin
Musical Direction by Ray Cook
Pianists: Daniel Troob and Albin
    Konopka
Musical Staging by Bob Howe
Scenery by Peter Docherty
Costumes by Florence Klotz
Lighting by Ken Billington
Scenery Supervision: Jay Moore
Musical Supervision: Paul Gemignani
Opened: Music Box, April 18, 1977
Performances: 384

Musical Numbers:
(Varied cast to cast) "Comedy Tonight,"
    "Love Is in the Air," "If Momma Was
    Married," "You Must Meet My
    Wife," "The Little Things You Do
    Together," "Getting Married Today,"
    "I Remember," "Can That Boy
    Foxtrot!" "Company," "Another
    Hundred People," "Barcelona,"
    "Marry Me a Little," "I Never Do
    Anything Twice," "Bring on the

Girls," "Ah, Paree!" "Buddy's Blues,"
"Broadway Baby," "You Could Drive
a Person Crazy," "Everybody Says
Don't," "Anyone Can Whistle,"
"Send in the Clowns," "We're Gonna
Be All Right," "A Boy Like That"/"I
Have a Love," "The Boy From . . ."
"Pretty Lady," "You Gotta Have a
Gimmick," "Losing My Mind,"
"Could I Leave You?" "I'm Still
Here," "Conversation Piece" (medley),
"Side by Side by Side"

Tony Award Nominations:
Best Musical, Best Actor—Featured
Role—Musical (David Kernan), Best
Actor—Featured Role—Musical (Ned
Sherrin), Best Actress—Featured Role
—Musical (Millicent Martin), Best
Actress—Featured Role—Musical
(Julie N. McKenzie)

Cast:
Millicent Martin, Julie N. McKenzie,
David Kernan, Ned Sherrin

Original London Production opened at
the Mermaid Theatre on May 4,
1976, and moved to Wyndham
Theatre on July 7, 1976

Sweeney Todd, The Demon Barber of Fleet Street

Music and Lyrics by Stephen Sondheim
Book by Hugh Wheeler
Based on a Version of "Sweeney Todd"
by Christopher Bond
Produced by Richard Barr, Charles
Woodward, Robert Fryer, Mary Lea
Johnson, Martin Richards
In Association with Dean and Judy
Manos
Directed by Harold Prince
Dance and Movement by Larry Fuller
Production Designed by Eugene Lee
Costumes Designed by Franne Lee
Lighting Designed by Ken Billington
Orchestrations by Jonathan Tunick
Musical Director: Paul Gemignani

Opened: Uris Theatre, March 1, 1979
Performances: 558

Musical Numbers:
"The Ballad of Sweeney Todd," "No
Place Like London," "The Barber and
His Wife," "The Worst Pies in
London," "Poor Thing," "My
Friends," "Green Finch and Linnet
Bird," "Ah, Miss," "Johanna,"
"Pirelli's Miracle Elixir," "The
Contest," "Wait," "Kiss Me," "Ladies
in Their Sensitivities," "Quartet,"
"Pretty Women," "Epiphany," "A
Little Priest," "God, That's Good,"
"Johanna," "By the Sea," "Not While
I'm Around," "Parlor Songs," "City
on Fire!" Final Sequence, "The Ballad
of Sweeney Todd"

Musical Numbers Deleted Prior to New
York Opening:
"Johanna" (Judge's song)

Tony Award Nominations:
*Best Musical, *Best Book (Hugh
Wheeler), *Best Score (Stephen
Sondheim), *Best Actor in a Musical
(Len Cariou), *Best Actress in a
Musical (Angela Lansbury), *Best
Director (Harold Prince), *Best
Scenic Design (Eugene Lee), *Best
Costume Design (Franne Lee), Best
Lighting Design (Ken Billington)

Winner: New York Drama Critics' Circle
Award for Best Musical

Cast:
Anthony Hope........Victor Garber
Sweeney Todd........Len Cariou
Beggar Woman........Merle Louise
Mrs. Lovett........Angela Lansbury
Judge Turpin........Edmund Lyndeck
The Beadle........Jack Eric Williams
Johanna........Sarah Rice
Tobias Ragg........Ken Jennings
Pirelli........Joaquin Romaguera
Jonas Fogg........Robert Ousley

Freely Adapted in 1974 by Burt
  Shevelove
Produced by the Yale Repertory Theatre
Staged by Burt Shevelove
Choreographed by Carmen de Lavallade
Scenery Designed by Michael H.
  Yeargan
Costumes by Jeanne Button
Lighting by Carol M. Waaser
Selections from William Shakespeare and
  George Bernard Shaw Selected and
  Arranged by Michael Feingold
Musical Direction by Don Jennings
Orchestrations by Jonathan Tunick
Opened: Yale Swimming Pool, May 20,
  1974
Performances: 8

Musical Numbers:
Prologos: "Invocation to the Gods and
  Instructions to the Audience," *Parodos*:
  "The Frogs," *Hymnos*: "Dionysos,"
  Parabasis: "It's Only a Play," *Paean*:
  "Evoe for the Dead," *Exodos*: "The
  Sound of Poets"

Cast:
Dionysos........Larry Blyden
Xanthias........Michael Vale
Herakles........Dan Desmond
Charon........Charles Levin
Hierophantes........Ron Recasner
Aeakos........Alvin Epstein
A Handmaiden........Carmen de Lavallade
An Innkeeper's Wife........Carmen de
  Lavallade
An Innkeeper........Stephen R. Lawson
Pluto........Jeremy Dempsey
William Shakespeare........Jerome Geidt
Bernard Shaw........Anthony Holland
Guards........Joseph Costa, Jonathan
  Marks, Gil Rochon, III, Paul
  Schierhorn
Flagbearers........Christopher Brown,
  Darryl Hill

Singers: Joan Berliner, Peter Bogyo,
  Alma Cuervo, Franchelle Stewart
  Dorn, Christopher Durang, Beth

Hatton, Brock Holmes, Richard
  Larsen, Stephen R. Lawson, Susan
  LeFevre, Robert Picardo, Ron
  Recasner, Gil Rochon, III, Stephen
  Rowe, Jeremy Smith, Kate McGregor-
  Stewart, Meryl Streep, David Thomas,
  Scott Ulmer, Bob Van Nest,
  Sigourney Weaver, Donald Woodall
Dancers: Diana Belshaw, Linda K.
  Harold, Ron Porter, Nora Peterson,
  Diana Raffman, Susan Strasburger,
  Alfonso Wilson, Kathryn Woglom
Frogs: Steve Edelson, Wade Agurcia,
  Michael Armstrong, Robert Barnett,
  Michael Cadden, Jack Callahan, Gary
  Cavaliere, Peter Crawford, David B.
  Fisher, Ed Hornsby, Alexander
  Lawler, Quentin Lawler, Frank
  Lawlor, Kevin Lawlor, Dave Lichten,
  Pat Monahan, Ralph Redpath, Curt
  Sanburn, Ted Stein, Jose A. Taboada,
  Richard Taas

Marry Me a Little (REVUE)

Songs by Stephen Sondheim
Conceived and Developed by Craig Lucas
  and Norman René
Directed by Norman René
Musical Direction by E. Martin Perry
Choreography by Don Johanson
Set Design by Jane Thurn
Lighting Design by Debra J. Kletter
Costume Design by Oleksa
Produced by Diane de Mailly
In Association with William B. Young
Originally Produced by The Production
  Company
Opened: Actor's Playhouse, March 12,
  1981
Performances: 96
(Original Production ran October 29—
  December 28, 1980)

Musical Numbers:
"Two Fairy Tales," "Saturday Night,"
  "Can That Boy Foxtrot!" "All Things
  Bright and Beautiful," "Bang!" "All

Things Bright and Beautiful (Part II)," "The Girls of Summer," "Uptown, Downtown," "Who Could Be Blue?" "Little White House," "So Many People," "Your Eyes Are Blue," "A Moment with You," "Marry Me A Little," "Happily Ever After," "Pour Le Sport," "Silly People," "There Won't Be Trumpets," "It Wasn't Meant to Happen"

Cast:
Craig Lucas, Suzanne Henry

Sunday in the Park with George (WORKSHOP)

Music and Lyrics by Stephen Sondheim
Book by James Lapine
Set Design by Tony Straiges
Costume Design by Patricia Zipprodt and Ann Hould-Ward
Lighting by Richard Nelson
Sound by Scott Lehrer
Musical Theatre Program Director: Ira Weitzman
Production Stage Manager: Frederic H. Orner
Musical Director: Paul Gemignani
Directed by James Lapine
Presented by Playwrights Horizons; Andre Bishop, Artistic Director, Paul Daniels, Managing Director
In Association with The Herrick Theatre Foundation
Opened: Playwrights Horizons, July 6, 1983
Performances: 25

Musical Numbers:
"Sunday in the Park with George," "Yoo-Hoo!" "No Life," "Color and Light," "Gossip," "The Day Off," "Soldiers and Girls," "Everybody Loves Louis," "Beautiful," "Sunday," "It's Hot Up Here," "Gotta Keep 'em Humming"

Cast:

1884
Georges........Mandy Patinkin
Dot........Bernadette Peters
Old Lady........Carmen Matthews
Nurse........Judith Moore
Franz........Brent Spiner
Boy in the Water........Bradley Kane
Young Man on the Bank........Kelsey Grammer
Pervert........William Parry
Louise........Danielle Ferland
Jules........Ralph Byers
Clarisse........Christine Baranski
Boatman........William Parry
Louis........Kevin Marcum
Celeste 1........Melanie Vaughan
Celeste 2........Mary Elizabeth Mastrantonio
Bette........Nancy Opel
Soldier........Kelsey Grammer
Mr.........Kurt Knudson
Mrs........Judith Moore

1984
George........Mandy Patinkin
Marie........Bernadette Peters
Dennis........Brent Spiner
Bob Greenberg........Charles Kimbrough
Naomi Eisen........Dana Ivey
Harriet Pawling........Judith Moore
Billy Webster........Cris Groenendaal
Photographer........Sue Ann Gershenson
Museum Assistant........John Jellison
Charles Redmond........William Parry
Alex........Robert Westenberg
Betty........Nancy Opel
Lee Randolph........Kurt Knudson
Blair Daniels........Barbara Bryne
Waitress........Melanie Vaughan
Elaine........Mary D'Arcy

Pacific Overtures (REVIVAL)

Music and Lyrics by Stephen Sondheim
Book by John Weidman
Additional Material by Hugh Wheeler
Directed by Fran Soeder

Originally Produced and Directed by
    Harold Prince
Presented by the Shubert Organization
    and Elizabeth McCann and Nelle
    Nugent
Based on the York Theater Company
    Production, March 1984
    Janet Hayes Walker, Producing
    Director
Scenic Design by James Morgan
Lighting Design by Mary Jo Dondlinger
Costume Design by Mark Passerell
Additional Costumes by Eiko Yamaguchi
Musical Director: Eric Stern
Orchestrations by James Stenborg
Dance Music by Daniel Troob
Original Choreography by Patricia Birch
Choreographed by Janet Watson
Opened: Promenade Theatre, October
    25, 1984
Performances: 109

Musical Numbers:
As before

Cast:
Reciter........Ernest Abuba
Lord Abe........Tony Marino
Shogun's Mother, British Admiral
    ....Chuck Brown
Kayama Yesaemon........Kevin Gray
Tamate, British Sailor........Timm Fujii
John Manjiro, Fisherman, French
    Admiral........John Caleb
Merchant........Ronald Yamamoto
Thief........Tim Ewing
Commodore Perry........John Bantay
Madame, Russian Admiral........Thomas
    Ikeda
Old Man, American Admiral........John
    Baray
Boy, Dutch Admiral, British Sailor
    ....Francis Jue
Warrior, British Sailor........Ray
    Contreras
Imperial Priest........Tom Matsusaka
Fencing Master's Daughter........Allan
    Tung
Proscenium Servants........Gerri Igarashi,

Gayln Kong, Diana Lam, Christine
Toy

Merrily We Roll Along (LA JOLLA PLAYHOUSE—REVIVAL)

Music and Lyrics by Stephen Sondheim
Book by George Furth
From the Play by George S. Kaufman
    and Moss Hart
Presented by La Jolla Playhouse through
    special arrangement with Music
    Theatre International
Des McAnuff, Artistic Director
Directed by James Lapine
Choreography by Lynne Taylor-Corbett
Set Design by Loren Sherman
Costumes Designed by Ann Hould-Ward
Lighting Designed by Beverly Emmons
Orchestrations by Jonathan Tunick
Musical Director: Michael Starobin
Makeup and Hair by Peg Shierholz
Sound Design by John Kilgore
Projections by Wendall Harrington
Opened: La Jolla Playhouse, June 16,
    1985
Performances: 24

Musical Numbers:
"Merrily We Roll Along," "That
    Frank," "Like It Was," "Franklin
    Shepard, Inc.," "Old Friends,"
    "Growing Up," "Not A Day Goes
    By," "Now You Know," "It's A Hit!"
    "The Blob," "Growing Up," "Good
    Thing Going," "Bobby and Jackie and
    Jack," "Not A Day Goes By,"
    "Opening Doors," "Our Time"

Musical Number Deleted from New
    York Production:
"Rich & Happy"

Cast:
Mary Flynn........Heather MacRae
Tyler Horton........Ray Gill
Scotty........Ralph Bruneau
Terry........Joy Franz
Kate........B.J. Ward
Jerome........Lawrence Raiken

Dory........Rosalyn Rahn
Ruben........Stephen McDonough
Rich Party Guest........Dick Decareau
Meg........Kathleen Rowe McAllen
Franklin Shepard........John Rubinstein
Gussie........Mary Gordon Murray
Joe Josephson........Merwin Goldsmith
George........Dick Decareau
Charley Kringas........Chip Zien
Newsman........Ralph Bruneau
Newswoman........Kathleen Rowe
   McAllen
Reporter........Joy Franz
Photographer........Stephen McDonough
Beth........Marin Mazzie
Mr. Spencer........Dick Decareau
Audience Member........Joy Franz
Ted the Pianist........Theodore Sperling
Audience Member........Rosalyn Rahn
Mrs. Spencer........B.J. Ward
Minister........Lawrence Raiken
Evelyn........Rosalyn Rahn

III. BROADWAY REVIVALS

West Side Story

Produced by The Musical Theater of
   Lincoln Center and Richard Rodgers,
   President and Producing Director
Direction and Choreography Re-
   Produced by Lee Theodore
Scenic Production by Oliver Smith
Costumes by Winn Morton
Lighting by Peter Hunt
Musical Director: Maurice Peress
Opened: New York State Theater, June
   24, 1968
Performances: 89

Cast:
The Jets
Riff, The Leader........Avind Harum
Tony, His Friend........Kurt Peterson
Action........Ian Tucker
A-Rab........Robert LuPone
Baby John........Stephen Reinhardt
Snowboy........George Ramos

Big Deal........Roger Briant
Diesel........Victor Mohica
Gee-Tar........Chuck Beard
Mouth Piece........Joseph Pichette
Tiger........Kenneth Carr

Their Girls
Graziella........Garet de Troia
Velma........Nancy Dalton
Minnie........Rachael Lampert
Clarice........Sherry Lynn Diamant
Pauline........Carol Hanzel
Pucky........Jeanne Frey
Anybodys........Lee Lund

The Sharks
Bernardo, The Leader........Alan Castner
Maria, His Sister........Victoria Mallory
Anita, His Girl........Barbara Luna
Chino, His Friend........Bobby Capo, Jr.
Pepe........Edgar Coronado
Indio........Peter de Nicola
Luis........Pat Matera
Anxious........Steven Gelfer
Nibbles........Ramon Caballero
Juano........Pernett Robinson
Toro........Byron Wheeler
Moose........George Comtois

Their Girls
Rosalia........Kay Oslin
Consuelo........Lee Hooper
Teresita........Connie Burnett
Francisca........Eileen Barbaris
Estella........Judith Lerner
Marguerita........Carol Lynn Vasquez
Felicia........Diane McAfee

The Adults
Doc........Martin Wolfson
Schrank........Joseph Mascolo
Krupke........Josip Elic
Gladhand........Bill McCutcheon

A Funny Thing Happened on the Way to the Forum

Presented by David Black
In Association with Seymour Vall and
   Henry Honeckman

Produced by Larry Blyden
Directed by Burt Shevelove
Choreography by Ralph Beaumont
Settings by James Trittipo
Costumes by Noel Taylor
Lighting by H. R. Poindexter
Musical and Vocal Direction by Milton
  Rosenstock
Opened: Lunt-Fontanne Theatre, April
  4, 1972
Performances: 156

Musical Numbers Added: "Farewell,"
  "Echo Song"
Musical Numbers Deleted:
"Pretty Little Picture," "That'll Show
  Him"

Tony Award Nominations:
*Best Actor—Musical (Phil Silvers),
  *Best Supporting Actor—Musical
  (Larry Blyden), Best Director (Burt
  Shevelove)

Cast:
Prologus........Phil Silvers
Senex, a Roman Citizen........Mort
  Marshall
Domina, his wife........Lizabeth Pritchett
Hero, his son, in love with Philia
  ....John Hansen
Hysterium, slave to Senex and Domina
  ....Larry Blyden
Pseudolus, slave to Hero........Phil Silvers
Lycus, a buyer and seller of courtesans
  ....Carl Ballantine
Erronius, an old man........Reginald
  Owen
Miles Gloriosus, a warrior........Carl
  Lindstrom
Tintinnabula, a courtesan........Lauren
  Lucas
Panacea, a courtesan........Barbara Brown
The Geminae, courtesans........Kerry
  McGrath, Trudy Carson
Vibrata, a courtesan........Keita Keita
Gymnasia, a courtesan........Lisa Clarson
Philia, a virgin........Pamela Hall
The Proteans........Joe Ross, Bill Starr,
  Chad Block

Gypsy

Produced by Barry M. Brown, Fritz
  Holt, Edgar Lansbury, Joseph Beruh
Directed by Arthur Laurents
Choreography Reproduced by Robert
  Tucker
Settings and Lighting by Robert
  Randolph
Costumes by Raoul Pène du Bois
Miss Lansbury's Costumes by Robert
  Mackintosh
Musical Director: Milton Rosenstock
Opened: Winter Garden, September 23,
  1974
Performances: 120

Tony Award Nominations:
*Best Actress—Musical (Angela
  Lansbury), Best Director—Musical
  (Arthur Laurents), Best Actress,
  Supporting or Featured—Musical
  (Zan Charisse)

Cast:
Uncle Jocko........John C. Becher
George........Don Potter
Clarence (and his classical clarinet)
  ....Craig Brown
Balloon Girl........Donna Elio
Baby Louise........Lisa Peluso
Baby June........Bonnie Langford
Rose........Angela Lansbury
Chowsie........Pee Wee
Pop........Ed Riley
Newsboys........Craig Brown, Anthony
  Marciona, Sean Rule, Mark Santoro
Weber........Charles Rule
Herbie........Rex Robbins
Louise........Zan Charisse
June........Maureen Moore
Tulsa........John Sheridan
Yonkers........Steven Gelfer
L.A.........David Lawson
Little Rock........Jay Smith
San Diego........Dennis Karr
Boston........Serhij Bohdan
Kringelein........John C. Becher
Mr. Goldstone........Don Potter

Miss Cratchitt........Gloria Rossi
Hollywood Blondes........Pat Cody, Jinny
   Kordek, Jan Neuberger, Marilyn
   Olson, Pat Richardson
Agnes........Denny Dillon
Pastey........Richard J. Sabellico
Tessie Tura........Mary Louise Wilson
Mazeppa........Gloria Rossi
Cigar........John C. Becher
Electra........Sally Cooke
Maid........Bonnie Walker
Phil........Ed Riley
Bougeron-Cochon........Serhij Bohdan

Candide

Music by Leonard Bernstein
Lyrics by Richard Wilbur
Additional Lyrics by Stephen Sondheim
   and John Latouche
Book by Hugh Wheeler
Adapted from Voltaire
Presented by The Chelsea Theater Center
   of Brooklyn
Artistic Director: Robert Kalfin
Executive Director: Michael David
Production Director: Burl Hash
In Conjunction with Harold Prince and
   Ruth Mitchell
Directed by Harold Prince
Choreographed by Patricia Birch
Assistant Director: Ruth Mitchell
Production Designed by Eugene and
   Franne Lee
Lighting Designed by Tharon Musser
Musical Direction by John Mauceri
Orchestrations by Hershy Kay
Opened: Broadway Theatre, March 10,
   1974
Performances: 740

Musical Numbers:
Overture, "Life Is Happiness Indeed,"‡
   "The Best of All Possible Worlds,"
   "O Happy We," "It Must Be So," "O
   Miserere," "O Happy We" (reprise),
   "Glitter and Be Gay," "Auto Da Fé
   (What a Day),"‡ "This World,"‡

‡New lyrics by Stephen Sondheim.

"You Were Dead, You Know," "I Am
Easily Assimilated," "I Am Easily
Assimilated" (reprise), "My Love,"
"Alleluia," "Sheep's Song,"‡ "Bon
Voyage," "The Best of All Possible
Worlds" (reprise), "You Were Dead,
You Know" (reprise), "Make Our
Garden Grow"

Tony Award Nominations:
*Best Book (Hugh Wheeler), Best Scenic
   Design (Eugene and Franne Lee),
   *Best Costume Design (Franne Lee),
   *Best Director (Harold Prince), Best
   Actor—Musical (Lewis J. Stadlen)

Cast:
Dr. Voltaire, Dr. Pangloss, Governor,
   Host, Sage........Lewis J. Stadlen
Chinese Coolie, Westphalian Soldier,
   Priest, Spanish Don, Rosary Vendor,
   Sailor, Lion, Guest........Jim Corti
Candide........Mark Baker
Huntsman, 1st Recruiting Officer,
   Agent, Spanish Don, Cartagenian,
   Priest, Sailor, Eunuch........David
   Horwitz
Paquette........Deborah St. Darr
Baroness, Harpsichordist, Penitente,
   Steel Drummer, Houri........Mary-Pat
   Green
Baron, Grand Inquisitor, Slave Driver,
   Captain, Guest........Joe Palmieri
Cunegonde........Maureen Brennan
Maximilian........Sam Freed
Servant, Agent of the Inquisition,
   Spanish Don, Cartagenian Sailor
   ....Robert Hendersen
2nd Recruiting Officer, Aristocrat,
   Cartagenian........Peter Vogt
Penitente, Whore, Houri........Gail
   Boggs
Penitente, Cartagenian, Houri
   ....Lynne Gannaway
Aristocrat, Cartagenian, 2nd Sheep
   ....Carolann Page
Bulgarian Soldier, Aristocrat, Fruit

Vendor, Sailor, Pygmy, Cow
........Carlos Gorbea
Bulgarian Soldier, Penitente,
   Cartagenian, Sailor, Cow........Kelly
   Walters
Westphalian Soldier, Agent, Governor's
   Aide, Pirate, Guest........Chip Garnett
Rich Jew, Judge, Man in Black,
   Cartagenian, Pirate, German,
   Botanist, Guest........Jeff Keller
Aristocrat, Cartagenian, Houri
   ....Becky McSpadden
Aristocrat, Whore, Houri (Cunegonde
   Alternate)........Kathryn Ritter
Lady with Knitting, Cartagenian, 1st
   Sheep........Renee Semes
Old Lady........June Gable
Swing Girl........Rhoda Butler

West Side Story (REVIVAL)

Based on a Jerome Robbins Conception
Book by Arthur Laurents
Music by Leonard Bernstein
Lyrics by Stephen Sondheim
Entire Production Directed and
   Choreographed by Jerome Robbins
Book Co-Directed by Gerald Freedman
Choreography Reproduced with the
   assistance of Tom Abbott, Lee Becker
   Theodore
Scenery Designed by Oliver Smith
Costumes Designed by Irene Sharaff
Lighting Designed by Jean Rosenthal
Co-Choreographer: Peter Gennaro
Musical Direction: John DeMain,
   Donald Jennings
Orchestrations by Leonard Bernstein
   with Sid Ramin and Irwin Kostal
Produced by Gladys Rackmil, The John
   F. Kennedy Center, and James M.
   Nederlander
In Association with Zev Buffman
Executive Producer: Ruth Mitchell
Opened: Minskoff Theatre, February 14,
   1980
Performances: 333

Musical Numbers: Same as Original

Tony Award Nominations:
Actress—Featured Role—Musical
   (Debbie Allen), Actress—Featured
   Role—Musical (Josie de Guzman),
   Reproduction—Play or Musical

Cast:
Riff........James J. Mellon
Tony........Ken Marshall
Bernardo........Hector Jaime Mercado
Maria........Josie de Guzman
Anita........Debbie Allen
Anybodys........Missy Whitchurch
Jets........Mark Bove, Todd Lester, Brian
   Kaman, Tim O'Keefe, Cleve Asbury,
   Reed Jones, Brent Barrett, G. Russell
   Weilandich, Stephen Bogardus, Mark
   Fotopoulos
Their Girls........Georgeanna Mills,
   Heather Lee Gerdes, Frankie Wade,
   Charlene Gehm, Nancy Louise
   Chismar
Sharks........Ray Contreras, Michael
   Rivera, Darryl Tribble, Adrian
   Rosario, Michael de Lorenzo, Willie
   Rosario, Gary-Michael Davies
Their Girls........Yamil Borges, Nancy
   Ticotin, Harolyn Blackwell, Stephanie
   E. Williams, Marlene Danielle, Amy
   Lester
Doc........Sammy Smith
Schrank........Arch Johnson
Krupke........John Bentley
Glad Hand........Jake Turner

IV. OPERA VERSIONS

Candide

Book Adapted from Voltaire by Hugh
   Wheeler
Lyrics by Richard Wilbur
Additional Lyrics by Stephen Sondheim
   and John LaTouche
Music by Leonard Bernstein
Orchestrations by Leonard Bernstein and
   Hershy Kay

Musical Supervision and Additional
  Orchestrations by John Mauceri
Conducted by John Mauceri
Directed by Harold Prince
Choreographed by Patricia Birch
Scenery Designed by Clarke Dunham
Costumes Designed by Judith Dolan
Lighting Designed by Ken Billington
Presented by the New York City Opera,
  Beverly Sills, General Director
Opened: The New State Theater,
  October 13, 1982
Performances: in repertory 1982, 1983,
  1984

Musical Numbers:
"Overture," "Life Is Happiness Indeed,"
  "The Best of All Possible Worlds,"
  "O Happy We," "It Must Be So,"
  "Fanfare, Chorale and Battle,"
  "Glitter and Be Gay," "Dear Boy,"
  "Auto da Fé," "Candide's Lament,"
  "You Were Dead, You Know," "I Am
  Easily Assimilated," "Quartet Finale,"
  "Entr'acte and Ballad: To the New
  World," "My Love," "The Old Lady's
  Tale (Barcarolle)," "Alleluia," "Sheep
  Song," "Governor's Waltz," "Bon
  Voyage," "Quiet," "The Best of All
  Possible Worlds" (reprise), "What's
  the Use?" "You Were Dead, You
  Know" (reprise), "Finale: Make Our
  Garden Grow"

Cast:
Voltaire........John Lankston
Candide........David Eisler
Huntsman........Don Yule
Paquette........Deborah Darr
Baroness........Bonnie Kirk
Baron........Jack Harrold
Cunegonde........Erie Mills
Maximilian........Scott Reeve
Servant of Maximilian........James
  Billings
Dr. Pangloss........John Lankston
Bulgarian Soldiers........Don Yule, James
  Billings

Westphalian Soldiers........Andy Roth,
  William Ledbetter
Don Issachar, the Jew........James
  Billings
Grand Inquisitor........Jack Harrold
Calliope Player........Bonnie Kirk
Heresy Agent........Ralph Bassett
Inquisition Agents........Gary Dietrich,
  William Poplaski
Judge........James Billings
Old Lady........Muriel Costa-Greenspon
Dons........Aurelio Padron, Andy Roth,
  Michael Rubino, Don Yule, William
  Ledbetter, Ralph Bassett
Businessman........John Lankston
Governor........John Lankston
Governor's Aide........Aurelio Padron
Slave Driver........Jack Harrold
Father Bernard........James Billings
Sailors........Gary Dietrich, William
  Poplaski, Andy Roth, Aurelio Padron
Pirates........John Henry Thomas,
  William Ledbetter
Pink Sheep........Ivy Austin, Rhoda
  Butler
Lion........James Sergi
Pasha-Prefect........Jack Harrold
First Gambler........James Billings
Second Gambler (Police Chief)........John
  Lankston
Sage........John Lankston

Sweeney Todd, The Demon Barber of Fleet Street

Music and Lyrics by Stephen Sondheim
Book by Hugh Wheeler
From a Play by Christopher Bond
Conducted by Paul Gemignani
Directed by Harold Prince
Scenery Designed by Eugene Lee
Costumes Designed by Franne Lee
Lighting Designed by Ken Billington
Choreography by Larry Fuller
Presented by the New York City Opera,
  Beverly Sills, General Director

Opened: The New York State Theater,
October 11, 1984
Performances: 8

Musical Numbers:
Same as before, with the addition of the
Judge's song "Johanna," and the
Beggar Woman's Lullaby.

Cast: (Second Cast in parentheses)
Anthony Hope........Cris Groenendaal
Sweeney Todd........Timothy Nolan
(Stanley Wexler)
Beggar Woman........Adair Lewis
Mrs. Lovett........Rosalind Elias (Joyce
Castle) (Elaine Bonazzi)
Judge Turpin........William Dansby
(Will Roy)
The Beadle........John Lankston
Johanna........Leigh Munro (Sheryl
Woods)
Tobias Ragg........Paul Binotto
Pirelli........Jerold Siena
Jonas Fogg........William Ledbetter
Ensemble........New York City Opera
Chorus

First presented at the Houston Grand
Opera, July 14, 1984

V. SPECIAL EVENTS

Sondheim: A Musical Tribute

Produced by Kurt Peterson
In Association with Craig Zadan and
Neil Appelbaum
Directed by Burt Shevelove
Choreographed by Donna McKechnie
Setting Courtesy of Boris Aronson
Lighting by Tharon Musser
Costume Coordination by Florence Klotz
Musical Direction by Paul Gemignani
Musical Coordination and Special
Arrangements by Jonathan Tunick
For the Benefit of A.M.D.A. and The
National Hemophilia Foundation
Shubert Theatre, March 11, 1973

Performance: 1

Musical Numbers:
Overture, "Side by Side by Side," "Do I
Hear a Waltz?" "Take the Moment,"
"If Momma Was Married,"
"America," "Something's Coming,"
"One More Kiss," "Broadway Baby,"
"You Could Drive a Person Crazy,"
"You're Gonna Love Tomorrow,"
"Love Will See Us Through," "Take
Me to the World," "I Remember,"
"Silly People," "Two Fairy Tales,"
"There Won't Be Trumpets," "Love Is
in the Air," "Your Eyes Are Blue,"
"Marry Me a Little," "Pleasant Little
Kingdom," "Too Many Mornings,"
"Me and My Town," "The Little
Things You Do Together," "Lovely,"
"Getting Married Today," "Buddy's
Blues," "Comedy Tonight," "Class,"
"So Many People," "Another Hundred
People," "Happily Ever After,"
"Being Alive," "We're Gonna Be All
Right," "Beautiful Girls," "Liaisons,"
"I'm Still Here," "A Parade in
Town," "Could I Leave You?" "Send
in the Clowns," "Losing My Mind,"
"Anyone Can Whistle," "What
Would We Do Without You?" "Side
by Side by Side"

Cast:
George Lee Andrews, Larry Blyden,
Susan Browning, Len Cariou, Jack
Cassidy, Dorothy Collins, Steve
Elmore, Harvey Evans, Hermione
Gingold, Laurence Guittard, Pamela
Hall, Ron Holgate, Beth Howland,
Glynis Johns, Justine Johnston, Larry
Kert, Mark Lambert, Angela
Lansbury, Victoria Mallory, Mary
McCarty, Donna McKechnie, John
McMartin, Pamela Myers, Kurt
Peterson, Alice Playten, Teri Ralston,
Chita Rivera, Marti Rolph, Virginia
Sandifur, Ethel Shutta, Alexis Smith,
Tony Stevens, Nancy Walker

Special Guests:
Harold Prince, Leonard Bernstein, Jule Styne, Burt Shevelove, Diana Shumlin, Sheldon Harnick, George Furth, James Goldman, Mary Rodgers, Goddard Lieberson, Anthony Perkins

A Stephen Sondheim Evening

Songs by Stephen Sondheim
Produced and Directed by Paul Lazarus as part of the Composers' Showcase series
Musical Direction by Paul Gemignani
Musical Supervision and Arrangements by Thomas Fay
Performance: Sotheby's, March 3, 1983

Musical Numbers:
"All Things Bright and Beautiful," "Invocation and Instructions to the Audience," "Saturday Night," "This Is Nice, Isn't It?" "Poems," "What More Do I Need?" "Another Hundred People," "With So Little To Be Sure Of," "Pretty Little Picture," "The House of Marcus Lycus," "Echo Song," "There's Something About a War," "Fear No More," "Being Alive," "You're Gonna Love Tomorrow," "Love Will See Us Through," "The Miller's Son," "Johanna," "Not a Day Goes By," "Someone in a Tree," "Send in the Clowns," "Old Friends"

Cast:
Liz Callaway, Cris Groenendaal, Bob Gunton, George Hearn, Steven Jacob, Judy Kaye, Victoria Mallory
Special appearance by Angela Lansbury, with Stephen Sondheim accompanying.

Follies in Concert with New York Philharmonic

Music and Lyrics by Stephen Sondheim

Book and New Continuity by James Goldman
Produced by Thomas Z. Shepard
Directed by Herbert Ross
Musical Direction by Paul Gemignani
Orchestrations by Jonathan Tunick
Assistant Director: Paul Lazarus
Dance Music by John Berkman
Choreography by Danny Daniels
Scenic Supervision by Tony Straiges
Sound Design by Jules Fisher and Paul Marantz, Inc.
Wardrobe Supervision by Karen Lloyd

Performances: 2
September 6 and 7, 1985, at Lincoln Center

Musical Numbers:
"Beautiful Girls," "Don't Look at Me," "Waiting for the Girls Upstairs," "Rain on the Roof," "Ah, Paree!" "Broadway Baby," "The Road You Didn't Take," "In Buddy's Eyes," "Who's That Woman?" "I'm Still Here," "Too Many Mornings," "The Right Girl," "One More Kiss," "Could I Leave You?" "Loveland," "You're Gonna Love Tomorrow," "Love Will See Us Through," "Buddy's Blues," "Losing My Mind," "The Story of Lucy and Jessie," "Live, Laugh, Love"

Cast:
Roscoe........Arthur Rubin
Sally Durant Plummer........Barbara Cook
Benjamin Stone........George Hearn
Buddy Plummer........Mandy Patinkin
Phyllis Rogers Stone........Lee Remick
Young Buddy........Jim Walton
Young Ben........Howard McGillin
Young Phyllis........Daisy Prince
Young Sally........Liz Callaway
Emily Whitman........Betty Comden
Theodore Whitman........Adolph Green
Dimitri Weismann........André Gregory
Solange LaFitte........Liliane Montevecchi

Hattie Walker........Elaine Stritch
Stella Deems........Phyllis Newman
Carlotta Campion........Carol Burnett
Heidi Schiller........Licia Albanese
Young Heidi........Erie Mills
Chorus........Ronn Caroll, Susan Cella,
   Robert Hendersen, Frank Kopyc,
   Marti Morris, Ted Sperling, Susan
   Terry, Sandra Wheeler
Dancers........Karen Fraction, Linda Von
   Germer, Jamie M. Pisano, Elvera
   Sciarra

VI. MOTION PICTURES

West Side Story

Presented by Mirisch Pictures
In Association with Seven Arts
   Productions
Released through United Artists
Directed by Robert Wise and Jerome
   Robbins
Choreographed by Jerome Robbins
Screenplay by Ernest Lehman
A Robert Wise Production
Released: October 1961

Academy Award Nominations:
*Best Picture, *Best Supporting Actor
   (George Chakiris), *Best Supporting
   Actress (Rita Moreno), *Best Director
   (Robert Wise and Jerome Robbins),
   *Best Color Cinematography (Daniel
   L. Fapp), *Best Color Art Direction
   and Sets (Boris Leven, Victor A.
   Gangelin), *Best Sound (Todd-AO),
   *Best Scoring of a Musical (Saul
   Chaplin, Sid Ramin, Johnny Green,
   Irwin Kostal), *Best Editing (Thomas
   Stanford), *Best Costumes (Irene
   Sharaff), Best Screenplay Based on
   Material from Another Medium
   (Ernest Lehman); Plus: Honorary
   Academy Award (Jerome Robbins)

Cast:
Maria........Natalie Wood

Tony........Richard Beymer
Riff........Russ Tamblyn
Anita........Rita Moreno
Bernardo........George Chakiris

The Jets
Ice........Tucker Smith
Action........Tony Mordente
Baby John........Eliot Feld
A-Rab........David Winters
Snowboy........Burt Michaels
Joyboy........Robert Banas
Big Deal........Scooter (Anthony) Teague
Gee-Tar........Tommy Abbott
Mouthpiece........Harvey Hohnecker
   (Evans)
Tiger........David Bean
Anybodys........Sue Oakes
Graziella........Gina Trikonis
Velma........Carole D'Andrea

The Sharks
Chino........Joe De Vega
Pepe........Jay Norman
Indio........Gus Trikonis
Luis........Robert Thompson
Rocco........Larry Roquemore
Loco........Jaime Rogers
Juano........Eddie Verso
Chile........Andre Tayir
Toro........Nick Covvacevich
Del Camp........Rudy Del Campo
Rosalia........Suzie Kaye
Consuelo........Yvonne Othon
Francisca........Joanne Miya
Lieutenant Schrank........Simon Oakland
Officer Krupke........Bill Bramley
Doc........Ned Glass
Glad Hand, Social Worker........John
   Astin
Madame Lucia........Penny Santon

Gypsy

Presented by Warner Bros. Pictures
Directed by Mervyn LeRoy
Screenplay by Leonard Spigelgass
A Mervyn LeRoy Production
Released: January 1963

Cast:
Rose........Rosalind Russell
Louise........Natalie Wood
Herbie Sommers........Karl Malden
Tulsa........Paul Wallace
Tessie Tura........Betty Bruce
Mr. Kringelein........Parley Baer
Grandpa........Harry Shannon
Baby June........Suzanne Cupito
Dainty June........Ann Jilliann
Baby Louise........Diane Pace
Mazeppa........Faith Dane
Electra........Roxanne Arlen
George........George Petrie
Mr. Beckman........James Millhollin
Mr. Willis........William Fawcett
Mervyn Goldstone........Ben Lessy
Pastey........Guy Raymond
Cigar........Louis Quinn
Yonkers........Danny Lockin
Angie........Ian Tucker
Farm Boy........Bert Michaels
Agnes........Lois Roberts
Delores........Dina Claire
Phil........Harvey Korman
Betty Cratchitt........Jean Willes

Academy Award Nominations:
Best Cinematography—Color (Harvey
    Stradling, Sr.), Best Costume Design
    —Color (Orry Kelly), Best Music—
    Scoring of Music Adaptation or
    Treatment (Frank Perkins)

A Funny Thing Happened on the Way to the Forum

Released through United Artists
Screenplay by Melvin Frank and Michael
    Pertwee
Produced by Melvin Frank
Directed by Richard Lester
Incidental Music by Ken Thorne
A Melvin Frank Production
Released: October 1966

Cast:
Pseudolus........Zero Mostel
Lycus........Phil Silvers

Erronius........Buster Keaton
Hysterium........Jack Gilford
Hero........Michael Crawford
Philia........Annette Andre
Domina........Patricia Jessel
Senex........Michael Hordern
Gymnasia........Inga Neilsen
Miles Gloriosus........Leon Green
Vibrata........Myrna White
Panacea........Lucienne Bridou
Tintinnabula........Helen Funai
The Geminae........Jennifer and Susan
    Baker
Fertilla........Janet Webb
High Priestess........Pamela Brown
Guard........Alfie Bass

Academy Award Nominations:
*Scoring of Music Adaptation or
    Treatment (Ken Thorne)

The Last of Sheila

(Nonmusical)
Written by Stephen Sondheim and
    Anthony Perkins
Produced and Directed by Herbert Ross
Production Designer: Ken Adams
Executive Producer: Stanley O'Toole
Music by Billy Goldenberg
"Friends" sung by Bette Midler
    Words and Music by Buzzy Linhart
    and Mark Klingman
Production Associate: Nora Kaye
Art Direction: Tony Roman
Costume Designer: Joel Schumacher
A Warner Bros. Presentation of a
    Herbert Ross Film

Cast (Principals):
........Tom........Richard Benjamin
Christine........Dyan Cannon
Clinton........James Coburn
Lee........Joan Hackett
Philip........James Mason
Anthony........Ian McShane
Alice........Raquel Welch

A Little Night Music

Presented by Sascha-Wien Film
In Association with Elliott Kastner
Executive Producer: Heinz Lazek
Producer: Elliott Kastner
Directed by Harold Prince
Screenplay by Hugh Wheeler
Music and Lyrics by Stephen Sondheim
Edited by John Jympson
Photographed by Arthur Ibbetson,
    B.S.C.
Costumes Designed by Florence Klotz
Choreography by Patricia Birch
Music Scored and Supervised by
    Jonathan Tunick
Musical Director: Paul Gemignani
Presented by Roger Corman—A New
    World Picture
Released: March 1978

Cast:
Désirée Armfeldt........Elizabeth Taylor
Charlotte Mittelheim........Diana Rigg
Fredrik Egerman........Len Cariou
Anne Egerman........Lesley-Anne Down
Mme. Armfeldt........Hermione Gingold
Carl-Magnus Mittelheim........Laurence
    Guittard
Erich Egerman........Christopher Guard
Fredrika Armfeldt........Chloe Franks
Kurt........Heins Marecek
Petra........Lesley Dunlop
Conductor........Jonathan Tunick

Academy Award Nominations:
*Original Song Score and Adaptation or
    Adaptation Score (Jonathan Tunick),
    Costume Design (Florence Klotz)

VII. TELEVISION

Evening Primrose

Music and Lyrics by Stephen Sondheim
Teleplay by James Goldman
Based on the Story "Evening Primrose"
    by John Collier

Produced by Willard Levitas
Executive Producer: John Houseman
For Gramercy Productions, Inc.
Directed by Paul Bogart
An *ABC Stage 67* Presentation
Telecast: November 16, 1966

Musical Numbers:
"I'm Here," "I Remember," "When?"
    "Take Me to the World"

Cast (Principals):
Charles Snell........Anthony Perkins
Ella Harkins........Charmian Carr
Mrs. Monday........Dorothy Stickney
Roscoe Potts........Larry Gates

Sweeney Todd, The Demon Barber of Fleet Street

In addition to credits of the original
    production:
Presented by RKO/Nederlander and The
    Entertainment Channel
Executive Producers: Ellen M. Krass,
    Archer King
Produced by Bonnie Burns
Directed by Terry Hughes
Executive in Charge of Production:
    James Rich, Jr.
Lighting Designed for Television by Bill
    Klages
Musical Conductor: Jim Coleman

Cast:
Anthony Hope........Cris Groenendaal
Sweeney Todd........George Hearn
Beggar Woman........Sara Woods
Mrs. Lovett........Angela Lansbury
Judge Turpin........Edmund Lyndeck
The Beadle........Calvin Remsberg
Johanna........Betsy Joslyn
Tobias Ragg........Ken Jennings
Pirelli........Sal Mistretta
The Birdseller........Spain Logue
The Passerby........Walter Charles
Jonas Fogg........Michael Kalinyen

The Company........Walter Charles, Roy Gioconda, Skip Harris, Michael Kalinyen, Spain Logue, Duane Morris, Patricia Parker, Meredith Rawlins, Stuart Redfield, Candace Rogers, Dee Etta Rowe, Carrie Solomon, Melanie Vaughan, Joseph Warner
Swings........Cheryl Mae Stewart, James Edward Justiss, William Kirk

Emmy Award Nominations:
*Outstanding Individual Performance in a Variety or Musical Program (George Hearn), *Outstanding Directing in a Variety or Musical Program (Terry Hughes), Outstanding Individual Performance in a Variety or Musical Program (Angela Lansbury), Best Video Tape Editing for a Limited Series or Special (Jimmy B. Frazier), Best Live and Tape Sound Mixing and Sound Effects for a Limited Series or Special (Doug Nelson—Production, Jerry Clemans—Post Production, Eric Lee Levison—Sound Effects)

Ace Award Nominations:
*Best Achievement in Directing a Theatrical—Musical Program (Terry Hughes), *Best Performance by an Actor in a Theatrical—Musical Program (George Hearn), *Best Performance by an Actress in a Theatrical—Musical Program (Angela Lansbury), *Excellence in a Single Program in a Theatrical—Musical Program

Sunday in the Park with George

In addition to the credits of the original production:
Executive Producers: Michael Brandman and Emanuel Azenberg in association with the Shubert Organization and American Playhouse
Produced by: Iris Merlis
Directed by: Terry Hughes
Executive in Charge of Production: Greg Sills
Lighting consultant: Bill Klages
Musical Director and Conductor: Paul Gemignani

Cast:
George........Mandy Patinkin
Dot/Marie........Bernadette Peters
Jules/Greenberg........Charles Kimbrough
Old Lady/Blair........Barbara Bryne
Yvonne/Naomi........Dana Ivey
Celeste #2/Elaine........Mary D'Arcy
Woman/Photographer........Sue Anne Gershenson
Louis/Billy........Cris Groenendaal
Man/Party Guest........John Jellison
Mr./Publicist........Frank Kopyc
Nurse/Mrs./Harriet........Judith Moore
Frieda/Betty........Nancy Opel
Boatman/Redmond........William Parry
Louise........Natalie Polizzie
Girl........Michele Rigan
Franz/Dennis........Brent Spiner
Celeste #1/Waitress........Melanie Vaughan
Soldier/Alex........Robert Westenberg

APPENDIX B: SONDHEIM · · ·
CAST ALBUMS

I. ORIGINAL BROADWAY CAST RECORDINGS

West Side Story
Columbia Records
   JS 32603
Album Produced by Goddard Lieberson

*Gypsy
Columbia Records
   PS 32607
Album Produced by Goddard Lieberson

†A Funny Thing Happened on the Way to the Forum
Capitol Records
   SW 1717
Album Produced by Andy Wiswell and
   Dick Jones

Anyone Can Whistle
Columbia Records
   KOS 2480
Album Produced by Goddard Lieberson

*Winner of the Grammy Award for Best Original
   Cast Show Album
†Nominated for the Grammy Award for Best
   Original Cast Show Album

†Do I Hear a Waltz?
Columbia Records
   KOS 2770
Album Produced by Goddard Lieberson

*Company
Columbia Records
   OS 3550
   CK 03550—Compact Disc
Album Produced by Thomas Z. Shepard

†Follies
Capitol Records
   SO 761
Album Produced by Dick Jones

*A Little Night Music
Columbia Records
   KS 32265
   CK 32265—Compact Disc
Album Associate Producer: Thomas Z.
   Shepard
Album Produced by Goddard Lieberson

Candide
Columbia Records
   S2X 32923

New Broadway Cast Recording
(complete show)
Additional Lyrics by Stephen Sondheim
Album Produced by Thomas Z. Shepard

†Pacific Overtures
RCA Records
  ARL1-4407
  RCD-4407—Compact Disc
Album Produced by Thomas Z. Shepard

*Sweeney Todd, The Demon Barber of Fleet Street
RCA Records
  CBL2-3379
  RCD1-5033—Compact Disc‡
Album Produced by Thomas Z. Shepard
‡Highlights only

Marry Me a Little
RCA Records
  ABL1-4159
Album Produced by Thomas Z. Shepard

†Merrily We Roll Along
RCA Records
  CBL1-4197
  RCD1-5840—Compact Disc‡
Album Produced by Thomas Z. Shepard
‡"It's a Hit," deleted from cast album,
  has been added to CD.

*Sunday in the Park with George
RCA Records
  HBC1-5042
  RCD1-5042—Compact Disc
Album Produced by Thomas Z. Shepard

II. OTHER ORIGINAL CAST RECORDINGS

The Mad Show
Columbia Records
  OS-2930
Album Produced by David Rubinson

Sondheim: A Musical Tribute
Warner Bros. Records
  2WS 2705
Album Associate Producers: Craig Zadan
  and Neil Appelbaum

Album Produced by Hal Halverstadt

Company
CBS Records
  70108‡
Larry Kert and Broadway Cast
Released for London Opening
Album Produced by Thomas Z. Shepard
‡This Broadway cast recording contains
  cuts tracked in by Larry Kert as a
  substitution for those originally
  recorded by Dean Jones.

Gypsy
RCA Records
  LBL 1-5004‡
Angela Lansbury and London Cast
Released for American Tour
Album Produced by Norman Newell
‡This American-released version of the
  London cast recording is remixed and
  contains different cuts from the same
  album released earlier in London.

†A Little Night Music
RCA Records
  LRL1-5090
  RCD1-5090—Compact Disc
Jean Simmons and London Cast
Album Produced by Thomas Z. Shepard

†Side by Side by Sondheim (Original London Cast)
RCA Records
  CBL2-1851‡
Album Produced by Thomas Z. Shepard
‡This London recording was also released
  as the original cast recording for the
  Broadway show.

†A Stephen Sondheim Evening
RCA Records
  CBL2-4745
Album Produced by Thomas Z. Shepard

Follies in Concert
RCA Records
  HBC2-7128
  RCD2-7128—Compact Disc‡
Album Produced by Thomas Z. Shepard
‡Cassette and CD also contain complete
  soundtrack album for *Stavisky*

Sondheim
Book-of-the-Month Club Records
   81-7515
   11-7517—Compact Disc
Album Produced by Max Wilcox

A Collector's Sondheim
RCA Records
   CRL4-5359
   RCD3-5480—Compact Disc‡
Album Produced by Thomas Z. Shepard
‡Deleted from CD: "Your Eyes Are
   Blue," "Welcome to Kanagawa," and
   "Silly People"

***West Side Story**
Deutsche Grammophon
   415253-1/4
   415253-2—Compact Disc
Album Conducted by Leonard Bernstein
Album Produced by John McClure

Candide (New York City Opera)
New World Records
   NW 340/341
   NW 340/341/2—Compact Disc
Album Produced by Elizabeth Ostrow

III. MOTION-PICTURE SOUNDTRACK RECORDINGS

West Side Story
Columbia Records
   OS 2070
Album Conducted by Johnny Green

Gypsy
Warner Bros. Records
   BS 1480
Album Supervised by Frank Perkins

A Funny Thing Happened on the Way to the Forum
United Artists Records
   UAS 5144
Album Musical Direction by Ken
   Thorne

Stavisky
RCA Records (American Release)
   ARL 1-0952
Polydor Records (European Release)
   2393 088
Music by Stephen Sondheim
Orchestrations by Jonathan Tunick
Original Soundtrack of a Film by Alain
   Resnais

A Little Night Music
Columbia Records
   JS 35333
Album Produced by Jonathan Tunick
   and Bob Hathaway

Reds
Columbia Records
   BJS 37690
Album Produced by Phil Ramone
Original Soundtrack of a Film by
   Warren Beatty

ACKNOWLEDGMENTS · · ·
First Edition

First, my deepest appreciation to author, playwright, and friend William Goyen, without whose persistence and belief this book would never have been initiated. I wish to thank Harold Prince, who helped me convince Stephen Sondheim that he was indeed ready for a "going over" at this point in his career. Without Jonathan Sand, my editorial assistant, who spent an eternity helping me prepare the taped transcriptions, the manuscript would have taken at least another year to put together. And most appreciatively, to Neil Appelbaum for his many hours of assistance and support throughout the writing of this book.

I would also like to thank the Dramatists Guild for permission to include portions of Mr. Sondheim's lecture on lyric writing (delivered at the 92nd Street YM-YWHA on May 2, 1971, and first published in the *Dramatists Guild Quarterly*, Autumn 1971). Thanks also to Warner Bros. Records for permission to include excerpts from Alan Rich's special account of *Sondheim: A Musical Tribute*.

In addition, I would like to thank the many others who contributed invaluable information and assistance: Tommy Valando, David Wolf, Bill Evans, Mary Bryant Publicity, Fred Ebb, Flora Roberts, Claire Heller, Roz Starr Agency, Merle Frimark, Hilary James, George Nelson, Barbara Meyers, Virginia Lord, Warner Bros. Pictures, Al Sullivan, Larry Gelbart, Van Williams, Joe Abeles, Martha Swope, Laura Rubin, Edwin and Michael Gifford, Marguerite Renz, Tom Trenkle, Larry Taylor, Jack Klugman, Ron Galella, Jewel Howard, Irini Res, Paul and Rhoda Gemignani, Harvey Evans, John Kander, Alexis Smith, Michael Misita, Larry Kert,

Dorothy Collins, Chuck Adams, Dean Jones, Gene Nelson, Mathilde Pincus, Al Miller, Charles Hansen, Annette Meyers, Chappell & Co., Lee Snider, Metromedia Music, Alan Eichler, John Lee, Peter Buckley, Michael Bennett, Keith Baxter, Herbert Ross, Arthur Laurents, Glenn Loney, Helen Nickerson, Doris Roberts, Verleah Brown, Columbia Records, Bill O'Connell, Bob Donaghey, Angela Lansbury, David Merrick, Noah Tree, Wakefield Poole, Leonard Bernstein, Steven Holmes, Thomas Z. Shepard, Irving Brown, Goddard Lieberson, Anthony Perkins, Jack Lyons, Edgar Lansbury, Herb Helman, George Martin, RCA Records, Larry Blyden, James Goldman, Milton Babbitt, John Grigas, Betty Lee Hunt Associates, George Oppenheimer, John Guare, Jack Cassidy, Ruth Mitchell, Diana Shumlin, Burt Shevelove, Hunt Downs, Jule Styne, Ed Naha, Bug Riesmeyer, Joan Hackett, Fritz Holt, Zero Mostel, Barry Brown, Jonathan Tunick, Boris Aronson, Richard Pilbrow, Sid Ramin, Chita Rivera, Jon Campbell, Tharon Musser, Florence Klotz, Sy Friedman, Shirley Rich, Rex Reed, Patricia Birch, Joanna Merlin, Daniel Langan, Len Cariou, Sy Sandler, Saul Richman, Hermione Gingold, Ralph Burns, Kermit Bloomgarden, Dyan Cannon, Glynis Johns, Jerome Whyte, The Drama Bookshop, Irving Goldman, Bernard B. Jacobs, Gerald Schoenfeld, Warren Caro, Philip Smith, Warner Bros. Records, Hal Halverstadt, Joe Smith, Billie Wallington, Liz Rosenberg, Cathy Galligan, Barry Nettles, Music Theatre International, Dean Pitchford, Joan Alleman Rubin, and finally, Martin and Muriel Bresloff, and Louis, Bertha, Murray, and Naomi Zadan.

C.Z.
New York City
1974

ACKNOWLEDGMENTS · · ·
Second Edition

I would like to thank several people who helped make the second edition of this book a reality: Thom Heinrichs, who first came up with the idea of going back and revising, updating, and expanding the original book; Joslyn Pine, whose belief in the book made it actually happen again; Jesse Green, my researcher, whose meticulous in-depth work made an enormous contribution; Fred Nathan and his associates Bert Fink and Dennis Crowley, who supplied me with endless hours of assistance and information when I was down to the crunch; Neil Meron, my associate, for the many hours of support; Lisé Johnson, my executive assistant, whose painstaking work and skill and sheer perseverance got the book completed; Dean Pitchford, whose support and advice got me through the writing of this edition as successfully as he got me through the first edition over a decade ago; Barbra Streisand for her friendship and generosity; Harold Prince, who started the whole thing, and whose contribution is deeply appreciated; and Stephen Sondheim for his cooperation and his support.

Special thanks to the photographers for their kindness in making the photos available: Van Williams, Joe Abeles, Henry Grossman, Don Perdue, Kenn Duncan and, especially, the wonderful Martha Swope and her associate Carol Rosegg.

I would also like to thank the Dramatists Guild for permission to include portions of Mr. Sondheim's lecture "The Musical Theater," first published in the *Dramatists Guild Quarterly*, Autumn 1978, and Mr. Sondheim and Mr. Prince's lecture "Author and Director: Musicals," first published in the *Dramatists Guild Quarterly*, Summer 1979.

In addition, I want to thank the many others who contributed invaluable information and assistance: Elaine Markson, Craig Nelson, Richard Baskin, Thomas Z. Shepard, Herb Helman, Peter Elliot, RCA Records, Patricia Sinnott, La Jolla Playhouse, David Levine and the Dramatists Guild, Arlene Caruso, Frank Verlizzo, David Edward Byrd, Columbia Records, Paul Grein, *Billboard* magazine, Margaret Mills, Larry Fuller, David Kernan, Andre Bishop, Ira Weitzman, Len Cariou, George Hearn, Bernadette Peters, Herbert Ross, Mandy Patinkin, Lonny Price, James Weissenbach, Lee Remick, Angela Lansbury, Flora Roberts, Michael Starobin, John Weidman, Hugh Wheeler, Tony Straiges, Beverly Sills, Craig Lucas, Bernard Jacobs, Betty Corwin, Lincoln Center Library, Laurence Jarvic, Tamara Rawitt, Annette Meyers, Tim Jacobi, Fran Soeder, Paul Gemignani, Anthony Perkins, Barbara Cook, Carol Burnett, James Lapine, Ron Field, Paul Lazarus, Robert Fryer, Patricia Birch, Terry Hughes, Peggy Hansen, Diana Riesman, Kenny Solmes, Lee Solters, Ellen Krass, Brent Oldham, Michael Austin, Bonnie Helwege, Eileen Nawrocki, Stephanie Gunning, and Theodore Chapin.

Thank you.

C.Z.
Los Angeles
1986

INDEX · · ·

Page numbers in *italics* refer to illustrations

Abbott, George, *64,* 66, 70, 71
Abuba, Ernest, *225*
Adams, Ken, 168
"Advantages of Floating in the Middle of the Sea,
    The," 215–16, *217*
"Ah, Paris!," 143
Allen, Debbie, 340, 341, *341*
Allen, Elizabeth, *98,* 100, 101, *103,* 104, 105,
    204
Allen, Lewis, 295
"All I Need Is the Girl," 41
"All Things Bright and Beautiful," 144
American Academy and Institute of Arts and
    Letters, 352
Anderson, Maxwell, 5
Andrews, George Lee, *187*
"Another Hundred People," 126, 157, 361
Anouilh, Jean, 181
Ansen, David, 198
Anyone Can Whistle, 60, 80, 81–95, *83, 86, 88,*
    91, 93, 155, 236–37, 362
    original cast recording of, 173–74
    rehearsals and Philadelphia tryouts, 85–87, 89
    reviews of, 92, 94
Aronson, Boris, *32, 134,* 147, 182, *211, 212,*
    213, 218, 221, 239
Aronson, Lisa, *32*
Atkinson, Brooks, 26, 28–29, 51
Ayers, Lemuel, 9
Azenberg, Emanuel, 308

Babbitt, Milton, 6–9, 12, 41
Ball, William, 100
"Ballad of Sweeney Todd, The," 252, *259,* 351
Bancroft, Anne, 100
Bantay, John, *225*
Barnes, Clive, 34, 59, 76, 127, 146, 190, 204,
    220–21, 258, 279, 312–13, 339
Barr, Richard, 244, 252, 260
Barrie, Barbara, 121
Barrow, Robert, 6
Baskin, Richard, 289, 292

Baum, Morton, 53
Baxter, Keith, 363
Beatty, Warren, 342
"Beautiful," 305
"Beautiful Girls," *137,* 147, 322
Becker, Lee, 19
Beggar on Horseback, 5
"Being Alive," 125, 126, 129, 159, 290, 360
Benjamin, Richard, 168, *171*
Bennett, Michael, 132, *134, 137, 149,* 240, 241,
    285, 316, *330*
    Company and, 121–24, 127, 129, *131*
    Follies and, 136, 138–41, 143–45, 147, 148,
    150
    Follies in Concert and, 321–22
Bennett, Tony, 162
Bergman, Ingmar, 181, 182
Berle, Milton, 67
Berlin, Irving, 38–39, 50, 147
Bernstein, Leonard, *10,* 11, 12, *31,* 115, 116,
    178, *207,* 230, 364–66
    Candide and, 162–63
    West Side Story and, 14–18, 20, 21, 23, 25, 26,
    28–29, 340
Beruh, Joseph, 54
Bettelheim, Bruno, 357
Beymer, Richard, 29, 179
Birch, Patricia, 186, 189, 191, 196, 215–16
Bishop, Andre, 298, 304, 308, 311, 315–16
Bizarre, 296
Black, Karen, 70
Bloomgarden, Kermit, 81, 84–87, 92, 95
Blyden, Larry, 75, 76, 77, *162, 164,* 204, *204*
Bogart, Paul, 114
"Bolero d'Amour," 140–41
Bolton, Whitney, 94
Bond, Christopher, 243–44, 260
Books of musicals (librettos), 61–63, 236–37
Book-of-the-Month Club Records, 351–52
"Bowler Hat, A," 216
"Boy From . . . , The," 162
"Boy Like That, A," 21, 338

Brando, Marlon, 29
Brecht, Bertolt, 115–17
Brisson, Freddie, 42
Broadway Album, The, 286, 288–93
"Broadway Baby," 143, 147, *151, 318*
Brown, Barry, 53, 54
Brown, Georgia, 339
Brown, Irving, 78
Brown, Lew, 147
Bryant, Jim, 179
"Buddy's Blues," 324, *325*
Burnett, Carol, *318,* 320–21, 326, *326, 331*
Burns, David, 67
Burns, Ralph, 154–59
Burthen Music, 79
Byrd, David Edward, *265, 266*
"By the Sea," 248, *348*

Calin, Micky, *24*
Callaway, Liz, 351
Canby, Vincent, 199
Candide, 12, 14, 15, 23, 162–63, 165, *166,* 296
    New York City Opera production of, 346
Cannon, Dyan, 168
"Can That Boy Foxtrot!," *142,* 143, 236, 351
Capitol Records, 175
Cariou, Len, 204, *205*
    A Little Night Music and, 184, *184,* 189–90,
        191, 193, 195–98, *197*
    Sweeney Todd and, *242,* 248, 249, *250, 253, 254*
Carr, Charmian, 114
Carroll, Kathleen, 198
Cassidy, Jack, *163,* 204, *204, 205,* 206
Casting, 108–11
Castner, Alan, *27*
Chapman, John, 25, 51, 94
Chappell & Co., 78–79, 82
Charisse, Zan, 54, *55,* 57, *57*
Chekhov, Anton, 117, 135, 189
Chelsea Theater Center, 162–63, 165, *166*
"Children and Art," 312
"Chrysanthemum Tea," 212, *214,* 218, 224
Church, Sandra, *39*
Coburn, James, 167, *171*
Coe, Richard, 71
Collector's Sondheim, A, 351
Collier, John, 114
Collins, Dorothy, *137,* 138, *149,* 156–57, 204,
    205
Collins, Judy, 287–88
"Color and Light," 301
Columbia Records, 173, 174, 176, 202
Comden, Betty, 37, 38, 47, *323, 329*
"Comedy Tonight," 71–72
"Come Over Here," 162
"Company," 121–22
Company, 34, 35, 79, 83, *112,* 117, *118,* 119–31,
    121, 122, 125, 128, 155, 157, 159, *162,*
    238, 253, 360–61, 365, 366
    idea for, 117, 119–20
    London production of, 130–31
    original cast recording, 174–75
    rehearsals for, 121–26
    reviews of, 126–27, 129
    writing songs for, 233, 234, 236, 238–40
Connelly, Marc, 5
Cook, Barbara, *327, 328,* 328–31, *329, 333*
Cooke, Sally, *56*
"Cool," 21, 366
Cool Million, A, 295, 296
Corman, Roger, 198
Corry, John, 272, 273

"Could I Leave You?," 324, 338, 360
Craig, David, 46
Crawford, Cheryl, 16–17
Crime and Variations, 352–53

Daniels, Danny, 322, 328, 331
Dankworth, John, 337
D'Arcy, Mary, *306, 352*
Davis, Clive, 176
Davis, Paul, 267
Davis, Peter G., 350
Day, Ernest, 169
"Day Off, The," 302, 303
De Carlo, Yvonne, 138, *142,* 143, 236
de Guzman, Josie, 340, 341, *341*
DeSylva, B. G., 147
Dexter, John, 100–2, 104, 119
Dietrich, Marlene, 266
Do I Hear a Waltz?, 103, 106
    casting of, 100–1
    recording of, *98*
    reviews of, 104–7
    try-outs of, 101–5
    writing of, 99–100, 235
Dolan, Judith, 279
"Don't Laugh," 162
D'Orsay, Fifi, *137,* 138, 143
Drake, Sylvie, 284
Drama Critics Awards, 147, 192
Dussault, Nancy, 339

"Echo Song," 76
Eder, Richard, 258, 260
Elliott, Patricia, *188,* 192
Enclave, The, 162
Engel, Lehman, 84
"Epiphany," 250
Epstein, Julius J., 9
Epstein, Philip G., 9
Evans, Edith, 185
Evans, Harvey, *141, 204*
Evening Primrose, 114–15, 184
"Everybody Ought to Have a Maid," 158–59
"Everything's Coming Up Roses," 41, 42, 45, 54
Exception and the Rule, The (Brecht), 115

Falla, Manuel de, 211
Farber, Stephen, 170–71
"Farewell," 75
"Fear No More," 351
Fiddler on the Roof, 73
Field, Ron, 144, 269, 272, 273, 276–77, 285
Fields, Dorothy, 147
Finch, Peter, 195
"Finishing the Hat," 304
Follies, 32, 34, 35, 79, 83, *134,* 135–53, *140–42,*
    145, 149, 151–53, 155, 158, 159, 183, 192,
    237, 241, 359, 365, 366
    casting, 138–39
    posters, *265, 266*
    rehearsals for, 139–41
    reviews of, 142, 146–47
Follies in Concert, 318, 318, 319–34, *321, 323,*
    325–30, 335, 366
    rehearsals for, 324, 326, 328–32
    reviews of, 333–34
    on television, 334
Ford, Paul, *318*
Fosse, Bob, 9, 131
Foster, David, 289
Fox, Pat, 70
Franchi, Sergio, *98,* 100, 101, *103,* 203

Frank, Mel, 75
Freedman, Gerald, 340
Freedman, Samuel G., 322
Frogs, The, 162, *164,* 351
Fryer, Robert, 252
Fujii, Timm, *220*
Fujimoto, Haruki, 215
Fuller, Larry, 197, 278–79
Funke, Lewis, 135
Funny Thing Happened on the Way to the Forum, A, 64
    on Broadway, *66,* 72–74
    casting of, 67–68
    motion picture of, *69,* 75
    recording of, *72,* 176
    reviews of, 70–72, 76
    revivals of, *73,* 74–77, *77*
    try-outs of, 70–71
    writing of, 37–39, 65–70, 158–59, 234, 236
Furth, George, 116, 117, 121, 124, 126, 162, 269, 272, 279, 282–83, *285*

Gabel, Martin, 11
Games and puzzles, *160,* 165, 167
Garber, Victor, *251*
Gates, Larry, 114
"Gavotte," 165
"Gee, Officer Krupke," 20, 21, 23, 26, 235
Gelbart, Larry, 37, *64,* 67, 68, 75
Gemignani, Paul, 96, 97, *172,* 196, 217, 252, 253, 310, *318, 324,* 326
Gershwin, George, 147
Gershwin, Ira, 147
Gilford, Jack, *66, 67*
Gill, Brendan, 279
Gingold, Hermione, 111, *180,* 184–86, *187,* 195, *204, 205,* 339
"Girls of Summer, The," 162
Girls Upstairs, The, 113, 116, 119, 120, 135, 144
"Glamorous Life, The," 186
Goldman, James, 70, 113, 114, 116, 119, 120, 135, 136, 141, 143, 148, 150–53, 190–91, 237, 322
"Goodbye for Now," 352
"Good Thing Going," 288
"Gotta Keep 'Em Humming," 303
Gottfried, Martin, 57, 138, 146–47
Gould, Jack, 114
Grammy nominations and awards, 287, 288
Gray, Kevin, *224*
Green, Adolph, 37, 38, 47, *323*
Greene, Herbert, 84
"Green Finch and Linnet Bird," 288
Grein, Paul, 287, 288
Grey, Joel, 70
Griffith, Robert (Bobby), *10,* 17–18, 66, 269
Grimes, Tammy, 184, 190
Groenendaal, Cris, 351
Gross, Ben, 114–15
Guardino, Harry, 81, 82, 85, *86, 87*
Guare, John, 115, 116
Guittard, Laurence, *184, 188*
Gunton, Bob, 351
Gussow, Mel, 129–30, 334, 344
Gypsy, 35, *36,* 37–59, *39, 40, 43, 44, 55, 56, 57, 58,* 61, 158, 235–36, 290
    casting of, 45–46
    movie version of, 52–53, *53*
    rehearsals for, 46
    reviews of, 47, 51, 56–57, 59
    revivals of, 53–57, 59
    writing of, 37–39, 41, 42, 44, 45

Hackett, Joan, 170, *171*
Hadjidakis, Manos, 162
Haines, Howard, 219
Hall, Pamela, *73, 202, 204*
Hammerstein, Dorothy, 5, 8
Hammerstein, James, 3, *5*
Hammerstein, Oscar, II, 3–5, *5,* 7, 8, 12, 38, 42, 70, 95, 99, 102, 232, 234
Hansen, John, *73*
"Happily Ever After," 125–26
Harburg, E. Y., 147
Hardy, Joseph, 116, 119, 120
Harnick, Sheldon, 22
Harris, Barbara, 70
Hart, Larry, 104
Hart, Moss, 269, 282, 283
Haun, Harry, 323
"Have I Got a Girl for You," 126
Hayward, Leland, 37, 38, 47, 65, 113, 119
Hearn, George, 260, 328, 331, 344, 346, *350,* 351
Hello, Dolly!, 52, 105, 267
Henahan, Donal, 346, 347
Henderson, Ray, 147
Henry, Suzanne, *342, 343*
Herman, Jerry, 177, 315
Hewes, Henry, 26
High Tor (Anderson), 5
Hirsch, Samuel, 142
Hirschhorn, Clive, 221
Hobe, 26, 258
Hobson, Harold, 130
Holden, Stephen, 288
Holgate, Ron, 204, *205*
Holliday, Judy, 162
"Hollywood and Vine," 162
Holt, Fritz, 53, 126
"Home Is the Place," 162
Hot Spot, 162
Houseman, John, 114
"House of Marcus Lycus, The," 351
Howland, Beth, 126, *204*
Hughes, Terry, 344, 357

"I Feel Pretty," 21, 22
"If Momma Was Married," 41
"I Know My Love," 161
Illya Darling, 162
"I'm Still Here," *142, 143, 200, 236,* 331
"In Betwixt and Between," 41
"In Buddy's Eyes," 156, 329
"I Never Do Anything Twice," 162, 339
Into the Woods, 354, 357
Invitation to a March, 162
"Invocation and Instructions to the Audience," 351
"It's a Hit!," 351

Jacob, Steven, 351
Jacobs, Bernard, 221, 226, 284, 315, 316
"Jet Song," *13,* 23
"Johanna," 347
Johns, Glynis, *180,* 184, 185, *187,* 189, 190, 192, *193, 204, 205,* 361
Johnson, Mary Lea, 252
Jones, Dean, *118,* 120–21, 127–30, *128*
June Moon, 162, *163*

Kael, Pauline, 198
Kahan, Judy, *180*
Kalem, T. E., 126, 219, 258, 340, 341
Kastner, Elliott, 195
Kaufman, George S., 5, 269, 282, 283

Kaye, Judy, *350, 351*
Kaye, Nora, 331
Keaton, Buster, 75
Kelly, Kevin, 124, 142, 188, 218
Kern, Jerome, 79, 147
Kernan, David, *336, 337*–39
Kerr, Jean, 165, 359
Kerr, Walter, 26, 72, 92, 94, 127, 146, 258, 340–41
Kert, Larry, *16,* 18, *19, 118, 121, 122,* 127–30, 204, *205,* 206, 339
"Kids Ain't," 24
Kilgallen, Dorothy, 51, 100
Kinser-Lau, Patrick, *220*
Kipness, Joseph, 9
Kirk, Lisa, 179
Kissel, Howard, 219–20, 279, 339, 340
Klotz, Florence, 147, 182, 192, 199, 221, 338
Klugman, Jack, *43, 46,* 47, *48,* 50–51, 52
Krasny, Diana (Diana Shumlin), 81–82, 85, 92
Kroll, Jack, 146, 219, 258, 313
Kukla, Fran, and Ollie, 339

La Cage aux Folles, 315, 362
"Ladies Who Lunch," *125,* 174, 231, 232, 291, 292
Laine, Cleo, 337
Lambert, Mark, *191*
Lane, Burton, 147
Lansbury, Angela, 81, 204, *204, 205,* 206, *350*
    Anyone Can Whistle and, *80,* 81–84, *83, 88, 91, 93,* 95
    Gypsy and, 54–57, *55, 57, 58, 59*
    Sweeney Todd and, *242,* 248–49, *250, 253,* 254–56, *257,* 258, *259,* 260, 261, 344, 346
Lansbury, Edgar, 54
Lapine, James, 177–78, 282–85, *294,* 295–301, 303–5, 307, 310–11, 316, 357
Lascoe, Henry, 85, 90
Last of Sheila, The, 167–71, *169, 171*
Latouche, John, 165
Laurents, Arthur, 11–12, *60,* 153, 162, 181, 230, 254, 359–61
    Anyone Can Whistle and, 81, 82, 84–87, 89–90, 95, 236–37
    on books of musicals, 61–62
    Do I Hear a Waltz? and, 99–102, 104
    Gypsy and, 38, 41–42, 45–48, 51, 54–57
    on musical staging, 132–33
    West Side Story and, 14–18, 26, 28, 30
Lawrence, Carol, *16,* 18, *22,* 203
Layton, Joe, 101
Lazarus, Paul, 324, 328, 331–32
Lee, Eugene, 162–63, 165, *166, 244,* 252, 255, 279
Lee, Franne, 162–63, 165, *166,* 255
Lee, Gypsy Rose, 37, 38, *40*
LeRoy, Mervyn, 52
"Lesson #8," 312
Lester, Richard, 75
Levitas, Willard, 114
"Liaisons," 185
Librettos (books), 61–63, 236–37
Lieber, Jerry, 115
Lieberson, Goddard, 95, *98,* 163, *172,* 173–76, 179
"Life Is Happiness Indeed," 165
"Little Lamb," 41, 47–48
Little Night Music, A, 27, 34–35, 79, 176, *180, 184,* 184–99, *187, 188, 191, 193, 194, 197,* 202, 233, 291, 361, 365, 366
    casting, 184–85

Little Night Music, A (cont.)
    motion-picture version of, 195–99
    reviews of, 188–90
"Little Things You Do Together, The," 175
Logan, Joshua, 65
Logan, Nedda, *5*
Lonoff, Jeffrey, 337
"Losing My Mind," 147, 159, *327*
Loudon, Dorothy, 260
"Loveland," 134, 140, 143, 147, 152
"Love Will See Us Through," *141,* 147
Lucas, Craig, *342, 343,* 344
Luna, Barbara, *27*
Lyric writing (songwriting), 229–41

McAnuff, Des, 283
McCann, Elizabeth, 221
McCarty, Mary, *137,* 138, 139, *204*
McClain, John, 25–26
McClure, John, 179
McKenzie, Julie N., *336,* 338
Mackintosh, Cameron, 338
McMartin, John, *137,* 138, *205*
MacRae, Heather, 283, *284*
McShane, Ian, 168, *171*
Mad Show, The, 162–63
Mako, 213, *214, 217*
Malden, Karl, 53
Mallory, Victoria, *27, 191, 350, 351*
Manos, Dean, 252
Manos, Judy, 252
Mao, Freddy, *220*
Margolis, Henry M., 11
"Maria," 21, 240
Marry Me a Little, 342, 343–44
Marshall, Ken, 340, *341*
Martin, Mary, 100
Martin, Millicent, *336,* 338
Marvin, Blanche, 260
Mason, James, 168, 170, *171*
Mathis, Johnny, 287
Matz, Peter, 289
May, Elaine, 25
"Me and My Town," 90
Measures Taken, The (Brecht), 115
Merlin, Joanna, 109–11, 214–15, 272
Merman, Ethel, 37, 38, *39, 40,* 41, *43, 44,* 46–50, *48, 49,* 52, 54, *55,* 179, 202
Merrick, David, 33, 35, *36,* 37, 47, 51, 65, 113, 114, 119, 153, 236, 267
Merrily We Roll Along, 34, 268, 269–85, *271, 273, 277, 280, 281, 284, 285,* 295
    original cast recording of, *281,* 282
    previews of, 275–80
    review of, 279
    revival of, 283–85, *284*
Meyers, Annette, 34, 215
Michell, Keith, 87
Mighty Man Is He, A, 161–62
Mills, Margaret, 352
Mitchell, Ruth, *32,* 165
Mizner, Wilson, 237
Mona Lisa, 296
Montevecchi, Liliane, *318, 329,* 331
Moreno, Rita, 29, 179
Morrison, Ann, *271, 272, 274, 280*
Mostel, Zero, 66, 67, 69, 72, *72*–75, 115, 116, 202, 203
Motown Productions, 352
"Move On," 301–2, *312*
"Mr. Goldstone," 41
Musical direction, 96–97

Musical staging, 132–33
Music publishing, 78–79
Musser, Tharon, 147
Myers, Pamela, *162*
My Fair Lady, 52
"My Friends," 248, 249, *250*

Nadel, Norman, 92
"Natives Are Restless, The," 90
Nelson, Gene, *137*, 138, 143–45, 203
Nelson, Richard, 315
Newman, Phyllis, 328, *329*
New York (magazine), 162
New York City Opera, 260, 346–47
New York Drama Critics Award, 130, 147, 192
"Next," 216
Nichols, Mike, 25, 162
"Night Waltz II," 351
Nixon, Marni, 179
Norton, Elliot, 142, 189
"Not a Day Goes By," 288
"Not While I'm Around," 291
Novick, Julius, 313
Nugent, Nelle, 221

"Officer Krupke," 20, 21, 23, 26, 235
"O Happy We," 23
Oklahoma!, 105
"Old Friends," 279, 351
"One Hand, One Heart," 21, 23
"One More Kiss," 147
On the Town, 12
Oppenheimer, George, 8, 11, 52, 104
Orchestration, 154–59
Ostrow, Stuart, 115, 116, 119

Pacific Overtures, 34, *208*, 209–27, *211, 212, 214,
    217, 220, 223*, 352
    reviews of, 218–21
    revival of, 221–24, *223–25*, 226–27
Papp, Joe, 267
Passionella, 162
Patinkin, Mandy, *297, 299*, 304–5, 308, *309*,
    311–12, *312*, 324, *325*, 326, 328, 331, 333
Pennebaker, D. A., 174
Perkins, Anthony, 114–16, 120–21, 129, 131,
    169, 366
    Crime and Variations and, 352–53
    The Last of Sheila and, 167–71
Peters, Bernadette, *299, 300, 302*, 308–9, *309,
    312*
Peterson, Kurt, *27, 141*
Photograph, 296
Pilbrow, Richard, 130
Playwrights Horizons, 298, 299, 303, 308, 357
Poole, Wakefield, 101, 104, 105
Pop recordings, 287–93
Porter, Cole, 38, 147, 234
Posters, *262*, 263–64, *265*, 266–67
"Prayers," 218
"Pretty Little Picture," 76
"Pretty Women," 249–50, 291, 292
Price, Lonny, 271–72, *271, 274*, 274–76
Prince, Daisy, 272, *320*
Prince, Harold (Hal), 7, *32*, 33–35, 94–95, 109–
    11, 113–14, 116, 133, 158, 181–83, 201,
    300–1, *330*, 359, 362–63
    Candide and, 162, 165, *166*
    Company and, *112*, 119–21, 124, 126, 128–30,
        141, 238
    Follies and, 135, 136, 138, 139, 141, 144, 147–
        48, 150, 153, 175, 183

Prince, Harold (*cont.*)
    A Funny Thing Happened on the Way to the Forum
        and, 65–67, 70–71
    The Girls Upstairs and, 119, 120, 135
    A Little Night Music and, 184–86, 189, 191,
        192, 194, 195, *197*, 198, 199
    Merrily We Roll Along and, 269–78, 280–81,
        285
    Pacific Overtures and, 209–10, 213–21, 226
    Side by Side by Sondheim and, 338–40
    Sweeney Todd and, 245, 248, 252, 254–56, 260–
        61, 344, *345*, 347
    West Side Story and, *10*, 17–19, 29, *31*
Prince, Judy, 269
Production Company, The, 343
Pulitzer Prize, 315
"Putting It Together," 289, 302–3
Puzzles and games, *160*, 165, 167

"Rag Me That Mendelssohn March," 161
"Rain on the Roof," 143, *323*
Ralston, Teri, *204*
Ramin, Sid, 158
RCA Records, 174, 281, 323–24
Reds, 342, 352
Reed, Rex, 56, 170, 198, 219
Remick, Lee, 81, 82, 84, 85, *86*, 90, *91*, 170,
    203, *321*, 324, 328, *328, 329*, 351
René, Norman, 343, 344
Rich, Alan, 205–7
Rich, Frank, 198, 216, 224, 279–80, 313, 333–
    34
Rich, Shirley, 108
Richard Rodgers Production Award, 352
Richards, Martin, 252
Rigg, Diana, 195
"Right Girl, The," 144, 331, 333
Ring Round the Moon, 181
Ritchard, Cyril, 339
Rivera, Chita, *16*, 18, *204, 204*, 206
"Road You Didn't Take, The," 237
Robbins, Jerome, *10*, 11, *16*, 25, 115, 132, 133,
    239
    A Funny Thing Happened on the Way to the Forum
        and, 37, 65–66, 71
    Gypsy and, 37, 38, 41, 45–48, 54
    West Side Story and, 14, 15, 17–21, 23, 30, 340
Robbins, Rex, *55*
Roberts, Flora, 12, 14, 25, 39, 50, 57, 65, 99–
    100, 120, 126, 153, 155, *164*, 183–84, 186,
    189, 243, 281
Rockwell, John, 174
Rodgers, Mary, 99, 162
Rodgers, Richard, 7, *98*, 99–102, 104, 105, *106*,
    107, 234, 235
Rogers, Ginger, 161
Rolph, Marti, *141*
Rosenstock, Milton, 179
Rosenthal, Jean, 341
"Rose's Turn," 38, 46–47, *49*, 54, 55, *58*, 290
Ross, Herbert, 89, 94, 104, 162, 167, 168–70,
    361–62
    Follies in Concert and, *318, 321*, 322–24, 326,
        328–31
Rossi, Gloria, 56
Rubinstein, John, 283, *284*
Rusk, Howard A., 30–31
Russell, Rosalind, 52, *53*

Saks, Jay, 177
Sandifur, Virginia, *141*
Saturday Night, 9, 11, 12, 351

Schoenfeld, Gerald, 221–22
Schwartz, Arthur, 5
"Send in the Clowns," 185, *193,* 196, 287–89,
    291, 351, 365
Serenade (movie), 11
Seurat, Georges, 264, 296–97, 301, 303, 308
Seven Percent Solution, The, 162, 339
Shaffer, Anthony, 167
Shakespeare, William, 351
Sharaff, Irene, 341
Shepard, Thomas Z., *128, 162, 172,* 174–79,
    281, 320, 323, 330–31, 334, 351
Sherrin, Ned, *336,* 337–39
Shevelove, Burt, 7, 8, 11, 18, 37, *64,* 67, 74–76,
    95, 99, 161, 162, *164,* 183, 201, *202*
Shimoda, Yuki, *208*
Shubert Organization, 308, 310, 314
Shumlin, Diana (Diana Krasny), 81–82, 85, 92
Shutta, Ethel, 143, *151,* 206
"Side by Side," 83, *122,* 123, 126, 360
Side by Side by Sondheim, 336, 338–40
Sills, Beverly, 260, 321, 346, 347
Silvers, Phil, 65, *69, 73,* 75–77, *77,* 202, 203
Simon, Carly, 288
Simon, John, 340
Simon, Neil, 150
Sinatra, Frank, 287, 288
Sleuth, 167
"Small World," 44–46, 232
Smiles of a Summer Night, 181–83
Smith, Alexis, 110, *137,* 138, *145,* 147, *149,*
    203, 204, 205, 266, 360
Smith, Liz, 275
Smith, Oliver, 18, 341
Soeder, Fran, 221, 222, 224, 226
"Soldiers and Girls," 303
"Someone in a Tree," 227
"Some People," 42, 50, 179, 290
Something for Everyone, 175–76
"Something's Coming," *19,* 21, 290
"Somewhere," 290, 292
Sondheim (album), 351–52
Sondheim: A Musical Tribute, 200, 201, *202*–5, 207
Sondheim, Stephen, *2, 10, 24, 31, 48, 60, 64, 98,*
    106, 128, 131, 160, 163, 169, 172, 194,
    205, 207, 228, 286, 294, 318, 331, 333,
    335, 345, 350, 358
    childhood and adolescence, 3–4
    on state of the theater, 367
    see also specific topics
Songwriting (lyric writing), 229–41
Sound of Music, The, 52
South Pacific, 366
Stage 67, 114
Staging musicals, 132–33
Stanley, Kim, 116
Starobin, Michael, 309–10
Stavisky, 162
Stein, Gertrude, 296
Stephens, Garn, 189
Stephens, Robert, 195
Stephen Sondheim Evening, A, 350, 351
Stevens, Roger, 16
Stevens, Tony, *204*
Stickney, Dorothy, 114
"Story of Lucy and Jessie, The," 143, 147, *321*
Straiges, Tony, *305, 306,* 310, 315
Streisand, Barbra, *286,* 288–93
Stritch, Elaine, 54, *112,* 121, *125,* 130, 174, 203,
    318, 326, 328–29, *329, 333*
Styne, Jule, 9, *36,* 38, 39, 41, 44–48, 50–52, 54,
    162, 234, 287, 290, *331,* 363–64

"Suite of Dances from *Pacific Overtures,*" 352
Summer, Bob, 281, 324
Summertime, 99
Sunday Afternoon on the Island of La Grande Jatte,
    296–97
"Sunday in the Park with George," 301, *302*
Sunday in the Park with George, 34, 289, 290, 294,
    297, 299, 302, 305, 306, 309, 312, 314,
    317, 361–63
    awards won by, 315
    Broadway production of, 308–17
    idea for, 296–97
    off-Broadway production of, 298–300, 303–7
    original cast recording, 177–78
    poster, 264, 266
    reviews of, 312–15
    on television, 357
    writing of, 297–98, 301–3, 308, 311
Swanson, Gloria, 136, *265,* 266
Sweeney Todd, 34, 242, 243–61, *244, 250, 251,*
    253, 257, 259, 296
    New York City Opera production of, *345, 346*–
      47
    original cast recording of, 177
    posters, *262, 263,* 264
    previews of, 254–56
    reviews of, 256, 258, 347
    on television, 344, 346
Syers, Mark Hsu, *220*

Tamblyn, Russ, 29
Taubman, Howard, 94
Taylor, Elizabeth, 195–99, *197*
Theatre Guild, 66–67
"There's Always a Woman," 90
"There's Something About a War," 351
"There Won't Be Trumpets," 90–91, 351
"This Is Nice, Isn't It?," 351
"This Turf Is Ours," 24
Tilstrom, Burr, 339
Time of the Cuckoo, The, 99
"Together, Wherever We Go," 54
"Tonight," 287
Tony nominations and awards, 35, 72, 76, 107,
    130, 147, 192, 221, 260, 315, 339, 341,
    362
"Too Many Mornings," 365
Topper (television series), 8
Tucker, Robert, 54
Tunick, Jonathan, 97, 146–47, 154–59, *162,*
    172, 199, 217, 309
Turpin, Gerry, 170
Twelve Dreams, 295
Twigs, 162
Tynan, Kenneth, 56–57

"Uptown Downtown," 143

Valando, Tommy, 79, 281, 324
Vaughn, Melanie, *306*
Verlizzo, Frank (Fraver), *262, 263*–64, 266
Viertel, Jack, 283–84

"Waiting for the Girls Upstairs," *137, 328*
Walker, Don, 155
Walker, Nancy, 75, 90, *200,* 204, *205*
Walton, Jim, *274, 276, 280*
Wand, Betty, 179
Watt, Douglas, 126, 146, 190, 219, 256, 258,
    279, 313, 339, 340
Watts, Richard, 94, 219
"We Do Not Belong Together," 301, 308–9

"Weekend in the Country, A," 27, 186
Weidman, Jerome, 209
Weidman, John, 209–10, 213, 214, 222, 227
Weissenbach, James, *271,* 273, 275–76
Weitzman, Ira, 308, 316, 357
Welch, Raquel, 168, *171*
"Welcome to Kanagawa," 218
West, Nathanael, 295, 296
Westenberg, Robert, *306*
West Side Story, 10, 12, *13,* 14–31, *16, 19, 22, 24, 27, 31,* 34, 42, 158, 178, 179, 290
   movie version of, 29–30, 179
   reviews of, 25–26
   revival of, 340–41, *341*
"What More Do I Need?," 351
"What Would We Do Without You?," *122,* 123
Wheeler, Hugh, 162, 163, 181, 182, 190, 192, 195, 196, *197,* 213
   Sweeney Todd and, 246, 250
Whitney Museum, 351
"Who's That Woman?," 139–41, *140,* 241, 322

Whyte, Jerome, 102
Williamson Music, 79
Wilson, Earl, 190, 203, 255
Wilson, John S., 343
Wilson, Mary Louise, *56*
Wise, Robert, 30
"With So Little to Be Sure Of," 84, 91
Wood, Natalie, 29, 53, *53,* 179
Woodward, Charles, 244, 245, 252
World of Jules Feiffer, The, 162
"Worst Pies in London, The," 249, *257*

Yale Repertory Theater, 162, *164*
"You Could Drive a Person Crazy," 83
"You'll Never Get Away from Me," 45, 46
Young Playwrights Festival, 350–51
"You're Gonna Love Tomorrow," *141,* 147

Zakariasen, Bill, 346
Zien, Chip, 283, *284*